The Open
University

ENVIRONMENTAL
·CONTROL · AND·
PUBLIC · HEALTH·

# A I R

# Units 14 – 16
# Air quality management

PREPARED BY THE COURSE TEAM

## T237 Environmental control and public health: Course Team

| | | | |
|---|---|---|---|
| Professor Andrew Porteous | Course Team Chairman | Caryl Hunter-Brown | Liaison Librarian |
| Judith Anderson | Course Manager | Dr Tony Jolly | BBC |
| Prof. Keith Attenborough | Technology | Dr Andrew Millington | BBC |
| Cameron Balbirnie | BBC | Dr Suresh Nesaratnam | Technology |
| Dr Rod Barratt | Technology | Dr John Newbury | Technology Staff Tutor |
| Lesley Booth | Course Secretary | Dr Brian Price | Unit writing consultant |
| Dr Keith Cavanagh | Project Officer | Janice Robertson | Editor |
| Dr David Cooke | Technology Staff Tutor | Ian Spratley | BBC |
| Sue Dobson | Graphic Artist | Doreen Tucker | Text Processing Compositor |
| Pamela Furniss | Technology | Bob Walters | BBC |
| Morine Gordon | Course Secretary | Dr David Yeoman | Unit writing consultant |
| Caroline Hailey | Graphic Designer | | |

In addition, the Course Team wishes to thank the following for reviewing this material (1992 designations):

External Assessor       Professor Jacob Lewin, Lewin Fryer & Partners, Consulting Engineers

Statistics and epidemiology: Elizabeth Overton, Public Health Laboratory Services

Wastes:                 Colin Palmer, Principal Assistant County Surveyor, Suffolk County Council;
                        John Birch, Managing Director (designate), Lincwaste

Air:                    Dr Jimi Irwin, Warren Spring Laboratory

## Contents of the course

| | | |
|---|---|---|
| Introduction | Unit 1 | Pollutants and pollution control |
| | Unit 2 | Biology |
| | Unit 3 | Environmental chemistry |
| | Unit 4 | Statistics and epidemiology |
| Water | Units 5–6 | Water quality, analysis and management |
| | Unit 7 | Water supply and sewage treatment |
| Wastes | Units 8–9 | Municipal solid wastes management |
| | Unit 10 | Hazardous wastes management |
| Noise | Unit 11 | Noise concepts and terminology |
| | Unit 12 | Fundamentals of noise control |
| | Unit 13 | Noise assessment, standards and legislation |
| Air | Units 14–16 | Air quality management |

This text has been printed on Savannah Natural Art™: at least 60% of the fibre used in the production of this paper is bagasse (fibrous residue of sugarcane, a waste byproduct of sugar processing) and the balance is softwood fibre which has undergone an oxygen bleaching process.

The Open University, Walton Hall, Milton Keynes, MK7 6AA.

First published 1993. Reprinted with corrections 1996.

Edited, designed and typeset by the Open University.

Printed in the United Kingdom by Hobbs the Printers Limited, Totton, Hampshire. SO40 3WX

This text forms part of an Open University Second Level Course. If you would like a copy of *Studying with the Open University*, please write to the Central Enquiry Service, PO Box 200, The Open University, Walton Hall, Milton Keynes, MK7 6YZ, United Kingdom. If you have not already enrolled on the course and would like to buy this or other Open University material, please write to Open University Educational Enterprises Ltd, 12 Cofferidge Close, Stony Stratford, Milton Keynes, MK11 1BY, United Kingdom.

ISBN 0 7492 6178 1

Edition 1.3

11637C/t237u14-16i1.3

# UNITS 14–16
# AIR QUALITY MANAGEMENT

## Contents

# AIMS AND OBJECTIVES

These three units on *air quality* management combine with two television programmes to give an introduction to the nature and sources of air pollution, together with an outline of waste minimisation and control technology. In particular, the aims of these units are:

- to show how air pollution may be caused by direct release or by atmospheric transformations of pollutants;
- to demonstrate dispersion of pollutants in atmospheres, and the significance of temporal variations in concentrations;
- to indicate typical adverse effects of air pollutants;
- to outline some principles of monitoring ambient and stationary sources of air pollutants;
- to demonstrate some representative techniques for minimising emissions to atmosphere;
- to introduce some representative techniques for the control of unavoidable emissions to atmosphere.
- by a combination of the previous aims, and through the medium of case study analysis, to develop an attitude towards practical problem solving.

After studying the material in these units and the associated audiovisual material, you should have the basic knowledge and skills to achieve the following objectives.

1 Define, explain and interpret correct descriptions of some principal air quality management terms, defined in this text or in the set book (Porteous, 1992), including:

| | |
|---|---|
| *absorption* | *ground-level concentration* |
| *adsorption* | isokinetic *sampling* |
| air pollution | *lapse rate* |
| atmospheric stability | *nuisance* |
| *bag house* | *odour threshold* |
| black *smoke* | plume, plume rise |
| dark smoke | precipitator |
| downwash, downdraught | *primary pollutant* |
| *emission factor* | *secondary pollutant* |
| *flare* | *temperature inversion* |
| fugitive emissions | *venturi* |
| *grit*, *dust* and *fume* | |

2 Recognise, define, interpret and give examples in the context of air quality management the acronyms and units as follows:

BPEO; BATNEEC; *VOC*; LCP; SCR; SNCR; CFC; *PAN*; UV-B; ppm; ppb; Dobson unit; odour unit.

3 Identify the main sources and characteristics of certain air pollutants of principal concern. [SAQs 1, 2, 4, 5,11–13, 34–40, 42, 52, 61]

4 Summarise the reasons for concern in terms of phytotoxicity, health effects, material damage or climatic change potentially caused by these pollutants. [SAQs 3, 8,11,41]

5 Describe the contribution that meteorological factors play in causing air pollution problems and in dispersion of pollutants. [SAQs 6–10, 34]

6 Outline the various goals, standards and guidelines for source and ambient air quality management. [SAQs 17, 25,29, 51]

7 Specify standard methods for the assessment of air quality as influenced by the principal pollutants. [SAQs 20, 22, 38]

8   Outline the measurement principles on which selected air quality assessment methods are based. [SAQs 20, 22,38]

9   Interpret measured air quality in relation to air quality standards and guidelines. [SAQs 17, 20, 21, 23–30, 39]

10   Interpret flowsheets and identify major causes of emissions of waste products to atmosphere from selected processes. [SAQs 35–37, 51, 53, 57, 59]

11   Estimate releases to atmosphere on the basis of emission factors and other relevant data. [SAQs 18, 19, 45, 62]

12   Compare emissions from mobile sources and stationary sources, and know some options for controlling mobile emissions. [SAQs 62–66]

13   Recommend actions to minimise the production of gaseous wastes. [SAQs 12,15, 35–39, 41, 59, 61]

14   Describe and select techniques to minimise the emission to atmosphere of unavoidable waste gases from specified processes. [SAQs 44, 47,48, 50, 59, 61]

15   Illustrate the role of dispersion as a final control option to reduce potential adverse effects of air pollutants. [SAQs 10, 54, 55, 60]

16   Investigate a local air pollution incident. [SAQs 10, 61]

17   Explain why buildings do not necessarily provide refuge against adverse air quality. [SAQ 67]

18   Interpret the main features of legal controls for air pollution control through provisions of the Environmental Protection Act 1990 and other legislation on clean air. [SAQs 31, 32, 33, 43]

# 1  INTRODUCTION

## 1.1  Clean air – a basic human need

Have you ever thought about how much air you need? The basic biological requirement for a person weighing around 68 kg is summarised in Table 1.

**Table 1**  *Air requirements for human activity*

| Activity | l min⁻¹ | l day⁻¹ | kg day⁻¹ |
|---|---|---|---|
| Resting | 7.4 | 10 600 | 12 |
| Doing light work | 28 | 40 400 | 45 |
| Doing heavy work | 43 | 62 000 | 69 |

So, your body needs something like 25 kg of air each day to provide its oxygen requirement. If you multiply this amount by a projected world population of around 6 thousand million by the year 2000, you will find that the total human need will be about 0.15 gigatonnes of air. Let us compare this with the amount of food needed. We eat about 1.5 kg of food each day, so our air requirement is slightly more than 15 times the food needed. This indicates why air quality is so important; any contamination needs to be so much lower in air than in food if we are to ensure that our total intake of potentially harmful substances does not put our health at risk.

We take the air for granted, but think how long you can go without food or water compared with the time you can hold your breath.

In our modern technological society, we also need air to burn fuels for heating and for transport. Look at the boiler in Figure 1.

To burn 0.8 litres of oil per minute needs 8.5 m³ of air per minute. A large boiler in a power station needs considerably more air. In Unit 3 we saw and calculated how much air is consumed by these processes, but also we saw that atoms in the fuels can rearrange to produce products which are discharged back into the air. We can do a similar analysis on the energy for transportation.

### Example: Determination of the stoichiometric air/fuel ratio for the complete combustion of petrol

Modern petrols are blends of hydrocarbons and additives, but we can represent an average formulation in terms of a single component, octene ($C_8H_{16}$). A balanced chemical equation for the combustion of this fuel is

$$C_8H_{16} + 12O_2 \rightarrow 8CO_2 + 8H_2O$$

For each mole of petrol, 12 moles of oxygen are required, and since the ratio of air to oxygen is 4.35 (Table 13 of Unit 3), we can produce the following relationships:

1 mole of octene ($C_8H_{16}$) = $8 \times 12 + 16 \times 1$ = 112 g

12 moles of oxygen needed for complete combustion = $12 \times 16 \times 2$ = 384 g

Hence the amount of air needed for complete combustion of 112 g of petrol is given by

$384 \times 4.35$ = 1670.4 g

So the stoichiometric air/fuel ratio is:

air/fuel = 1670.4/112 = 14.9

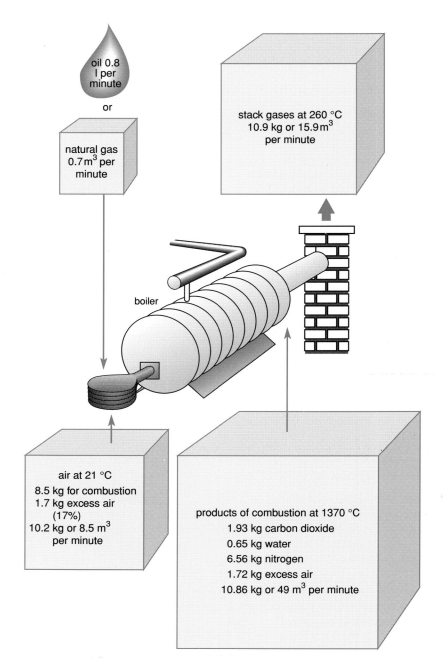

**Figure 1**   *Fuel and air requirements for a typical central heating and hot water boiler.*

Therefore, each mass unit of petrol needs about 15 mass units of air. We will see the significance of this ratio in Section 6. Think how many cars are on the roads in the UK. If each kg of fuel needs 15 kg of air for combustion in the engine, you should be able to work out how much air you need for your car each day. The car exhaust also contaminates the air we breathe. You can see that the air is an indispensable resource, which we contaminate by using it.

In these units we will examine some aspects of air quality, look at how the air behaves, and see how we can minimise our impact on what may be regarded as our most precious resource.

## 1.2   What is air pollution?

The United Kingdom is where the industrial revolution began, bringing with it a legacy of damage to the natural environment and public health. Resources such as water, coal and minerals were exploited, and by the middle of the nineteenth century the air and water were choked with industrial emissions. Measures to protect the environment can be traced back to this period, and later we will look at some of the early decisions relating to the improvement of air quality. The air is obviously an important part of the environment to protect – it is essential for the survival of all higher forms of life on the planet. While seemingly vast, the atmosphere accounts for only about 1% of the diameter of the Earth. It is also continuous and so may be contaminated by activities perhaps hundreds or even thousands of miles away. We usually refer to this contamination as *air pollution*. The World Health Organisation has defined air pollution as:

> The presence in the outdoor atmosphere of one or more contaminants, such as dust, fumes, gas, mist, odour, smoke or vapour, in quantities or characteristics, and of duration such as to be injurious to human, plant or animal life or to property, or which unreasonably interferes with the comfortable enjoyment of life and property.

While this is a lengthy definition it ignores some important aspects. For example, it does not acknowledge that we spend over 70% of our time indoors, nor does it refer to energy as a pollutant. Broader definitions of pollution are found in Unit 1 and in the set book, but to put it simply:

> Pollution is something in the wrong place at the wrong time in the wrong quantity.

## 1.3 Air quality

In Unit 3, we showed a table with the approximate composition of dry air from the *troposphere* (lower atmosphere). It is repeated in Table 2 below, with a few additions.

**Table 2** *Approximate composition of dry tropospheric air*

| Gas | Symbol | Typical concentration in air (vol. per vol./ppm) | (mass per vol./$\mu g\ m^{-3}$) |
|---|---|---|---|
| *Essentially permanent* | | | |
| nitrogen | $N_2$ | $781 \times 10^3$ | $976 \times 10^6$ |
| oxygen | $O_2$ | $209.5 \times 10^3$ | $229 \times 10^6$ |
| argon | Ar | 9340 | $16.7 \times 10^6$ |
| neon | Ne | 18.36 | 16 400 |
| helium | He | 5.24 | 940 |
| krypton | Kr | 1.14 | 4263 |
| xenon | Xe | 0.09 | 527 |
| *Variable* | | | |
| hydrogen | $H_2$ | 0.5 | 45 |
| methane | $CH_4$ | 2 | 1430 |
| nitrous oxide | $N_2O$ | 0.33 | 648 |
| carbon dioxide | $CO_2$ | 340 | $0.668 \times 10^6$ |
| ozone | $O_3$ | $(1–5) \times 10^{-2}$ | |
| *Very variable* | | | |
| carbon monoxide | CO | 0.05–0.25 | |
| nitrogen dioxide | $NO_2$ | $(0.1–5) \times 10^{-3}$ | |
| ammonia | $NH_3$ | $(0.1–10) \times 10^{-3}$ | |
| sulphur dioxide | $SO_2$ | $(0.03–30) \times 10^{-3}$ | |
| hydrogen sulphide | $H_2S$ | $(<0.006–0.6) \times 10^{-3}$ | |
| water | $H_2O$ | 10 ppm to 4% | |

Undoubtedly, the troposphere contains many other compounds not shown in Table 2, but the gases shown are among the most important in any consideration of air quality. In addition, **aerosols** or **particulate** matter are present, and include substances such as trace metals and a variety of organic compounds. From this, you should appreciate that there is no such thing as 'pure air', for air is a mixture. The composition of the minor, or trace, components is very variable in space and over time, and the variable components are those that are considered air pollution. All of those shown in the table have natural sources, but are also produced from human activities. When concentrations increase to an extent that local or global air quality deteriorates, we can regard this as air pollution. As we will see later, even the major components nitrogen and oxygen take part in chemical reactions in which pollutants may be formed. There is no space to review the nature, sources and effects of all air pollutants, and so only a selection will be covered. Our selection includes several of the more important air pollutants, which in regulations under the **Environmental Protection Act** 1990 are known as 'prescribed substances' (Table 3).

**Table 3**   *Chemical substances released to air which are classified as 'prescribed substances' in regulations issued under the Environmental Protection Act 1990*

Oxides of sulphur and other sulphur compounds

Oxides of carbon

Metals, metalloids and their compounds

Halogens and their compounds

Particulate matter

Oxides of nitrogen and other nitrogen compounds

Organic compounds and partial oxidation products

Asbestos (suspended particulate matter and fibres), glass fibres and mineral fibres

Phosphorus and its compounds

### 1.3.1   Sulphur

Atmospheric sulphur compounds include $SO_2$, $SO_3$, sulphuric acid, sulphate salts and reduced compounds such as hydrogen sulphide. (Recall from Unit 3 the chemical use of the word 'reduced'.) Estimates suggest that up to half of the atmospheric sulphur is as $SO_2$ from human activities, with the remainder being generated as reduced sulphur from natural processes. Unfortunately, human activities tend to be concentrated in a global sense, and so give rise to local high levels of sulphur pollutants. Hence there have been many air pollution problems related to $SO_2$ concentrations building up in cities. The acid which is produced when $SO_2$ from the contaminated air dissolves in water also contributes to the phenomenon known as **acid rain**, which is of concern over wider areas, and will be discussed in more detail in Section 3.5. An additional problem is that emissions of $SO_2$ from human activities are increasing on a global scale, and predictions suggest that they will soon overtake natural emissions. In the UK, however, concentrations have declined at ground level (Figure 2 and set book under **ground-level concentration**). Fuel changes may have accounted for this trend in part, but the control philosophy of dispersing combustion products from tall chimneys has also played an important role. While this approach may avoid an impact on the local environment, it contributes to long-range transport of air pollutants. We will explore some features of this in the context of acid rain.

### 1.3.2   Nitrogen

Nitrogen oxides are intimately associated with air pollution problems known as **photochemical smog**, the **ozone hole**, and **acid rain**. These are described in the set book, and will be covered in more detail later. We can deduce from Table 2 that the troposphere is about 80% nitrogen by volume. The second most abundant nitrogen compound is nitrous oxide ($N_2O$). At normal concentrations it is not harmful to health,

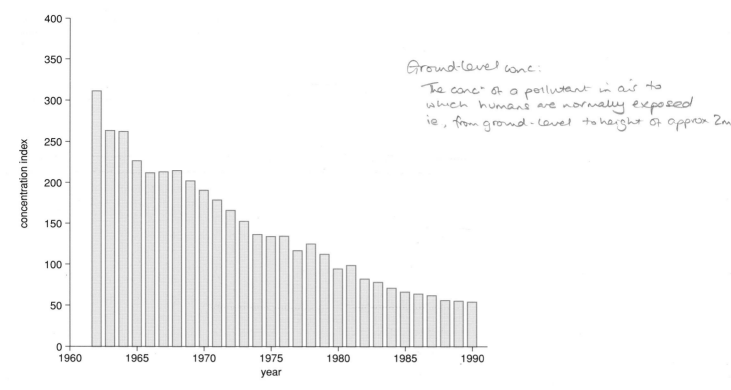

Ground-level conc:
The concⁿ of a pollutant in air to
which humans are normally exposed
ie, from ground-level to height of approx 2m

**Figure 2** *The decline in ground-level concentrations of sulphur dioxide over the last 30 years. (The sulphur dioxide concentration is represented as a concentration index – a relative scale rather than an absolute concentration scale.)*

and is in fact the anaesthetic known as 'laughing gas'. It is generated by natural processes and is only present at an average 0.33 ppm by volume in the air. Its major significance is in the contribution to the ozone hole, as will be outlined in Section 3.4.2.

The most important reactions of nitrogen in the troposphere relate to the formation of other oxides during combustion. From many sources, including motor vehicles and furnaces, nitric oxide (NO) is produced by the chemical reaction

$$N_2 + O_2 \rightarrow 2NO$$

Very little NO is produced at room temperature, but at flame temperature very much more NO is formed. Figure 3 depicts how the amount of NO varies within the normal range of combustion temperatures. Above 1200 °C, so called 'thermal' nitric oxide is produced, initiated by the oxidation of molecular nitrogen by oxygen *radicals*. The rate of reaction increases rapidly with temperature, and is significant above 1700 °C. Maximum thermal nitric oxide formation takes place using near stoichiometric air/fuel ratios, especially with fuels giving high flame temperatures.

Free Radicals
- atoms or molecule
with odd number of
bonding electrons
eg., $HO_2$, $Cl$, $NO_3$
responsible for most
atmospheric chemical
reactions.

---

### SAQ 1

Suggest how thermally produced NO from a combustion system may be minimised.
— lower flame temperatures

---

Another mechanism for nitric oxide formation involves the reaction of molecular nitrogen with hydrocarbon radicals derived from the fuel. This is a less significant route than the first, but can be important under fuel-rich conditions.

A third mechanism involves oxidation of nitrogen compounds contained in the fuel, but is minimal for clean gaseous and distillate fuels.

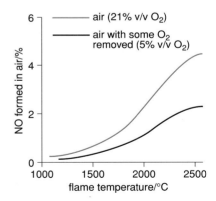

**Figure 3** *Formation of NO from air as a function of flame temperature.*

Nitric oxide undergoes an equilibrium reaction with oxygen to produce nitrogen dioxide ($NO_2$):

$$2NO + O_2 \rightarrow 2NO_2$$

The ratio of $NO:NO_2$ increases with temperature, and at ambient conditions favours $NO_2$ formation. At higher temperatures (say 500 °C) the equilibrium is about equal, but because the reaction is relatively slow, the typical proportion of $NO_2$ in combustion gases may be less that 10% of the total oxides of nitrogen.

Nitric oxide has no adverse health effects, but is slowly converted in the atmosphere to produce nitrogen dioxide ($NO_2$), which is toxic and forms *secondary pollutants*.

Another compound of nitrogen, ammonia ($NH_3$), is also important as an air pollutant. It is a colourless gas having a characteristic sharp, pungent odour. With water, ammonia produces an alkaline solution which can react with acids to produce ammonium compounds, such as ammonium sulphate and ammonium nitrate, which make up many airborne particles.

### 1.3.3   Carbon

Carbon monoxide (CO) and carbon dioxide ($CO_2$) are the main carbon compounds of concern as primary air pollutants from combustion processes. The significance of these gases will be covered in more detail in later sections.

In addition, many organic compounds contribute to odour problems and to the formation of secondary air pollutants. Of increasing concern are the *volatile organic compounds (VOCs)*, which include many solvents used in paints and adhesives, as well as hydrocarbons evaporating from fuels such as petrol.

VOC's
Organic compounds & hydrocarbons eg. benzene, styrene, acetone. Which readily evaporate and cause air pollution directly or via chemical reactions (to produce for example ozone)

## 1.4   Effects of air pollutants

Atmospheric pollution may have adverse effects on human health, the biosphere, natural resources (especially water and soil), buildings, and materials.

The extensive range of air pollutants and their potential effects on human, animal and plant life, on buildings and materials, and on climate, rivers and land are too numerous to cover in detail. Table 4 summarises some of the principal air pollutants and their effects. Some of the terminology may be unfamiliar at present, but this and some of the effects will be amplified in more detail as we progress through this text. Table 5 reviews some problems of particulate matter. Notice that the term 'particulate matter' refers to anything in a condensed phase, whether liquid or solid. A comprehensive review of the effects of air pollutants is beyond the bounds of this part of the course, so we will examine only a few aspects here. Certain air pollutants will be considered in more detail later.

**Table 4**  *Major sources and principal effects of some common air pollutants*

| Pollutant (and physical properties) | Major sources through human activities | Natural sources | Principal effects |
|---|---|---|---|
| Sulphur dioxide (colourless gas with irritating, pungent odour; detected by taste at 0.3–1 ppm (v/v); very soluble in water) | Fuel combustion (coal, oil, cellulosic material); industrial processes such as metal and petroleum refining | Atmospheric oxidation of organic sulphides | Sensory and respiratory irritation; plant damage; corrosion; potential health effects; contribution to acid deposition problems |
| Oxidants – of which ozone is an indicator species (ozone is a colourless, toxic gas, slightly soluble in water) | Atmospheric photochemical reactions involving nitrogen oxides, organic vapours and solar radiation | Natural atmospheric chemistry; transport from upper to lower atmosphere | Sensory and respiratory irritation; plant damage; reduced visibility through formation of photochemical aerosols; adverse health effects; material damage (e.g. polymers) |
| Carbon monoxide (colourless, odourless, flammable gas, slightly soluble in water) | Transportation; fuel combustion for space heating and industrial processes | Atmospheric oxidation of methane and other hydrocarbons of biological origin | Reduction in the oxygen-carrying capacity of the blood (see Units 2 and 3); toxic at high concentration |
| Non-methane hydrocarbons | Transportation; fuel combustion; industrial processes; solvent evaporation | Vegetation (e.g. pine forests) | Visibility reduction, plant damage and sensory irritation; contribution to photochemical pollutant formation |
| Nitrogen oxides ($NO_2$ is a reddish brown gas with a sharp odour; is toxic and corrosive, giving an acid gas in solution; absorbs light over much of the visible spectrum. NO and $N_2O$ are colourless, odourless gases, only slightly soluble in water) | Transportation; fuel combustion; industrial processes | Bacterial action produces NO and $N_2O$; natural combustion and lightning | Visibility reduction, plant damage; sensory irritation through formation of photochemical pollutants; direct health effects of nitrogen dioxide; contribute to stratospheric ozone loss and global warming; contribute to acid deposition |
| Carbon dioxide (colourless, odourless gas, moderately soluble in water giving an acid solution) | Combustion | Natural combustion | Global warming |
| Hydrogen sulphide (colourless, flammable gas; highly toxic and having a characteristic odour of 'bad eggs' | Coke-making; tar distillation; viscose rayon manufacture; chicken feather processing; natural gas and petroleum refining | Biological decay; volcanoes and geothermal activities | Odour *nuisance*; a toxic gas in high concentrations |
| Hydrogen fluoride (colourless gas dissolving in water to give an acidic solution; highly toxic) | Heating to high temperatures certain ores, clays or fluxes containing fluorine, e.g. in steel, ceramic, aluminium and superphosphate fertiliser manufacture | | Damage to plants; weakens teeth and bones of livestock grazing on forage contaminated by atmospheric fluoride |
| Lead | Vehicles using leaded petrol; industrial emissions | | Interference with metabolic processes; toxic in high doses |

**Table 5** *Particulate pollution of the atmosphere*

| | |
|---|---|
| Health problems | Respiratory effects caused by large concentrations of particles <1 μm, and fibrous particles such as asbestos. |
| | Toxicity caused by components such as fluorides, lead, cadmium, beryllium, etc. |
| | Eye or skin irritation caused by acid mists or small particles. |
| Aesthetic problems | Soiling by large mass emission rates, tarry or sticky emissions. |
| | Low visibility caused by small particles <1 μm which cause great light scattering. |
| | Odour. |
| Economic problems | Material damage caused by corrosive particles. |
| | Cleaning costs related to soiling. |
| | Secondary economic problems caused by neighbourhood deterioration. |
| Toxicological aspects | Particulate matter may be toxic through: |
| | (a) intrinsic toxicity of the particles; |
| | (b) interference with clearance mechanisms of respiratory tract; |
| | (c) particles carrying toxic substance. |
| | Evaluation on the basis of mass or concentration alone is insufficient; particle size must be considered. |
| | Sub-micrometre particles are more active physiologically than larger particles. |
| | Some particulate matter aggravates the effect of irritant gases (synergism). |

*[Handwritten margin notes:]*
*non-methane hydrocarbons*
*carbon monoxide*
*(+ smoke, sulphur dioxide, nitrogen oxides, & carbon dioxide)*

*non-methane hydrocarbons*
*(oxidants produced indirectly)*

*oxidants (from photochemical reactions)*

## SAQ 2

By reference to Table 4, identify the major pollutants you may expect from:
(a)  incomplete combustion;
(b)  solvent use;
(c)  photochemical reactions in the atmosphere.

### *1.4.1 Human health effects*

The adverse effects of air pollutants on human health depend on both the amount and concentration of pollutants. Non-toxic particulate matter in the form of dusts may present more of an irritation than a harmful effect, although excessive amounts of dusts may cause harm, as Table 5 indicates. Overloading the clearance mechanisms of the respiratory system may be one cause of irritation, although this may lead to a decrease in resistance to disease. An alternative case is where a dust contains components that are inherently toxic, such as asbestos fibres from damaged insulation, lead from vehicle exhausts, vanadium from oil burning or dioxins from combustion processes in general.

In short-term exposure, the human body may be exposed to a concentration of pollutant that causes no unfavourable reaction, but such concentrations differ widely from one pollutant to another. When such a threshold is exceeded, the body may react by resistive or adaptive processes in which it attempts to eliminate the pollutant. Coughing is one of the automatic defence mechanisms that operates when we enter a polluted atmosphere that we can detect by our senses. Unfortunately, we are not able to sense all harmful pollutants.

The effects of high concentrations of many air pollutants have been most clearly established. For example, fluorides released from ceramic processes and aluminium smelting have adverse effects on bones and teeth, as well as on the calcium level in the blood. Hydrogen sulphide is notorious as causing the smell of bad eggs, but is also very toxic and may cause death. Carbon monoxide is also very toxic, but is odourless and tasteless, which may increase the hazard of this pollutant. Hydrocarbons include many compounds, but substances such as aldehydes and ketones are particularly important, being irritant to the eyes and nose, as well as having effects on the central nervous system. Nitrogen oxides are worthy of note because nitrogen dioxide in particular has a delayed effect on the respiratory system, which it may also sensitise to damage by other pollutants.

It is important to recognise that we are not exposed to a single air pollutant, but to a cocktail of pollutants, each of which by itself may not be harmful. As Table 5 indicates, irritant gases (such as sulphur dioxide) and particulate matter may produce ill-health effects far greater than simply adding together their effects. We will return to this phenomenon of *synergism* later.

## 1.4.2 Effects on vegetation

Plants respire carbon dioxide and draw it in for photosynthesis through the *stomata* on the undersides of leaves. The stomata are designed to allow free passage of gases and are non-selective; plants are consequently sensitive to air pollution. Records of plant injury go back to the last century, but damage to vegetation has received most publicity since the 1970s and the increased awareness of the phenomenon known as acid rain. This is more correctly called 'acid deposition' as its effects are not due to wet deposition in rainfall alone, but include dry deposition when gases come into contact with a surface. The acid gases contributing to acid deposition are primarily sulphur oxides and nitrogen dioxide, although other pollutants also play important roles. For example, ozone contributes to the formation of the acidic oxides. Deciduous trees seem to absorb more sulphur dioxide than evergreens, but tend to be more resistant to its effects. The plant injury depends on the concentration and exposure time, in a similar manner to human health effects. Likewise, coniferous trees may suffer chronic (long-term, low concentration) injury, reflected in premature loss of older needles and ultimately death of the tree. At higher concentrations, acute damage to needles occurs, with chlorophyll decomposition being apparent through discoloration of needles within as short a time as a few hours.

Fluorides are another form of air pollution causing severe plant injury. If you refer to the entry for *gladioli* in the set book, you will see that these plants have been used as sensitivity indicators for fluorides. Linking vegetation injury to air pollutants is notoriously difficult, however, because certain effects resemble those of stress through water stress, frost damage, or soil contamination. Nevertheless, there is convincing evidence of injury due to air pollutants resulting in reductions in crop yields.

## 1.4.3 Effects on animals

Domestic and other animals suffer from the effects of air pollution directly by breathing polluted air in a manner similar to humans, and also indirectly through eating vegetation contaminated by air pollutants. However, as domestic livestock are often slaughtered for market at relatively young ages, the effects are often unnoticed. Certain effects are well known, such as the blindness of chickens due to ammonia in poorly managed intensive units. Fluorides have also caused considerable economic loss due to fluorosis in cattle, although this is less widespread than in the past.

## 1.4.4 Effects on materials

Corrosion by the action of acidic air pollutants has important economic consequences and requires continuous efforts to protect and maintain structures, usually by painting. It is ironic that painting itself is a major cause of air pollution by hydrocarbons or volatile organic compounds (VOCs) as we will see later. Substances that increase the corrosive effects of the atmosphere on steel and other metallic structures are notably the acid gases sulphur dioxide, nitrogen dioxide and hydrogen chloride, which in combination with atmospheric humidity produce the corresponding acids. The life-time of organic materials (rubber, plastics and paints) is also decreased by pollutants such as the oxidants ozone, chlorine and nitrogen oxides. Construction materials such as brick and natural stone also suffer from damage by air pollutants, and many ancient monuments, such as the Parthenon in Athens, have suffered considerable damage due to air pollution this century. Sulphur dioxide is especially harmful to limestone. It converts the calcium carbonate to calcium sulphate, and the resulting volume change leads to surface cracking. This surface damage allows water to enter, and although the calcium sulphate is not soluble, freezing of the water causes further physical damage. The damage to buildings is consequently increased and the expense of maintenance multiplied several times. At least the soiling of buildings by *smoke* tends to be a lesser problem now than in the first half of this century, and it is economically practi-cable to clean buildings as they will remain clean for longer than in the past.

Many other effects on materials could be listed; I will mention merely two. Electrical components containing copper are readily damaged by even small amounts of nitrates in the air as a result of the combined effect of nitrogen oxides and atmospheric humidity. Paper is also damaged by air pollutants, and air conditioning with air purifi-cation is often provided for library archives containing old manuscripts.

## 1.5 What are the causes of air pollution?

We shall see in these units that air quality is closely linked with weather conditions, and that human activities are major contributors to air pollution. Figure 4 summarises some of the causes of air pollution. As we go through this text we will see how these causes may be dealt with.

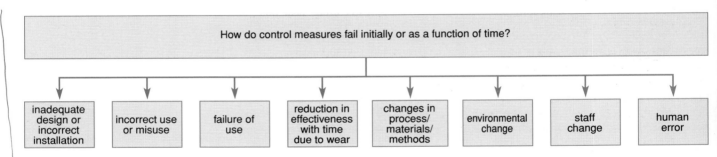

**Figure 4**

# 2   A DIVERSION INTO HISTORY

The health effects of air pollution from fuel use have long been known.

> And they took ashes of the furnace, and stood before Pharaoh; and Moses sprinkled it up towards heaven; and it became a boil breaking forth with blains upon man, and upon beast.
>
> *(Exodus 9.x)*

The chronology of more recent events is perhaps more impressive. The thirteenth century seems to have been the time when air pollution made itself felt in England; there were no less than four commissions to investigate the phenomenon between 1285 and 1310.

> 20 May 1285: Commission to Roger de Northwode, John de Cobenham and Henry de Galleys to enquire touching certain lime kilns constructed in the city and suburbs of London and Southwark of which it is complained that whereas formerly the lime used to be burnt with wood it is now burnt with sea coal, whereby the air is infected and corrupted to the peril of those frequenting and dwelling in these parts.

There was no change in the growth rate of medieval cities or of industry at that time, and the problems with pollution seem to have been brought about by a change in fuel use. As we will see later, fuel use by society may have a great impact on environmental quality. In the middle ages, the primary source of air pollution was combustion processes, just as today. Domestic heating must have needed large amounts of fuel, but though widespread the individual sources would not have been large. At the low end of the industrial scale, the bakers, dyers, chandlers and brewers would all have caused annoyance in the crowded cities of the day, but they were small in scale compared with the production of building materials, pottery and tile kilns, iron making and the lime industry.

In homes the domestic smokeless fuel for cooking was charcoal. The charcoal burners themselves must have caused a great deal of air pollution, but they usually worked in the forests, close to their raw material and away from the towns and cities. We can look at this as a good example of early planning controls, with industrial zoning of polluting sources away from residential areas; in practice, it was probably convenience rather than public policy.

It seems that the price of wood soared between 1270 and 1290, while the price of coal, transported by sea essentially as ballast, remained stable; so the switch to so-called sea-coal may initially have been on financial grounds. However, the properties of the fuel were so attractive that its use increased.

In 1273 the use of coal in London was prohibited as being 'prejudicial to health', but the popularity of coal was so great that its use continued, and so did the pollution. There is record of an action in 1377 brought against Stephen atte Frythe, armourer, complaining of the nuisance by smoke from his forge in Watling Street and of the great hammers causing so much noise and vibration that they shook the stone and plaster walls of his neighbours' houses, which deprived them of rest day and night and thickened and spoiled the wine in their cellars.

In 1661 the pollution of London had become so bad that it prompted John Evelyn to write the publication 'Fumifugium, or the Inconvenience of the Aer, and Smoake of London Dissipated', which he submitted to Charles II and Parliament. It is clear, however, that early attempts to control air pollution by legislation failed.

The principal industries associated with air pollution in the centuries before the Industrial Revolution were metallurgy, ceramics and animal products. In the nineteenth century the chemical industry emerged, including the notorious Leblanc process for the manufacture of sodium carbonate from sodium chloride. The process resulted in copious emissions of hydrochloric acid gas, which escaped to the atmosphere. The resulting pollution caused considerable concern and resulted in the Alkali Act of 1863. This introduced the Alkali Inspectorate, whose successors form part of HM Inspectorate of Pollution (HMIP).

## 2.1  Recent air pollution disasters

This century has seen great changes in technology both in the production and in the control of air pollution. We have also seen some of the worst air pollution disasters resulting in considerable loss of life and severe illness. These episodes have been the subject of epidemiological studies of the type introduced in Unit 4 (Section 3). Table 6 summarises some of the important features of these episodes. Certain terms introduced in this table (such as those relating to weather conditions) may be unclear, but we will explain them in Section 3.

**Table 6**  *Comparison of three major air pollution crises: Meuse Valley, 1930; Donora, Pennsylvania, 1948; London, 1952*

| Conditions | Meuse Valley, 1930 | Donora, 1948 | London, 1952 |
|---|---|---|---|
| Weather | Anticyclonic, inversion, and fog | Anticyclonic, inversion, and fog | Anticyclonic, inversion, and fog |
| Topography | River valley | River valley | River plain |
| Most probable source of pollutants | Industry (including steel and zinc plants) | Industry (including steel and zinc plants) | Household coal-burning |
| Nature of the illness | Chemical irritation of exposed membranous surfaces | Chemical irritation of exposed membranous surfaces | Chemical irritation of exposed membranous surfaces |
| Deaths among those with pre-existing cardiorespiratory disease | Yes | Yes | Yes |
| Time of deaths | Began after second day of episode | Began after second day of episode | Began on first day of episode |
| Ratio of illnesses to deaths | Not available | 75:1 to 300:1 | Illness rates not in expected proportion to those of deaths |
| Autopsy findings | Inflammatory lesions in lungs | Inflammatory lesions in lungs | Inflammatory lesions in lungs |
| Suspected proximate cause of irritation | Fluorides and sulphur oxides with particulates | Sulphur oxides with particulates | Sulphur oxides with particulates |

Source: Air Pollution Monograph Series, World Health Organization, Geneva, 1961.

One episode occurred in the Meuse Valley between Huy and Liège in Belgium. The valley is 15 miles long, about 0.75 miles wide and about 120 m deep; it was densely populated and a centre of heavy industry. Between 1 and 5 December 1930, prolonged stable weather conditions resulted in drainage of cold air from uplands to the valley, producing severe fogs under a *temperature inversion*. Several hundred people became ill and some 60 died as a result of respiratory illness; this was ten times the figure expected for the period, and we could say that there were some 54 excess deaths. We met the concept of an expected number of deaths in Section 4.3 of Unit 4. Livestock also suffered from the effects of the air pollution and many cattle had to be slaughtered. No measurements of air quality were made either during or before the episode, but after excluding other possibilities an official enquiry concluded that illnesses and deaths were due to poisonous waste gases from the factories accumulating under unusual climatic conditions. Sulphur dioxide was thought to be a primary cause, but a subsequent investigation revealed 15 factories in the area which could have emitted fluorine compounds. Thus the ill effects may have been acute fluorine intoxication aggravated by immense quantities of suspended particulate matter in the air. The possibility of many components in the environment contributing to adverse effects is a common example of multiple causality, which may make it difficult to identify the best way of dealing with a problem. The absence of air quality data from the Meuse Valley episode meant that lessons could not be learned to prevent subsequent problems.

Donora is an industrial town situated in the valley of the River Monongahela some 30 miles south of Pittsburgh, USA. The setting is similar to that in the Meuse Valley. Heavy industry in Donora included many steel works, smelting works and sulphuric acid plant. The main fuel in the area was coal. Visible smog was common in the area until about 10 a.m, but in spring and autumn this commonly persisted throughout the day. From 25 to 31 October 1948 very stable weather conditions produced conditions similar to those in the Meuse Valley. The fog accumulated day by day until rain dispersed it on 31 October. Once again there was a striking increase in respiratory tract complaints, with some 42% of the population of 14 000 suffering some illness. Twenty people died, mainly on the third day, and of these a pre-existing cardiac or respiratory disease was common. A follow-up study ten years later indicated that those who became ill in the 1948 episode showed higher mortality and illness than others in the town at the time. The highest illness rates were in smokers who became ill during the episode.

An examination of Donora's mortality statistics revealed that a similar increase had occurred in 1945, but a link with environmental factors had not been recognised at that time. As in the Meuse Valley, no environmental measurements were made, but it was estimated that sulphur dioxide levels reached 1.4–5.5 mg m$^{-3}$, and particulate matter was also undoubtedly high. The fog remained dense, yet calls for medical assistance ceased abruptly on the Saturday evening. This suggests a change in the nature of particulate matter (smoke), perhaps an increase in the size of the particles suspended in the air, allowing them to be filtered out or to deposit in the upper airways of the human respiratory system.

Epidemiological links between air pollution and ill-health are no more marked than in London where, as we have shown in Table 6, there was the disaster of 1952. A fog of unprecedented scale descended over the city from 5 to 8 December. One of the earliest signs of problems was illness among livestock at the annual Smithfield Show, but human health problems soon followed. Mortality was mainly due to respiratory and cardiovascular disease, with over 90% of the deaths in people over the age of 45, while deaths in children under 1 year of age were doubled. Illnesses were unusually sudden in onset, typically on the third or fourth day of the episode. Shortness of breath, some fever and an excess of fluid in the lungs were found. The mortality remained high for several weeks after the air quality improved, suggesting that acute pollution may start a process which subsequently continues, e.g. lowered resistance to infection.

Data for the then County of London are shown in Table 7.

**Table 7**   *Mortality in the London fog of 1952 (central London)*

| Cause | Seasonal norm (deaths per week) | Deaths in week after fog | Excess deaths |
|---|---|---|---|
| Bronchitis | 75 | 704 | |
| Other lung diseases | 98 | 366 | |
| Coronary heart disease, myocardial degeneration | 206 | 525 | |
| Other diseases | 508 | 889 | |
| Total | 887 | 2484 | |

### SAQ 3

Complete Table 7 to show the number of excess deaths attributed to the 1952 London smog episode.

Fortunately, measurements of smoke and sulphur dioxide have been carried out in the UK since 1912. In fact, these two pollutants have been synonymous with air pollution to many people until relatively recent times, although the possible role of other pollutants cannot be discounted. Nevertheless, the adverse health effects of smoke and sulphur dioxide are well documented, and data are available for the UK. A close relationship was found between the excess mortality and the atmospheric concentrations of the two pollutants – as seen from the entry **sulphur oxides** in the set book, which illustrates the link between air quality and deaths. While this relationship does not necessarily imply causes, the linkage of the two pollutants with respiratory disease has been well established and, as we shall see later, has enabled **air quality standards** to be developed for their control.

Before continuing on our journey through time we should note that the public outcry from the London disaster resulted in legislation in the form of the Clean Air Act of 1956 and its subsequent regulations and amendments. Strong evidence on air quality, knowledge about the adverse health effects of the pollutants concerned, and the public outcry following the disaster forced the government of the day to decide on legislation. This Act was one of the first principal pieces of legislation to deal with air pollution anywhere in the world. Through the controls over smoke emissions, and the requirements to fit gas-cleaning plant to furnaces, the levels of pollution by smoke have been reduced considerably. One major reason for this was another fuel change, but unlike that in the thirteenth century when coal use increased, the switch was away from coal to gas. As we can see from Table 6, domestic coal burning was strongly implicated in the London smog episode, particularly because the smoke from domestic chimneys is emitted at a relatively low level compared with industrial chimneys. Consequently, it has a significant impact at ground level where we go about our daily business. In the 1950s coal tended to be replaced by cleaner and more convenient gas for home heating, while those wanting to keep coal fires had to use smokeless fuels or fireplaces that burned coal without producing smoke.

Likewise, the local pollution by sulphur dioxide has also fallen, but this has been primarily through using tall chimneys to disperse the pollution over great distances, thereby reducing concentrations but not the total discharge. Nowadays we are recognising the folly of over-reliance on this choice of control, which contributes to long-range transport of pollution in the form commonly known as acid rain. While the Clean Air Act provided a legal framework for the control of air pollution, it is arguable that other factors were also important. Industry recognised that smoke going up the chimney was wasted energy, which they could not afford to waste, and so combustion efficiency was improved. This is an important example of waste reduction or **waste minimisation**, which you will find defined in the set book. Oil and gas, which were cheaper and more convenient than coal, were increasingly used – to the benefit of air quality since they are less likely to produce smoke. Similarly, as we have mentioned earlier, at home it was cheaper and more convenient to use these fuels than coal. So now we have turned the full circle from the thirteenth century. A fuel change then caused a deterioration in air quality, whereas in the middle of the twentieth century a fuel change brought about improvements.

As we can see from Table 8, there have been other episodes in London before and since that of 1952. We should comment particularly on the remarkable worldwide episode that occurred in 1962. That episode produced serious health effects as it swept from west to east between 27 November and 10 December. Between 27 November and 5 December high pollution levels were noted in Washington DC, Philadelphia, New York and Cincinnati. In New York City an increase in respiratory symptoms was detected. Between 5 and 7 December sulphur dioxide levels in London exceeded those of the 1952 episode, but particulates were lower; 700 excess deaths were reported. Between 2 and 7 December sulphur dioxide reached five times the normal level in Rotterdam, and mortality and hospital admissions increased, while from 3 to 7 December in Hamburg sulphur dioxide reached over five times its normal level and particulates over twice the normal. Increased pollution was also reported in Paris, Frankfurt, Prague and Osaka. There was no increase in pollution recorded on the west coast of the USA nor in Australia. This episode illustrates the global perspective of air pollution, which has been emphasised in more recent years by concerns about acid deposition, global warming, deterioration of stratospheric ozone, and incidents such as that at **Chernobyl**.

**Table 8** *Some air pollution episodes in London*

| Date | Pollutants (conc. in $\mu g\ m^{-3}$) | Meteorology | Health effects |
|---|---|---|---|
| 9–11/12/1873 | | fog | 650 excess deaths |
| 26–29/1/1880 | | fog | 1176 excess deaths |
| 26/11–1/12/1948 | smoke 200–2800 $SO_2$ 250–2100 | visibility 24–400 m wind 0–4.6 mph | 700–800 excess deaths |
| 5–9/12/1952 | peak $SO_2$ 3800 peak smoke 4500 | vis. 20–210 m wind to 5.8 mph fog | bronchitis, emphysema, cardiovascular disorders, dyspnoea, wheezy chests, fever, 4000 excess deaths |
| 3–6/1/1956 | smoke to 2400 $SO_2$ to 1500 | | 1000 excess deaths |
| 5–10/12/1962 | peak smoke >4000 peak $SO_2$ >4000 | | 700 excess deaths |
| 14–16/12/1975 | peak smoke 811 | peak $SO_2$ 1238 | |
| 13/12/1991 | 382 ppb (v/v) $NO_2$ | anticylonic | None reported, but worst air quality for $NO_x$ since measurement began in 1976 |

With the decline in visible smoke, concern has turned to different air pollution problems such as those mentioned above. In particular, we should note the expansion of the chemical industry, which over the period 1950 to 1985 registered an increase in the production of organic chemicals from 7 million tonnes to 250 million tonnes. Against the benefits from these products must be weighed the accidents resulting in significant releases of potentially hazardous chemicals. The scale of the incident in 1984 at Bhopal in India is demonstrated by the 2800 deaths, 50 000 injuries and

200 000 evacuees resulting from the release of methyl isocyanate to the atmosphere. Methyl isocyanate (MIC) is used as a raw material in the manufacture of the insecticide carbaryl; it is a highly reactive chemical and several precautions are necessary for its safe storage. These include:

- storage only in stainless steel tanks;

- tanks only half full, or empty tank kept for emergency evacuation;

- inert nitrogen atmosphere above MIC;

- refrigerating the MIC storage tank using inert fluid;

- providing a *scrubber* to clean emissions in case of MIC escape.

## 2.2   What happened on 2 December 1984?

There was apparently a leak in the MIC plant and so it failed to get pressurised with nitrogen on the morning of 2 December. When plant operators started washing some pipelines, some water entered through leaking valves and ultimately entered the MIC tank.

The unexpected release of toxic gas from reaction of MIC with water frustrated any concerted effort to prevent the consequences. The lack of emergency advice allowed many to die, while the failure to provide toxicity data limited the role of the medical services.

Decisions to apply standard risk management practices, such as remote siting, early warning, evacuation plans and hazard communication, never materialised. All would have been particularly important with a high risk plant in a densely populated urban area such as Bhopal.

## 2.3   Our increasing use of energy

For thousands of years we have lived on Earth, but our impact on it has been mainly within the past millennium. Until about 8000 BC we were hunter–gatherers of wild produce and had no domestic animals or crops. We ate fruit and berries, whose seeds were dispersed as they are today by birds and animals. Our wastes were dispersed over the land and served to fertilise it, as did our decaying remains after death. We were insignificant in the ecosystem.

As we turned to agriculture, our effect on the environment increased. Some crop growing has gone on for perhaps ten thousand years, although arable farming has a history of half that time. Broadcast sowing made hand weeding the only practicable option, but as drilling in rows was introduced in the last century, weeding was easier, especially as labour was cheap. As wages rose, technology developed to aid the farming processes. Mechanisation and the wide use of pesticides (including herbicides) cut labour costs, increased crop yields to feed the growing population and also increased pollution.

The transition from an agricultural to a technological economy implies a large increase in energy consumption. Industrial production is clearly a major energy consumer, but transportation requires a substantial share of the energy supply, as does the increasing domestic consumption as standards of living rise. These issues generate much international political debate as less developed countries concentrate on economic and industrial growth to meet the needs of their growing populations, and so go through the cycle that developed countries have followed. While the debate between developed and less developed countries reflects each side's priorities, the distance between the two has diminished as global concerns have grown, but unfortunately remains. There is little doubt that the combustion of the fossil fuels (coal, oil and natural gas) represents the greatest source of air pollution. Among the variety of combustion products, sulphur dioxide, particulate matter and nitrogen oxides have the greatest potential health impact, while carbon dioxide has a significant role in global warming, and hence climatic change. The relative contributions of different sources to emissions of air pollutants in the UK are shown in Figure 5, and Figure 6 represents

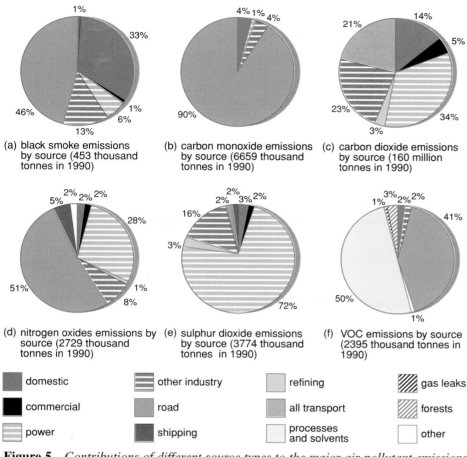

**Figure 5**   *Contributions of different source types to the major air pollutant emissions in 1990 in the UK.*

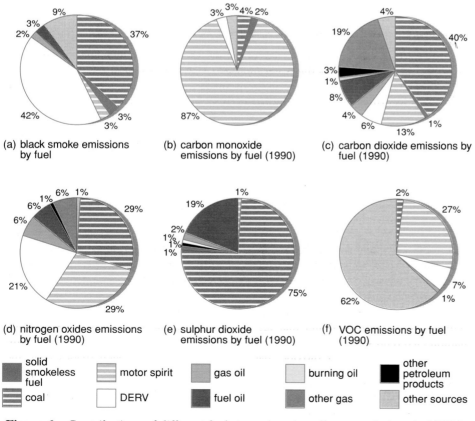

**Figure 6**   *Contributions of different fuels to major air pollutant emissions in 1990 in the UK.*

the contributions from different fuels. Large stationary combustion installations such as power stations produce over 70% of the total sulphur dioxide and over 40% of the nitrogen oxide emissions.

## SAQ 4

From Figures 5 and 6, identify the major fuels and sources contributing to emissions of the principal air pollutants in the UK in 1990.

The volatile organic compounds (VOCs) have been gaining increased attention in recent years, and by the time you are reading this text there will almost certainly be more controls over their production, both from vehicle emissions and a wide range of manufacturing processes. We will return to this important topic later. Energy consumption by traffic also produces pollutants such as lead, which have caused great concern over the last 20 years or so.

## Exercise

It has been estimated that about 70 million tonnes of petrol was consumed in the EC in 1973. Assuming that the average lead content of petrol was 0.55 g $l^{-1}$, the specific gravity of petrol was 0.7, and that 30% of the lead was retained in the engine and exhaust system, how much lead was emitted into the air from vehicle exhausts throughout the EC?

## Answer

The emission of lead is calculated by the relationship:

volume of petrol × average Pb content per litre × % Pb emitted

We can also calculate that the volume of petrol = total mass/specific gravity, so:

$(70 \times 10^6$ tonnes/0.7$) \times (0.55$ g/1 l$) \times (1$ kg/1000 g$) \times (70/100)$

$= 38.5 \times 10^3$ tonnes of Pb

(Notice how the dimensions cancel to yield the right units.)

Therefore, 70 million tonnes of petrol released $38.5 \times 10^3$ tonnes of lead into the atmosphere throughout the EC in 1973.

## SAQ 5

(a)  UK government statistics indicate that 23.9 million tonnes of petrol were consumed in 1989, compared with 18.7 million tonnes in 1979. Noting that in 1986 the limit on lead in petrol was reduced to 0.15 g $l^{-1}$ and assuming that the lead content of petrol before 1986 was 0.4 g $l^{-1}$, determine whether the releases to the atmosphere increased or declined over the decade.

(b)  Statistics for 1991 indicate that 24 million tonnes of petrol were used, of which 9.85 million tonnes were unleaded. Estimate the lead emissions from motor cars in 1991, assuming other data as in the previous Exercise.

From your calculation you will have seen that emissions of lead have been considerable. The associated health risks generated great public pressure for control over these emissions, and the trend towards unleaded petrol also provides another example of how a fuel change has a great impact on air quality. The global impact of lead as an air pollutant is demonstrated by its presence in Greenland snow, but the phased reduction in leaded petrol internationally is having an impact. Recent observations in Greenland have shown this effect and we will look at this in more detail in Section 5.2.5.

While lead emissions may be decreasing, the contribution of motor vehicles to other forms of air pollution is increasing, and we will return to this later in the course. However, in general, this text will deal mainly with so-called stationary sources of air pollution, i.e. boilers, furnaces and similar processes. Mobile sources make very important contributions to air pollution, as Figure 5 illustrates. In TV 7, you will see some research on assessing the significance of these mobile source emissions and in Section 6 we take a look at some aspects of transport emissions. In general, however, control of mobile source emissions is largely in the hands of vehicle and engine manufacturers. By comparison, emissions from stationary sources may depend much more on the way they are used and operated. As individuals, we must never forget that we have direct involvement and influence over emissions from stationary sources, but also have control over how much (and how) we drive.

As a final comment on the links between air pollution and changes in energy use, we may note the emergence of a competitor to coal and oil in power stations, namely *orimulsion*. Raw bitumen from the Orinoco Belt in eastern Venezuela has a very high viscosity at ambient temperatures and is unsuitable for direct use in power stations. By mixing the bitumen with about 30% water and a surfactant, a stable emulsion is obtained, known as orimulsion. This fuel behaves similarly to fuel oil and has performed well in trials in Canada, USA, Japan and in three power stations in the UK. While financially attractive compared with its competitors, the environmental costs of orimulsion are potentially greater. First of all, orimulsion has a relatively high sulphur content (2.9%), which necessitates gas cleaning equipment to remove the sulphur dioxide produced if the fuel is burned in power stations. The sulphur emission per unit of thermal energy released is greater than that of fuel oil. An application in 1992 to burn the fuel at Pembroke power station elicited an unusual response from the National Rivers Authority which was concerned about the impact of aerial emissions on waterways and acid sensitive soils already suffering from the effects of acid deposition. Up to 28% of streams and rivers in Wales have been claimed to be too acidic. A further problem related to the uncertainty of how the fuel would disperse if a spillage at sea occurred. Orimulsion is dense and most of it would sink in water, thereby making conventional marine pollution controls ineffective. The volume of ash produced by the combustion of orimulsion is less than from coal, but more than from oil, and most can be collected by gas cleaning equipment such as electrostatic precipitators, which we describe later. The ash consists mainly of magnesium oxide and relatively high concentrations of vanadium and nickel compounds. There is a market for the ash, for the commercial recovery of these compounds, but any waste would be classified as special waste, and must go to a suitably licensed landfill site.

Any future developments of this potential fuel change and of others that may emerge must be watched with interest by all concerned about air pollution and environmental quality in general.

## 2.4   Summary

Air quality is a term we may use in describing the composition of the air, which can never be 'pure' owing to its nature as a mixture of many chemical components. Deterioration of air quality by the introduction into the air of substances or energy which may cause harm or interference with use of the air as a resource is known as 'air pollution'. Until well into this century, air pollution was synonymous with smoke, and several pollution episodes through history have been associated with the problems of smoke and other pollutants in the atmosphere. Mortality and morbidity statistics demonstrate the impact of air pollution on human health, but effects on plants, materials and the environment itself are equally of concern. Smoke has its origins in combustion of fuels, and fuel use has very strong links with air pollution, although nowadays the emphasis is on the invisible pollutants: gases such as nitrogen oxides, sulphur oxides, carbon dioxide and carbon monoxide. We have come to realise that smoke is a manifestation of the inefficient use of fuels, and by improving the process using the fuel we may reduce the emissions of smoke. Legal controls over fuel quality and fuel use offer another means of preventing air pollution. Attention is increasingly being given to other pollutants and their sources, notably contributions from transport and solvent use.

# 3  AIR POLLUTION METEOROLOGY

You may have noticed that sometimes weather forecasts comment on air quality, with reference to sulphur dioxide, or nitrogen oxides in the winter, and ozone in the summer. You may conclude from this that air quality and meteorology (the science of the atmosphere) are connected, and in this section we shall examine some of the links.

## 3.1  The greenhouse effect

Let us start by looking at the effect of the atmosphere on the temperature of the Earth's surface. The source of heat is sunlight (short-wave radiation of wavelength around 0.2–4 µm), which reaches us at a rate ($E$) given by:

$$E = S(1 - A)\pi R^2 \text{ watts} \tag{1}$$

where $S$ is the **solar constant** ($1360 \pm 20$ W m$^{-2}$), $A$ is the albedo, or fraction of solar radiation reflected back into space (about 0.3), and $R$ is the Earth's radius ($6.37 \times 10^6$ m).

At equilibrium, this balances the energy loss to space, which is given by the Stefan-Boltzmann law. This states that the total energy emission ($E$) by a unit area of blackbody surface in terms of its absolute temperature is:

$$E = \sigma T^4$$

where $\sigma$ is the Stefan-Boltzmann constant ($5.67 \times 10^{-8}$ W m$^{-2}$ K$^{-4}$), and $T$ is the absolute temperature (°C + 273).

So for the Earth, the radiant energy loss is given by:

$$E = 4\pi R^2 \sigma T^4 \tag{2}$$

where $T$ is the surface absolute temperature.

If you equate the expressions for heat loss and heat gain, and solve for $T$, you will find an answer of 255 K, or −18 °C. This is done in the *Mathematics* supplement, but try this calculation for yourself to confirm the answer, which is what the Earth's surface temperature would be in the absence of an atmosphere.

As mentioned above, sunlight is electromagnetic radiation of wavelength between 0.2 and 4 µm, with a maximum in the visible spectrum at 0.5 µm. A cloudless sky is transparent to this radiation. However, the radiation from the Earth occurs between 2 µm and 40 µm (Figure 7) with a maximum around 10 µm. If you refer back to Figure 18 in Unit 3 *Environmental chemistry* you will see that this is in the infra-red region. Unlike sunlight, which is in the ultraviolet region, not all infra-red radiation can pass through the atmosphere. There is a great deal of water vapour in the atmosphere, and, as shown in Figure 6, this vapour absorbs infra-red radiation across a wide part of the spectrum under consideration (see **absorption** in the set book), but leaves a 'window' between about 8 and 14 µm. Carbon dioxide absorbs between 12 and 18 µm, and so effectively makes the window smaller. The radiation absorbed by gases such as water vapour and carbon dioxide is re-emitted in all directions. So only about half of the energy goes out into space, with the other half radiating back to the surface which it heats (Figure 8). As a result, the Earth's surface is not −18 °C, but a more comfortable average of 15 °C. This warming effect is called the greenhouse effect as an analogy with the functioning of a greenhouse, although other processes such as the containment of warmed air and exclusion of cold draughts contribute to the latter. The greenhouse effect is thus a natural process upon which we depend for our survival. It also accounts for the hot climate on Venus, with its carbon-dioxide-rich atmosphere, and the coldness of Mars, with little carbon dioxide. Perturbations in this natural process on Earth will be covered later (Section 3.6).

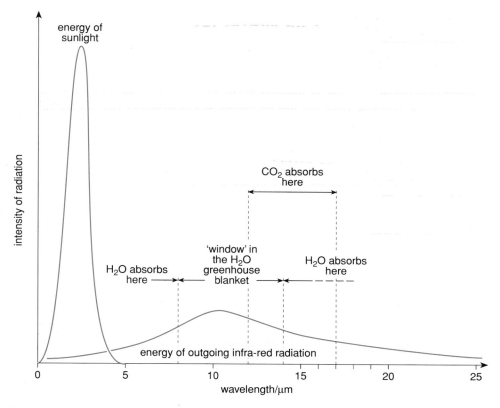

**Figure 7** *Incoming and outgoing radiation and contributions to the greenhouse effect.*

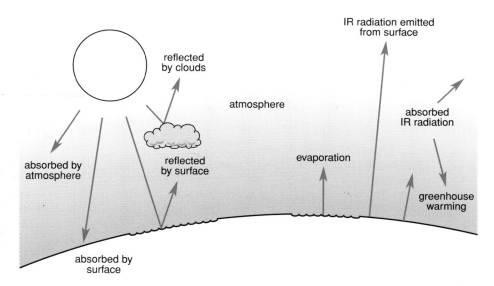

**Figure 8** *Some atmospheric interactions leading to the greenhouse effect by the warming effect of absorption of infra-red (IR) radiation.*

## 3.2 The vertical temperature profile

The dispersion of air pollutants through the atmosphere depends to a large extent on the speed and direction of the winds, but the vertical mixing is influenced strongly by differences in temperature with altitude. We have seen that the Earth's surface is warmed by sunlight and the greenhouse effect. A hypothetical parcel of air next to the surface is warmed and rises as it becomes less dense. In rising, it moves to a lower pressure region and so expands. Assuming that the parcel neither gains nor loses energy from its surroundings (we call this an adiabatic expansion), the energy for expansion comes from within the parcel, and so it cools. It can be calculated that the resulting temperature gradient is about −1 °C for each 100 m rise in altitude. This is known as the *dry adiabatic **lapse rate***, and its value is usually written as $-1\,°C\ 100\ m^{-1}$. If there were no other influences, then there would be a **stable** stratified atmosphere characterised by the temperature gradient associated with the dry adiabatic lapse rate.

If the air is moist, the cooling effect may allow water to condense and form clouds, with the release of enthalpy of evaporation (latent heat) reducing the cooling rate.

As the atmosphere is not quiescent, variable heating of the ground from one area to another and over time causes the lapse rate in the lowest few hundred metres of the atmosphere to show marked variations throughout the day. If you were to measure the temperature at various heights in the atmosphere you would be measuring the *environmental lapse rate*, and this may not be the same as the dry adiabatic lapse rate.

The vertical temperature gradient, or lapse rate, is generally used as an indicator of *atmospheric stability*, which, simply, is the tendency of the atmosphere to resist or enhance vertical motion. Some examples of vertical temperature profiles are shown in Figure 9, in which the broken line represents the 'ideal' or dry adiabatic lapse rate, while the solid lines are examples of the environmental lapse rate. We will see later that it is the gradient of the line that is important rather than the absolute values associated with it. The figure also shows the ways in which plumes discharged from chimneys (or 'stacks') tend to behave under different conditions of atmospheric stability. The resulting effect on the ground-level concentration of pollutants from the plume is also shown in the form of typical recorder traces from air quality measurement instruments.

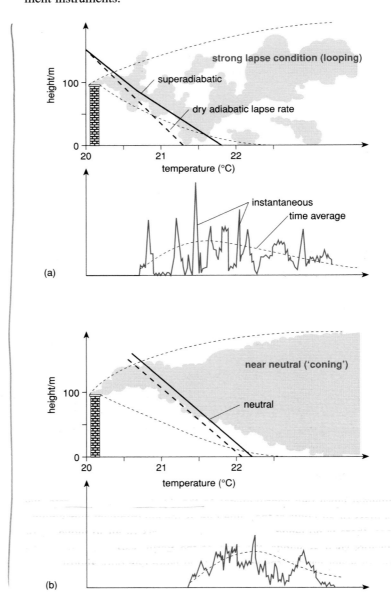

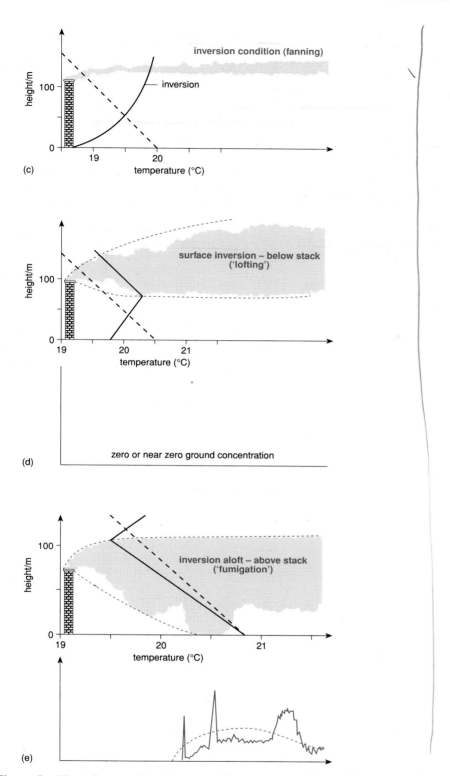

**Figure 9** *The influence of environmental lapse rates on plume behaviour and ground-level concentrations of pollutants: (a) strong lapse condition (looping); (b) near neutral ('coning'); (c) inversion condition (fanning); (d) surface inversion below stack ('lofting'); (e) inversion aloft above stock ('fumigation').*

### 3.2.1  Neutral conditions

When the environmental lapse rate approximates to the dry adiabatic lapse rate, we can envisage that a mass of air cools at the same rate as the environment surrounding it. As a consequence, there is no tendency for a displaced mass of air to move up or down. Owing to factors such as winds, the spin of the Earth, variable heating and cooling, and the role of water vapour, the environmental lapse rate only approximates to the 'ideal' dry adiabatic lapse rate if there is thorough mixing of the air. This is the case with neutral conditions. Neutral conditions are associated with overcast skies and moderate to strong winds; the clouds prevent solar radiation from reaching the surface, while the wind mixes the air and smooths temperature differences. Such conditions are common in the UK. A plume discharged under these conditions spreads out from the chimney as a steadily expanding but slightly tilted cone. This is depicted in Figure 9(b). Sooner or later the lower edge of the expanding cone or waste gases will reach the ground, although dispersion and dilution will continue downwind. Beyond the point of first contact and in a horizontal direction, the ground-level concentration of a pollutant tends to rise rapidly to a maximum at progressively greater distances, before slowly declining. In the absence of other discharges, the pollution will continue to fall to the background concentration. Figure 9(b) represents this behaviour over open level country. The behaviour over uneven landscape and around buildings is more complicated and will be described in Section 5.4. The coning plume is the basis of many atmospheric dispersion models which are widely used in air quality management. The use of these models is outside the scope of this course, but is introduced in T334 *Environmental monitoring and control*.

### 3.2.2 The superadiabatic case

When strong solar heating occurs or when relatively cold air is transported over a much warmer surface, the temperature gradient is usually greater than $-1°\ 100\ \mathrm{m}^{-1}$. This is represented by the solid line in Figures 9(a) and 10, which represents merely one example of lapse rate (the starting point of ground-level temperature may be any value on the temperature axis).

Extreme superadiabatic conditions give rise to mirages. Imagine a mass of air moving upwards from say 200 m to 300 m. It will cool according to the theoretically calculated rate of $-1°\ 100\ \mathrm{m}^{-1}$. This lapse rate is shown as the broken line in Figure 10. We can see that the mass of air cools from, say, 13 °C to 12 °C while its surroundings are at a lower temperature. The mass of air is warmer than its surroundings and therefore more buoyant. As a result of this, any small air volume displaced upwards, such as a chimney discharge, is less dense than its surroundings and continues its motion upwards. Such conditions generally favour strong convection and turbulence in the air. We call this an unstable atmosphere, and typically occurs under strong solar heating. The ground is heated by the sun and in turn heats the air next to it, but the air cannot redistribute itself to accommodate the heat input. So up to 50 m of the atmosphere is unstable. The instability is good for dispersing pollutants, but it is possible for a plume to develop 'looping' characteristics, and reach the ground quite close to the source before much dilution of pollution has occurred. Under such circumstances high pollutant concentrations may result, as shown in Figure 9(a). Large-scale unstable lapse rates are rare because the buoyancy forces cause the air to redistribute and form neutral conditions.

### 3.2.3 Inversion

A ***temperature inversion*** occurs when temperature increases with altitude, as Figures 9 (c to e) and 11 represent.

---

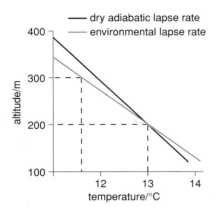

**Figure 10** *The superadiabatic lapse rate.*

---

### SAQ 6

Following a similar line of reasoning to that given in Section 3.2.2, predict the behaviour of a parcel of air moving from 200 m to 300 m under the inversion conditions of Figure 11.

---

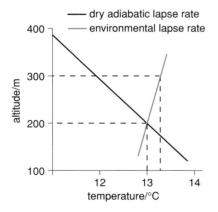

**Figure 11** *Typical inversion conditions.*

Inversions are significant from an air pollution standpoint because they allow little mixing or dilution of pollutants. Inversions form through cooling from below or warming from above. *Radiation inversions* occur frequently when the ground cools by radiation loss on clear nights. A nocturnal radiation inversion commonly causes fogs, as droplets of water vapour condense from the cooled air. The presence of particulate matter (such as smoke) may serve as a nucleus for the droplets and so stabilise the fog. Such conditions gave rise to the notorious London smog of 1952, the name of which was invented in the early part of this century by H. A. Des Voeux from SMoke and fOG. Ground-based or surface inversions may also occur through horizontal movement of an air mass from over a warm surface (such as land) to over a cool surface (such as water). At night the relative temperatures may be reversed. The inversion under these circumstances is shown in Figure 12 and is called an *advective inversion*. A frontal inversion can form at the interface of two air masses of different temperatures. In a weather forecast, you may have heard of a cold front, which is where cold air is advancing. The warm air overrides the cold air, and in doing so leads to condensation and rain, which follows the position of the front.

Inversions resulting from heating from above involve the sinking and compression of an air mass as it moves horizontally. Where the sinking and compression process causes a sufficiently great rise in temperature, a *subsidence inversion* results. This type of inversion may be associated with a high pressure weather system, or *anticyclone*.

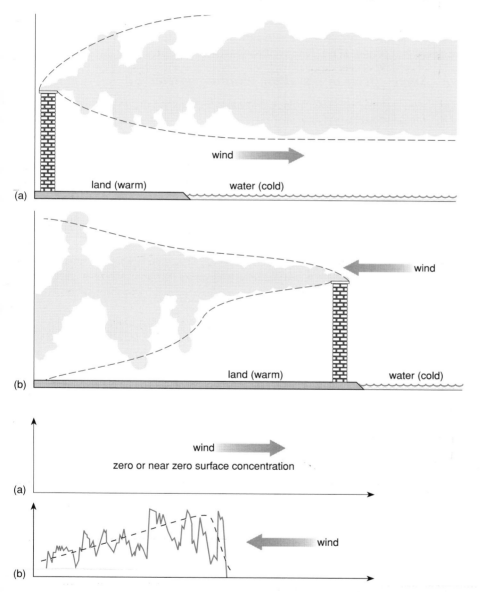

**Figure 12** *An inversion established at the land–sea interface.*

*How to read a weather map*

If you look at a typical weather chart on television or in a newspaper, you will see various types of symbols representing different meteorological features.

Thin lines represent isobars, which indicate areas of equal atmospheric pressure. 'HIGH' means a high pressure area or anticyclone, which in summer usually makes the weather warm and sunny, while in winter it often causes cold weather and fogs. A ridge is a high pressure region which is not at the centre of an anticyclone. 'LOW' means a low pressure region, depression, or cyclone, which is usually associated with wind and rain. A trough is an area of low pressure away from the centre of a depression.

Bold lines with marks are fronts, where air masses of different temperatures meet. Cold fronts (marked with sharp symbols) have a narrow belt of rain ahead of them, but as the front passes, brighter weather follows. Warm fronts (marked with semi-circles) show rain, but once they have passed they are followed by wet, cloudy weather. Occluded fronts are areas where warm and cold fronts meet. Ahead of them is rain, but they are followed by dry, bright weather.

The trapping of pollutants under inversions may lead to serious pollution problems. Figures 9 (c to e) show the behaviour of chimney plumes under inversion conditions, which may effectively act as a lid on the atmosphere, and prevent good dispersion. Ideally a chimney discharge rises above the inversion layer (a lofting plume) which hinders the return of pollutants to ground level. We will return to this aspect in Section 5.4.

## 3.3    Some typical weather effects on air quality

Air quality is influenced by many factors, but we may broadly classify these under human and weather effects (Figure 13).

Human activities are influenced to some degree by weather patterns, as in our demand for energy for lighting and heating buildings, all of which generate air pollutants, but the greatest influence of the weather is on transport and removal of pollution. We have already seen how certain conditions of atmospheric stability may trap pollution, but wind and rain influence removal mechanisms. An understanding of the links between air quality and weather conditions is useful in predicting conditions under which air pollution episodes may occur, and you are sure to have noticed air quality bulletins on weather forecasts. We will now look at some typical weather patterns in more detail and comment on their implications for air quality.

*Not examined*

### 3.3.1    Some effects of travelling weather systems

Easterly type weather patterns (Figure 14) have a characteristic feature of air streams from continental Europe passing over the North Sea. In winter, very cold air is heated slightly and becomes correspondingly damper as it passes over the sea. An extensive or strong anticyclone over Scandinavia may give protracted cold spells in winter, with the result that combustion-generated pollution from space-heating in dwellings and other buildings may increase, especially where inversions occur.

In contrast, a northerly or north-easterly flow (Figure 15) occurs when pressure is high to the west and low to the east, and may be particularly marked in spring. A northerly wind brings cold, unstable showery air, but a veer to the north-east brings

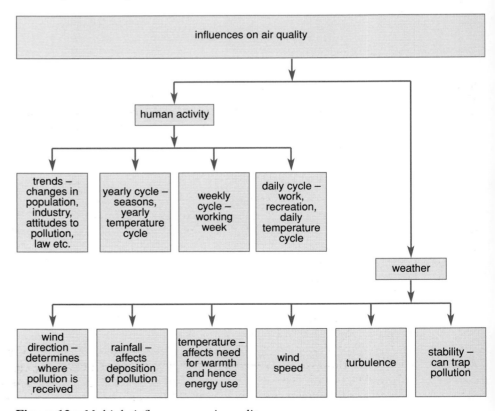

**Figure 13**  *Multiple influences on air quality.*

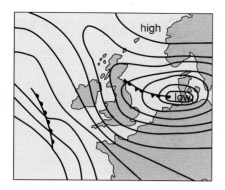

**Figure 14** *A typical easterly weather pattern over the UK.*

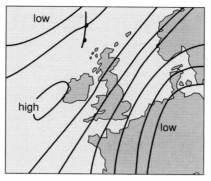

**Figure 15** *A typical northerly and north-easterly weather pattern.*

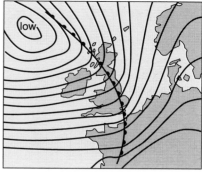

**Figure 16** *A typical south-westerly to westerly weather flow.*

polar continental air with squally snow showers. While the cold air stimulates heating needs, pollution levels are not high as a result of the dilution caused by the winds.

South-westerly to westerly winds dominate the weather pattern in the UK (Figure 16). They occur when there is high pressure to the south of the country, low to the north, and usually come in a sequence of ridges and depressions travelling eastwards across the Atlantic Ocean. When the anticyclone to the south intensifies and pushes north-wards, the air may be of maritime tropical origin, which is stable and produces stratus clouds and drizzle. Air quality may deteriorate in the stable regime. More common, however, is maritime polar air, which is warm at the surface and cold aloft; this is unstable and is characterised by cumulus clouds. Pollution is not usually a problem under these conditions.

North-westerly flows occur when depressions are passing on a track to the north-east of the country (Figure 17). Cold, polar, maritime air loses its squally, unstable properties in passing over the country, and clear air is an associated feature. Pollution levels may rise, but are usually low.

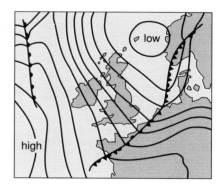

**Figure 17** *A typical north-westerly weather flow.*

A cyclone is also known as a depression or low pressure system (Figure 18). The weather is typically wet, with marked changes in the conditions as fronts pass through. Pollution is low as a result of dilution by winds and rain washing pollutants from the air.

Anticyclones or high pressure systems may also be centred over or near a region and give rise to fair, stable conditions as a result of the clear skies and light winds. Notice that under these meteorological conditions, described in Figure 19, pollution from the UK flows in the air stream towards Scandinavia, and this is the basis of concerns that have been expressed by the Scandinavian people about the contribution of emissions from the UK to acid rain pollution in that region. Surface inversions are common under anticyclonic conditions and lead to fogs in low-lying areas. The cold weather stimulates combustion-generated air pollution, which may stagnate under the stable conditions, and severe pollution episodes may occur, especially if subsidence inversions also form.

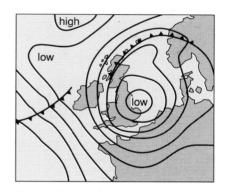

**Figure 18** *Typical cyclonic weather conditions.*

Look back at Tables 6 and 8, which show that anticyclonic conditions applied when several major episodes occurred in the past. Such conditions were occurring when this section was being planned in December 1991 and January 1992, and weather forecasts and newspaper reports regularly noted the very poor air quality (Figure 20). We will refer to the particular incident on 13 December 1991 again, and you will also see reference to it in TV 7.

Skies are usually clear under anticyclones, and strong sunshine may generate secondary pollutants which may be trapped under inversion conditions as the 'Foggy days' article in Figure 19 illustrates. We will examine these secondary pollutants in more detail in Section 3.4.3. However, other pollutants may also be trapped under similar meteorological conditions, and Figure 21 illustrates the weather map and measured lapse rate relating to an air pollution incident in May 1987.

# Foggy days, everywhere but in London town

Unseasonal weather across Europe, bringing a remarkably warm winter, has also brought alarming levels of air pollution to major cities and urgent calls to limit the volume of traffic emitting toxic fumes.

Paris and Milan and the usually sparkling cities of Switzerland have been shrouded in fog. Ironically, although Britain is suffering similar high levels of air pollution, London has been enjoying bright sunshine and crisp breezes. Yesterday it was 61°F, the same as Bahrain and warmer than Majorca and Tunis.

Ice-cream sellers were doing better business than roast-chestnut salesmen and there were sunbathers in the parks. The forecast was for two more warm days before unsettled weather returns. Meanwhile, in Europe, they were seeking solutions to the pall of smog now only a dim memory for Londoners.

In Paris, despite a weekend of unusually low pollution levels due to high winds and reduced traffic, the authorities may be forced to consider banning certain types of vehicle.

Several days of an *alerte du smog* last week, attributed to the inversion effect of the anti-cyclone covering much of Western Europe, have focused the attention of the Government and the Greens alike on what is acknowledged to be the principal source of pollutants — the cars so beloved of the French.

The Environment Minister, M Brice Lalond, has been talking about the urgent need for motorists to accept

**Round-Europe survey from Alan McGregor, Geneva; Ian Murray, Bonn; Paul Bompard, Rome; Philip Jacobson, Paris; and David Rowan, London**

some limitations on access to the capital, where traffic is now increasing at an ominous 5 per cent every year. Motorists should be encouraged to steer clear of the seriously congested city centre or take pains to travel with a full load of passengers.

But the ministry emphasizes that there is no plan to slap a comprehensive ban on the flow of traffic. In fact, the Environment Minister has no power to do so.

If anything as dramatic as that occurred, it would be for the Prefect of Paris to forbid the movement of certain categories of vehicle, for instance heavy lorries.

Pollution levels in Paris at the weekend dropped, thanks to a shower of rain, reduced traffic and the shutting down of four electricity generating units. The level of pollutants which is derived principally from motor car exhausts dropped from a high of 143 microgrammes to a nearly tolerable 94 microgrammes on Sunday.

**Geneva** — and much of the lake area, including **Lausanne** — has been in a smog belt for the past three weeks, and the authorities have requested that private cars be used "only in case of serious necessity". Appeals to use public transport have been largely

ignored and the smog is expected to last at least another week.

Around **Milan** a freak winter with no rain and very little wind has brought a vast cloud of smog.

At the end of January the first official alarm was raised; the mayor, Signor Paolo Pillitteri, announced that samples of the city's air showed a content of sulphur dioxide and carbon dioxide in excess of the first maximum safety level. He appealed to the Milanesi, to use their cars as little as possible and to turn down central heating systems. They ignored him. ·

In the days that followed pollution levels remained high, dipping slightly only when a rare, light breeze swept across the city. Then, last week, he ordered that theb 9.000 lorries a day that normally come into the city to go through Customs, should be processed outside Milan.

An emergency meeting of the city administration was called with the Minister for the Environment, Signor Giorgio Ruffolo, and the Minister for Urban Areas, Signor Carlo Tognoli, himself an ex-mayor of Milan. The first result was to earmark 15 billion lira (£6 million) of state money to buy electric buses and to convert diesel buses to methane gas fuel. Everyone vowed, as usual, to push for the adoption of lead-free petrol.

An ugly, black beret of pollution also crowns **Madrid**. In January air pollution reached a crisis and levels have remained high for the past month. An emergency proclamation from the mayor banning the use of central heating systems during the day

and putting city streets off-limits to non-residents has been gathering dust in the offices of the town council.

In cities all over Europe noxious fumes, mainly carbon monoxide from motor vehicles, have been trapped at street level by a layer of unseasonably warm air. WHO figures put 10 microgrammes of carbon monoxide per cubic metre over eight hours as the maximum permissible level. Fifteen times in the four months to the end of January London recorded levels of 19-25 microgrammes, according to London Scientific Services.

**Record levels of car sales are adding** to the problem in Britain where new vehicles are not required to have the catalytic converters which are now mandatory in the United States.

In the popular imagination a basic villain has emerged: the diesel engine. In. Italy diesel fuel costs, by the litre, 60 per cent of the price of petrol, and is anyway more economical. The result is that when the popularity of diesel engines peaked two years ago, one out of three new cars registered had a diesel engine.

A spokeswoman for the Department of the Environment in London, said that the EEC directive on the levels of pollutants in vehicle emissions, to which vehicles must conform by 1992, will "make a vast difference" to the quality of air.

Greenpeace, the environmental organisation, agrees that lead-free petrol is essential, but Mr Steve Elsworth, the group's Air Pollution Campaigner, believes that not enough is being done to decrease other toxins.

## Paris drivers urged to walk or stay home

### By Suzanne Lowry
### in Paris

WITH THE Eiffel Tower half swathed in yellow-grey smog and pollution readings at danger level, Parisians were urged last night not to drive their cars in the next few days.

The air of Paris has suffered from the mild weather over Europe since the end of December.

According to meteorologists, there is now a thick layer of warm, polluted air holding down a layer of rather colder atmosphere below, creating a fog that gets dirtier and dirtier.

Car exhausts are one of the worst offenders which is why a Government spokesman on television asked Parisian drivers to stay at home.

London will not suffer the same fate, said the London Weather Centre, because the foggy air over southern England was being blown towards the Continent.

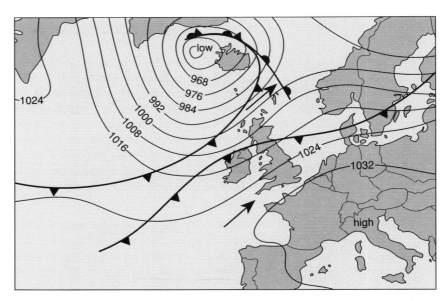

**Figure 19**   *A weather map and reports relating to a typical anticyclonic weather pattern on 3 February 1989.*

# London endures worst air pollution on record

BY NICK NUTTALL, TECHNOLOGY CORRESPONDENT

LONDON and its surrounding areas yesterday suffered their worst air pollution since records began, as the anti-cyclone which has brought freezing temperatures to western Europe continued. The London Weather Centre said that the pollution was coming from traffic fumes being trapped by the still air.

The environment department, which monitors nitrogen dioxide and sulphur dioxide levels across the country, asked the public to restrict its use of cars and to switch to public transport to reduce exhaust emissions. It said that levels of nitrogen dioxide, a gas which, in high concentrations, can increase respiratory problems, pneumonia, asthma attacks and viral infections, had reached 382 parts per billion (ppb) in central London, 388 in west London and 423 in southwest London. Air quality, which the department has monitored since 1976, is deemed good up to 49 ppb and very poor above 300.

The weather centre said that the anti-cyclone was likely to begin shifting away over the weekend. Temperatures rose towards seasonal daytime averages of around seven degrees celsius in the South and Midlands yesterday and around 5° in the North and Scotland. Over the weekend and into next week, it should remain sunny and dry in the South but it will still be quite cold at night. Unsettled weather from the North could arrive on Wednesday, bringing rain.

Despite the improvements in temperatures, several sporting fixtures over the weekend have been cancelled due to the cold. Two race meetings have been cancelled, along with five football league matches and seven rugby union championship games.

Yesterday William Hill, the bookmaker, said that it had tightened the odds for one or more snowflakes falling on Christmas day after punters increased their bets. The odds of it snowing on any weather centre roof in Britain are now 8-1.

● The severe frost is likely to push up the price of Brussels sprouts and other Christmas vegetables, as farmers have been unable to lift them from the frozen ground. Alan Hewitt, chairman of the National Farmers' Union's vegetables committee, said: "I would like to assure shoppers that the increase largely reflects the higher labour and marketing costs and the crop losses incurred. The problem is exacerbated by the fact that the cold snap has increased demand for vegetables for hot meals."

Carrot growers have had to spread straw over their crops to protect them from the cold. That slows the rate at which they can be harvested, and is estimated to increase production costs by between £30 and £60 a ton.

(a)

(b)

(c)

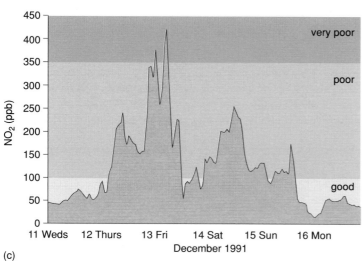

**Figure 20** *(a) Report and (b) weather map relating to air pollution on 13 December 1991; (c) central London nitrogen dioxide episode, December 1991.*

35

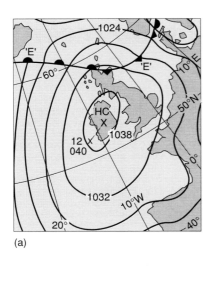

(a)

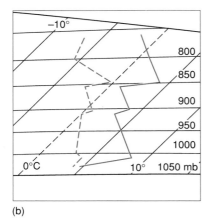

(b)

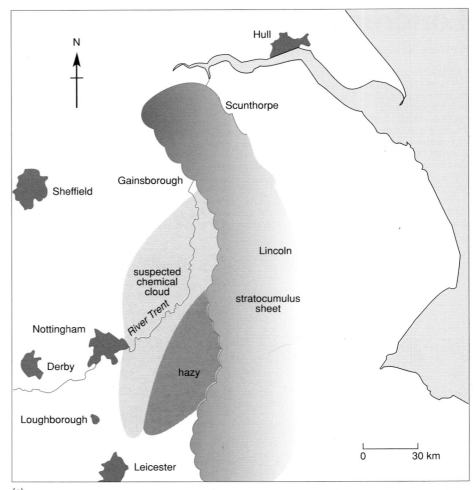

(c)

**Figure 21**   *(a) The synoptic situation, 6 May 1987 at 00 h GMT; (b) the upper air temperature (solid line) and dewpoint (broken line) at 00 h GMT, 6 May 1987 at Hemsby, Norfolk; (c) the position of the suspected vapour cloud relative to the River Trent and the major towns.*

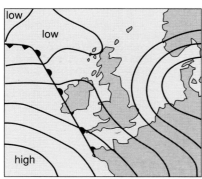

**Figure 22**   *Typical weather conditions leading to a col.*

A col (Figure 22) is also associated with poor air quality. It often occurs when an anticyclone is over Scandinavia and another lies south-west of Eire. Conditions are similar to anticyclonic, but usually of shorter duration.

Clearly there is nothing we can do to prevent the formation of inversions, but we can minimise releases of pollutants into the atmosphere so that they are not likely to build up under such weather conditions. We will examine ways of minimising these releases in Section 5.

So far we have considered the temperature profile or lapse rate in the atmosphere near to ground level. This region is known as the ***troposphere***. Above it is the ***stratosphere***, in which the temperature increases with height (Figure 23). The reason for this increase and the related atmospheric chemistry are examined in Section 3.4.2.

### SAQ 7

Name three types of inversion in the atmosphere, summarise their cause and comment on their implications for air quality.

### SAQ 8

Interpret the meteorological data provided in Figure 21 to explain the build-up of air pollution on 6 May 1987.

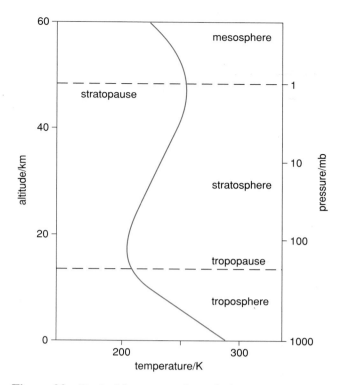

**Figure 23**   *Typical lapse rate through the troposphere and stratosphere.*

### 3.3.2   *The directional influence of winds*

While there is an overall balance in the incoming and outgoing solar radiation reaching Earth, the balance is uneven at a given point. This is due to the cloud cover, the latitude and the nature of the surface (albedo over sea, land, snow, soil, etc.). Towards the polar regions, a given amount of solar energy passes through more atmosphere and impinges on a greater surface area than at the Equator. This uneven distribution of energy input to the surface combined with the albedo differences leads to the large-scale air movements across the Earth which serve to transport energy through a permanent air flow from the tropics to the poles and restore equilibrium. The large-scale air movements are made more complex by factors such as the rotation of the Earth, but the overall effect is that they cause the weather patterns and winds.

Wind direction is important in that any receptor is only at risk if situated downwind of a source of air pollution. The importance of this seemingly obvious statement must not be underestimated. Wind direction has perhaps the greatest impact on air quality at a given point, for changes in wind direction have a great effect on the pollution received from a source. However, wind varies both in time and position. As an example, it is usual for the wind speed to approximately double between 10 m and 1 km above ground, and also to change direction. It is the roughness of the surface due to such obstacles as buildings and trees that slows the wind at ground level. Further complications that structures bring to air and therefore pollutant movements will be dealt with in Section 5.4.

Wind direction is a primary measurement in air pollution studies. The proportion of time that wind blows in a given direction is usually represented as a ***wind rose***. For example, data from a local weather station showed the following distribution of wind direction according to time.

| Wind direction | N | NW | W | SW | S | SE | E | NE | Calm |
|---|---|---|---|---|---|---|---|---|---|
| Proportion of time (%) | 14 | 10 | 14 | 20 | 15 | 10 | 8 | 7 | 2 |

We can represent this diagrammatically as in Figure 24. In this diagram, the length of each 'arm' is proportional to the amount of time the wind blows *from* the respective direction.

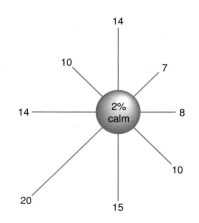

**Figure 24**   *A wind rose.*

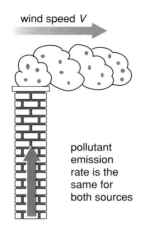

wind speed *V*

pollutant emission rate is the same for both sources

wind speed 2*V*

**Figure 25**   *The influence of wind speed on concentration. Doubling the wind speed halves the pollutant concentration for a given emission rate.*

It is possible to relate wind direction with air quality measurements by a pollution rose in which the length of each arm is drawn in proportion to the average pollutant concentration when the wind blew from that direction. A pollution rose therefore suggests the direction in which a source of pollution lies.

Wind speed has the effect of diluting pollutants. Thus if the air flow over a point doubles while the pollutant emission rate is constant, the effect is to halve the pollutant concentration (Figure 25).

The combined effect of variations in emissions from pollutant sources, the effects of wind speed, direction and other factors indicated in Figure 13 make air quality vary continuously. This may be seen by examining the record from a continuous pollution monitor, of which Figure 26 is typical. This trace shows the combined effect of all the factors that influence air quality, as indicated in Figure 13. How we measure air quality and make sense of such a complex set of data is covered in Section 5.

### SAQ 9

Meteorological measurements for an air quality sampling station gave the following data:

| Wind direction | N | NE | E | SE | S | SW | W | NW |
|---|---|---|---|---|---|---|---|---|
| Proportion of time (%) | 7 | 15 | 8 | 12 | 14 | 25 | 9 | 8 |

For the rest of the time the weather was calm. Draw a wind rose for the site.

### SAQ 10

A major source of sulphur dioxide is located 2.5 km to the NW of a sampling station on the boundary of a town. Meteorological records for the same periods as air quality data are as follows:

| Wind direction | N | NE | E | SE | S | SW | W | NW |
|---|---|---|---|---|---|---|---|---|
| Relative $SO_2$ concentration | 10 | 20 | 18 | 30 | 23 | 18 | 6 | 12 |

Draw a pollution rose from the data and interpret its significance.

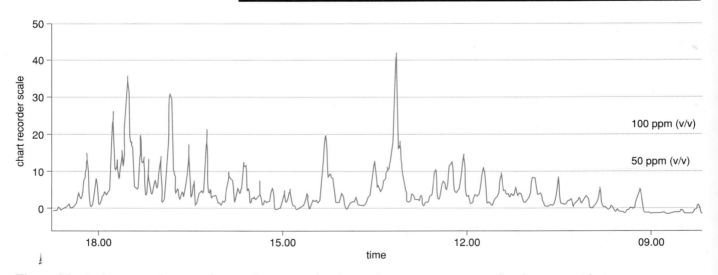

**Figure 26**   *A chart recorder trace from an instrument for the continuous measurement of carbon monoxide.*

## 3.4   Atmospheric ozone chemistry

In Unit 3 we introduced **ozone** as an allotrope of oxygen, with the molecular formula $O_3$. Popular belief used to suggest that ozone at the seaside was beneficial to health, but in fact ozone is a highly toxic and irritant gas. Its name comes from the Greek word meaning to smell, and if you've been beside a photocopier or similar electrical equipment, you may have noticed the characteristic pungent odour. Ozone readily breaks down to produce oxygen, and this makes ozone a powerful oxidising agent which can readily react with other substances in the atmosphere to produce other harmful gases. Ozone occurs in the troposphere and in the stratosphere, but its formation and significance in both zones could not be more different. The problems of ozone illustrate the global perspective of air pollution.

### 3.4.1   Measurement units

Amounts of ozone are usually represented by two different units. Ground-level concentrations, and hence air quality standards, use conventional units of $\mu g\ m^{-3}$ or ppm and their derivatives. These relate to measurement by drawing air samples through analytical instruments which record the amount of ozone in the samples. *Dobson units* (DU) are used for representing amounts of ozone throughout the atmosphere. The Dobson instruments measure the ratio of radiation intensities simultaneously received at two UV wavelengths, one in the UV-B range (280–320 nm) partly absorbed by ozone, and one in the UV-A range where there is little absorption. No other gas is an important absorber of UV-B radiation, so changes in the ratio relate to changes in the amount of ozone between the instrument and the sun. A layer of pure ozone at the ground equal to the total amount in the atmosphere might typically be 3 mm thick; this is equated to 300 DU. The total ozone is measured from the ground at Dobson spectrophotometric stations, which give local data at over 30 sites around the world. Records go back to 1930, but only for about a quarter of the Earth. More recent data over the whole globe are now available from Nimbus satellite-based instruments.

### 3.4.2   Stratospheric ozone

Ozone is formed in the stratosphere from oxygen, which absorbs short wavelength sunlight. We can represent light energy by $E$ and so write a chemical equation:

$$O_2 + E \xrightarrow{250\,nm} O + O \tag{3}$$

The oxygen atoms may then react in the presence of something else (let's call it $M$) which takes away the excess energy when oxygen molecules are reformed:

$$O + O + M \rightarrow O_2 + M \tag{4}$$

$$\Delta H = -493\ kJ\ mol^{-1}$$

You should recall from Unit 3 that we can represent the energy change in a chemical reaction by $\Delta H$, and when this is shown as a negative value it indicates that the reaction 'system' loses energy.

The oxygen atoms may react with oxygen molecules to form ozone:

$$O + O_2 + M \rightarrow O_3 + M \tag{5}$$

$$\Delta H = -100\ kJ\ mol^{-1}$$

but the ozone may itself react with oxygen atoms:

$$O + O_3 \rightarrow 2O_2 \tag{6}$$

$$\Delta H = -390\ kJ\ mol^{-1}$$

or absorb solar radiation, which breaks it down:

$$O_3 + E \xrightarrow{215-295\,nm} O_2 + O \tag{7}$$

The overall effect is a balance between the formation and destruction reactions resulting in a maximum concentration of ozone in the stratosphere at a height of between 15 and 35 km. Some 90% of atmospheric ozone exists in the stratosphere.

### SAQ 11

Write down the reaction producing ozone and the two in which it is destroyed. Comment on the overall energy changes in the sequence of reactions.

The series of reactions shown above is a simplification, and the amounts of ozone measured in the 1950s were lower than predicted from them. Perhaps other reactions occurred to reduce the ozone concentrations. Several chemical species are believed to take part in such reactions, and include oxides of nitrogen, which may react as:

$$NO + O_3 \rightarrow NO_2 + O_2 \tag{8}$$

$$\Delta H = -200 \text{ kJ mol}^{-1}$$

Where the ozone concentration is greatest, this reaction removes far more ozone than the earlier reaction with oxygen atoms.

Oxides of nitrogen come from microbial activity and combustion of fossil fuels, but a major route involves the reaction:

$$O + N_2O \rightarrow 2NO \tag{9}$$

First, however, $N_2O$ has to reach the stratosphere, and this is believed to occur through the normal weather mechanisms. In the troposphere air is warmed at the Earth's surface and rises, to be replaced by colder air as we saw in Section 3.3. Pollutants are taken into the stratosphere by the rising air currents generated by the upward movements of tropical storms, although it may take several years after release in the troposphere for pollutants to enter the stratosphere.

In the 1970s, consideration turned to whether chlorine compounds could enter the stratosphere. If chlorine atoms were produced, these may react rapidly with ozone:

$$Cl + O_3 \rightarrow ClO + O_2 \tag{10}$$

subsequently regenerating chlorine:

$$ClO + O \rightarrow Cl + O_2 \tag{11}$$

The effect of chlorine is very much greater than that of nitrogen oxides.

In 1974, Molina and Rowland suggested that **chlorofluorocarbons** (CFCs) were a potential source of chlorine. The compounds found wide use as aerosol propellants, refrigerants, plastic foam expansion agents and industrial solvents in the electronics industry, and had been designed for their low toxicity and high chemical stability (i.e. low reactivity). There are many CFCs and these compounds have a unique system for naming, which we will describe in the footnote to Table 9. As CFCs were chemically unreactive, it was reasonable to expect them to remain in the atmosphere indefinitely. However, over a long period of time, upward diffusion into the stratosphere was possible, and in that region breakdown may occur due to absorption of solar energy, e.g.

$$CCl_2F_2 + E \rightarrow CClF_2 + Cl \tag{12}$$

It has been found that there are reservoirs which take the Cl out of circulation and put it in a non-active form such as hydrogen chloride (HCl) and chlorine nitrate (ClONO$_2$), e.g.

$$ClO + NO_2 + M \rightarrow ClONO_2 + M \tag{13}$$

As the reservoir molecules are reactive chemicals, they can break down to produce atomic Cl again, which can go round the cycle many times. Thus a single Cl atom may destroy perhaps 100 000 ozone molecules, until eventually it diffuses down into the troposphere as HCl, which may be removed by rain.

*What is the ozone hole?*

Measurements have shown that there are quite large variations in stratospheric ozone, both over time and across the globe. Reports suggest that for several years monitoring from satellites had indicated a large drop of some 40% in total ozone over the Antarctic region during the southern spring, but NASA computers had been programmed to reject differences greater than ± 30%, which may have resulted from instrumental drift or natural variability. It was not until Farman and his colleagues of the British Antarctic Survey reported the difference in 1985 in a letter to the journal *Nature* that the unexpected effect of a reduction was confirmed. (An important lesson to be learned here! Don't ignore results simply because they are unexpected.) The report showed that by October 1984 (i.e. Antarctic spring) the average October ozone concentration recorded over Halley Bay had decreased from about 320 DU in the 1960s to less than 200 DU. Figure 27 shows more recent measurements of the effect known as the 'ozone hole'. Subsequently, depletion at other latitudes has been observed, including in the northern hemisphere. The ozone hole over Antarctica has been growing year by year, and by 23 September 1992 it extended to 8.9 million square miles – almost as large as the area of North America. On 4 October 1992 the 'hole' covered inhabited land for the first time when it extended over Tierra del Fuego before moving over the Falkland Islands three days later. Data from Nimbus-7 satellite measurements showed readings of about 170 DU over Tierra del Fuego and 220 over the Falklands.

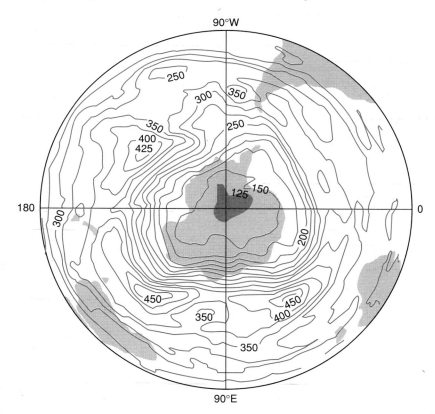

**Figure 27**   *The 'ozone hole' as revealed by contours of ozone concentrations through the depth of the atmosphere in Dobson units. Measurements by satellite-based instrumentation.*

*Why should the ozone hole occur at the poles?*

We have seen that the stratosphere is relatively warmed owing to the absorption of UV radiation by ozone. However, during the polar night the stratosphere becomes very cold, especially at the Antarctic (typically 180–190 K). At these temperatures, even the dry stratospheric air becomes saturated and polar stratospheric clouds form. It is these that contribute to the unusual behaviour of the region. Reactions between the reservoir species HCl and $ClONO_2$ on the surface of the ice particles in the polar stratospheric clouds release $Cl_2$. Sunlight breaks this down to form Cl atoms, which react with ozone according to equation (10). As the generation of Cl is initiated by sunlight, ozone depletion occurs in the Antarctic spring when the sun begins to shine.

*Major concerns*

Look back at equation (7). You will notice that it involves absorption by ozone of solar radiation in the 215–295 nm region. Consequently the ozone acts as a shield protecting the surface of the Earth from this wavelength band, which is in the ultra-violet region and is known as UV-B radiation. Several key biomolecules, including DNA, absorb and are damaged by light beginning at around 300 nm and extending towards the ultraviolet. Ozone provides an effective shield in this region, and its depletion in the stratosphere may have a deleterious effect on humans, on plants or on food chains. For example, one suggestion has been made that there could be an increased death rate from melanoma skin cancer in Britain of between 9% and 18% in the year 2030 compared with 1970. Other suggestions are that the incidence of disease may increase because UV-B radiation could depress the human immune response, and there may also be increases in the incidence of eye cataracts.

Concerns over the potential for reduced crop yields as a result of increased UV exposure to plants depend on what increases occur and the resultant decrease in photo-synthesis (and hence yield). Aquatic larvae and plankton are sensitive to small increases in UV exposure, and effects through the food chains and webs have the potential of presenting greater problems than human cancer effects.

*Control*

As a result of Molina and Rowland's work, pressure mounted in the USA for reductions in the use of CFCs, especially in aerosol sprays, and by 1978 their use in many sprays was banned. Nevertheless, concentrations of CFCs in the atmosphere continued to grow as a result of their many other uses. Continuing concern eventually led to the Montreal Protocol. In 1987 in Montreal, a conference supported by most of the CFC-using countries agreed a protocol for a 50% reduction in CFC use by the year 2000. Continuing studies showed that such reductions would still result in doubling the amount of chlorine in the stratosphere by that date, and so a further con-ference was held in 1990. It was agreed that use of CFCs and other ozone-depleting chemicals would be cut by 50% by 1995, 85% by 1997 and completely phased out by 2000. Some countries have agreed an earlier phase-out.

The policy of changing from CFCs to less harmful substances is an example of the first stage in the hierarchy of 'waste minimisation', and practical ways of achieving this will be covered in Section 5 on air pollution control.

### 3.4.3   Tropospheric ozone

It is perhaps paradoxical that at the same time as a depletion in stratospheric ozone has occurred, there has been an increase in tropospheric ozone. Natural sources are the downward transport of ozone from the stratosphere and production from naturally occurring nitrogen oxides, but on top of the natural background is the formation of ozone as a result of human activities. However, ozone is not a *primary pollutant* but is formed in the atmosphere by a complex series of reactions mainly involving hydro-carbons and oxides of nitrogen. Ozone is therefore a *secondary pollutant*. As we saw for the stratospheric ozone, sunlight is also involved in the formation of tropospheric ozone by photochemical reactions. Ozone is therefore a component of ***photochemical smog***.

A simple outline of the formation of ozone starts with the action of sunlight on nitrogen oxides. High temperature combustion produces nitric oxide (NO), which is slowly oxidised in the atmosphere to nitrogen dioxide ($NO_2$). This reaction can be reversed by sunlight which releases very reactive oxygen atoms:

$$NO_2 \rightarrow NO + O$$

with the oxygen atoms being able to combine with oxygen molecules:

$$O + O_2 \rightarrow O_3$$

Ozone can react with nitric oxide to reform nitrogen dioxide:

$$NO + O_3 \rightarrow NO_2 + O_2$$

Overall, there is an equilibrium, which results in no build-up of ozone:

$$NO_2 + O_2 \underset{}{\overset{sunlight}{\rightleftharpoons}} NO + O_3$$

However, we have seen that the air is a mixture of many components, and some interfere with this equilibrium. In particular, the action of sunlight on hydrocarbons produces very reactive chemical species called *free radicals*. These can convert nitric oxide to nitrogen dioxide and so cause a build-up of this and of ozone:

accumulates $\quad\xrightarrow{\text{sunlight}}\quad$ accumulates

$$NO_2 + O_2 \qquad\xleftarrow{\hspace{2cm}}\qquad NO + O_3$$

free radicals
sunlight
hydrocarbons

The role of sunlight and the sequence of formation of nitrogen dioxide and then ozone is apparent from records of air quality throughout the day, as seen in Figure 28 and part of the mobile air quality monitoring laboratory sequence in TV 7. Both records show an important feature that the greatest intensity of photochemical smog occurs in the middle of the day. This makes an important distinction from conventional smog which, resulting from nocturnal radiation inversions, tends to diminish during the day as the sun disperses it.

Other photochemical reactions also occur, leading to the formation of substances such as peroxyacylnitrates including *peroxyacetylnitrate* (PAN).

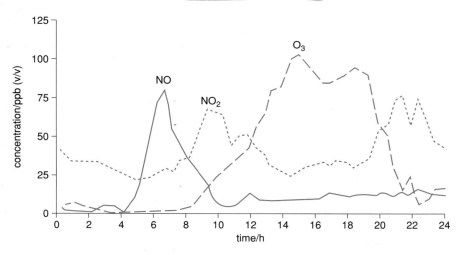

**Figure 28** *Diurnal variations of pollutant concentrations.*

Photochemical smog first came to notoriety in Los Angeles, and hence it has been called 'Los Angeles smog'. It has, however, been recorded in many other areas, including Mexico City, Tokyo, Sydney and Athens, where the reduction in visibility, eye irritation, smell and health problems have been serious. In view of the role of strong sunlight, one may think that the UK may be relatively free of the problem. Evidence of photochemical activity comes from ground-level ozone measurements, and these first began in the UK in 1971. High ozone concentrations are normally produced on warm days with high solar radiation, light winds and inversion conditions. An anticyclone over north-west Europe or Scandinavia gives ideal conditions. In 1976, a prolonged heatwave gave the highest levels of ozone since measurements began. Figure 29 traces the air mass trajectory carrying precursors of ozone; similar trajectories may be seen in the forecasting system in TV 7.

---

*Case study*

On 27 June 1976, air quality measurements at Warren Spring Laboratory showed ozone concentrations of over 14 pphm (parts per hundred million by volume), which being in excess of the US air quality standard at the time, were indicative of photochemical activity. Back trajectories of the air mass (see Figure 29) showed it to be moving at about 500 km d$^{-1}$ in winds of 4–10 km h$^{-1}$. This placed the air mass over southern Poland on 25 June, when injection of primary pollutants could occur, but as temperatures were low, photochemical activity would have been low. On 26 June, the air mass was over Germany. Clear skies and temperatures of 30 °C were good for photochemical activity, and further primary pollutants could be released into the air. On 27 June at midday, the air mass was over London, where more primary pollutants could be released, and weather conditions again favoured the reactions.

In summary, over three days, the air mass was passing over several countries from which primary pollutants were released, while on two days there was full sunlight and high temperatures for photochemical smog formation. Clearly, dealing with regional air pollution problems of this nature demands international action.

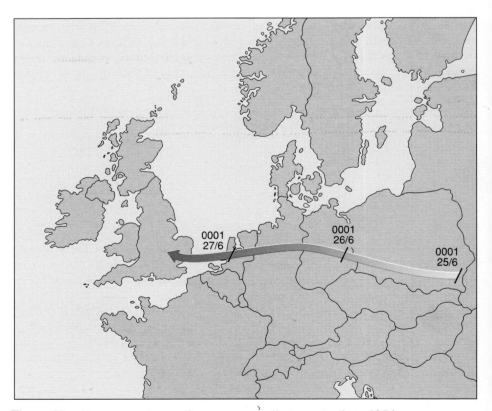

**Figure 29**  *Air mass trajectory for an ozone pollution episode in 1976.*

## SAQ 12

We have seen that photochemical smog formation depends on nitrogen oxides and hydrocarbons being released as primary pollutants. Look back at Figure 5 showing the sources of pollutants and identify where control efforts should be directed.

*[handwritten: nitrogen oxides from road transport & power stations*

*hydrocarbons (VOC's) from also road transport but mainly from processes & solvents]*

# 3.5   Acid deposition

Acid deposition, or 'acid rain' to use its more familiar name, has been much in the news in recent years, although it is not a new phenomenon. Robert Angus Smith, the first member of what later became known as the **Alkali and Clean Air Inspectorate**, published in 1872 an account of his measurements of the composition of air and rain, and described rain at least as acidic as any found today. Many serious air pollution problems of the past have been reduced by techniques such as 'dilute and disperse'. By releasing discharges to atmosphere from tall chimneys, we believed that we were solving these problems. Only in more recent years have the adverse effects of diluted pollutants at great distances from their sources been recognised, together with the significance of the phenomenon first recognised by Smith.

Rain is naturally acidic owing to carbon dioxide dissolving in the water, and this suggests that rain has a pH value of around 5.6 rather than 7. Lower levels (say 4.7) may be produced exceptionally by sea or volcanic-derived sulphate: for example, as part of the natural sulphur cycle. Overall, a global background of around pH5 is expected, and this is confirmed by measurements in remote areas. In industrial areas, much lower pH values have been observed. You will recall from Unit 3 that the pH scale is logarithmic, and so apparently small changes involve great changes in the hydrogen ion concentration, with potentially great biological impact.

Sulphur oxides and nitrogen oxides from fuel burning are major contributors to the acidification. Both gases dissolve in water to produce acidic solutions. Further oxidation to other acids, as well as conversion to sulphates and nitrates, have an acidifying influence. Reactive hydrocarbons from motor vehicles and industrial solvent use are important in the production of ozone and other photochemical pollutants. These compounds are not only aggressive to structures and living tissue in their own right, but also are involved in the conversion of sulphur and nitrogen oxides to acids. Further reactions, such as that between ammonia and sulphur dioxide, form ammonium sulphate as fine particulate matter. Removal of these pollutants from the air can be categorised as dry deposition or wet deposition. The former proceeds without the aid of (meteorological) precipitation, and denotes the direct transfer of gaseous and particulate air pollutants to the surface of the Earth, plants, structures, etc. Wet deposition, on the other hand, includes all processes by which air pollutants are transferred to surfaces in aqueous form. We commonly talk of 'acid rain' because most studies have concerned wet deposition; it is much easier to measure and study than dry deposition. However, the correct term for the total phenomenon is 'acid deposition'.

Since the 1950s and 1960s, observations of acid deposition have been linked with ecological effects, especially in Scandinavia and eastern North America. Patterns of rainfall acidity have also been observed in the UK, especially through the work of the UK Review Group on Acid Rain, whose reports summarise the main features of the phenomenon. Lowest rainfall acidity (i.e. highest pH) occurs in north-west Scotland, Northern Ireland, west Wales and south-west England according to reports from the UK acid deposition networks established by the Department of the Environment. You will have examined the nature of rainfall in your own environment as part of the home experimental programme of this course. An analysis of previous years' data from the course is included in Porteous and Barratt (1989); the results agree with UK network reports and confirm the west to east gradient of increasing acidity. However, the greater intensity of rainfall in the west means that these areas can suffer from the effects of acid deposition and this partly explains the concerns about these areas.

## 3.6 Global warming

Carbon dioxide is always released when fuels containing carbon are burnt. Its importance in the carbon cycle was described in Unit 2 *Biology*. As a natural and necessary part of life, we have tended to discount it as an air pollutant. Now, however, it is of particular concern in respect of its contribution to global warming.

Since the beginning of the industrial revolution in the nineteenth century, the rate of burning fossil fuels has increased dramatically. You may also recall that the increases in carbon dioxide emissions were calculated in the *Mathematics and Modelling* supplement. Over the same time period there has been substantial worldwide deforestation as a result of new farming practices. The combined result of these changes is that the carbon dioxide released into the atmosphere is no longer balanced by the rate of removal. Consequently, atmospheric concentrations have been found to increase steadily worldwide.

The worldwide increase of about 1.3 ppm each year in the background concentration of carbon dioxide remote from industrial areas is illustrated graphically in Figure 30. The annual cyclic variations superimposed on the general rising trend are due to seasonal changes in the rates of emission and absorption. For several years, this rising trend has caused concern, and conflicting theories have been proposed to predict the effect on world climate. You will recall from Section 3.1 that carbon dioxide absorbs infra-red radiation and contributes to the greenhouse effect on which we depend for the survival of life on Earth. The 1980s saw the five warmest years on record and some extreme climatic disturbances such as major droughts. All helped raise the profile of the greenhouse effect. Remember that, from an air pollution perspective, we are concerned with the 'enhanced greenhouse effect' which is attributed to atmospheric pollution.

$CO_2$ CFC's, $CH_4$, $N_2O$

In addition to carbon dioxide and water (see Figure 7), many other gases contribute to global warming (Figure 31). The main contributing pollutants produced by human activity are carbon dioxide, chlorofluorocarbons, methane, and nitrous oxide (Table 9). As a result of the growing concerns and the complexities of the problem, the Intergovernmental Panel on Climate Change (IPCC) was established in 1988 to carry out an 18-month assessment of the issues. The conclusions of the IPCC are set out in the box below.

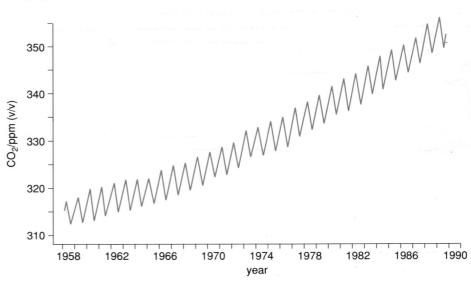

**Figure 30** *Observations of carbon dioxide in the atmosphere at Mauna Loa, Hawaii.*

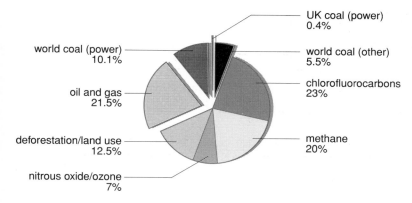

**Figure 31** *Contributions to global warming. The slices drawn out of the pie represent the contributions from carbon dioxide.*

---

*Summary of IPCC conclusions*

We are certain that:

- There is a natural greenhouse effect which already keeps the Earth warmer than it would otherwise be.
- Emissions resulting from human activities are substantially increasing the atmospheric concentrations of the greenhouse gases ($CO_2$, $CH_4$, CFCs and $N_2O$). These increases will enhance the greenhouse effect, resulting on average in an additional warming of the Earth's surface.

We confidently calculate that:

- $CO_2$ has been responsible for over half the enhanced greenhouse effect in the past, and is likely to continue to do so.
- Atmospheric concentrations of the long-lived gases ($CO_2$, $N_2O$ and CFCs) change only slowly in response to emission changes. Continued emissions of these gases at present rates would commit us to increased concentrations for centuries ahead.
- The long-lived gases would require immediate reductions in emissions from human activities of over 60% to stabilise their concentrations at today's levels; methane would require a 15–20% reduction.

Based on current model results, and subject to the many uncertainties in our predictions with regard to timing, magnitude and regional patterns, we predict:

- The IPCC business-as-usual emissions of greenhouse gases will result in a likely increase in global mean temperature of about 1 °C above the present value by 2025 and 3 °C before the end of the next century.
- Land surfaces will warm more rapidly than the oceans, and high northern latitudes will warm more than the global mean in winter.
- Regional climate changes will differ from the global mean, although our confidence in the prediction of detail of regional changes is low. For example, temperature increases in southern Europe and central North America are predicted to be higher than the global mean, accompanied on average by reduced summer precipitation and soil moisture.
- Global mean sea-level will rise at an average rate of about 6 cm per decade over the next century.

Our judgement is that:

- Global-mean surface temperature has increased by 0.3 °C to 0.6 °C over the last 100 years, with the five global-average warmest years being in the 1980s. These increases have been neither smooth in time nor globally uniform.
- The size of warming is broadly consistent with predictions of climate models, but is also of similar magnitude to natural climate variability.
- Unequivocal detection of the enhanced greenhouse effect is unlikely for a decade or more.
- There is no firm evidence of greater variability in climate over the last few decades.
- Ecosystems affect climate, and will be affected by a changing climate and increasing carbon dioxide concentrations.

**Table 9**  *Greenhouse gas characteristics and trends*

|  | $CO_2$ | $CH_4$ | CFC-11[a] | CFC-12[a] | $N_2O$ |
|---|---|---|---|---|---|
| Atmospheric concentration (v/v): |  |  |  |  |  |
| pre-industrialisation, 1750–1800 | 280 ppm | 0.8 ppm | 0 ppt | 0 ppt | 288 ppb |
| recent, 1990 | 353 ppm | 1.72 ppm | 280 ppt[b] | 484 ppt | 310 ppb |
| Current rate of change (% $y^{-1}$) | 0.5 | 0.9 | 4 | 4 | 0.25 |
| Atmospheric lifetime (years) | 50–200[c] | 10 | 65 | 130 | 150 |
| Global warming potential (°C, 100 y horizon) | 1 | 21 |  |  | 290 |
| 1990 emissions ($Tg^d$) | 26 000 | 300 | 0.9 (total) |  | 6 |
| Reduction required to stabilise concentration at present values (%) | >60 | 15–20 | 70–75 | 75–85 | 70–80 |

[a]Chlorofluorocarbons (CFCs) are referred to by a numbering system. This system can be interpreted by adding 90 to the number and translating the three-digit number as follows. The right digit gives the number of fluorine atoms, the middle digit is the number of hydrogen atoms, and the left digit is the number of carbon atoms. Thus for CFC-11, we first add 90 to give 101. This implies one carbon atom, no hydrogen atoms and one fluorine atom. The number of chlorine atoms equals the number of carbon bonding sites in the methane or ethane skeleton that are not taken up by fluorine or hydrogen. So CFC-11 must contain three chlorine atoms and is trichlorofluoromethane ($CFCl_3$).

[b]Parts per trillion ($10^{12}$).

[c]The complex ways $CO_2$ is removed from the air by seas and plants does not allow a single value to be given for its lifetime in the atmosphere.

[d]Tg represents teragrams ($10^{12}$ g).

Seeking abatement options requires some knowledge of the relative impacts, sources and control options of the greenhouse gases so that efforts may be directed in the most productive direction. Table 10 summarises the sources.

**Table 10**  *Main sources of greenhouse gases*

| Gas | Source |
|---|---|
| Carbon dioxide | fossil fuel burning |
|  | deforestation and land use changes |
|  | cement manufacture |
| Methane | rice cultivation |
|  | ruminants (sheep, cows. etc.) |
|  | biomass burning and decay |
|  | releases from fossil fuel production |
| CFCs | manufactured for solvents, refrigerants, aerosol spray propellants, foam packaging, etc. |
| Nitrous oxide | fertilisers |
|  | fossil fuel burning |
|  | land conversion for agriculture |
| Precursor gases involved in ozone and methane chemistry: |  |
| nitrogen oxides | fossil fuel burning |
| non-methane hydrocarbons | evaporation of liquid fuels and solvents |
| carbon monoxide | fossil fuel and biomass burning |

I hope that you can appreciate how steps such as replacing 'warming' gases such as CFCs, or reducing uncontrolled landfill gas discharges to the atmosphere, will combat global warming. Controlling landfill gas is beneficial in that it cuts methane release and also the recovered gas can be used to replace other energy sources, since emissions of methane from UK landfill sites are equivalent to about 45 million tonnes of carbon dioxide over a ten-year timescale. However, it is impossible to capture all the methane generated in landfill, and other options, such as combustion of municipal solid waste with heat recovery, may be more practicable overall.

Avoiding extensive deforestation is another possible step to reduce global warming because forests remove carbon dioxide from the atmosphere. However, direct removal of carbon dioxide from combustion gases is a daunting prospect because it is a primary product of combustion. We will examine some of the practicable options later in this text.

### SAQ 13

(a) Derive the chemical formula and name for CFC-12.
(b) Derive the CFC numbers for $CHClFCF_3$ and $CCl_2FCClF_2$.

### SAQ 14

From Tables 9 and 10, deduce what is the dominant activity contributing to the greenhouse effect, and the area where greatest attention is justified to reduce the impact?

### SAQ 15

Suggest practicable approaches to reducing the amount of $CO_2$ released to the atmosphere by burning fuels.

## 3.7  Summary

The heating effect of solar radiation reaching the Earth is enhanced by the greenhouse effect due to the atmosphere, and this enhancement makes the Earth's temperature suitable for sustaining life. The energy imbalance set up between the Equator and the poles results in travelling weather systems such as depressions and anticyclones, which influence both climate and air quality. The temperature of the lower part of the atmosphere (the troposphere) changes with altitude, and the manner of change influences atmospheric stability. When the temperature decreases with altitude, vertical mixing occurs to a greater or lesser extent, but when the temperature increases with altitude, an inversion exists and the atmosphere is said to be stable. Under stable conditions, vertical mixing is suppressed, and pollution levels may increase. Inversions often occur under anticyclonic weather systems.

Atmospheric ozone presents two contrasting problems. In the stratosphere, where it protects us from harmful UV radiation, there is a depletion, while in the troposphere the levels have been increasing. Both effects are due to air pollution. Substances such as chlorofluorocarbons are stable in the lower atmosphere, and eventually migrate to the stratosphere where peculiar polar meteorology allows them to break down to produce chlorine. This reactive chemical destroys ozone.

In the troposphere, a mixture of air pollutants, including many resulting from transport, react together under the influence of sunlight to produce photochemical smog. This irritant cocktail includes ozone, which is used as an indicator of photochemical activity. Photochemical smog is most intense during strong sunlight, and this distinguishes it from traditional smog, which may be dispersed by sunlight.

Enhancement of the natural greenhouse effect is known as global warming, which may have considerable impact on our planet. Carbon dioxide concentrations have been shown to be increasing, as have other gases which contribute to global warming by absorbing infra-red radiation and trapping it in the atmosphere. Dealing with the build-up of gases which contribute to global warming involves a combination of substitution and greater efficiency in the use of resources.

# 4   MANAGING AIR QUALITY – MEASUREMENT

## 4.1   Introduction

We saw in Section 1.3 that air pollution may be regarded as the state when air quality has deteriorated, perhaps by an increase in one of the components of air. To check whether such a change has occurred, we need to analyse the air to assess any change in composition. Identifying what pollutants are involved may also help in identifying the source(s) and hence where control need be applied. As we shall see later, there are several ambient air quality standards established by law, and the existence of a standard implies that there must be a 'standard' way of assessing whether the standard is met. Unfortunately, air quality measurement is complicated by most components of the air needing a different measurement method. We do not have the space or the time to examine them all here, so we will concentrate on a few for which air quality standards apply and for which standard measurement methods are set. You will see several standard methods applied in TV 7.

Measuring air quality is now an extensive and expensive exercise, with many networks of air quality monitoring stations operating throughout the UK and globally. These networks measure *ambient* air quality, i.e. the quality of the air around us. However, it is also necessary to measure the quality of emissions released from processes. Emission testing also serves to assess compliance with standards, many of which are now set under the provisions of the Environmental Protection Act (EPA) 1990.

An essential feature of the control of air pollution under the provisions of the 1990 Act is the specification of emission limits. The substances for which these apply and the limits themselves vary according to the particular process. Details are given in guidance notes issued by HM Inspectorate of Pollution (HMIP) for specific processes, and individual values need not concern us in this course. Common to many processes, however, are the following statements which include several terms that are likely to be unfamiliar to you at present.

> Emissions from combustion processes should in normal operation be free from visible smoke and in any case should not exceed the equivalent of Ringelmann Shade 1 as described in British Standard BS 2742: 1969.

> The reference test method for particulate matter emissions in chimneys or ducts is that of British Standard BS 3405: 1983…

and

> The aim should be that all emissions are free from offensive odour outside the process boundary…

The first two statements relate to emission measurement, while the last is another requirement for ambient measurement. These issues, together with the previously undefined terms, will be examined in this section.

## 4.2   Emission measurement

The chemical species of interest for emission measurements are those on the prescribed list for air (see Table 3). However, Section 7(2)(a) of EPA 1990 requires not only that prescribed substances be rendered harmless, but also includes 'any other substance which might cause harm if released into any environmental medium'. Potentially this could include a very wide range of substances, but for practical purposes we need only consider pollutants specified in process guidance notes issued by the Secretary of State for the Environment. The main pollutants for which release limits are specified in these notes are listed in Table 11, and you should compare the pollutants listed here with those in Table 3. You will then notice that Table 11 expands on Table 3 by mentioning specific chemical compounds.

**Table 11**   *Substances for which release limits are specified in guidance notes issued under provisions of EPA 1990*

| | |
|---|---|
| amines and amides | lead |
| ammonia | mercaptans |
| cadmium | nitrogen oxides (NO, NO$_2$) |
| carbon monoxide | non-methane hydrocarbons |
| formaldehyde | organic and inorganic sulphides (including mercaptans) |
| hydrogen chloride | oxygen |
| hydrogen fluoride | particulate matter (**smoke, grit, dust** and **fume**) |
| hydrogen sulphide | sulphur oxides (SO$_2$, SO$_3$) |
| isocyanates | volatile organic compounds |

*(handwritten annotations: $<2\,\mu m$ ; $1-76\,\mu m$ ; $>76\,\mu m$ ; $<1\,\mu m$)*

If we consider a waste gas stream flowing from a process through ductwork to a chimney and then being released to atmosphere, we may look at the composition of the gas stream at any point in that flow. In terms of release of pollutants to atmosphere it may appear logical to assess the composition as release occurs at the top of the chimney. Another approach may be to measure the gas composition in the chimney or ductwork, while yet again we may take a sample from the gas stream and analyse that sample. The options are represented in Figure 32. All are used and we will look briefly at some examples.

---

**SAQ 16**

*(handwritten note: it is present in waste gases due to excess air supplied for combustion. Therefore levels of it indicate performance of combustion system →)*

Notice from Table 11 that oxygen is included. It is not a pollutant, so suggest why it may be included among the components to be measured in releases to atmosphere.

---

### 4.2.1   Remote sensing

Assessing pollution as it is discharged from a chimney by pointing a measuring device at the plume from a remote point (Figure 32a) has several attractions, not the least being convenience and safety. Perhaps the simplest emission measurement method, the **Ringelmann chart**, falls into this category. The Ringelmann chart was invented in the last century and has been widely used internationally since. It is a British Standard method of measurement (BS 2742: 1969) and comprises a series of cross-hatched squares (Figure 33), which appear as shades of grey when viewed from a distance of more than 15 m.

The chart is placed in line between the observer and a chimney, with the sun preferably to the side. The darkness of smoke emerging from the chimney top is compared with the shades on the chart, and the Ringelmann number most closely matching the darkness of the smoke is recorded.

Nowadays, more sophisticated remote methods, often based on laser spectrometry, are available for assessing the degree of pollution, but being expensive techniques, they are less widely used than traditional methods.

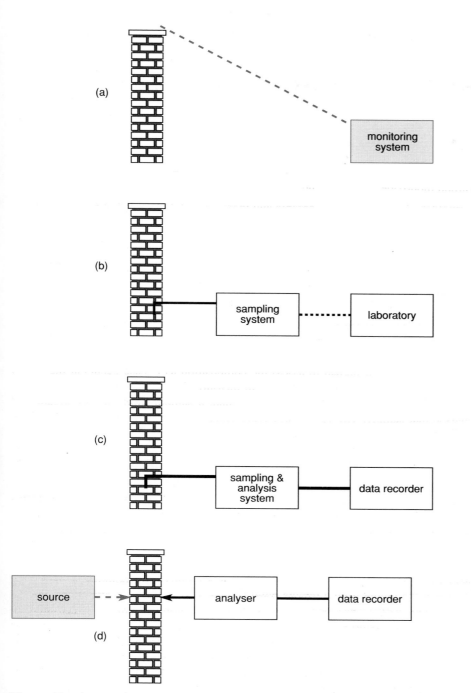

**Figure 32** *Approaches to emission testing: (a) remote sensing; (b) extractive; (c) continuous; (d) in-situ.*

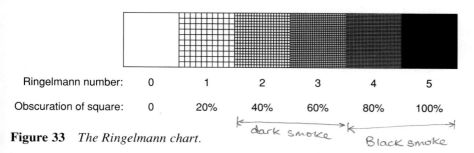

**Figure 33** *The Ringelmann chart.*

**SAQ 17**

What shades on the Ringelmann chart correspond to 'dark smoke', 'black smoke' and the smoke emission limit allowed in process guidance notes under the Environmental Protection Act 1990?

### 4.2.2  *Extractive methods*

It is possible to extract a sample from the gas stream in a duct or chimney and analyse its composition in a laboratory (Figure 32b). This is the basis of British Standard BS 3405:1983 for the measurement of particulate matter in emissions. The gas flow from a process to a chimney may be considerable, as we can see by looking back at Figure 1 – and that was for a relatively small-scale process. It would be impossible to collect all the emission and separate the component of interest for analysis, and so we have to take a *sample*. A sample must be representative of the whole. For gases, which are uniformly mixed, we only have to withdraw a sample for analysis, but for particulate matter in a gas stream, the situation is much more difficult. Particles may not be uniformly distributed throughout a flowing gas stream. Large particles may tend to settle or, through their inertia, may impact on obstructions in the gas stream while the gas itself flows round the obstruction. Small particles may behave more like the gas, and so flow around obstructions. These behaviour patterns have important implications for sampling particulate matter from gases. Isokinetic sampling (see *sampling, isokinetic* in the set book) is essential if the sample is to represent the whole gas stream. This technique involves extracting the sample at the same velocity as the existing gas flow in the duct or chimney. Notice from Figure 34 how the flow may be disturbed and lead to an unrepresentative sample being obtained.

A schematic diagram of one type of equipment for isokinetic sampling of particulate emissions is shown in Figure 35. In this equipment, some of the gas stream is drawn into a nozzle by suction and the particulate matter is separated from the gas stream by a *cyclone*. This uses centrifugal force for the separation in a similar manner to the cyclone shown in TV 1 for oil separation from water, and also in gas cleaning for air pollution control; this will be covered later in Section 5.3. The cyclone alone is adequate for many purposes, but when specific monitoring requirements make it necessary to measure particulate matter below about 5 µm, it is necessary to use a filter to collect this *grade* of material. This is because the cyclone is inefficient at collecting small particles. The particulate matter collected in the cyclone (and filter if used) is weighed for calculation of the emission. Chemical analysis of the particulate matter may also be done to assess emissions of pollutants such as metals.

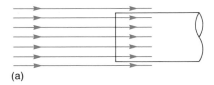

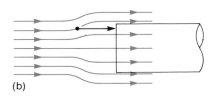

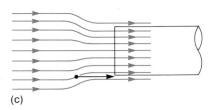

**Figure 34**  *Isokinetic and anisokinetic sampling – the effect on particle size distribution.*

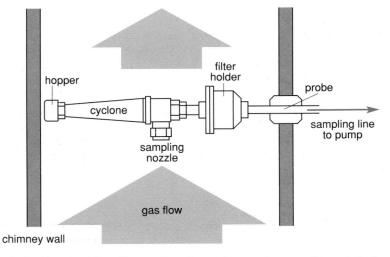

**Figure 35**  *Cyclone, filter and probe equipment for sampling particulate matter from a flue.*

The air flow through the duct or chimney is usually measured with a pitot tube (Figure 36). You may visualise how this works by imagining going out on a windy day. You experience the atmospheric pressure (or static pressure) all around your body and so do not notice it, but the dynamic pressure of the wind is experienced as the additional force resisting your movement towards the wind. This dynamic pressure is proportional to the air speed, and so may be used to measure this. The pitot tube comprises two concentric tubes, of which one has holes around its circumference and effectively is exposed to the static pressure within the duct. The other (inner) tube is open only at its tip and so experiences the static pressure plus the velocity pressure. The pressure difference (which represents the dynamic pressure) is measured with a suitable pressure gauge or electronic pressure transducer, and the reading is converted to air speed using published conversion tables.

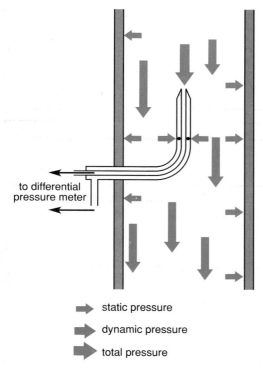

to differential
pressure meter

static pressure

dynamic pressure

total pressure

**Figure 36**  *Schematic representation of the mode of operation of a pitot tube for gas flow measurements. Dynamic pressure is the total pressure less the static pressure.*

The air flow across and at different positions in a duct is measured with a pitot tube in order to identify the best sampling positions. Bends, constrictions and other factors may lead to uneven flow patterns, while sampling in horizontal ducts may give misleading results owing to particle sedimentation. The ideal sampling position is usually in a flue gas duct just before discharge, where the gas flow is vertical and the distribution of solids should be reasonably uniform, but access and safety constraints may make it necessary to sample elsewhere. It may also be necessary to sample upstream and downstream of pollution control equipment (arrestment plant) in order to check on its performance. Figure 37 indicates typical sampling positions. If we know the air flow at the sampling position, the rate at which the gas stream is sampled into the cyclone and probe may be adjusted so that the sampling rate and gas flow rate in the duct are the same. Sampling will thereby be isokinetic.

### 4.2.3  Continuous emission monitoring

Where measurement is required for checking compliance with emission limits, modern practice prefers the use of continuous monitors which measure the pollutant directly on an extracted sample (Figure 32c). Several types are available and only one or two examples will be given. Monitors for sulphur dioxide and carbon monoxide are usually based on the absorption of electromagnetic radiation in the infra-red band of the spectrum. These devices are similar to those used for ambient carbon monoxide

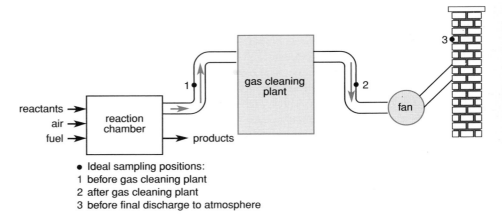

● Ideal sampling positions:
1 before gas cleaning plant
2 after gas cleaning plant
3 before final discharge to atmosphere

**Figure 37**   *Typical sampling positions for emission measurements of air pollutants.*

measurement, and the principle of operation and some of the problems will be described in the next section. You see the application of this type of instrument in TV 7. Hydrogen chloride and hydrogen fluoride may be measured by adding the sample to a solution in which the component of interest dissolves. The resulting ion concentration in solution may be measured automatically by an ***ion selective electrode*** which responds to the ion in a manner similar to the way the pH electrode in your home experiment kit responds to hydrogen ion concentration. Continuous emission monitors are also available for particulate matter, nitrogen oxides, oxygen, and volatile organic compounds. Some systems are known as in-situ monitors (Figure 32d) and operate by measuring the absorption or scattering of a light beam across a stack.

### 4.2.4   Emission data

Measurement of gaseous components in an emission is relatively more straightforward than the measurement of particles in a gas stream. Sampling downstream of fans should give good mixing. Uniform mixing allows a sample to be extracted very simply without the need to consider isokinetic conditions. In addition, the concentrations of pollutant gases are much greater than in the ambient air, so measuring their concentrations is so much easier. It becomes more and more difficult to measure something as its concentration decreases; often we have to take a larger sample in order to collect a sufficient amount of the component of interest, and then separate the component from the bulk before measuring it. The high concentrations in emissions simplify this problem, although they may present another. We often talk in terms of sampling emissions in a 'hostile environment', because the high concentrations may present new problems of corrosiveness, toxicity and high temperature.

Often the methods for measuring gases in emissions are similar to those for ambient measurement, allowing for the different orders of concentrations. You will see some of the problems of emission measurement and typical instrumentation in TV 7. Sometimes it may not even be necessary to measure emissions of certain gaseous pollutants other than for test purposes. An ***emission factor*** may allow the emission to be calculated relatively simply. For example, the concentration of sulphur dioxide in the combustion gases from an oil-fired furnace must be related to the sulphur content of the fuel and the amount of fuel used. If both are known, it is relatively simple to estimate the emission rate.

The contribution of shipping to air pollution was indicated in Figure 5. Typical emission factors for shipping as derived using techniques similar to those shown in TV 7 are shown in Table 12. Emission factors may be used in compiling an ***emission inventory*** and in the assessment of environmental impact through air pollutant emissions, as the pollution contour maps in TV 7 illustrate.

*Emission factor*
*mass of pollutant produced relative to each unit of process eg, unit mass, item of production*

*Map of distribution of emissions*

**Table 12** *Typical exhaust emission factors from shipping under steady state operation*

| Pollutant | Emission factor/ (kg per tonne fuel) |
|---|---|
| $NO_x$ | 59 |
| CO | 8 |
| Hydrocarbons | 2.7 |
| $CO_2$ | 3250 |
| $SO_2$ | $(21.9 \times S) - 2.1$ where $S$ is the sulphur content of the fuel (% by weight) |

Source: Lloyds Register of Shipping (1990) *Marine Exhaust Emission Research Programme: Steady State Operation.*

## Exercise

A car ferry consumes 24 l min$^{-1}$ of light fuel oil of density 0.99 kg l$^{-1}$ at 15 °C when running at a speed of 22 knots. The sulphur content of the fuel is 3.8% (by mass). How much carbon dioxide is emitted over 1 hour at constant speed?

## Answer

The fuel consumption is equivalent to

24 l min$^{-1} \times$ 0.99 kg l$^{-1}$ = 23.76 kg min$^{-1}$

= 0.024 tonne min$^{-1}$

Hence in one hour, using the emission factor quoted in Table 12, the emission of carbon dioxide is

3250 kg t$^{-1} \times$ 0.024 t $\times$ 60 = 4.7 t

## SAQ 18

Calculate the emissions of the other pollutants emitted from the car ferry over one hour under the conditions quoted above.

## SAQ 19

Efficiency improvements to a gas-fired furnace for curing paint on metal will result in annual energy savings of 1070 GJ. Assuming that the emission factor for $NO_x$ production is 44 g GJ$^{-1}$, calculate the annual reduction in $NO_x$ emissions.

## 4.3 Ambient air quality measurement

Measurement can be relatively simple. Consider measuring the size of this page with a ruler. The ruler is reliable, rugged, cheap, requires little training to use it and is self-contained. It also does not require a sampling stage, and is direct reading, i.e. does not need calibrating against a standard before we use it. If only components of the atmosphere could be measured as easily. Unfortunately, as I mentioned previously, many air components require different techniques for their measurement. There are many methods available, and these may be classified in a similar manner to that shown previously for emission measurements. Thus Figure 38 shows three approaches: manual, continuous and long-path monitoring. We will consider only one or two examples, starting with a traditional manual method for assessing sulphur dioxide and suspended particulate matter, as represented in Figure 39.

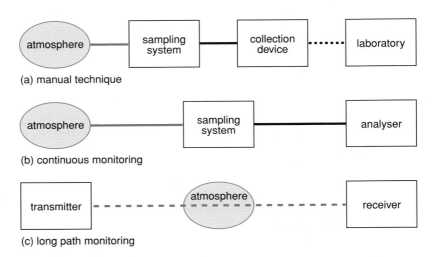

(a) manual technique

(b) continuous monitoring

(c) long path monitoring

**Figure 38**   *Options for sampling and measuring ambient air quality.*

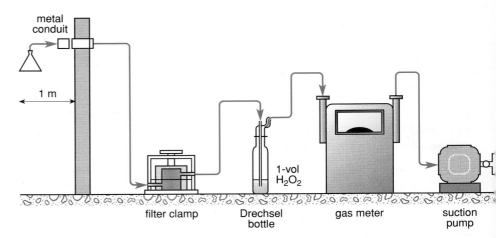

**Figure 39**   *Traditional British Standard method for measuring ambient sulphur dioxide and smoke.*

Measurements of sulphur dioxide and airborne particulate matter have been carried out throughout the UK since the 1920s. The number of sites at which measurements were made as part of the **National Survey of Air Pollution** increased over the years to a maximum of around 1200, but in the early 1980s the numbers were cut back to about 280. This was partly because air pollution from these two pollutants had decreased considerably in many areas, making continued surveillance across such a wide area less important.

The method used in the National Survey involved a known amount of air being drawn through a filter paper; the suspended particulate matter in the air was retained on the filter to form a stain – a *smoke stain*. The darkness of the stain depends on the amount of particulate matter and its nature. Thus coal smoke and diesel exhaust are very dark, while cement dust is light in colour. In the past, smoke came mainly from coal burning, and the intensity of the smoke stain was a measure of the amount of coal smoke in the air. The intensity of the smoke stain can be assessed with a reflectometer, in which a steady light beam is directed on to the stain and the reflected light is measured by a photocell, which gives a reading on a micro-ammeter. The darker the stain, the less reflection from the filter paper and so the lower the reading. By calibrating the reading against a 'standard smoke' the air pollution by smoke may be assessed. This method of measuring 'smoke' is used in many countries, but different calibrations apply. So, for example, in the UK a British Standard calibration is used, whereas elsewhere in Europe the OECD (Organisation for Economic Cooperation and Development) calibration graph is used. We must remember this when we come to consider air quality standards in Section 4.5.

### SAQ 20

Suggest a problem with the principle behind the 'smoke stain' method of measuring air-borne particles.

*[handwritten margin notes: — originated from coal smoke — dark and reflective / other smokes eg cement dust — light coloured / also no indication of mass.]*

The National Survey apparatus also included a 125 ml drechsel (bubbler) bottle containing 50 ml of 0.3% wt/vol aqueous solution of hydrogen peroxide ($H_2O_2$) to absorb sulphur dioxide from samples of ambient air. As air is bubbled through the solution, any $SO_2$ is oxidised rapidly to sulphuric acid thus:

$$SO_2 + H_2O_2 \rightarrow H_2SO_4$$

With an air flow rate of about 1.5 litres $min^{-1}$, some 2 $m^3$ of air will pass through the solution in 24 hours. After this sampling time, the amount of $SO_2$ collected can be estimated by using an alkaline solution of sodium tetraborate to titrate the acidified hydrogen peroxide back to a pH value of 4.5. [You use this same basic technique of titration in home experiment activities.] The National Survey method measures acidity due to sulphur dioxide, whereas titration to pH7 would also measure the acid produced by carbon dioxide in the air dissolving in the water. Another source of acid in the air may be hydrogen chloride, which is formed when plastics such as PVC are incinerated, while ammonia from farming activities (animal wastes) can neutralise acids in the solution. These factors may introduce uncertainties in the measurement method, which relies on the net acidity of the solution. Now, however, exposed peroxide solutions can be analysed by ion chromatography (IC). This method is $SO_2$ specific and more sensitive than titration by sodium tetraborate. By substituting different absorbing solutions and using different chemical analyses, the technique can be used for measuring other components of the air.

As with the smoke stain reflectometer readings, the $SO_2$ results are coordinated by Warren Spring Laboratory*, which serves as the national centre for UK networks. The inherent simplicity of the method favoured its widespread use over many decades, and continued use allows comparison of data with historical patterns. This is a very important point. When data are compared (for example, to see what improvements of air quality have been made over a period or to compare one site with another), the measurement methods must be comparable too. The method just described relates the amount of suspended particulate matter to the darkness of a stain. I hope that you recall that the soiling power is not related directly to the mass of particles – what about light-coloured cement dust? Likewise, the sulphur dioxide is measured by the acidity of a solution, and again this is not a property specific to sulphur dioxide. Other techniques for measuring these pollutants use different properties, such as the β-radiation attenuation technique you see in TV 7. The variety of methods may not give comparable data without calibration.

It is not possible to detect concentrations smaller than 10 μg of $SO_2$ in 50 ml of solution with this method, so this constraint determines both the minimum sampling period and the range of concentrations over which acceptable measurements can be made. For this reason, the equipment usually collects a sample over 24 hours; this gives sufficient material to analyse. We say the method has a 24-hour averaging period. This introduces another fundamental point we must explore further.

### 4.3.1  The effect of averaging time

We saw from Figure 26 that air quality varies continuously. Modern sensitive instruments of the type we will consider shortly may give instantaneous values, while with many older techniques enough sample over a period of time has to be collected in order to have enough to detect. We may draw a parallel here with the integrating sound level meter. Effectively, collecting a sample over a given time period is an

---

* Since this unit was written, the Government announced that the activities at Warren Spring Laboratory were to be transferred to a national environmental technology centre in Oxfordshire.

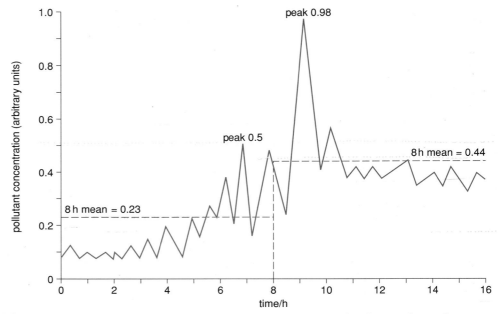

**Figure 40**   *The effect of continuous air quality variations, peak values and sample averaging time on representative data.*

averaging technique. This has an advantage of simplifying the data we have to interpret, but we must be aware of the consequences.

Let us consider a typical variation in the concentration of an air pollutant in Figure 40. The peaks and troughs may indicate how air quality varies with time and other factors, but the variations are overwhelming. We can lose or smooth out some of the variations by averaging over a time period. The period chosen will affect how much definition we lose from the data. Some obsolete methods of measuring air pollutants used to sample over 30 days, and it was impossible to relate these 30-day averages to an event occurring on one or two days. Figure 40 shows how such averaging loses definition by concealing the peaks which may result from plant malfunction, unusual meteorological conditions or other reasons. It can also be seen how sampling over a period may give a different value from that over the same length of period at a different time.

---

### SAQ 21

The following list shows the maximum sulphur dioxide concentrations observed over different averaging times throughout a three-month period. Plot the data on the graphical scales below (logarithmic scales). Summarise what the graph shows and suggest how the resulting graph may be used.

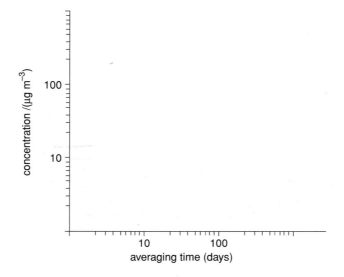

| Concentration/($\mu$g m$^{-3}$) | Averaging time (days) |
|---|---|
| 424 | 1 |
| 166 | 7 |
| 94 | 30 |
| 82 | 90 |

We have seen that the sampling period may be determined by the time required to collect sufficient component to measure, but we should also relate the sampling period to the effect under investigation. For example, odours are sensed by our noses in a matter of a second, and for this reason we need to be aware of instantaneous peaks when dealing with odour pollutants. Similarly, plants may succumb to the adverse effects of air pollutants after short periods of exposure. By comparison, lead pollution from, say, motor car exhausts has a cumulative effect on our bodies, and so long-term averages are more meaningful than short-term peaks. We will see these features reflected in air quality standards in Section 4.5. Overall, we can say that the sampling period is a compromise based on the measurement method, the relevant effect, and inevitably the number of samples we can handle.

### 4.3.2 Continuous ambient air quality monitoring

Many techniques are available for measuring continuously the concentrations of components of the atmosphere (see Figure 38) but certain methods have been found to be most reliable. Such methods have been designated for use in assessing compliance with air quality standards, and many of these methods are based on spectrometric principles which were introduced in Section 8.2.1 of Unit 3. Here we will outline the principles of only two methods – one for measuring sulphur dioxide and one for carbon monoxide.

### 4.3.3 Sulphur dioxide

While the net acidity method for routine surveillance of sulphur dioxide concentrations is still widely used in many countries, modern networks use continuous analysers (Figure 41).

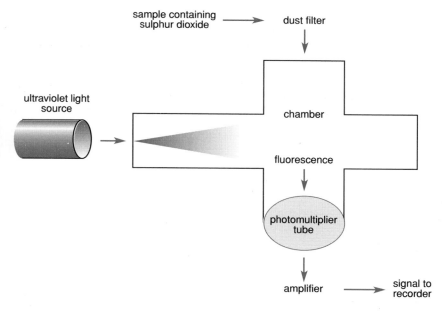

**Figure 41** *The principle of UV fluorescence for measuring sulphur dioxide. Sulphur dioxide molecules absorb UV light, which is re-emitted as fluorescence, and measured at right angles to the incident beam. In this way only the emitted light is measured.*

### 4.3.4   Carbon monoxide

The standard method for measuring CO in atmospheres relies on absorption of infra-red radiation. Such instruments are simpler than those used in laboratory analysis, in which prisms or diffraction gratings are used to split the radiation into wavelength bands characteristic of certain molecules (Section 8.2.1 of Unit 3). Infra-red pollution analysers use optical filters to isolate the required wavelength region, and pure gases sensitise the instrument to the component of interest. For this reason the instruments are called 'non-dispersive' since the light is not dispersed into bands of different wavelengths. Figure 42 illustrates a typical arrangement in an instrument.

Infra-red radiation emitted by hot filaments passes through two analysis tubes and falls on the two halves of the detector, each of which contains a pure, dry sample of the gas to be detected (CO in this case). The receiving chambers of the detector have windows in their upper faces transparent to the wavelengths in use, while the two halves are separated by a thin diaphragm. This diaphragm is made of one plate of an electrical capacitor. The gas in the detector absorbs energy at its own specific wavelength, and so becomes heated, which increases the pressure in each chamber. If the same energy reaches both halves of the detector, the pressure increase will be identical and the diaphragm will not be affected. However, if non-absorbing gas is in one analysis tube and air containing the pollutant of interest is in the other, a pressure imbalance is set up across the diaphragm, which is distended. This changes the electrical capacitance of the cell, which is converted to an electrical output proportional to concentration.

Notice that the principle used in this instrument, namely the absorption of infra-red radiation by a pollutant, is essentially the same as that which occurs in the atmosphere and contributes to the greenhouse effect.

Non-dispersive infra-red analysis was the technique by which the data in Figure 26 were obtained, and is also a technique seen in TV 7 for both ambient and emission measurement.

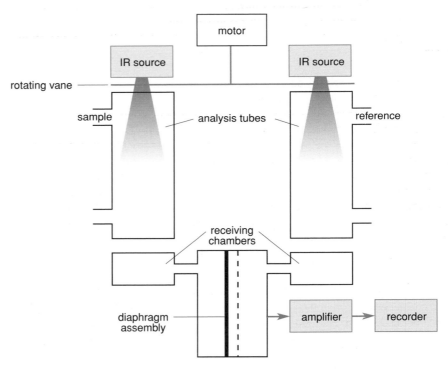

**Figure 42**   *Schematic diagram of a non-dispersive infra-red analyser for carbon monoxide measurement.*

---

**SAQ 22**

Suggest a possible problem when a non-dispersive carbon monoxide analyser is used directly on an ambient air sample.

*the infra-red absorption region of H2O can interfer with CO. Solved by freeze drying or absorbing water first.*

---

### 4.3.5   Remote or long-path monitoring

Traditional ambient monitoring has been performed as point monitoring using instruments of the types described previously; such equipment forms the backbone of the present national networks in the UK. However, increasing interest is focused on long-path optical measurement, shown as the third approach in Figure 38. The techniques employ a beam of optical radiation (usually infra-red or ultraviolet) as the gas sensor, which is transmitted across a path which may extend from a few metres to several kilometres in length. By selecting a wavelength at which selective absorption by a gas of interest occurs, the average amount of that gas in the air is measured.

The technique overcomes one of the problems indicated at the start of this section, namely that traditional methods of air quality monitoring require different instruments for each pollutant. With long-path monitoring, a range of gases may be measured by simply changing to a different wavelength. Unfortunately, the complexity of these instruments is reflected in their high costs, and comparison of results with those from other techniques is difficult because it means comparing point measurements with averages over a long distance.

### 4.3.6   Continuous air quality monitoring networks

Networks of instruments to measure air quality have been in operation in several countries in Europe and the USA for several years. In the UK, the origins of the National Survey of Air Pollution can be traced back to around 1912, but more advanced monitoring is of more recent introduction.

Ground-level concentrations of nitrogen dioxide and airborne lead are monitored for compliance with EC directives. A network for urban carbon monoxide, sulphur dioxide and nitrogen dioxide together with a rural ozone network have been in operation in the UK for several years. In 1992 a new urban network became operational. Initially, sulphur dioxide, nitrogen oxides, ozone, carbon monoxide and particulate matter will be monitored continuously at sites in London, Cardiff, Birmingham, Newcastle, Belfast and Edinburgh, with other locations to be added in the future. Techniques similar to those shown in TV 7 are used to provide continuous information on air quality at the selected sites. The networks include on-line data telemetry and access by terminal links, allowing air quality bulletins to be provided. Rapid dissemination of air quality data to newspapers and the television during high pollution episodes began in October 1990. The direct datalink through the network control centre at Warren Spring Laboratory to the Meteorological Office provides the basis of the Government's air quality information service, which operates every day of the year. This concept of a public information system on air pollution is shown in TV 7, and is common in many countries.

### 4.3.7   Calibration

We have seen from the few examples given that air quality monitors do not measure the amount of a component in air directly, but relate the concentration to a property of that component. For example, sulphur dioxide may be measured by the net acidity produced when it dissolves in water, or by the UV-fluorescence produced. In fact, there are scores of different methods for measuring this gas, and many use different properties of the gas. So, unlike the case of a ruler for measuring the size of this page, we must *calibrate* the instruments. This is usually done by introducing air containing none of the pollutant of interest ('*zero gas*'), and then a gas mixture of accurately known composition (a '*standard*') into the instrument, and adjusting its response to give the respective readings. Primary standard gas mixtures may be stored in gas cylinders which are specially coated to prevent losses of the traces of pollutant standard.

Another technique for preparing standards involves the use of a **permeation tube**. Figure 43 illustrates a typical design and method of use.

Calibration is fundamental to securing good and reliable data, as TV 7 illustrates, but it is also complicated and an extra cost. A national air quality calibration centre exists at Warren Spring Laboratory.

A common feature of all these measurement techniques is that they produce a large amount of data. How we analyse the data is the topic of the next section.

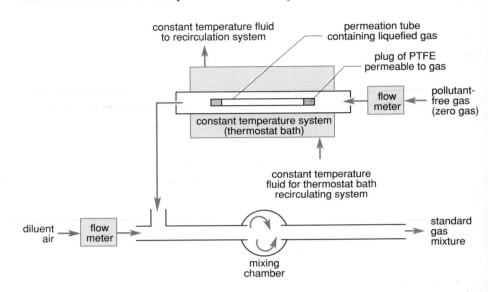

**Figure 43**   *Schematic diagram of a typical permeation tube within a permeation system for producing standard mixtures of pollutant gases in air.*

## 4.4   *Reduction of data to characterise a site*

As a consequence of the many source-related and meteorological factors influencing air quality at a site, a continuous record of a pollutant concentration shows wide variations. Even when measurements are made by collecting samples over 24 hours, a list of daily mean concentrations quickly becomes cumbersome. The quantity of data must be reduced to a manageable amount so that its basic characteristics can be appreciated. The data reduction process may begin by taking the arithmetical mean (AM), of all the observed values. As we saw in Unit 4, the arithmetic mean is not the best indicator of typical air quality. Depending on the averaging period chosen, the result obtained may represent typical air quality at the site, but while this allows one site to be compared with another, taking averages may conceal the high values, or peaks, which could cause nuisance such as odour, or at worst damage health. Figure 40 showed how averaging over longer periods loses definition of short-term fluctuations. The data may be inspected to pick out the maximum concentrations that might cause adverse environmental effects, but a simple list of large values is not very useful.

Conventionally, the individual observations, taken over a chosen period such as a month, six months, or a year, are sorted into a convenient sequence. The values are placed in an ascending order of increasing concentrations:

$$C_1, C_2, C_{3...}, C_i..., C_N$$

where $C_i$ is the $i$th concentration in the observed set of $N$ values, $N$ is the number of observations, and $i$ is any integer number between 1 and $N$. As you will recall from Unit 4, the difference between the smallest value ($C_1$) and the largest concentration ($C_N$) is called the *range*. If there are $N$ observations, and $N$ is odd, the middle value is called the *median*, which was introduced in Section 2.3 of Unit 4. If $N$ is even, the median is conveniently taken to be the mean of the two middle values. By further dividing up the set of observations into four parts, or *quartiles*, we can define additional statistics about the spread of observations by giving the individual values at the dividing points. Dividing up the observations into 10 equal parts gives us *deciles*.

The process can be continued still further by dividing up the set of observations into 100 groups to obtain *percentile* values. For example, you will recall from Unit 4 that the 50th percentile concentration corresponds to the median value. When a data set of $N$ values is placed in an ascending order, the $P$th percentile corresponds to the $(P \times N/100)$th value. Quite often this ratio will not be an integer value; various procedures are then available to overcome the difficulty.

## SAQ 23

What may we call the pollutant concentration at the second quartile and fifth decile?

## SAQ 24

As an example of a set of data and to remind you of the important concepts you learned from Unit 4, consider all the integer numbers (i.e. whole numbers) from and including 5 to 44 inclusive.

(a) What is the range?

(b) What is the median value?

(c) What are the values of the first and third quartile?

(d) What is the seventh decile?

TV 7 shows that data from air quality monitoring networks in the UK are processed by computer at Warren Spring Laboratory. Data are subjected to extended analyses and data reduction, and the results are regularly published. Figure 44 shows an extract from a report on the network for smoke and sulphur dioxide which serves in part to meet the requirements of the EC Directive (80/779/EEC). The yearly period runs from the beginning of April to the end of the following March. This enables the six months in each warmer or cooler half-year period to be grouped together and they appear consecutively. The winter and summer values are therefore given separately, including the winter median (WMD).

Each site is identified by a name and number. Letters classify the site within the basic urban network (A), the EC Directive Survey (B), the rural network (D) and whether it was in operation before 1982 as part of the then National Survey on Air Pollution (F). Each site is also classified by code to indicate the nature of the surrounding area and its potential for air pollution. For example, A2 in Figure 44 indicates:

> Residential area with high-density housing (probably terraced) or with medium-density housing in multiple occupation, in either case surrounded by other built-up areas, and interspersed with some industrial undertakings.

Other coded characters indicate the pollution potential of the surrounding area by reference to different categories of high or low density housing, industry, commerce or rural community.

The first rows of printed figures against both smoke and $SO_2$ give the arithmetical mean of the daily mean concentrations, each calculated over a 4- or 5-week period based on the calendar months. Below each line, a second row of figures indicates the highest daily mean concentration of smoke or sulphur dioxide within each period. Below the second line, additional figures give the number of days in each period during which the daily concentrations of smoke or $SO_2$ exceeded the values specified in the left-hand column.

Next, the daily mean values are aggregated into the Sum(mer) and Win(ter) 6-month periods. Similar analyses yield the arithmetical mean, the highest daily concentrations of smoke and $SO_2$, and the total number of days in each 6-month period during which each specified concentration is exceeded.

At this point we must leave further interpretation of the air quality data in order to introduce air quality standards. Later we will return to these data to interpret them in relation to the standards.

Handwritten annotations:

*Limits for median values: for the chronic effects of long term exposure*
*Limits for 98th percentile for the acute effects of short term peaks on some people*

*arithmetic mean* (→ AM)
*winter median values* (→ WMD)
*Geometric mean – represents typical value over the year without undue influence from one or two very high peaks* (→ GM)
*median of daily values for the year* (→ 50%)

**Site name and number:** Belfast 13  
**Survey code:** ABF  
**Classification code:** A2

| | A | M | J | J | A | S | O | N | D | J | F | M | Sum | Win |
|---|---|---|---|---|---|---|---|---|---|---|---|---|---|---|
| **Smoke** $\mu g\,m^{-3}$ | 37 | 22 | 16 | 9 | 15 | 21 | 34 | 97 | 113 | – | 21 | 20 | 20 | 54 |
| highest conc. | 68 | 41 | 26 | 23 | 27 | 42 | 77 | 186 | 688 | 49 | 49 | 40 | 68 | 688 |
| days over 100 | | | | | | | | 10 | 12 | | | | | 22 |
| days over 150 | | | | | | | | 3 | 7 | | | | | 10 |
| days over 200 | | | | | | | | | 6 | | | | | 6 |
| days over 250 | | | | | | | | | 4 | | | | | 4 |
| **SO₂** $\mu g\,m^{-3}$ | 80 | 56 | 32 | 20 | 28 | 39 | 46 | 93 | 197 | – | 54 | 44 | 42 | 85 |
| highest conc. | 171 | 91 | 81 | 38 | 51 | 64 | 118 | 206 | 936 | 137 | 109 | 102 | 171 | 936 |
| days over 200 | | | | | | | | 1 | 10 | | | | | 11 |
| days over 250 | | | | | | | | | 7 | | | | | 7 |
| days over 350 | | | | | | | | | 7 | | | | | 7 |
| days over 500 | | | | | | | | | 1 | | | | | 1 |

**Annual summary**

| | Smoke | SO₂ |
|---|---|---|
| AM | 37 | 63 |
| WMD | 28 | 55 |
| GM | 24 | 47 |
| SGD | 2.23 | 2.05 |
| 1% | 5 | 6 |
| 5% | 8 | 18 |
| 20% | 14 | 27 |
| 50% | 22 | 45 |
| 80% | 44 | 76 |
| 90% | 74 | 118 |
| 95% | 116 | 159 |
| 98% | 194 | 342 |
| 99% | 262 | 405 |

−, incomplete data; AM, arithmetic mean; GM, geometric mean; SGD, standard geometric deviation; WMD, winter median. For ABF and A2 see text.

**Figure 44** *Example of smoke and sulphur dioxide summary statistics for a UK monitoring site, adapted from the 1989/90 summary tables, courtesy of Warren Spring Laboratory.*

*do not learn the details but be able to interpret them of air quality standards*

# 4.5 Air quality standards

*This section must begin with a health warning! You will find many detailed tables of air quality standards in this section, and the aim is to enable you to interpret standards. You do not have to learn the values cited.*

Environmental guidelines, goals, admissible limits, control limits, maximum admissible concentrations and many similar terms may differ in their scope and legal basis, but all are 'environmental standards'. They all serve to describe the region of 'no adverse effect' or, more exactly, a given low probability of effect in a defined but small fraction of the population exposed to a pollutant.

The form of an environmental standard may be a single value, such as a concentration in drinking water, or a pair of values relating to concentration and time as applied to air pollutants. In experimental toxicology it is relatively easy to set limits, but it is very much more difficult when we try to apply standards to human populations or to long-lived ecosystems such as forests. One reason for the problem is that a standard relates to the absence of an effect. The nearer one gets to the 'limit', the more uncertain becomes the effect. The relationship between human disease and exposure to pollution is rarely simple, or fully understood. A spectrum of responses is possible. Moreover, some members of the population, particularly the very young, the very old and the sick, may be especially sensitive to environmental factors.

Another problem is that in the environment we are not exposed to a single pollutant but a cocktail of many. Let us look at the problem by considering the well-studied pollutants, sulphur dioxide and smoke. These have often been used as 'indicator pollutants' to give a general picture of air quality in an area.

Sulphur dioxide is a colourless gas with a sharp smell and a choking taste – typically the smell when we strike a match. Humans can sense the gas at concentrations of 1000–3000 $\mu$g m$^{-3}$, but the effects of the gas are not lasting in healthy individuals. Smoke is more difficult to relate to ill-health effects because it is by nature a mixture of substances. Some ill-health effects may be the result of a specific chemical in a smoke from a specific source. Generally, however, in the absence of specific toxic materials in smoke, concentrations of typically 1000 $\mu$g m$^{-3}$ are unlikely to produce adverse health effects.

So, either smoke or sulphur dioxide at concentrations of 1000 $\mu$g m$^{-3}$ would not seem to be a matter of great concern, other than perhaps causing some discomfort. However, if you look back to our discussion of air pollution episodes, you will see that London smog conditions of typically twice these concentrations for both pollutants seemed to cause a great number of excess deaths. This suggests that the consequences of the two pollutants together is much greater than simply adding the effects that each would produce alone. This is what we call *synergism*.

*Synergistic effects of smoke & SO₂*

There may be several mechanisms for synergism. Sulphur dioxide is very soluble in water and so will dissolve in the mucous fluid in the nasal cavity; the effect of this is to reduce the effectiveness of the removal of particles in the nose and throat. Sulphur dioxide will also adsorb on the surface of the particles of smoke – as these can now reach the lung, so will the adsorbed gas. In addition, some sulphur dioxide may be oxidised to sulphuric acid, a process which will occur more readily on the surface of particles which may include catalysts, and sulphuric acid aerosol is regarded by some as a major contributor to the health effects.

In addition to there being many pollutants present in the air, their concentrations vary widely due to the uncontrollable meteorological and topographical conditions, and chemical reactions between the individual pollutants can take place to produce new pollutants. Such reactions are often stimulated by strong sunshine or high humidity.

In 1972 the World Health Organisation invited a number of scientists to form a committee to prepare a document on air quality criteria and guides for the more common air pollutants. One of the purposes of this work was to provide a basis for national governments or larger groups such as the European Community to set standards for air pollution control. As air pollution control has economic consequences, this justifies a phased programme for improvements. The programme starts with establishing the criteria, which relate concentrations with effects, and then long-term goals, which are levels tentatively set at what might be called zero-effect levels. Air pollution standards then provide the mechanism for a stepwise movement towards meeting the goals.

The committee found that for some of the pollutants the available evidence was sometimes difficult to interpret, but they were able to agree on the most relevant points. Table 13 shows the criteria for sulphur dioxide and particulates. Notice how both daily means and annual geometric means are used. Look back at Section 2.4 of Unit 4 if you are unclear about geometric means. They are used to represent the typical value over a year without undue influence being exerted by one or two very high values. The daily mean, however, is derived from a practical measurement. By sampling air continuously over 24 hours and measuring the amount of pollutants collected from the air volume sampled, analysts can express the result as a 24-hour mean.

**Table 13**  *Expected health effects of air pollutants on selected population groups*

| Concentration/($\mu g$ $m^{-3}$) | | Effect |
|---|---|---|
| $SO_2$ | Smoke (particulates) | |
| 500[a] | 500[a] | Excess mortality and hospital admissions |
| 500–250[a] | 250[a] | Worsening of patients with pulmonary disease |
| 100[b] | 100[b] | Respiratory symptoms |
| 80[c] | 80[c] | Visibility and/or human annoyance effects |

[a]daily averages; [b]annual arithmetic mean; [c]annual geometric mean.

Values for sulphur dioxide and suspended particles apply only in conjunction with each other. Specific measurement methods apply, and some were covered in Section 4.2.

Another aspect of the expert committee's work in 1972 was to establish long-term goals; these are set out in Table 14.

**Table 14**  *Long-term goals for limits of pollutants*

| Pollutant | | Limit/($\mu g$ $m^{-3}$) |
|---|---|---|
| Sulphur dioxide | annual mean | 60 |
| | 98% of daily values below | 200 |
| Suspended particulates | annual mean | 40 |
| | 98% of daily values below | 120 |
| Carbon monoxide | 8 hour average | 10 mg $m^{-3}$ |
| | 1 hour maximum | 40 mg $m^{-3}$ |
| Photochemical oxidants | 8 hour average | 60 |
| | 1 hour maximum | 130 |

Values for sulphur dioxide and suspended particles apply only in conjunction with each other. Specific measurement methods apply, and some were covered in Section 4.2.

As noted above, the goals were to be reached by the setting of intermediate standards for pollution control, and the next step came in 1980. European Community Directive 80/779/EEC was the first directive to set mandatory air quality standards throughout the Community (Table 15). These standards related to smoke and sulphur dioxide and were intended to protect human health and the environment.

**Table 15**  *EC air quality standards for suspended particulates and sulphur dioxide*

| *Ground-level concentration* | | *Limit/($\mu$g m$^{-3}$)* |
|---|---|---|
| *Smoke (suspended particulates):* | | |
| Yearly (median of daily values throughout the year) | | 68 |
| Winter (median of daily values from 1 Oct to 31 Mar) | | 111 |
| Peak (98 percentile of daily values throughout the year) | | 213 |
| *Sulphur dioxide:* | | |
| Yearly: | if smoke <34 $\mu$g m$^{-3}$ | 120 |
| | if smoke ≥34 $\mu$g m$^{-3}$ | 80 |
| Winter: | if smoke <51 $\mu$g m$^{-3}$ | 180 |
| | if smoke ≥51 $\mu$g m$^{-3}$ | 130 |
| Peak: | if smoke <128 $\mu$g m$^{-3}$ | 350 |
| | if smoke ≥128 $\mu$g m$^{-3}$ | 250 |
| | | *Guide value/($\mu$g m$^{-3}$)* |
| *Smoke* | | |
| Year (arithmetic mean of daily mean values) | | 34 to 51 |
| 24 h (daily mean value) | | 85 to 128 |
| *Sulphur dioxide* | | |
| Year (arithmetic mean of daily mean values) | | 40 to 60 |
| 24 h (daily mean value) | | 100 to 150 |

You may think that in view of the round figures quoted previously for criteria and goals, the EC limit values for smoke appear exact. In fact the values given in the Directive are in round figures derived from calibration for smoke according to the OECD method. The values given in Table 15 above and used in the UK relate to the BSI calibration for smoke stain. (The relationship between the two is OECD value = BSI value/0.85.) You will also notice how complicated the standard seems by comparison to giving a single concentration. In the case of sulphur dioxide and smoke we obviously have to consider the synergistic aspect, and this means relating the concentration of one pollutant to the other. By giving standards for medians, the chronic effects of long period exposure are acknowledged, while the 98 percentile allows for short-term peaks which may cause acute problems in some people, yet still allows for one or two days of high levels. These limit values are generally lower than the concentrations that criteria suggest will cause ill-health effects in large sections of the population, but they still have some way to go to reach the WHO long-term goals.

Since the 1980 Air Quality Directive, more air quality standards have been introduced by the EC. These are summarised in Table 16.

**Table 16**   *EC ambient air quality standards\**

| Ground-level concentration | Limit/($\mu g\ m^{-3}$) |
|---|---|
| *Lead (Directive 82/884)* | 2 |
| Mean annual value | |
| *$NO_2$ (Directive 85/203)* | |
| 98th percentile of mean hourly values throughout year. | 200 |
| *$O_3$ (draft)* | |
| Health protection threshold (lengthy exposure): | |
| for mean value over 8 h | 110  (55 ppb) |
| Vegetation protection threshold: | |
| for mean value over 1 h | 220  (100 ppb) |
| for mean value over 24 h | 65  (32.5 ppb) |
| Health protection warning value (short exposure): | |
| for mean value over 1 h | 175  (87.5 ppb) |

\*For $SO_2$ and suspended particulates, see Table 15.

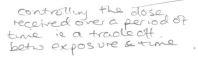

*controlling the dose received over a period of time is a trade off betw exposure & time .*

In 1987, the World Health Organisation published a further set of air quality guidelines for Europe, and among the many values were the data presented in Table 17. For a definition of **time-weighted average**, you should refer to the entry in the set book. You will notice that the entries in Table 17 suggest a downward revision by comparison with the WHO long-term goals for smoke and sulphur dioxide seen previously in Table 14. This trend is always a feature of 'standards' in that they tend to be revised downwards as expectations rise for a better quality of life. It is also found that standards become more stringent as the ability to measure concentrations and/or effects become more refined. Notice also from Table 17 that averaging times range from 10 minutes to 1 year for different pollutants and even vary for the same pollutant. This will influence the way air quality measurement data are processed, because it is essential that the appropriate averaging period is used if a comparison with a guideline or standard is to be meaningful.

### SAQ 25

What interpretation can you draw from the WHO guidelines for carbon monoxide?

We can now return to the air quality data for Belfast presented previously in Figure 44, and see how they relate to air quality standards.

The final columns in Figure 44, headed 'Smoke' and '$SO_2$', are particularly relevant to the EC Directive on smoke and sulphur dioxide. The main features of the Directive are set out in Table 15 which gives the current *limit* and guide values for smoke and sulphur dioxide that should not be exceeded. The Directive refers to suspended particulate matter but you will recall that the measurement method in the UK assesses particulate matter by a smoke stain with a BSI calibration, and so the term 'smoke' is often used by tradition. The limiting values for sulphur dioxide depend on the corresponding concentration of smoke as a result of synergism.

Look at the first line in Table 15. During a year, the median daily value of smoke should not exceed a concentration of 68 $\mu g\ m^{-3}$ (using the BS calibration). If the median smoke concentration is less than 34 $\mu g\ m^{-3}$, the median daily concentration of $SO_2$ should not exceed 120 $\mu g\ m^{-3}$. If the smoke concentration equals or exceeds 34 $\mu g\ m^{-3}$, then the median daily $SO_2$ concentration should not exceed 80 $\mu g\ m^{-3}$.

**Table 17**   *Air quality guidelines for Europe: guideline values for individual substances based on effects other than cancer or odour/annoyance*

| Substance | Time-weighted average | Averaging time |
| --- | --- | --- |
| Cadmium | 1–5 ng m$^{-3}$ | 1 year (rural areas) |
| | 10–20 ng m$^{-3}$ | 1 year (urban areas) |
| Carbon disulphide | 100 μg m$^{-3}$ | 24 hours |
| Carbon monoxide | 100 mg m$^{-3a}$ | 15 minutes |
| | 60 mg m$^{-3a}$ | 30 minutes |
| | 30 mg m$^{-3a}$ | 1 hour |
| | 10 mg m$^{-3}$ | 8 hours |
| 1:2-Dichlorethane | 0.7 mg m$^{-3}$ | 24 hours |
| Dichloromethane (or methylene chloride) | 3 mg m$^{-3}$ | 24 hours |
| Formaldehyde | 100 μg m$^{-3}$ | 30 minutes |
| Hydrogen sulphide | 150 μg m$^{-3}$ | 24 hours |
| Lead | 0.5–1.0 μg m$^{-3}$ | 1 year |
| Manganese | 1 μg m$^{-3}$ | 1 year$^b$ |
| Mercury | 1 μg m$^{-3c}$ (indoor air) | 1 year |
| Nitrogen dioxide | 400 μg m$^{-3}$ | 1 hour |
| | 150 μg m$^{-3}$ | 24 hours |
| Ozone | 150–200 μg m$^{-3}$ | 1 hour |
| | 100–120 μg m$^{-3}$ | 8 hours |
| Styrene | 800 μg m$^{-3}$ | 24 hours |
| Sulphur dioxide | 500 μg m$^{-3}$ | 10 minutes |
| | 350 μg m$^{-3}$ | 1 hour |
| Tetrachloroethylene | 5 mg m$^{-3}$ | 24 hours |
| Toluene | 8 mg m$^{-3}$ | 24 hours |
| Trichloroethylene | 1 mg m$^{-3}$ | 24 hours |
| Vanadium | 1 μg m$^{-3}$ | 24 hours |

[a]Exposure at these concentrations should be for no longer than the indicated times and should not be repeated within 8 hours.

[b]Due to respiratory irritancy it would be desirable to have a short-term guideline, but the present data base does not permit such estimations.

[c]The guideline value is given only for indoor pollution; no guidance is given on outdoor concentrations (via deposition and entry into the food chain) that might be of indirect relevance.

*Note*: When air levels in the general environment are orders of magnitude lower than the guideline values, present exposures are unlikely to present a health concern. Guideline values in those cases are directly only to specific release episodes or specific indoor pollution problems.

Source: WHO Regional Publications, European Series No.23 (1987).

Back in Figure 44, the median concentrations of smoke and sulphur dioxide during the winter six-month period are shown against the letters WMD. The 98th percentile concentrations of smoke and $SO_2$ appear near the bottom of the last two columns of Figure 44 against 98%.

## SAQ 26

Examine the data given in Figure 44 and decide whether or not the concentrations of smoke and sulphur dioxide recorded at this site exceeded the EC guide values or both the guide and limiting values.

The tests that have been described are performed routinely by the computer used to process the data from survey sites. This enables any breach of the EC limits to be detected automatically and a warning issued so that remedial measures can be put in hand.

It may be helpful now to pause and review the position we have reached on the basis of Unit 4 combined with this section. When $N$ observations are divided up into 100 groups, the top 1% of the largest observed values will all be greater than the pollution concentration represented by the 99th percentile. Similarly, 2% of the observations will exceed the 98th percentile value, and 10% will be greater than the 90th percentile. You should notice a difference between the terminology used in air quality management compared with noise control. In relation to air quality the 98th or 90th percentiles represent peaks, while in noise control the $L_{90}$ indicates the background. Obviously, by definition, when there is an even number of observations, half of them must be greater than the median value. As discussed in Unit 4 and without resorting to a mathematical explanation, you should recognise intuitively that these statements about the concentrations represented by percentiles are all expressions of the probability that any particular concentration will be exceeded.

You should also recall from Unit 4 that, inconveniently, most air quality data do *not* conform to a normal distribution, but tend to be clustered towards the lower end of the range of observed data. However, the (natural) logarithms of the observed pollution concentrations are usually found to follow a normal distribution quite closely. The set of data is therefore said to have a log-normal distribution. The probability that any specified large concentration will be exceeded can then be estimated quite easily.

Statistical calculations of probability are aided by using special graph paper with a scale of normal probability along one axis. When a normal distribution of values is plotted against a linear scale on the other axis, all the data points tend to lie on a straight line. Similarly, when a log-normal distribution is plotted against a logarithmic scale on the second axis, these data points will also tend to lie on a straight line.

I have done this to produce Figure 45. The plotted points represent the distribution of smoke concentrations that were set out in Figure 44 under the annual summary column headed 'Smoke'. The logarithmic scale on the vertical axis represents pollutant concentrations in $\mu$g m$^{-3}$. The normal probability scale on the horizontal axis is used to plot percentiles, and is labelled: 'cumulative frequency/(% less than stated value)'. This acknowledges that the distribution of the percentile concentrations (i.e. the 1st, 5th, 20th,…median,…98th and 99th) along this axis is a transformation of, and directly equivalent to, the probability that each of these percentile concentrations will be exceeded by the set of $N$ observations. (Here you should accept that the mathematical reason for this is outside the subject area of the course.)

Figure 45 illustrates an extremely helpful way of visualising the pollution characteristics of any site by plotting the percentile concentrations. We can see immediately that the background concentration of smoke in the area represented by, say, 10% of the observations is below 10 $\mu$g m$^{-3}$. At the other extreme, points representing the 90th percentile and higher appear to depart slightly from the straight line representing a normal distribution. This departure at higher concentrations is common and you should recognise that it relates to the comparatively few observations (i.e. about 10% of the year) when smoke concentrations exceed the 90th percentile. Clearly, these are the days in November and December.

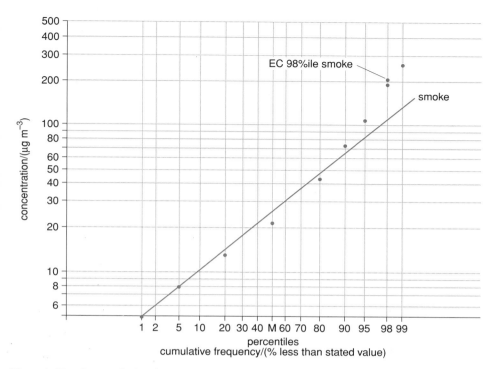

**Figure 45**  *A cumulative frequency distribution of the daily mean concentrations of smoke plotted from the data given in Figure 44.*

---

### SAQ 27

Now use the data in Figure 44 and plot the percentile concentrations of sulphur dioxide on Figure 45.

(a)  How does the range of $SO_2$ concentrations compare with the corresponding range of smoke concentrations?

(b)  How does the 10% background concentration of $SO_2$ compare with the corresponding background level of smoke?

---

Perhaps you feel that the answers to SAQ 27 could have been deduced by inspection of the data given in Figure 44, but inspection could not have shown whether the data were consistent, nor whether there were any unusual features requiring further investigation and explanation. It must not be assumed that the large concentrations of each pollutant coincide. Clearly, the data tabulated under November and December show that they may, although the specific days are not indicated. High smoke concentrations tend to occur during the winter, but there is also the possibility that large concentrations of smoke might be due to a local fire, or to stubble burning in the summer, a practice that is now being phased out. Remember also that there are other sources of airborne particulate matter. It is consequently much more important to look at the form of the graph representing the smoke concentrations rather than a few extreme values. It can also be instructive to mark the EC limit and guide values onto Figure 45 so that their relevance to the data becomes more immediately obvious. This has been done for the smoke 98th percentile, and you can see that the line passes below the standard.

---

### SAQ 28

Mark the EC Directive 98th percentile for $SO_2$ on Figure 45 and use your mark to interpret the significance of the data.

---

A visual presentation of data in the form of the log-normal distribution is thus an extremely convenient way of reducing large quantities of data to a manageable form, and of comparing the pollution characteristics of one site with any other. These analytical procedures can be extended and developed as a powerful tool for making predictions about the distribution of pollutant concentrations and the maximum concentration to be expected in areas covered by monitoring sites. Related procedures are useful for estimating the likely maximum concentration over shorter sample periods such as an hour or 30 minutes.

### 4.5.1    Air quality bulletins

You are sure to have seen or heard weather reports including reference to air quality being 'very good', 'good', 'poor' and 'very poor'. This is part of the UK Air Quality Bulletin system which was introduced in October 1990. This section and part of the television broadcast TV 7 summarises how this public information system operates.

Section 4.3 introduced the concept of national air quality monitoring networks providing data for public information. At 3 pm each day, the automatic network is scanned for data from the previous 24 hours. After checking, the data are sent to the Meteorological Office, converted to a bulletin and distributed to the news media. Bulletins are also available by telephone. The air quality monitoring networks produce quantitative data, but we have seen that interpreting these data is not straightforward. The bulletins from the Meteorological Office include concentrations, but this information would be of little use to members of the public who have not studied air pollution. Consequently, air quality is described in the qualitative terms 'very good', 'good', 'poor' and 'very poor'. The charts in Figure 46 show how these terms relate to quantitative data and also to standards and other guidelines.

### SAQ 29

What qualitative description would apply to the air quality on 13 December 1991, when measurements in London showed 388 ppb (v/v) in terms of nitrogen dioxide?

Before moving on to the next step in the use of standards, we should bear in mind that so far we have only considered health protection. What about environmental protection? Vegetation is an example of another component of the ecosystem sensitive to pollution. Plants are susceptible to air pollutants and may suffer acute or chronic injury. Figure 47 shows a typical response curve, and you should be able to see that plants can also suffer acute or chronic exposure. Putting this another way, plants may be able to tolerate a short period at a high concentration or a longer period at lower concentrations before ill effects are caused. You may have noticed from Table 16 that the draft EC air quality standard for ozone reflects this.

We have now looked at a typical set of health protection standards for air pollution control. At this point I should remind you that the term 'air pollution control' refers to both engineering control of processes and to the legal and administrative framework. To deal with an air pollution problem we can imagine a chain of events between a source of pollution and the ultimate effects on health. These links in the chain are:

- *Health effects*. The principal concern is related to the dose of pollutants (i.e. the amount of material passing through the body defence mechanisms to target organs) received by the population. The effects depend also on factors such as sex, smoking habits and previous health.

- *Dose* is determined by a person's total exposure to each pollutant and to other factors such as the respiration rate while engaged in various activities, and the size of particles.

- *Exposure* is determined by the concentrations of air pollutants in each place where people spend time, and the time spent at that place.

- *Concentration* at a location depends on the ventilation, chemical and physical changes, and the behaviour of emission sources.

- *Emissions* may be produced by many types of sources, but combustion processes have always been of most concern. Activities such as paint spraying and other forms of solvent use are of increasing interest.

- *Source:* the type and quality of the source may suggest the potential for harm.

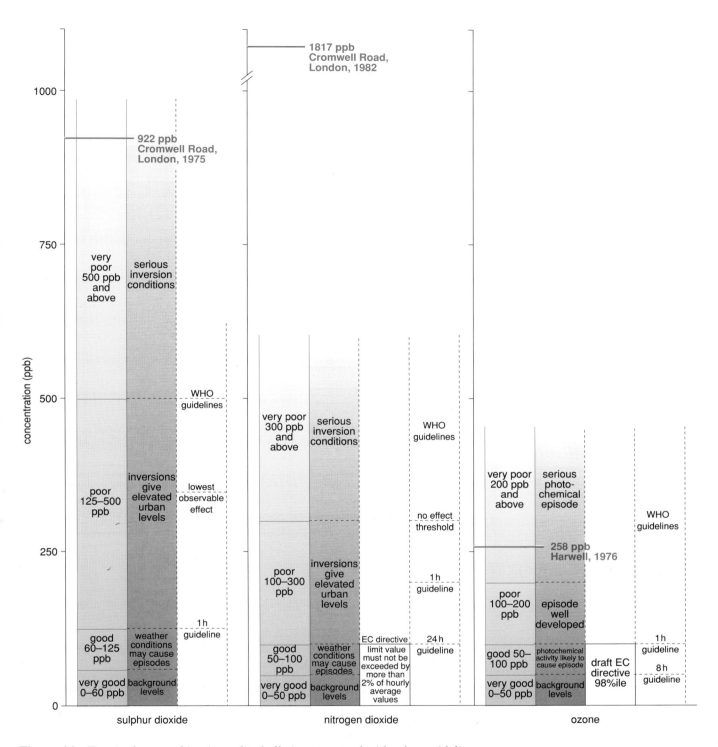

**Figure 46**  *Terminology used in air quality bulletins compared with other guidelines.*

So you can see that in order to control the air quality likely to have an effect on our health, we have ultimately to control the source of pollution. Unfortunately in the past we have used tall chimneys to discharge pollutants at high level in the expectation that dilution in the atmosphere will lower the concentrations to a level that will present no problem. We now know that this is one possible cause of 'acid rain' or long-range transport of pollution. The modern approach is to try to reduce the amount of waste products by changing the process in some way. One legal mechanism for doing this is to use emission standards, i.e. standards that limit the amount of pollutants that may be discharged from a source.

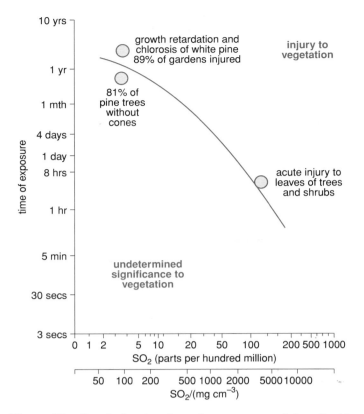

**Figure 47**   *Graph showing time of exposure to sulphur dioxide against concentration, producing effects on plant life.*

### SAQ 30

Why is the WHO guideline for ozone for 1 h greater than the 8 h value?

## 4.6   Summary

Measurement of air quality is an essential component of an air quality management programme. An understanding of what components are present in an atmosphere and of their concentrations is needed before decisions can be made on the risks of harm to the environment and the optimal control options. Measurement of emissions requires techniques capable of operating in hostile environments owing to the high temperatures and high concentrations that often exist. Ambient measurements on the other hand are made difficult by the need to measure low concentrations, and some techniques require sampling over long time periods in order to collect enough material to measure. This approach may lead to some loss in definition of the data, and care is needed in their interpretation. The log-normal distribution of air quality data also needs to be recognised if representative values are to be quoted. Many methods are available to measure air quality, and most are selective to particular components of an atmosphere. Legislation and air quality standards specify preferred methods of measurement, and careful calibration is essential if results are to be reliable. Modern air quality measurement networks use continuous analysers to provide near real-time data for use in public information systems.

# 5 MANAGING AIR QUALITY – CONTROL

'Air pollution control' is a term that refers both to the technology for dealing with air pollution and also to the legal and administrative system associated with protection of the air environment. We will consider first the latter use of the term, because legal pressures are increasingly driving new technological developments and applications in environmental protection.

## 5.1 A little law

The control of air pollution from industrial and other stationary sources is divided between local authorities and national inspectorates. In England and Wales HM Inspectorate of Pollution (HMIP) operate 'integrated pollution control' (IPC) to the potentially most polluting or technologically complex industrial processes. In Scotland a similar but separate system of IPC applies with regulation by HM Industrial Pollution Inspectorate. Control of mobile sources is the responsibility of the Department of Transport.

The largest number of processes is controlled by local authority environmental health departments. Most air pollution results from combustion sources. While clean air legislation can be traced back over several centuries, one of the most important legal developments was the introduction of the Clean Air Act 1956. This was introduced as a direct result of the notorious London smog of 1952, which we considered in some detail in our historical review. The Act introduced major controls over smoke and particulate matter emissions, and also introduced the concept of *smoke control areas* (not 'smokeless zones', which is an incorrect term used by many people). Many regulations were issued dealing with specific technical features of the Act, and the Clean Air Act 1968 introduced a number of amendments to the principal Act. Subsequently, the Control of Pollution Act 1974 and the Health and Safety at Work etc. Act 1974 brought in further controls over air pollution. More recently, the major development has been the Environmental Protection Act 1990. At the time of writing these units (1992), a Clean Air Bill aiming to consolidate many of the features of clean air legislation preceding EPA 1990 had been circulated for consultation. In view of this, only a general outline of the legal provisions under local authority control will follow, and reference to specific acts, regulations and clauses will be omitted.

*Clean Air Act of 56 & 68 consolidated by Clean Air Act 1993*

*EPA 1990 Section 2 Prescribed Processes and substances*

*Environment Act 1995 Part IV – assessment/management of air quality*

### 5.1.1 Dark smoke

All emissions of smoke from chimneys of buildings or chimneys serving boilers or industrial furnaces are controlled by law. In law, smoke 'includes soot, ash, grit and gritty particles emitted in smoke', and emissions from chimneys must not exceed specified intensities or permitted periods. Similar controls apply to vessels in certain waters. The intensity of smoke is defined in terms of the Ringelmann chart described previously, and you should remind yourself now of the definitions of dark smoke and black smoke. In any legal proceedings for an offence of smoke emissions, it may be a defence to prove that:

*Ringelmann Nos.*
*Dark smoke   2, 3*
*Black smoke   4, 5*

- the contravention was solely due to lighting up a furnace from cold;
- the contravention was solely due to unforeseen failure of plant;
- the contravention was solely due to unsuitable fuel being used as a result of suitable fuel being unavailable; or
- a combination of two or more of these causes.

In all cases, all practicable steps must be taken to prevent or minimise the emissions.

Emissions of dark smoke from industrial or trade premises, as distinct from emissions from chimneys, are also controlled by law. These provisions relate to emissions from activities such as bonfires on industrial sites, and a defence may be to prove that the contravention was inadvertent and all practicable steps were taken to prevent or minimise the emission of dark smoke.

### 5.1.2   Smoke, grit, dust and fumes

No furnace may be installed in a building unless the furnace is so far as practicable capable of being operated smokelessly when burning fuel of a type for which it was designed. Before any furnace controlled by law is installed, the local authority must be notified of the intention, and prior approval that the plant is capable of smokeless operation may be sought. In examining an application for approval, the technical specification and operational features of the plant are examined. Domestic furnaces are not covered by this control, but may be covered by smoke control area restrictions (see Section 5.1.4).

In law, domestic furnace means any furnace which is:

(a)  designed solely or mainly for domestic purposes; and

(b)  used for heating a boiler with a maximum heating capacity of less than 55 000 British thermal units per hour.

Although some legislation still uses Imperial units, we may convert the rating of the furnace to SI equivalent units as follows.

55 000 Btu h$^{-1}$ is equivalent to 55 000/3600 Btu s$^{-1}$ = 15.28 Btu s$^{-1}$

From Appendix IV in the set book, 1 Btu = 1.055 kJ.

Hence the rating of the boiler is

15.28 Btu s$^{-1}$ × 1.055 kJ Btu$^{-1}$ = 16.1 kJ s$^{-1}$

or 16 kW, since the definition of *watt* is J s$^{-1}$.

Turning to grit, dust and fume emissions, we first need to define these terms. **Grit** was first defined in the Clean Air (Emission of Grit and Dust from Furnaces) Regulations 1971 as 'particles exceeding 76 µm in diameter', and **fume** was defined in the Clean Air Act 1968 as 'solid particulate matter smaller than dust'. However, while there is no definition of **dust**, it is generally taken to be particulate matter between 1 and 76 µm. Limits on the emissions of grit and dust from furnaces may be prescribed by regulations under clean air legislation. To meet such limits, equipment to collect the dust from flue gases (*arrestment plant*) may be required.

Where a furnace in a building is used:

(a)  to burn pulverised fuel; or

(b)  to burn at a rate of 100 pounds or more an hour, any other solid matter; or

(c)  to burn, at a rate equivalent to 1.25 million or more British thermal units an hour, any liquid or gaseous matter,

the furnace must have arrestment plant to the approval of the local authority, unless an exemption has been made. Furthermore, the local authority may require measurements to be made of emissions of grit, dust and fumes from the furnace. However, where the furnace burns:

(a)  at a rate less than 1 ton an hour, solid matter other than pulverised fuel; or

(b)  at a rate less than 28 million British thermal units an hour, any liquid or gaseous matter,

the occupier of the building in which the furnace is situated may request the local authority to measure the grit, dust and fume emissions. Measurements must be made by an approved method, which implies isokinetic sampling, which we considered in Section 4.2.2.

Local authorities may also require occupiers of buildings to furnish information on furnaces within the buildings, and also on the fuel or waste burned in the furnaces.

---

### SAQ 31

A furnace designed for coal firing is seen to be emitting excessive amounts of smoke. On investigation you find that the operator is also burning waste materials. Discuss the legal position.

---

---

**SAQ 32**

Convert the ratings of 1.25 million and 28 million British thermal units an hour to SI units. Refer to the *Mathematics and Modelling* supplement and Appendix IV of the set book if you have difficulty with this.

---

### 5.1.3   Chimneys

Waste gases, fumes, dust and other emissions often escape through doors, windows, roof louvres and other openings of factory buildings, but major emissions to atmosphere are preferably collected together by ventilation systems and discharged as a plume from a chimney. A legal definition of chimney includes

> structures and openings of any kind from or through which smoke, grit, dust or fumes may be emitted and, in particular, includes flues...

A furnace may not be used unless the height of the chimney serving it has been approved by a local authority, and the operator complies with any conditions subject to which the approval was granted. In determining an application for chimney height approval, the local authority must be satisfied that the height will be sufficient to prevent, so far as is practicable, the smoke, grit, dust, gases or fumes emitted from becoming prejudicial to health or a nuisance. In doing this, regard is given to:

(a)  the purpose of the chimney;

(b)  the position and descriptions of buildings near to it;

(c)  the levels of neighbouring ground, and any other relevant matters.

We have already seen some factors influencing plume behaviour, and consequently influencing chimney heights, and we will examine others in Section 5.4.

### 5.1.4   Smoke control areas

A local authority may make an order declaring part or all of its district a smoke control area. If smoke is emitted from a chimney of any building in such an area, it is an offence unless it can be proven that the smoke came from an *authorised fuel*. These are fuels declared by regulations of the Secretary of State to be fuels which have been tested and shown to be capable of burning without smoke in any appliance, and include fuels such as natural gas, electricity, anthracite and *carbonisation* products such as Homefire™, Coalite™ and Sunbrite™. Other fuels may be used in a smoke control area provided that they are burned in an *exempted fireplace*. Such fireplaces are furnaces, grates or stoves which have passed tests showing them to be capable of essentially smokeless operation. Exempted fireplaces include those for liquid fuels, and various coal and wood burning appliances which have satisfactorily met the test requirements. A smoke control order may exempt a specific fireplace, such as an industrial furnace, not covered by a national regulation.

---

**SAQ 33**

In what circumstances may coal, oil, gas and logs be burned in a smoke control area?

---

### 5.1.5   Regulations on fuel quality

Regulations may be made to impose requirements on the composition and contents of any fuel used in motor vehicles. Under these provisions, limits on the lead content of petrol and on the sulphur content of gas oil (diesel) for vehicles have been made. Similarly, regulations setting limits on the sulphur content of oil fuel for furnaces have been made.

### 5.1.6   The Environmental Protection Act 1990

At the beginning of Section 5.1 we pointed out that releases to atmosphere from many specialised processes are controlled by local authorities (Environmental Health

Departments), by HMIP or by HM Industrial Pollution Inspectorate using provisions in EPA 1990. While earlier legislation such as the Clean Air Acts gave certain powers of prior approval of plant such as furnaces, arrestment plant and chimneys, EPA 1990 extends the principle and requires that no process listed in regulations (*prescribed processes*) may be operated without an authorisation provided by a local authority or HMIP. Guidance notes specific to prescribed processes (process guidance notes) have been issued by the Secretary of State for many industrial processes with significant potential for producing air pollution problems. All refer to the objective set down in Section 7(2)(a) of the EPA which is:

> …ensuring that, in carrying on a prescribed process, the best available techniques not entailing excessive cost (BATNEEC) will be used
>
> (i)   for preventing the release of substances prescribed for any environmental medium into that medium or, where that is not practicable by such means, for reducing the release of such substances to a minimum and for rendering harmless any such substances which are so released; and
>
> (ii)  for rendering harmless any other substances which might cause harm if released into any environmental medium.

This wordy phrase merely sets out the sequence of control philosophy described previously, while the BATNEEC duty includes 'minimisation of offence to any of man's senses'.

The guidance notes also require chimneys and vents to be of heights that take into account the ground-level concentrations of pollutants resulting from them, bearing in mind local meteorology, landscape and buildings. You will recall that chimneys serving combustion plant such as industrial boilers are controlled by clean air legislation, and similar factors have to be taken into account before plans for a chimney are approved as part of an authorisation. Guidance on the heights of chimneys required to meet ground level air quality is available in the form of mathematical equations and graphical schemes. (These guidelines are not covered in this course, but you will gain experience in their use if you study the course T334 *Environmental monitoring and control*.) It should be evident from the previous discussion that a major criterion for an acceptable chimney height is that its effluent on reaching ground level should neither be prejudicial to health nor should it cause a nuisance. It is important to realise that a nuisance is a subjective response, variable in interpretation and difficult to establish in law:

> Whether anything is a nuisance or not is a question to be determined, not merely by an abstract consideration of the thing itself, but in reference to its circumstances; what would be a nuisance in Belgrave Square would not necessarily be so in Bermondsey.
>
> *(Thesiger, L.J. in Sturgess v. Bridgman (1879), 11 Chancery Division, 856)*

EPA 1990 restates and develops the law on *statutory nuisances* (i.e. nuisances defined in law) and includes the following definitions of specific relevance to air pollution:

(a)  any premises in such a state as to be prejudicial to health or a nuisance;

(b)  smoke emitted from premises so as to be prejudicial to health or a nuisance;

(c)  fumes or gases emitted from premises so as to be prejudicial to health or a nuisance;

(d)  any dust, steam, smell or other effluvia arising on industrial, trade or business premises and being prejudicial to health or a nuisance.

Local authorities are obliged to inspect their areas to detect statutory nuisances and, if satisfied that a such a nuisance exists or is likely to occur or recur, to serve an *abatement notice* to ensure the abatement or prevention of the nuisance. Where any requirement of an abatement notice is ignored, the local authority must take legal action or take whatever action is necessary to abate the nuisance. Legal action in the Magistrates Court may be taken, but it is a defence to prove that the ***best practicable means (BPM)*** was taken to prevent or counteract the effects of the statutory nuisance. Where any requirement of an abatement notice has been contravened or not complied with,

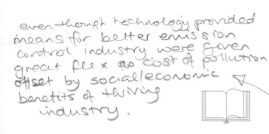

even though technology provided means for better emission control industry were given great flex as cost of pollution offset by social/economic benefits of thriving industry.

and the local authority is of the opinion that action in the Magistrates Court may prove inadequate, the local authority may take action in the High Court. While the High Court may take account of BPM, it does not appear to be a statutory defence by this route.

## 5.2   Pollution prevention and waste minimisation for air pollution control

Integrated pollution control has a principal objective of preventing or minimising the release of substances which are potentially harmful or polluting to the environment. This objective may be achieved by using the 'best available techniques not entailing excessive cost' (BATNEEC). In this phrase, 'best' means the most effective in preventing, or minimising and rendering harmless, polluting emissions. The aim of this section is to illustrate some options for minimising releases of some air pollutants described previously in this text.

### 5.2.1   A general approach

To remind you of the principles of preventing or minimising pollution, there are four key steps.

1   Reformulate the product – develop a non-polluting or less-polluting product or process, by using different raw materials or feedstock;

2   Modify the process – change the process to control by-product formation or to incorporate non-polluting raw materials;

3   Change the equipment – make the equipment more efficient or allow it to use by-products from another process;

4   Recover resources – recycle by-products for own use or use by others;

Only after minimising wastes released to any domain of the environment do we proceed to other levels in the management hierarchy. This hierarchy was represented in Unit 10 in a manner applicable to gaseous, liquid or solid wastes.

More detailed examples of waste minimisation which alone or in combination with others can minimise air pollution include:

1   replacing chemical processes with mechanical ones – produces more manageable emissions;

2   replacing organic solvent-based inks, paints and coatings with water-based ones – reduces emissions of volatile organic compounds;

3   replacing halogenated compounds with non-halogenated – reduces the impact on stratospheric ozone;

4   replacing mercury, cadmium and lead with other less toxic substances – reduces emissions as particulate matter or as vaporised metal;

5   improving technology to minimise producing pollutants from the process stream, or to return useful products to the process;

6   installing improved process-monitoring equipment to make it possible to improve and continuously maintain optimum process conditions – this improves all-round efficiency and so reduces emissions.

We will examine these approaches in turn and apply them to some of the air pollution problems introduced previously. The content of TV 8 also addresses these issues and illustrates some of the difficulties facing industry.

### 5.2.2   Replacing chemical processes with mechanical ones

In this section we will introduce some very important concepts and terms relating to particulate matter. As this may come from a wide variety of sources, it is a common cause of air pollution problems.

It is generally accepted that particulate matter in the atmosphere forms a trimodal size distribution, i.e. the distribution has three modes (look back in Unit 4 if you are unsure of the term 'mode'). Figure 48 shows a common representation of this.

*[handwritten margin note: management hierarchy  1. Minimise waste]*

Three approximately log-normal distributions are the nucleation mode (less than 0.08 µm), the accumulation mode (0.08 – 1.5 µm) and the coarse mode (greater than 1.5 µm). Other terms are sometimes used: for example, grit, dust and fume as we defined previously. As the size of particles decreases, the difficulty of collecting them from a gas stream increases, as we shall see in Section 5.3. So it is easier to control emissions from a process producing larger-sized particles. Figure 48 shows that particles from condensation of vapours, together with particles produced by reaction between gaseous pollutants contribute to 'fume', and so are difficult to collect owing to their small size. Mechanically generated particles are larger and therefore more easily controlled. An additional problem is that particles between 0.1 and 1 µm are of similar size to the wavelength of light, and so scatter light, which makes an emission of such particles readily visible and a source of potential complaint. Mechanical processing rather than chemical treatment is often a way of relieving these problems. In some cases, however, chemical treatment may offer advantages. Thus, paint stripping by chemicals generates less air pollution than mechanical stripping. In every case there is a need to find the 'best' technique.

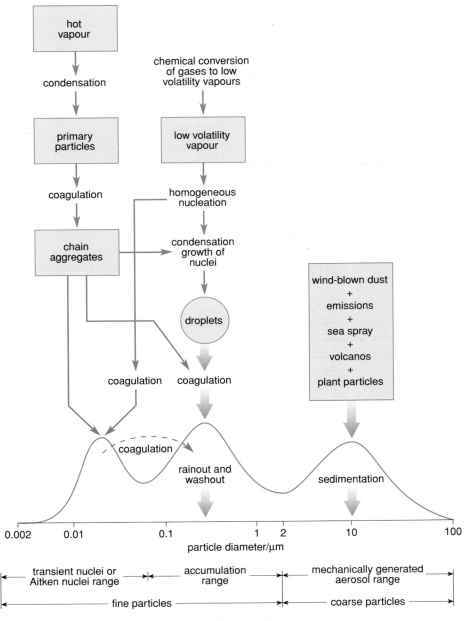

**Figure 48**   *Origins of the trimodal distribution of particulate matter.*

### 5.2.3   *Replacing organic solvent-based materials with water-based ones*

In manufacturing processes, organic solvents find many uses. Organic compounds such as grease and oil are removed with solvents during manufacture or maintenance of engines, moulds and many products. Fabrics are cleaned with organic solvents, while paints, adhesives and aerosols use many organic compounds as carriers. Applications in the electronics industry will be covered in the next subsection.

Guidance on the control of air pollution from various processes subject to provisions of the EPA 1990 includes the aim of reducing and eventually eliminating the use of volatile organic compounds. In surface coatings, this may be achieved by:

* using water-based coatings (i.e. low organic solvent content, typically less than 10% by weight);

* using higher solids content coatings;

* using powder coatings.

The use of low solvent content or solvent-free inks and adhesives are other examples of substitution. Far from being new developments, water-based adhesives are among the earliest, and, in addition to their environmental benefits, they are less toxic, less flammable, easier to store, and more easily removed than solvent-based counterparts.

The journal *Clean Air* (Vol. 20) included a report of Volvo's aim to reduce the emission of solvents by over 80%. Water-borne paints, pioneered by Volvo in association with ICI, contain less than 25% of the organic solvents used in conventional paints. The penalty of water-borne paints is a tenfold increase in drying time. Volvo's conventional paint shop consumes almost 3 million cubic metres of air per hour, but a recirculating system in the new plant reduces air consumption to less than 10% of the previous level while giving the same performance. This major energy saving leads to a reduction in carbon dioxide emissions. As you will notice from TV 8, water-borne paints are not the solution for all applications, and some of the problems facing the aircraft industry are addressed.

Another example of minimising solvent (VOC) emissions comes from the foundry industry. A pattern of the article to be made is first made from resins, and then is covered in a series of coats of silica, alumina or zircon. Binders to hold these particles together generally contain ethanol or isopropanol. Under EPA 1990, BATNEEC is required to prevent or minimise the release of the organic compounds which are prescribed substances. Add-on abatement options include wet systems coupled with biological digestion, incineration or carbon **adsorption**. These techniques will be covered later. The alternative is to move to a cleaner process involving a water-based technique. Currently the technical merits of the competing systems are the subject of much debate.

*adsorption*
*molecules of substance are taken up and held on the surface of the adsorbent material.*

### 5.2.4   *Replacing halogenated compounds with non-halogenated*

This area has gained prominence as a result of concerns over the ozone hole. Replacements for CFC aerosol propellants were quickly found when CFCs were banned in the USA in the late 1970s. Gases such as propane and isobutane were introduced, while alternative delivery systems such as pump-valves for hair sprays and roll-on deodorants emerged.

Another example concerns the specific application of solvents in the electronics industry. During the manufacture of printed circuit boards, solder is applied with flux to help it flow properly, and when the board is finished the flux is removed with a solvent. Likewise, in the precision cleaning of electronic components, CFC solvents have been found ideal. The relatively low cost of the solvents has provided little incentive to prevent release of their vapours. Several options are now available to avoid the resulting air pollution. The best option for flux removal is to use new fluxes which do not require removal, but halogen-free solvents are also available. Alcohol and aqueous washes are available, but aqueous cleaners may contain components such as phosphates or surfactants (see Unit 3) which are not readily biodegradable; we may simply be exchanging air pollution for water pollution. Another option is to use terpenes, i.e. organic cleaners whose active ingredients occur naturally in most living plants.

Refrigerators emit small amounts of CFCs, usually at the end of the product's life. Alternative refrigerants are available and some are described in the entry for *chlorofluorocarbons* in the set book. While they still contain halogens, their ozone-depletion potential is relatively low, and they contribute negligibly to global warming. Other refrigerant mixtures under investigation require modified refrigeration systems, but again offer benefits of improved efficiency and therefore lower energy consumption, lower operating costs and lesser contribution to global warming.

Another use of CFCs is in 'plastic foam blowing' in which the evaporation of the CFC produces the air bubbles in foam packaging. Cardboard is, of course, a competitor for some packaging, while foam blowing with alternatives to CFCs will become competitive.

### 5.2.5   Replacing mercury, cadmium and lead with other less toxic substances

If you refer to the entry *lead* in the set book, you will appreciate some of the reasons for the concerns over lead as an environmental pollutant. A major source has been the use of tetraethyl lead as an additive in petrol since the 1920s. Studies reported in 1969 showed evidence of a more than 200-fold increase in the lead concentrations in the ice and snow in Greenland since ancient times. The investigation was carried out by analysing the lead in samples from different depths, which represented the airborne lead scavenged from the air at the time the snow fell. This evidence indicated the global dispersion of lead from petrol, and contributed to the development of policies by several governments to introduce unleaded petrol. (If you have studied T102 *Living with technology* you may recall examining this as a detailed case study in decision making.) Lead additives are now being phased out, and the quality of petrol is being maintained by modifications to the refining process or through other additives which impart the desired anti-knock properties. Research published at the end of 1991 provided evidence of the benefits in terms of reduced lead pollution of the troposphere of the northern hemisphere. Once again, the study involved taking sections cut through the ice and snow and analysing their metal content by atomic absorption spectrophotometry using a graphite furnace, a technique introduced in Unit 3.

Figure 49 shows the variations in lead pollution with time. Although these data were obtained at widely dispersed locations, it seems reasonable to put them together as the concentrations of major impurities such as sodium, aluminium and sulphates are similar at these sites. The figure illustrates that after the great increase (~200 fold) from several thousand years ago to the mid-1960s, lead concentrations decreased rapidly (by a factor of ~7.5).

The study also showed a decline in pollution by cadmium. This is another pollutant which is being used in products less and less. As one major source of airborne cadmium is waste incineration, its replacement in products minimises subsequent pollution on disposal of the products. Similarly, the use of mercury in batteries is being phased out to minimise release of this volatile metal to the environment.

### SAQ 34

Examine Figure 49 and attempt to explain the sharp changes in the trend lines.

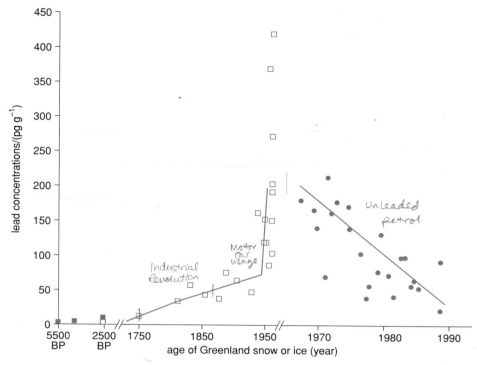

**Figure 49** *Changes in lead levels in Greenland snow and ice from 5500 years ago to present. Closed circles (right): data from 1967 to 1989, from Summit. Open squares (centre): 1753 to 1965, from north-west Greenland. Closed and open squares (left): 5500 to 2700 BP (before present), data from Camp Tuto and Camp Century respectively.*

### 5.2.6  Pollution prevention by improved technology

In any combustion process using air to supply oxygen, some nitric oxide will be formed. As we saw in Section 1.3.2 and in Figure 3, the rate of formation of nitric oxide depends on the temperature of the gases as they pass through the combustion zone. Keeping the temperature below 1200 °C ensures a low rate of formation, with insignificant amounts of nitric oxide being formed. Several burner modifications reduce thermal NO formation. As this approach needs only burner replacement without modifying the furnace, it is relatively inexpensive. One approach uses 'two-stage combustion' and may be used for all fuels. Primary combustion is kept fuel-rich by controlling the combustion air. Then fuel-lean combustion follows in a secondary stage where more air is introduced (Figure 50).

Another example under this category of minimising wastes is using the acidity of a flue gas due to the presence of $SO_2$ to neutralise an alkaline liquid effluent, such as may be produced from bottle washing or metal cleaning processes. In this way both air pollution and water pollution problems are reduced. The use of vapour recovery systems to recover solvents is a further possibility, and some technology for this will be outlined later, as well as being addressed in TV 8. This programme also shows the

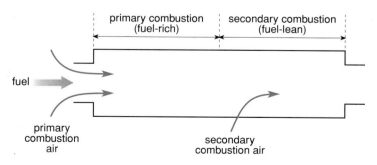

**Figure 50** *The principle of two-stage combustion for nitrogen oxide control.*

pollution problems of conventional paint spraying. Alternative technologies may be applied to minimise the overspray and so reduce the pollution. For example, dipping, roller coating or electrophoretic paint deposition (using electrical attraction between the article and paint droplets) are possible approaches for appropriate applications.

### 5.2.7   Optimising process conditions by monitoring

You will recall from the historical review in Section 2 that combustion plant have always been and still remain major sources of air pollution. Operating combustion plant efficiently ensures that the minimum amount of fuel is burnt to achieve the purpose of the plant, and by burning less fuel, we produce less pollution. This aspect of energy efficiency has assumed greater prominence with the concerns over global warming, for there is at present no way of controlling the emissions of carbon dioxide that inevitably come from the combustion of fossil fuels.

In Unit 3 we introduced some combustion theory, from which you should recall that the efficient combustion of a fuel depends on the correct amount of excess air being present and the temperature in a combustion zone being high enough for the chemical reactions to occur. We say that the temperature must be above the ignition temperature.

In Unit 3 we also calculated the stoichiometric amount of air needed for the combustion of a fuel, and stated that practical combustion systems require some air in excess of this stoichiometric quantity.

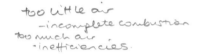
too little air
  —incomplete combustion
too much air
  —inefficiencies.

---

### SAQ 35

Suggest what will be the effect of having too little excess air and also of having too much excess air.

---

We need to know the optimal amount of excess air, and how we can monitor this. Fossil fuels all contain carbon, so if we first consider a fuel comprising 100% carbon, this will burn according to the equation

$$C + O_2 + 3.76N_2 = CO_2 + 3.76N_2$$

in which we have allowed for the nitrogen in the air.

From this equation, 1 mole of oxygen produces 1 mole of $CO_2$, and from the definition in Unit 3, we can also say that 1 volume of oxygen produces 1 volume of $CO_2$. If we take into account the nitrogen in the air, we calculate that the amount of $CO_2$ in the combustion products is

$$\% \ CO_2 = (1/4.76) \times 100 = 21\%$$

---

### SAQ 36

How much carbon dioxide will be present in the combustion products from burning pure carbon with 100% excess air?

---

In practice, a fuel is not pure carbon, so the carbon dioxide content of flue gases will be less than 21%. It is also found that fossil fuels do not need 100% excess air for efficient burning; only municipal waste with its unpredictable composition needs so much excess air.

We can now summarise what happens in a furnace diagrammatically (Figure 51). This shows that under air deficiency, unburnt fuel is found in the flue gases, but as the air supply increases, more carbon dioxide is produced. As the stoichiometric proportions are approached, the carbon dioxide approaches its maximum, and oxygen begins to appear in the flue gases. Adding more air in excess of the stoichiometric ratio dilutes the carbon dioxide.

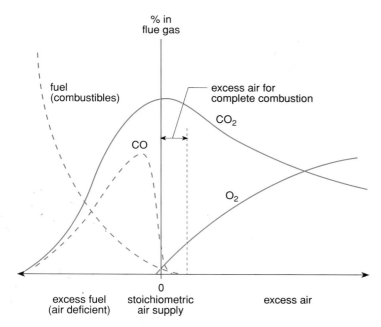

**Figure 51**   *Flue gas composition as a function of air supply.*

---

### SAQ 37

Explain the change in carbon monoxide (CO) concentration with excess air.

*burning C containing fuels with insufficient air may produce CO. Amount produced increases as excess fuel decreases. Eventually a point is reached where there is sufficient air for the CO to burn*

---

As we can see from Figure 51, the excess air can be correlated with the combustibles, carbon dioxide, oxygen or carbon monoxide in the flue gases. Combustibles may appear as smoke, and as the aim is to eliminate this, smoke monitors in the flue may serve as a warning device for furnace operators; such instruments do little for ensuring efficient combustion. Measuring $CO_2$ was long used for optimising combustion because it was relatively easy to do, and the aim was to maintain a maximum value corresponding to the region at the top of the curve in Figure 51. However, we can see that at the optimal value, the rate of change of $CO_2$ is small, and this would give poor sensitivity. The maximum also depends on the type of fuel, as shown in Figure 52.

---

### SAQ 38

By inspecting Figure 51 identify another problem in measuring $CO_2$.

---

Oxygen serves as a useful indicator of efficient combustion conditions, and instruments have used this parameter in automatic combustion optimisation for several years in preference to $CO_2$ because it is less fuel dependent. It may, however, be relatively insensitive, and the ideal excess oxygen in the flue gas does not necessarily mean that there is not a local problem at the burners giving rise to inefficient combustion. In addition, air leaking into a flue may give an erroneous reading.

The most sensitive measurement of flue gas composition for good combustion performance is carbon monoxide. It is directly related to the completeness of combustion, and is unaffected by air in-leakage. Theoretically, CO should be zero in the presence of excess oxygen, but optimal efficiency is usually found with CO values around 100–300 ppm (v/v).

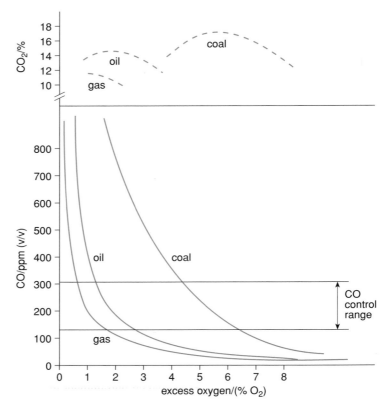

**Figure 52**   *Excess oxygen and carbon monoxide in the flue gas from a boiler.*

---

### SAQ 39

Suggest why a low concentration of CO in the flue gases of a boiler gives better efficiency than zero.

---

For the above reasons, modern control systems and combustion testing equipment rely on oxygen and/or carbon monoxide measurement. Control systems adjust the correct air supply to maintain efficient combustion.

While the efficient use of energy through good combustion is clearly important to minimise emissions to atmosphere, there are many other routes to energy efficiency. Many may be categorised by the key words 'time', 'level' and 'efficiency' as summarised in Table 18.

### 5.2.8   What can individuals do?

If you study the examples in Table 18, you will notice that most are associated with action (or inaction!) by individuals. This table gives you a checklist of some opportunities for you to minimise air pollution through efficient energy use at work or at home. All energy savings contribute to reducing global warming.

**Table 18**   *Good housekeeping energy management*

|  |  | *Examples* |
| --- | --- | --- |
| Time | Is plant in operation when it could be off? | Lights on |
|  |  | Heating on |
|  |  | Boiler/furnace on standby |
|  |  | Exhaust ventilation on with no production |
| Level | Are control levels correct? | Steam pressure (the higher the pressure the greater the leak potential) |
|  |  | Too much lighting |
|  |  | Compressed air pressure too high |
|  |  | Oil storage temperature too high |
|  |  | Refrigeration set too low |
|  |  | Room thermostat too high |
| Efficiency | Is equipment used to the best advantage at all times? | Lighting clean |
|  |  | Boiler combustion efficiency |
|  |  | Excessive air entrainment in ventilation |
|  |  | Dust on ventilator/heater grilles |
|  |  | No insulation |
|  |  | Dirty windows |

## Exercise

Work out how great your own contribution is to global warming.

Examine your energy bills and calculate your total energy use over a twelve-month period to account for seasonal effects. Fill in the following table.

|  | *Total consumption over year* | *$CO_2$ produced/kg* |
| --- | --- | --- |
| Coal | ...... tonnes × 2700 |  |
| Gas | ...... therms × 5.9 |  |
| Electricity | ...... kWh × 0.06 |  |
| Oil | ...... litres × 3 |  |
| Petrol | (...... annual car mileage)/(...... miles per gallon) = ...... gallons × 11.4 |  |
|  | (If you use a diesel-fuelled vehicle, multiply by 12.8 instead of 11.4) |  |
|  | Total $CO_2$ produced by me in one year is |  |

## SAQ 40

Refer back to Unit 3 and calculate the volume occupied by your annual production of $CO_2$.

**SAQ 41**

It is often said that pollution control is a non-productive cost to an organisation. Summarise the benefits of waste minimisation in the context of air pollution.

## 5.3   Air pollution control techniques

This section, together with TV 8, reviews some of the techniques that are available for reducing and controlling the emission of air pollutants. Relevant legislation will be indicated as appropriate.

The costs of maintaining current standards of air quality have to be met from the profits of our industrial economy. Any amendment to existing law or new legislation tends to increase this burden on industry, and the introduction of the Environmental Protection Act 1990 was greeted by cries of anguish from several industrial sectors. Improvements must be based on proven techniques that are demonstrably effective and practicable, and this is inherent in the BATNEEC approach. Moreover, any extension of air pollution control should move in step with our understanding of atmospheric reactions, the dispersal process and the mechanisms of environmental damage.

There are three broad ways in which air pollution can be reduced by control at source. They are:

1   modification of the processes to minimise the production of, or to avoid releasing wastes to atmosphere;

2   collection of particulate materials;

3   absorption of toxic gases.

Some techniques can be used to control both particulates and gases; others are applicable to only one of the categories. The following subsections review some of the options available.

### 5.3.1   Particulate emissions: the control of smoke

Dark smoke tends to be released wherever carbon-bearing fuels are burnt inefficiently. Often this is because the combustion temperature is too low or the supply of air is inadequate.

You should recall from the legal outline in Section 5.1 and reference to the set book that dark smoke is defined in law by reference to the Ringelmann chart, which is used to assess the visual aspect of smoke emissions. All heating installations larger than a domestic boiler must be able to operate continuously without emitting smoke. The problems of poor combustion during start-up and during periodic boiler cleaning by soot blowing have been recognised and allowed for in legal regulations, but for most of the time the discharge of smoke is prohibited.

Combustion control for efficient burning is achieved by careful attention to the design of the combustion chamber and the control of the fuel and air supplies, as we saw in the previous section.

Another potentially large source of urban smoke is the domestic fire. If you live in a smoke control area, you will know that only approved smokeless fuels should be burnt in approved heating appliances. By designating and enforcing smoke control areas, any semblance of the smoke emissions giving rise to the 1952 episode in London has been largely prevented in our towns and cities. It is an offence for an occupier of premises in a smoke control area to allow smoke emission from a chimney unless it serves an exempted fireplace, or unless the smoke is caused by the use of an authorised fuel (see Section 5.1.4). This applies to both households and industry. So, in law, gas and smokeless solid fuels are authorised fuels, but coal and oil are not. However, both may be burned in an exempted appliance.

Evidence from government statistics now suggests that motor vehicles contribute more smoke to the atmosphere than do domestic fires. SAQ 42 illustrates the trends.

## SAQ 42

Complete the following table by calculating the percentage rise in pollutant emissions from road transport over the decade to 1989.

| Pollutant | Emission (thousand tonnes) | | % of current UK emissions | 1979–1989 10-y rise (%) |
|---|---|---|---|---|
| | 1979(a) | 1989(b) | (c) | $((b-a)/a) \times 100$ |
| black smoke | 121 | 198 | 39 | 64 |
| sulphur dioxide | 55 | 60 | 2 | 9 |
| nitrogen oxides | 908 | 1298 | 48 | 43 |
| volatile organics | 490 | 762 | 37 | 56 |
| carbon monoxide | 3992 | 5751 | 88 | 44 |
| carbon dioxide | 21 000 | 29 000 | 19 | 38 |

The massive increase in smoke emissions over the decade is clear, and compares with no increase from other sectors of the economy. Diesel-fuelled vehicle emissions are usually linked with this increase. You should also notice the magnitude of the increase in emissions of other pollutants from transport, and this is the justification for increasing attention being given to transport emissions, as TV 7 illustrates. Compare the statistics in column (b) of SAQ 42 with the statistics in Figure 5, and notice the changes in the contribution from transport between 1989 and 1990.

## 5.3.2 The control of grit, dust and fume emissions from industrial plant

Assuming that smoke emissions may be prevented by improving combustion efficiency, there are broadly five ways in which the escape to atmosphere of particulate matter can be prevented or controlled at source. As is clear from TV 8, there is a great variety of particulate matter that may cause potential air pollution problems, but in all cases it is particle size and particle shape that are major factors in selecting a solution. It is important to note that for many particulate collectors, the efficiency of collection varies with the particle size or **grade**. A graph showing the variation of collection efficiency with particle size is called a *grade efficiency curve*. (The use of these is beyond the scope of this course, but you will apply them if you study T334 *Environmental monitoring and control*.)

## SAQ 43

Define grit, dust and fume.

Control of grit, dust and fume is preferably done by modification of the process to prevent material becoming airborne. If this should prove to be impracticable, airborne particulate material can be separated out of any contaminated gas stream by use of:

- gravity and inertial forces in a mechanical separator;
- a liquid for washing;
- a fabric filter; or
- electrostatic forces in an electrostatic precipitator.

These are four active processes and they may require a considerable amount of energy to be expended. Each will be considered in turn later.

*Dust control by protective enclosures*

It is often said that prevention is better than control, and this must be true of any measures that are taken to prevent fine particles becoming airborne in industrial processing or manufacturing plant. Problems of dust might often be prevented by attention to detail during the design stages of new equipment. Wherever possible, fine material should not be shaken up in the air, nor be allowed to fall freely through air, nor have air passed through it. Even large molten or liquid droplets can result in the production of fine airborne particles by the evaporation of a liquid or solvent fraction. Fine ash or fume are likely to be discharged from many combustion or high temperature processes that could with advantage be modified at the design stage, as we saw previously.

If the release of grit, dust or fume cannot otherwise be prevented, suitable enclosures or hoods must be built around the process. Fans and ducting will be installed to lead the contaminated air to where it can be cleaned by an appropriate gas scrubber, filter or inertial separator. Sometimes it is necessary to 'condition' the gas stream. This may involve cooling it to a temperature that will not harm the gas cleaning plant, warming it to prevent condensation of water vapour, or introducing additives to improve the collection efficiency. A typical complete system is represented in Figure 53.

There are many different kinds of dust-removal device, and descriptions of a few representative types will be given in the following subsections.

*The separation of particles by gravity and inertial forces*

When a gas stream carries only large particles, they will tend to settle out naturally if the air is slowed down to give them sufficient time to do so. This occurs when a duct carrying dust-laden air is led through a simple expansion type of settling chamber (Figure 54). The gas velocity is reduced as it passes through the expansion chamber, the dust settles, and the accumulated material can be drawn off from hoppers set into the floor. This device is suitable only for large particles, since it is generally uneconomic to make the equipment long enough to allow sufficient passage of time for the smaller particles to fall through the full height of the chamber.

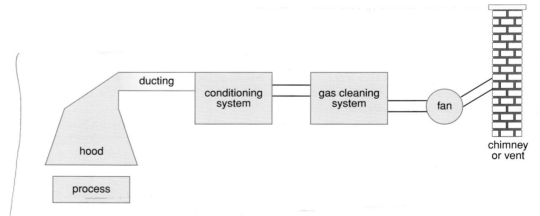

**Figure 53** *A typical system for particulate collection and control.*

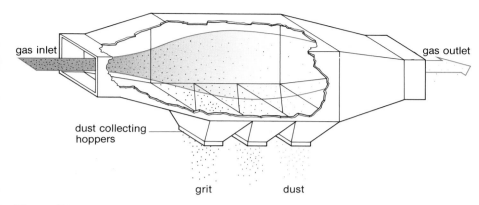

**Figure 54** *A simple horizontal flow settling chamber. The increase in cross-section of the duct causes the gases to slow down so that the entrained dust particles settle out and can be collected in hoppers.*

*Centrifugal separators*

The gravitational separation may be enhanced by centrifugal force, and an application of the principle for separating oil from water was shown in TV 1. In a **_cyclone dust separator_**, the spin given to a dust-laden gas stream throws the dust particles to the walls of the cone from where they fall into a hopper. The penalty is a considerable increase in the amount of energy that must be supplied. Again there are many design variants, each of which is claimed to give some small improvement in efficiency over some part of the working range (Figure 55).

The inlet gases are forced to rotate at high speed about a vertical axis by any one of several different tangential, spiral or vane-directed inlet designs. The gases spiral downwards towards a dust collection hopper, before reversing direction to spiral back upwards through the centre. Because of their inertia the heavier dust particles are less easily deflected by the gas flow into a circular path round the vortex. They therefore impinge on the cyclone walls and, with their velocity destroyed, they fall into the collecting hopper below. Only the smallest particulate fraction continues with the gas stream.

In any centrifugal separator, great care must be taken with the detailed geometry, aerodynamic design, quality of construction and the dust hopper sealing arrangements in order to minimise the load on the fan motor and maximise the separation efficiency.

In principle, a cyclone could be designed to remove particles over any size range, and the overall efficiency may be increased by operating two cyclones in sequence. However, the minimum particle size for efficient collection, at a realistic cost, rarely extends below the size range of 5–20 µm. For the efficient collection of these smaller particles, the inner lining of the cyclone must be irrigated to trap the dust more effectively, and water sprays are often required to prevent re-entrainment of the accumulated material into the high speed airflow.

*The control of particulate emissions by wet methods*

Particulate collection by wet procedures is achieved in plant called *scrubbers* or simply *wet arrestors*. These offer several advantages over comparable dry methods, principally the avoidance of risk of fire or explosion. Coarse dust is trapped effectively, and collection can be extended down to much smaller particle sizes with only a moderate fall in efficiency. This efficiency is largely independent of the scale of the plant and, as the wet equipment tends to be more compact overall, it can have a lower capital cost.

By selecting an appropriate scrubbing liquid, some gaseous contaminants can be removed at the same time as the particulate matter, while the corrosive effect of other materials can be effectively neutralised to prevent damage to the equipment, or avoided by using corrosion-resisting materials. (The removal of gases will be covered in Section 5.3.4.)

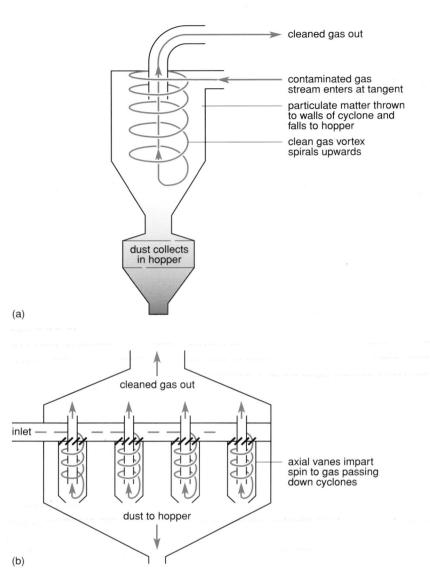

cleaned gas out

contaminated gas
stream enters at tangent

particulate matter thrown
to walls of cyclone and
falls to hopper

clean gas vortex
spirals upwards

dust collects
in hopper

(a)

cleaned gas out

inlet

axial vanes impart
spin to gas passing
down cyclones

dust to hopper

(b)

**Figure 55**  *Cyclone dust separators showing the vortex flow. The two types of
cyclone entry are: (a) tangential; (b) axial vane directed, used in multicyclone
configurations. In both types, the dust can be drawn off from a hopper at the base of
the equipment. A recirculating eddy may tend to form near the top of the vortex, and
dust-contamination of the outflow must be prevented by careful attention to the
design configuration.*

 Wet gas-cleaning methods are generally insensitive to changes in gas temperature near
to the **dewpoint** where condensation could be troublesome with alternative dry
methods. Where necessary, gas cooling and dust removal can be accomplished within
one process, although recovery of useful low-grade heat may be better achieved in
other ways. Problems of handling sticky dusts are conveniently avoided, and the
waste material is recovered in a liquid **slurry** which can be pumped. There are consequently no secondary dust problems during its final disposal. Wet collection methods
also offer a design and operational advantage of a constant gas pressure drop over the
system, but there are a number of disadvantages.

Chief of these is the need for a water supply and slurry treatment plant, both of which
add to the operational costs of the system. There is always the possibility that the
water will freeze during cold weather, or an unexpected chemical reaction may lead to
corrosion, flow obstruction or some other operational difficulty. Solids can be
deposited, or the scrubbing liquid may form a gel or foam of stable bubbles, any of
which can cause a handling problem. Alternatively, the collected material may
become slow to settle out in the dewatering process.

Efficient collection of the smallest material requires a large pressure drop across the system and it is therefore expensive in the consumption of energy, but if the small material remains uncollected the final discharge could be visible and obtrusive. Since the overall collection efficiency is unlikely to approach 100% for any particle size, wet collection procedures are not necessarily suitable for very large dust loadings, nor is the cleaned air generally suitable for recirculation within the workplace. With the waste gases being cooled, there must be some loss of buoyancy in the final discharge, and any visible plume of condensed water vapour may add to local nuisance through precipitation or loss of amenity.

### Simple dedusters and demisters

Wet methods of gas cleaning normally use water as the scrubbing liquid, although if necessary it can be made either acidic or alkaline to prevent corrosion or to react with a gaseous contaminant. The liquid may be spread as a fine film over internal surfaces, or may be dispersed as a fine spray. With a fine spray, some form of mist eliminator will usually be required downstream, and it is here that there is an overlap between the simple procedures for removing mists and airborne dusts, and the collection of droplets carried over from energy-intensive scrubbing systems.

The capture of airborne particles is by impaction on a wetted surface, or on droplets. The tendency for capture is determined by a balance between the inertia of each particle, which continues to carry it towards a wet surface, and the aerodynamic forces of the gas flow, which tend to carry it round or past the obstruction. As a result, larger, heavier and faster moving particles are captured more easily than the lighter ones that are moving more slowly. A high efficiency in removing the smallest particles therefore depends on inducing a large relative velocity between them and the droplets of scrubbing liquid. The collection efficiency is also enhanced when minute droplets can be induced to coalesce, and when water or vapour is able to condense onto the airborne material, which implies that the gas stream is saturated with water. There are many design variants using wet collection methods and quite often one device will incorporate several different features, each intended to improve collection efficiency.

One of the simplest wet devices is the traditional method of cleaning the emission from a *cupola* (a shaft-type melting funnel used in a foundry for recycling scrap metal) (Figure 56). The device combined a baffled expansion chamber and water irrigation of the baffle on which airborne particles impact. The liquor was separated from the solid matter in a settlement tank. The method of gas cleaning was not highly efficient and nowadays is unacceptable on large cupolas.

Simple droplet and mist eliminators incorporate large easily wetted surfaces in the form of baffles, embossed plastic sheets or other complex shapes that ensure an intimate contact with the mist-laden air (Figure 57). This type of device is often required on the downstream side of commercial cooling and air-conditioning plant to prevent a local nuisance from the fallout of water droplets.

Mists and droplets can be filtered from gases by a variety of fabrics and filter materials. One eliminator for corrosive mists uses pads of uniformly crimped, stainless steel wires to capture large droplets (Figure 58).

Fine mists and dusts can be removed by felted pads of fine fibrous materials. The pads work more efficiently if they are irrigated, or mounted on a rotating drum or disc that is repeatedly wetted as it passes through a liquid reservoir. The general aim is to maximise the area of liquid surface in contact with the waste gases while minimising the resistance to gas flow through the equipment.

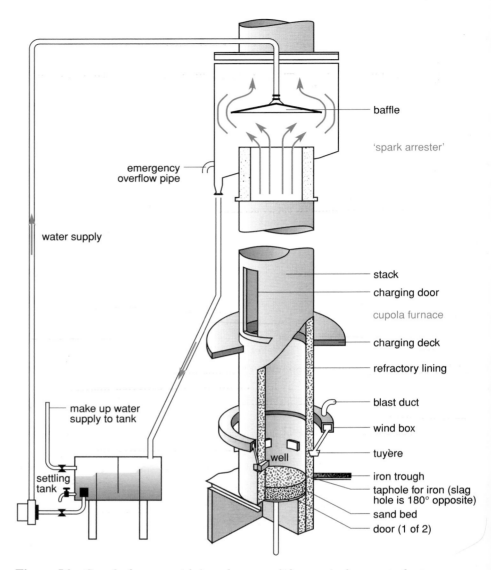

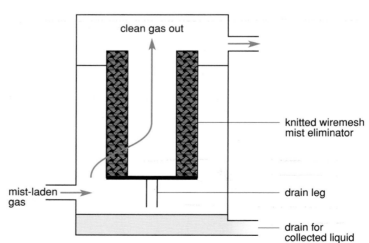

**Figure 56**   *Cupola furnace with 'spark arrester' for particulate control.*

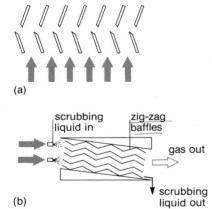

**Figure 57**   *Simple mist eliminators: (a) horizontal baffles or louvres intercept mist droplets in a slowly rising column of gases; (b) a chevron spray eliminator can be used for simple scrubbing or the removal of large droplets.*

**Figure 58**   *Knitted wiremesh mist eliminator.*

*Packed scrubbers*

There is a variety of more complex designs of wet arrestors that use packed beds of coke, broken stone or proprietary ceramic, metal or plastic packing components in the form of rings, saddles or spheres. These designs will also remove small dust loadings, but the difficulty of cleaning the accumulated solid material from the packed beds generally precludes their use for collecting large concentrations of dust (Figure 59). The problem of obstruction by accumulated dust is largely overcome in a floating bed scrubber (Figure 60). A packing of light plastic spheres is suspended in a fluidised state by a rising gas flow. Movement of the spheres is claimed to give a self-cleaning action so that the collected solid particles can be carried away easily by the scrubbing liquid.

*Tower scrubbers and self-induced spray scrubbers*

In tower scrubbers the emphasis is placed on minimising the resistance to gas flow. There are many designs in which the liquid is retained in layers on horizontal plates mounted one above the other (Figure 61).

Spaced holes in the plates allow the contaminated gases to move upwards, while the scrubbing liquid simply cascades downwards. Various types of baffle are provided to allow air bubbles to form and these cover each hole. Particles in the gas flow are captured by the fine spray at the edges of the baffles. The particle collection efficiency is maximised if the gas flow is saturated with water vapour before it enters the tower.

Another option for particle collection involves one of several designs of self-induced spray scrubber. An example is shown in Figure 62. The collected material accumulates in the base of the unit from where it can be removed automatically by a simple drag-link conveyor. The gain in gas cleaning efficiency is, however, counterbalanced by an increased energy loss due to the pressure drop across the system. These systems are available as ready-made package units, and so are attractive for smaller operations.

*High-energy scrubbers*

In an alternative line of development, energy is expended to gain a relatively large velocity between droplets of the scrubbing liquid and the waste gas flow. In Figure 63, the airflow becomes turbulent as it passes the flooded disc. This effectively breaks up the liquid into a fine spray on which any particulate material impacts. Effectively, the droplets make the dust particles larger, enabling their removal from the gas flow in a downstream cyclone separator. By adjusting the disc either up or down in an axial direction, the annular area between the disc and the conical-shaped throat can be varied for control of the gas flow.

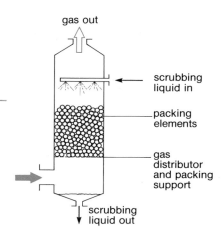

**Figure 59**   *A simple bed of packed elements facilitates the removal of mist and a limited amount of dust from contaminated gases.*

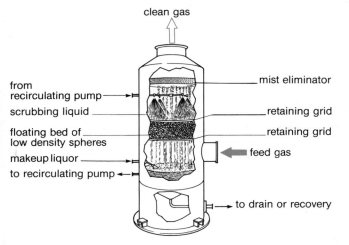

**Figure 60**   *A floating-bed scrubber contains low-density plastic spheres and avoids the tendency of particles and sticky materials to collect and 'plug' or obstruct the air flow.*

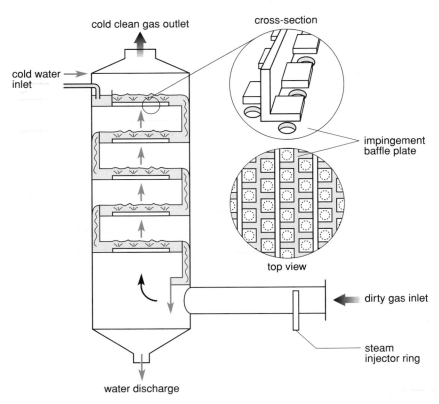

**Figure 61**   *Diagram of a tower scrubber with impingement baffles suspended over each plate. The scrubbing liquid flows across each plate in turn as it passes down through the tower.*

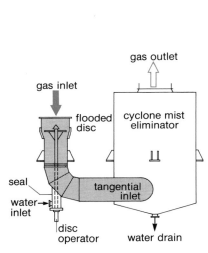

**Figure 63**   *A flooded disc scrubber: the contaminated airflow becomes turbulent as it passes between the flooded disc and the pipe walls. This causes the scrubbing liquid to break into a fine spray on which fine particles impact. The spray droplets are removed from the gas stream in a cyclone mist eliminator.*

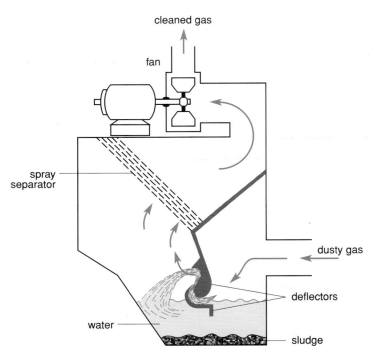

**Figure 62**   *A proprietary self-induced spray scrubber. The collected particulate material accumulates in the base from where it is removed by a chain-link conveyor.*

By extending this principle, the efficiency in collecting very small particles can be greatly improved. The high-energy *venturi* scrubber will deal with material down to sub-micrometre sizes (Figure 64). This improvement in efficiency is achieved by accelerating the dust-laden gas through a narrow constriction (called a venturi) in the

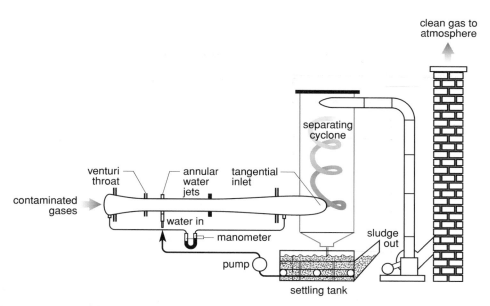

**Figure 64**   *The operation of a venturi scrubber. The gas to be cleaned is accelerated to a high velocity through the venturi constriction; annular water jets are broken up into fine droplets by the fast moving gas stream. The water droplets and contaminants move into a cyclone separator and clean air is discharged.*

pipe or duct. The scrubbing liquid is introduced upstream of the venturi as a finely divided spray. The very large gas velocity through the venturi then ensures an intimate mixing and impaction of the fine particles on the spray droplets.

Achieving high-efficiency gas cleaning depends upon the way moisture can be induced to condense onto the smallest particles by the reduction in pressure through the venturi section. This enables them to increase in size, agglomerate and become impacted on spray droplets. The overriding disadvantage of the venturi scrubber is the very large pressure drop across the device which must be maintained by the use of large amounts of energy in a powerful fan motor. For this reason, high-energy systems such as this may be preferred for short-term duty rather than for continuous operation.

*Fabric filters*

Perhaps the most obvious way of collecting dust from a gas stream is to pass it through a filter of finely woven fabric or felt, as in the domestic vacuum cleaner. Collecting efficiencies can easily be maintained above 99%, even for particle sizes below 1 μm.

Unfortunately, although many different natural and synthetic materials for filters are now available, most may be damaged by temperatures of over 100–200 °C, or by corrosive constituents in the air flow. With flammable dusts, there is an ever-present risk of serious fire or explosion. Sticky materials, or too much water, can hinder the routine cleaning of the filter medium that becomes necessary whenever the pressure drop across it becomes too great, as we shall see later. Handling and disposal of the collected material pose difficult problems if a secondary dust nuisance is to be avoided. Despite all these disadvantages, fabric filters are in general and widespread use as a result of the high-efficiency collection they offer, with the ability to meet statutory emission limits under EPA 1990.

The design process begins with the selection of a suitable filter medium that is sufficiently permeable to allow the carrying gas to pass, but of adequate density to retain the suspended particulate matter. A balance has to be drawn between the minimum acceptable filtering characteristics, and the routine costs of replacement. The choice includes cotton and wool, which are able to withstand working temperatures of 80 °C or 90 °C. Nylon and polypropene have better resistance to abrasion and chemical attack. Different characteristics are found in other synthetic materials. Acrylic, polyester, PTFE and glass-fibre fabrics are available to extend the maximum working temperature in steps from 127 °C to 260 °C.

In general for the same bulk, fine fibres are more efficient than coarse, while needle felts tend to give a better performance than woven fabrics for the same resistance to airflow. Once particles have been captured, they are retained by a complex mechanism involving electrostatic, molecular, and (if moisture is present) capillary forces of attraction acting in opposition to the aerodynamic drag force seeking to displace them. Material is deposited both within the thickness of the fabric and on the upstream face. As the dust load builds up into a cake, it takes over the filtering function. This is allowed to continue until the air pressure drop across the filter becomes excessive and much of the material must be removed, although some residue enhances collection efficiency (Figure 65).

Dust removal is achieved periodically by:

1   mechanical shaking or displacement of the filter;

2   temporary reversal of the airflow; or

3   intermittent reverse pulsing by compressed air.

The evolution of these fabric filter-cleaning options is outlined in TV 8.

To achieve the largest ratio of filtering surface area to volume, fabric filters are usually arranged in groups of long narrow envelopes, tubes or sleeves. These are suspended vertically in a weather-proof housing called a **bag house,** so that when the accumulated dust cake is displaced, it will fall directly into a suitable collecting hopper below. A typical arrangement is shown diagramatically in Figure 66, and in TV 8. The cleaned air permeates inwards through the open-topped bags to leave the collected material on the outside of the sleeves.

*Electrostatic precipitators*

Electrostatic forces of attraction can be used effectively on their own to capture a wide variety of both wet and dry particles. The principle of electrostatic attraction is demonstrated in TV 8, which also illustrates an array of electrostatic precipitators used in a power station.

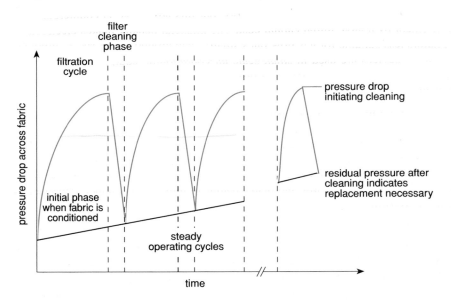

**Figure 65**   *Representation of behaviour of fabric filter over several operating cycles. In the initial phase some dust collects on the bags and improves filtration efficiency, but eventually the pressure drop across the bags becomes excessive. At a certain pressure drop the bags are cleaned and the cycle begins again. Eventually the residual dust causes an unacceptable pressure drop indicating that it is time to change the bags.*

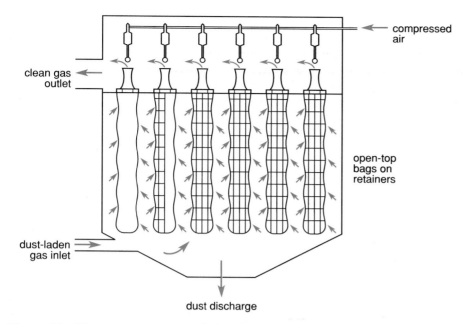

**Figure 66**  *The components in a tubular sleeve filter house; this arrangement displaces the accumulated material by reversed jets of compressed air.*

The electrostatic precipitator will work efficiently with gases contaminated by a range of dust burdens, and it can be designed to operate successfully over a range of gas pressures and temperatures up to 500 °C. If special care is taken with the design, these conditions can be extended to temperatures of 800 °C and pressures of up to $6 \times 10^5$ Pa. The equipment can be made resistant to abrasion and corrosion, and it will deal with gases close to their dewpoint or contaminated with acid fumes and tar.

The principal operating advantage is a low air pressure drop across the system, with a correspondingly small consumption of energy, but this advantage is counterbalanced to some extent by a large initial capital cost. The financial penalty makes electrostatic precipitators less suitable for gas flow rates smaller than around 10 m³ sec⁻¹, although some simple devices are used in small-scale air conditioning equipment. The size of electrostatic precipitators may also be a problem, especially when considering fitting them to an existing process.

Figure 67 will remind you of the operating principle and layout of the device. In out-line the electrostatic precipitator consists of an arrangement of closely spaced parallel wires suspended vertically between pairs of tall metal plates. The plates are earthed and in large installations the wires are held at a controlled negative potential typically between 45 000 and 55 000 volts. As a result of this large voltage difference, the air in the small gap between the wires and plates begins to ionise and conduct a small electric current to earth.

Gas molecules in the air gap become ionised where the voltage gradient is greatest. Under the intense electric field, the positive ions move towards the wires, where more electrons are released to join those already moving away. The visible effect is a characteristic glow discharge or corona from any surface irregularity. The wires are therefore usually fitted with sharply pointed barbs at regular intervals to spread the corona discharge evenly over the whole area.

Current to maintain the discharge is supplied from a variable low-voltage source via a transformer–rectifier system. The corona is stabilised by an automatic control on the primary side which constantly readjusts the negative voltage to a level just below that which would provoke excessive or continuous sparking. The aim is to maintain the largest practicable space charge of electrons just outside the region of the corona and so take account of any changing dust burden.

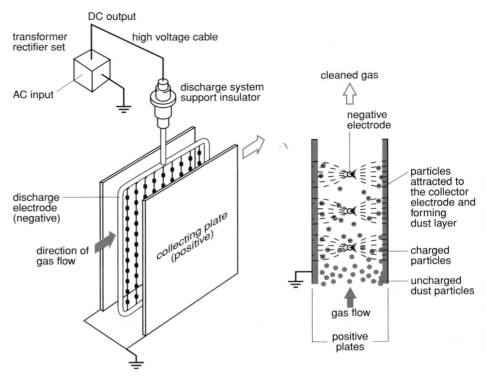

**Figure 67** *Removal of dust by electrostatic precipitators. Most uncharged dust particles receive a negative electrical charge from the central discharge electrodes which causes them to migrate towards one of the earthed collecting electrodes. In a typical installation, several pairs of electrodes would be energised in parallel from one transformer–rectifier set. The gases to be cleaned would be passed sequentially through two or more fields. The capacity of the installation is made up by parallel gas paths through other units.*

Most of the solid or liquid droplets, comprising the bulk of the airborne material entering the system, will collide with electrons to become negatively charged. Under the influence of the strong electric field, these particles migrate across the gas flow to form an agglomerated layer on the positive earth electrodes. A much smaller proportion of the airborne material will receive a positive electric charge on passing directly through the corona and colliding with positively charged ions. This material will be drawn towards the negative electrodes and will accumulate on the array of wires.

Liquid droplets collecting on the electrodes tend to coalesce and drain away, but solid or tarry material builds up and must be removed at intervals. If they are dry enough, most deposits will be dislodged by a simple rapping mechanism using a motor-driven hammer. Suitable collecting hoppers are built below the electrode arrays, and there are many ingenious mechanical designs of electrode to ensure that the falling dust does not short-circuit the high voltage supply and put the device out of action. Alternatively, the electrodes used for collecting acid mists or tar can be flushed with a liquid (normally water) to remove the accumulated material as a slurry. This of course requires further treatment before disposal. Likewise, care must be taken to avoid pollution by the fine dust collected in the hoppers when they are emptied from time to time.

Electrostatic precipitators work best if the electrical resistivity (i.e. effectively a measure of the electrical insulating power) of the collected material lies within certain, quite wide, limits. If the resistance is too low, the electric charge will leak away too quickly, and the material may become re-entrained in the gas flow. Alternatively, if the electrical resistance is too high, an insulating layer may be formed on the electrodes which will prevent the proper corona discharge and reduce the collection efficiency. The temperature of the gas stream is quite important in this respect, since the resistivity of many materials varies over a wide range with changing temperature. Some high-resistance dusts that are difficult to collect can be precipitated more effectively by prior conditioning. For example, changing from a high- to a low-sulphur coal results in a higher resistivity fly ash that is more difficult to collect. The use of sulphur trioxide, ammonia or proprietary chemicals for preconditioning the flue gases offers a way in which the performance of electrostatic precipitators may be improved.

In large installations, the specified collection efficiency is usually achieved by passing the gas flow through the electric fields of two or more precipitators in sequence. The volume of the gas flow is then accommodated by operating several gas paths in parallel. Individual units are dimensioned to ensure that there is always spare cleaning capacity to cover routine maintenance or equipment failure.

The design performance of any collection system will be maintained only so long as it is adjusted and operated correctly. As with any other dust removal equipment, electrostatic precipitators do not contribute directly to the profits of a company. With insufficient incentive or supervision there can be an understandable tendency to skimp on inspection and maintenance. For example, if the dust hoppers are simply left unemptied for too long, the electrodes will be 'short circuited' and cleaning will be interrupted. The electrodes will no longer be freely suspended and the insulated system could be damaged by the rapping mechanism. 'Equipment-failure' would then be an inadequate and quite improper excuse for any severe dust fall over the neighbourhood.

### 5.3.3   Selecting the 'best' available technique for particulate matter

In this section I will give some guidelines on how to choose techniques for controlling particulate air pollution emissions that are produced in spite of attempts at pollution prevention. In this it is necessary to distinguish between point sources, such as furnaces and other equipment or processes, and *fugitive* sources, which are emissions emitted from locations other than the main vent or chimney. We also need to consider separately the different approaches to organic vapours, inorganic gases and vapours, and we will address control options for these pollutants in the next section. In all cases, however, the applicability of the best available technique for control depends on the characteristics of the waste gas stream.

*Particulate emissions control – point sources*

As emission standards become more demanding, the options for controlling large or hazardous releases of air pollutants to atmosphere tend to focus on fabric filters, electrostatic precipitators and venturi scrubbers. The efficiency and applicability of any of these options depend on the physical, chemical and electrical characteristics of the particulate matter, while the choice of technique depends also on the characteristics of the waste gas stream. Table 19 summarises the major characteristics of the three control options in relation to the properties of waste gas streams, and should allow a likely match to be selected. In some cases it may be necessary to use pretreatment equipment (such as cyclones, gas cooling or heating systems) upstream of the control device to bring the characteristics of the emission stream within the ranges outlined in the table. For example, the temperature of the emission stream should be 25–50 °C above its dewpoint if fabric filters or an electrostatic precipitator are to be used, otherwise corrosion of metal surfaces or 'blinding' of filters may occur as a result of condensation.

*Tables 19–22*
*- Know general principles*
*+ some examples*
*not the details*

**Table 19**   ***The applicability of high-efficiency gas cleaning systems to particulate emission streams***

| Control device | Efficiency achievable | Particle size range | Sensitivity to: | | |
|---|---|---|---|---|---|
| | | | Temperature | Corrosion or electrical resistance | Moisture |
| Fabric filter | over 99% | Least efficient with particles of diameter 0.1–0.3 μm | Typically not to exceed 300 °C, but depends on fabric | Special fibres required to resist corrosion | Poor efficiency with emission streams of high or variable moisture content |
| Electrostatic precipitator | over 99% | Often least efficient with particles of diameter 0.2–0.5 μm | Generally up to 500 °C | Corrosion-resistant materials needed; gases containing highly resistant particles may need conditioning | Can be designed to handle high moisture content, but is sensitive to moisture changes |
| Venturi scrubber | over 99% | Usually best with particles over 0.5 μm | No limits | May need special materials for corrosive streams | Not sensitive to moisture content |

Some additional information on the three techniques is given in Table 20. While not directly affecting the technical feasibility of an option, some factors may nevertheless influence the final choice, as may other factors such as costs.

**Table 20** *Advantages and disadvantages of high-efficiency particulate control techniques*

| | Advantages | Disadvantages |
|---|---|---|
| Fabric filter | Very efficient for fine particles; lower pressure drop than venturi (e.g. <15 mbar compared with >100 mbar) for fine particulate matter; can collect resistive particles; with mechanical shaking or reverse air cleaning the efficiency is independent of inlet loading; simple to operate. | cannot control streams with high moisture content; erosive particles may damage filter; mechanical collector required upstream if large amounts of large (>20 μm) particles are present; needs special fabrics for corrosive streams. |
| Electrostatic Precipitator | Can control small (<0.1 μm) particles with high efficiency; low operating costs with low pressure drop (1 mbar); can collect corrosive and tarry mists; low power requirements for continuous operation; wet precipitators can collect gaseous pollutants. | High capital cost; not readily adapted to changing conditions; conditioning agents may be needed for resistive particles; more sensitive to particle loadings than the other options in this table; space requirements may be greatest. |
| Venturi scrubber | Low capital cost; little space required; can control sticky, flammable or corrosive matter with few problems; can collect particulate matter and gases simultaneously; simple to operate with few moving parts. | High operating cost owing to high pressure drop (100 mbar or more) especially for small particles; wastewater treatment and disposal problems and costs; least efficient with particles below diameter of 0.5 μm. |

Finally, Table 21 illustrates common applications of particulate control plant to some industrial operations.

**Table 21** *Summary of typical uses of gas cleaning plant for particulate control in some industries*

| Activity | Concentration[a] | Particle sizes[b] | Typical gas cleaning plant used in industry | | | | |
|---|---|---|---|---|---|---|---|
| | | | Cyclone | High efficiency cyclone | Wet deduster | Fabric filter | Electrostatic precipitator |
| Ceramics: raw product handling | light | fine | rare | seldom | frequent | frequent | no |
| Chemicals: material handling | light to moderate | fine to medium | occasional | frequent | frequent | frequent | rare |
| Chemicals: crushing, grinding | moderate to heavy | fine to coarse | often | frequent | frequent | frequent | no |
| Chemicals: pneumatic conveying | very heavy | fine to coarse | usual | occasional | rare | usual | no |
| Coal mining and power plant: material handling | moderate | medium | rare | occasional | frequent | frequent | no |
| Fly ash: coal burning on grate | moderate | fine to coarse | rare | usual | no | no | rare |
| Coal burning: pulverised fuel | heavy | fine | rare | frequent | no | no | frequent |
| Foundry: abrasive cleaning of items | moderate to heavy | fine to medium | no | occasional | frequent | frequent | no |
| Flour and feed mills: grain handling | light | medium | usual | occasional | rare | frequent | no |
| Metal melting: ferrous cupola | moderate | varied | occasional | occasional | frequent | frequent | rare |
| Mining and rock products: material handling | moderate | fine to medium | rare | occasional | usual | considerable | no |
| Cement kiln | heavy | fine to medium | rare | frequent | rare | considerable | considerable |
| Metal working: grinding, scratch brushing | light | coarse | frequent | frequent | considerable | considerable | no |
| metal working: buffing | light | varied | frequent | rare | frequent | rare | no |
| Woodworking machines | moderate | varied | usual | occasional | rare | frequent | no |
| Woodworking: sanding | moderate | fine | frequent | occasional | occasional | frequent | no |

[a]Light concentrations are approximately $<5$ g m$^{-3}$; moderate are 5–12 g m$^{-3}$; heavy are $>12$ g m$^{-3}$

[b]Fine implies 50% $<5$ μm; medium implies 50% in range 5–15 μm; coarse is 50% $>15$ μm.

## SAQ 44

By reference to Table 21 and the text of Section 5, identify which particulate control option you would apply in the following situations. Justify your recommendation.

(a)  Roadstone preparation and coating at a quarry.  *wet venturi system*

(b)  Sanding operations in a furniture manufactory.  *fabric filters*

(c)  Grinding in a metal fabricating workshop.  *wet self induced spray or fabric filters*

(d)  Collection of sub-micrometre fume containing hygroscopic (moisture attracting) *irrigated knitted wire filter* ammonium chloride from hot dip galvanising of steel.

(e)  Pulverised coal burning at a power generating station.  *electrostatic precipitators.*

*Relative efficiency of gas cleaning equipment*

Typical particulate concentrations in waste gases cover a wide range. Concentrations that may be released from cement works, power stations, iron and steel works, incinerators and many other processes are defined in specific process guidance notes issued by the Secretary of State for the Environment.

## Exercise

Suppose that a hypothetical municipal waste incinerator produces $10^5$ m$^3$ of waste gases each hour in which the particulate concentration is 400 g m$^{-3}$.

(a)  What is the minimum cleaning efficiency required of suitable gas cleaning plant to be fitted to an existing incinerator burning up to 6 tonnes of waste per hour, in order to meet a release limit of 100 mg m$^{-3}$ under the requirements of the EC directive and the EPA process guidance note?

(b)  What quantity of particulate material could be released from this works to atmosphere each hour without exceeding the release limit?

## Answer

(a)  The efficiency of collecting particulate matter from the waste gases is equivalent to:

(concentration removed/total concentration) × 100

$= ((400 - 0.1 \text{g m}^{-3})/400 \text{ g m}^{-3}) \times 100 = 99.98\%$

(b)  The amount of material that can be discharged each hour without exceeding the release limit of 100 mg m$^{-3}$ is just less than:

$(10^5 \text{ m}^3 \text{ h}^{-1} \times 0.1 \text{ g m}^{-3}) = 10 \text{ kg h}^{-1}$

## SAQ 45

If the incinerator described in the preceding example burns more than 6 tonnes of waste per hour, it has to meet a release limit of 30 mg m$^{-3}$. What efficiency is required to achieve this performance standard?

The answers to the example and SAQ demonstrate how little inefficiency can be tolerated in the gas cleaning equipment of a large works. In our particular example, the particulate material would have to be removed at a rate of almost 40 tonnes per hour to avoid breaching the release limit. The problems posed by large concentrations of very fine material should now be obvious. It is also clear that any deterioration in cleaning performance must be dealt with immediately, and why standby plant must be provided to cover the possibility of breakdown.

*Particulate control malfunction*

From the beginning of this text you will recall that failure of gas cleaning plant during operation is a potential cause of a local air pollution problem. In considering the causes of plant failure it is important to remember the overall system, which generally breaks down into four principal components (see Figure 53):

- a hood;
- the ductwork;
- the particulate separation equipment;
- the prime mover (fan) to draw air through the system.

Ineffective particulate control may result in the hood region when:

- air entrainment through the hood is too low owing to a fault in the fan or leaks in the system;
- the hood is poorly designed or ill-fitting;
- suction into the hood is unable to capture all the dust owing to low air velocity because the hood cannot be placed close enough to the source.

You should remember that it is pointless having highly efficient gas cleaning when all of the emission is not captured at the source; clearly, this is an important area to correct any malfunction.

In the ductwork, progressive deposition of dust may reduce air-flow at the hood, increase suction at the fan, or, at worst, cause the ductwork to collapse through the weight of dust. Causes of deposition can include poor original design of the ductwork, with defects or projections causing eddies. Air leaks in through poor joints may also allow deposition of dust, while large or moist particles may settle and not be resuspended in the air-flow. Continual vigilance and maintenance are essential to help avoid these problems.

A major cause of malfunction, however, is with the arrestment plant itself. Provided that it is suitable for the task to which it is applied, is well designed and well made, then any reduction in performance should be capable of rectification.

With cyclones, inefficiency in particulate collection often appears in the form of a visible effluent. Potential causes include:

- unnecessarily high dust burdens entering the system;
- blocking of the cyclone, perhaps by large objects;
- blockage of the dust discharge system from the cyclone, especially when manual removal is used;
- leakage of air into the cyclone.

Wet collectors are often more efficient than cyclones, but may give impaired performance if:

- water levels are low;
- choking of pipework or spray eliminators occurs;
- too much dust is retained in the recirculating water, leading to reduced water flow at sprays;
- foaming occurs through water and dust interactions in the turbulent environment.

---

### SAQ 46

How could you check on malfunction of particulate arrestment plant through many of the aforementioned causes?

---

### SAQ 47

List the main physical principles on which fabric filters depend for removing particles from a flow of waste gases. How is the accumulated material displaced from the filter medium?

---

### SAQ 48

Look at the following sentences, and complete them in your own words to preserve the correct meaning or intention.

A    It is an offence for the occupier of premises in a smoke control area to allow smoke emissions from a chimney unless (a) the emission is caused by the use of *authorised smokeless fuel* ........ or (b) the fireplace discharging into the chimney is on a list of *exempted fireplaces* ............

B    In venturi and certain tower scrubbers the particle collection efficiency is maximised if the upstream gas flow is *saturated* before passing through the device.

C    The complete cleaning of fabric filters is neither *necessary* nor *desirable* since *dust* retained within the filter reduces the pore size and increases the gas cleaning efficiency.

D    The purpose of the high voltage across the electrodes of an electrostatic precipitator is to maintain a space ............so that ............ become ............ charged and are attracted to the positive electrode.

## 5.3.4   The control of gaseous pollutants

So far this review of air pollution control techniques has only covered methods for abating particulate emissions. There is still an enormous variety of gases and vapours that escape to atmosphere.

This subsection will describe just a few representative methods for preventing the escape of some typical gaseous and volatile organic air pollutants. Much debate concerns the benefit, practicability and cost of reducing emissions of the acid gases $SO_2$, $SO_3$ and $NO_x$, which hitherto have been dispersed from tall chimneys. Another problem of growing concern is that of volatile organic compounds. Some aspects of dealing with these are covered in TV 8, and so we will look at organic compounds first, and then consider some inorganic compounds.

*Volatile organic compound control – point sources*

Uncontrolled releases to atmosphere have been common, but it is increasingly necessary to control systems to minimise releases. Add-on control options for volatile organic compound (organic vapour) control tend to be either combustion or recovery systems, with the former often being more favoured owing to the high removal efficiencies that are possible. Combustion systems include *flares*, conventional furnace systems, and thermal and catalytic incinerators. Recovery systems include *adsorption, absorption* and condensation. We will summarise the main features of each before addressing the question of which to use for a particular application.

*Flares*

Flares often serve to dispose of waste gases during unusual process events, such as start-up or shut-down, and in emergencies, and are simply a vent to atmosphere at which flammable gases are burnt. They are also used as process control devices as you saw in TV 1, in which the flare on the offshore platform regulates the gas pressure in the 3-phase separators handling the well fluids (oil, gas and water). Flares can be used for many volatile organic compounds and are usually considered where the calorific value of the emission cannot easily be recovered owing to uncertain or intermittent flow, such as in relief gas flows from oil refineries and chemical works, as well as for dealing with landfill gas at some waste disposal sites. As efficient combustion of a flare burning in the open air is difficult to ensure, it may be preferable to burn the waste gas in a conventional furnace.

*Furnaces*

It may be possible to direct a waste gas stream containing organic compounds to an existing furnace such as a boiler or process heater. The waste gases from steelmaking processes have long been used as a source of heat by burning their combustible components in heat recovery systems. On a smaller scale, it may be possible to use waste air containing volatile organics as the combustion air for a boiler. Destruction efficiencies over 98% are possible at relatively small capital cost, but care is necessary to ensure that the waste air flow is not excessive for efficient combustion within the boiler.

*Thermal incinerators*

Thermal incinerators (Figure 68) may be used to control a wide variety of continuous emission streams containing organic compounds. The technique is typically applied to dilute mixtures of organic compounds in air, with the greatest concentration in air usually being limited by safety considerations to 25% of the lowest concentration that may allow an explosion (the *lower explosive limit*). Waste gases may have sufficient energy content to sustain a flame directly, or may require a supplementary fuel. The cost of supplying this fuel is a disincentive to maintain high temperatures (say 800 °C) necessary for the destruction of organic compounds and possible odours, and lowering the temperature may result in pollution problems, such as odours from partial combustion products. It may be possible to recover some heat from the effluent from the incinerator for preheating the incoming gases. Variable flows of waste gases may not allow good mixing for combustion, and so thermal incinerators may not be well suited to such applications.

*Catalytic incinerators*

Catalytic incinerators are similar in design to thermal incinerators, except for the addition of a catalyst to enhance the rate of combustion. As a result of the catalyst, such incinerators may be operated at lower temperatures, so offering significant fuel savings, which may be further enhanced by incorporating heat recovery (see Figure 68). The catalytic technique is not so widely applicable as thermal incineration because the catalysts are sensitive to pollutant characteristics. Materials such as phosphorus compounds, lead, antimony, mercury, iron oxide, sulphur and halogens can poison the catalyst, while dust or liquid particles may coat the catalyst and impair its performance. High concentrations of organic compounds may also cause the catalyst to overheat, and should not be treated by this technique without dilution. With correct operating conditions, a catalyst may operate satisfactorily for three to five years.

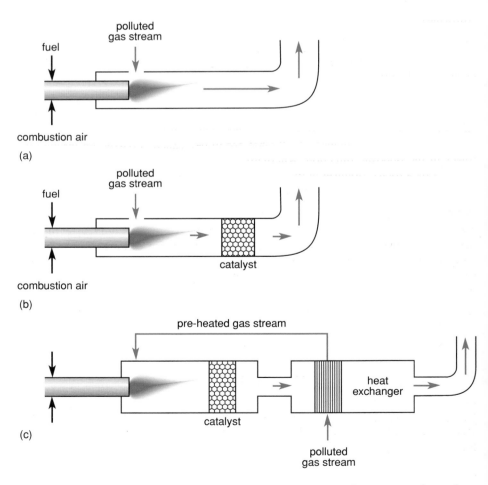

**Figure 68** *Incineration options for the control of gaseous pollutants: (a) thermal incinerator; (b) catalytic incinerator; (c) catalytic incinerator with heat recovery.*

*Carbon adsorbers*

Carbon adsorption is used both for pollution control and solvent recovery, and in contrast to incineration options is attractive when the organic compounds have a commercial value.

Activated charcoal is especially useful for intercepting a variety of offensive odours, recovering solvents for reuse, or for trapping hazardous gases and vapours. The sorbent (i.e. adsorbing material) is activated by thermal or chemical processing to develop an open pore structure in the small carbon particles. The resulting large ratio of surface area to weight provides the greatest receptive area where gas molecules can become physically bound (adsorbed) onto the solid material.

In some instances, the carbon may be pretreated with other substances so that the chemical reactions take place with the unwanted pollutant and enhance the collection effect by a process called *chemisorption*. For low flow rates, the gas to be cleaned is passed through a thin uniform layer of the activated carbon held in any convenient bed or filter pack. For larger flow rates, arrangements which enhance the contact between carbon and gas stream are used, e.g. fluidised beds, or rotating screens. Pollutant gas or vapour coming into contact with an unoccupied part of the adsorbent is held until most of the carbon surface is covered with a unimolecular layer. The sorbent material must then be removed for disposal or regeneration by treatment with steam or some other hot clean gas.

Adsorption is a technique that is sensitive to waste gas stream conditions. High molecular mass compounds (>130), which characteristically have low volatility, are strongly adsorbed and consequently are difficult to remove during regeneration, while highly volatile materials with molecular mass below 45 do not adsorb readily. High humidity, high temperatures or the presence of particulate matter are conditions that may require pretreatment.

*Absorbers*

The procedures for controlling gaseous pollutants often involve dissolution or simple chemical reaction. Many applications, especially for the control of odours, involve chemical oxidation.

Most gas washing or scrubbing processes rely on bringing the polluted waste gas stream into close contact with the absorbing reagent. The most obvious way of doing this is to allow the liquid to trickle or cascade down through a tower that is packed with obstructions. Simultaneously, the hot gas to be cleaned is passed up through the tower in the opposite direction. Alternatively, the liquid can be broken up into fine droplets by a rotary atomiser at the top of the reactor vessel, or by pumping it through suitable spray nozzles. Figure 69 illustrates two typical designs.

What are the characteristics of a simple representative wet scrubbing installation? Some are like the scrubbers used for particulate materials. There are many competing designs, each one involving different trade-offs between the various interrelated factors that must be taken into account. Early designs sought to minimise the operational problems of scaling and blockage. There was consequently a move towards very simple devices to reduce this risk. With a better understanding of the phenomenon, more attention was then paid to improving the collection efficiency and reducing costs. These aims call for:

1   a good gas-to-liquid contact;
2   a low pressure drop across the system;
3   an even distribution of scrubbing liquid in the absorber.

All three factors influence the amount of energy expended in the gas and liquid pumping system. Finally, there is the need to maintain or restore plume buoyancy so that there is sufficient dispersion and dilution of the remaining combustion products that must be discharged.

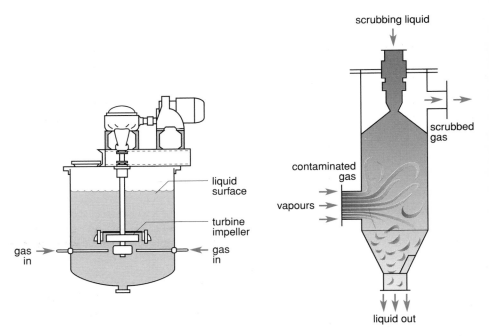

**Figure 69**   *Two typical designs of absorption systems for gaseous pollutant control.*

Absorbers (or scrubbers) may be used for emission control of volatile organics, but are more commonly used for the control of inorganic vapours. One of the most important factors is the availability of a suitable solvent in which the pollutant is readily soluble. I hope that you will recall from Unit 3 that many organic compounds are not very soluble in water, which is the most readily available solvent. However, aqueous solutions, such as sodium hypochlorite, may serve to control emissions, but this is usually by chemical reaction rather than for recovery. Absorbers may also have to be very large to deal with low concentrations in an emission, and this may not be cost effective. Another consideration is disposal of the absorber effluent: it is clearly unacceptable to convert an air pollution problem to a water pollution problem.

*Condensers*

Condensers are widely used for recovery and as preliminary air pollution control devices before other systems such as incinerators. The type of coolant used for the condenser is a critical factor, and water may be unable to meet the low emission limits often required. Other coolants such as chilled water or brine may have advantages, but the technique is more suitable for pretreatment than as a single stage process. You will notice that condensers are an integral part of the pollution control on degreasing tanks shown in TV 8.

*Option selection*

The choice of control option depends mainly on the emission stream rather than on the type of source, and Table 22 identifies the key emission stream characteristics influencing the applicability of each technique. Matching the characteristics of a waste gas stream to the key points in the table will help you to identify potential techniques for a specific application. Figure 70 indicates typical removal efficiencies for total organics from a waste gas.

---

### SAQ 49

Using the knowledge of combustion gained in Unit 3, summarise why a fluctuating flow of waste gas from a ventilation system contaminated with organic compounds may present difficulties when used as the air supply for a boiler.

---

**Table 22   Waste gas characteristics relating to the selection of control techniques for organic vapours**

| | Emission stream characteristics | | | | Pollutant characteristics | | | |
|---|---|---|---|---|---|---|---|---|
| Control device | Organic content/ ppm(v/v) | Calorific value/ (MJ m⁻³) | Moisture content | Flow rate/ (m³ s⁻¹) | Temperature (°C) | Molecular mass | Solubility | Vapour pressure at ambient temperature /mbar |
| Thermal incinerator | >20 (<25% of LEL) | | | <50 | | | | |
| Catalytic incinerator | 50–10000 (<25% of LEL) | | | <50 | | | | |
| Flare | | >10 | | <10⁶ kg h⁻¹ | | | | |
| Boiler | | >5 | | steady | | | | |
| Carbon adsorber | 1000–10000 (<25% of LEL) | | 50% | 0.15–50 | 40–100 | 45–130 | | |
| Absorber | 250–10000 | | | 0.5–50 | | | must be readily soluble in water or other solvent | |
| Condenser | >5000 | | | <1 | | | | >10 |

LEL, lower explosive limit.
The absence of an entry indicates that the characteristics are of less concern.

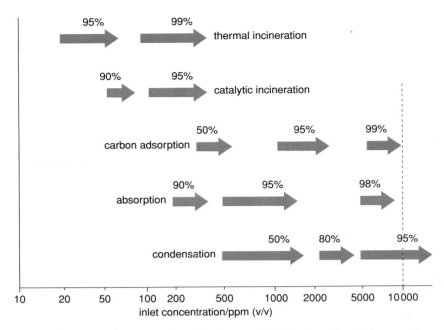

**Figure 70**   *Typical ranges of application and efficiencies of volatile organic compound control techniques. The arrows indicate the applicable concentration ranges.*

*Inorganic vapour emissions – point sources*

Inorganic vapour emissions typically include gases such as ammonia, hydrogen sulphide, carbon disulphide and certain metal compounds such as carbonyl complexes or cyanides. Only a limited number of control options are applicable to inorganic vapour emissions. For example, combustion techniques are not applied in general, but one notable exception is the use of flares to control hydrogen sulphide from gas processing and fuel wells. Absorption is by far the most common method, offering efficiencies over 95%, but as with organic compounds, a most important factor is the solubility of the pollutant in the solvent. Water is the ideal choice of solvent, particularly in terms of cost, but, as discussed previously, it is imperative to incorporate a wastewater treatment plant within the overall system. Typically, pH adjustment may be needed to precipitate metals before separation and disposal to a licensed landfill.

Adsorption using conventional or chemically impregnated carbons offers an alternative approach for certain inorganic gases and vapours, provided that conditions similar to those for organic compounds are met.

Table 23 summarises some control options for inorganic pollutant vapours.

**Table 23**   *Control options for certain inorganic vapours*

| Inorganic vapour | Absorption | | Adsorption | |
| --- | --- | --- | --- | --- |
| | *Removal efficiency (%)* | *Solvent* | *Removal efficiency (%)* | *Adsorbent* |
| mercury | 95 | brine/ hypochlorite solution | 90 | sulphur-impregnated activated carbon |
| hydrogen chloride | 95 | water | | |
| hydrogen sulphide | 98 | sodium carbonate/ water | 100 | ammonia-impregnated activated carbon |
| hydrogen fluoride | 85–95 | water | 99 | calcined alumina |
| chlorine | 90 | alkali solution | | |

## SAQ 50

Propose a suitable control option for the following emissions, and justify your choice.

(a) vapour degreasing using trichloroethylene;

(b) dry cleaning solvent emissions in retail premises;

(c) odours produced by the thermal treatment of paint ('paint baking') during car body manufacture;

(d) odours caused by hydrogen sulphide in waste gases at an oil refinery.

*Fugitive emissions*

So far we have considered the control of releases from processes and activities where the emissions are confined – so-called point sources. When emissions are less readily collected into hoods and ducted along flues, we use the term *'fugitive emissions'*. The term is also used to describe emissions that occur through windows, doors and other routes of egress from a building rather than from a chimney. Table 24 suggests ways of dealing with some fugitive emissions.

**Table 24  *Some control options for organic/inorganic fugitive emission sources***

| Emission source | Control technique | Effectiveness of control (%) |
|---|---|---|
| pumps | regular leak detection/repair | 61 |
| | use seal-less pumps | 100 |
| dual seal systems | vent seal area to control device | 100 |
| | | 100 |
| pressure relief valves | vent seal area to control device | 100 |
| compressors | mechanical seals with vent to control device | 100 |
| valves | leak detection and repair | 73 (gas); 46 (light liquid) |
| | diaphragm valves | 100 |

## 5.3.5  *Control options for sulphur dioxide and nitrogen oxides*

While sulphur dioxide and nitrogen oxides are inorganic compounds and therefore capable of control by the options described in the preceding section, their widespread sources and the magnitude of their emissions justify a separate discussion.

There are two EC directives which relate specifically to emissions of $SO_2$ and $NO_x$; these are the 'Framework' Directive (84/360) on the Combating of Air Pollution from Industrial Plants, and a daughter directive, the Large Combustion Plant (LCP) Directive (88/609/EEC).

## SAQ 51

(a) Look back at Figure 5 and identify the contribution made by large combustion plant in the UK to emissions of $SO_2$ and $NO_x$.

(b) A 2000 MW power station is 30% efficient in generating electricity from coal containing 1.7% sulphur. The calorific value of the fuel is 25 MJ kg$^{-1}$. Calculate the rate of release of sulphur dioxide to the atmosphere assuming no retention of the pollutant.

The LCP Directive applies to plant of more than 50 MW$_{th}$ heat input. If you are unsure what the subscript 'th' means, refer to the entry *energy* in the set book. The Directive sets stringent emission limits for $SO_2$, $NO_x$ and particulate matter, and also sets programmes for reducing emissions of these pollutants from existing plants. For the UK, the current requirements are to reduce $SO_2$ emissions from existing large combustion plant to:

> 3.106 million tonnes in 1993 (20% below calculated 1980 emissions)
>
> 2.330 million tonnes in 1998 (40% reduction on 1980 baseline)
>
> 1.553 million tonnes in 2003 (60% reduction)

For $NO_x$ the required reductions are to:

> 0.864 million tonnes in 1993 (15% below 1980 baseline)
>
> 0.711 million tonnes in 1998 (30% reduction)

Let us see what options we have to meet the requirements of the directive, especially with respect to $SO_2$.

We know from Unit 3 that when coal or fuel oil are burnt in a furnace, the sulphur in the fuel is oxidised and converted to sulphur dioxide. In the case of coal, some of the sulphur (typically 10%) remains chemically bound in the ash, but for oil all the sulphur is released as the oxide. In addition, perhaps 1–2% of the sulphur dioxide produced is further oxidised to sulphur trioxide.

The first decision is on how we can control the sulphur oxides emissions. Some of our options include:

(a)  replace fuels containing sulphur, e.g. replace coal and oil with gas or change to nuclear power;

(b)  replace existing fuels by, for instance, imported low-sulphur coals;

(c)  remove sulphur from the fuel before it is burnt (fuel desulphurisation);

(d)  capture the sulphur dioxide immediately it is formed;

(e)  remove the sulphur dioxide from the flue gases after they leave the boiler or furnace (flue gas desulphurisation).

The first two decisions are largely political, but let us look at the technological options (c) to (e).

### Fuel desulphurisation

Sulphur is present in coal both as chemically bound to coal and as minerals, such as iron pyrites, mixed with the coal in the coal seams. Coal as mined is 'washed' in order to lower the mineral content, and this reduces the sulphur content by perhaps 15%. Unfortunately, only some of the mineral matter can be removed in this way, and none of the chemically bound sulphur is removed. The development of more complicated coal cleaning methods involves crushing the coal to release more of the mineral matter, but the separation system has to be more complicated. A point of diminishing economic return is reached when coal losses begin to outweigh sulphur removal.

For oil, it is common practice to desulphurise distillate gas oil (diesel for furnace and motor vehicles) in order for it to comply with fuel standards that are made under the Control of Pollution Act 1974. However, it is not economically viable to desulphurise the residual fuel oil in the UK in view of the price difference between oil and coal. You may notice that the fuel standards for distillate oils offer another way of controlling air pollution. In fact, there have been limits on the sulphur content of oils that may be used as fuel in London for many years. The limits on the lead content of petrol and the introduction of unleaded petrol are also examples of fuel standards, and, as we shall see later, fuel specification for waste oil burning furnaces is part of the control scheme for those furnaces.

### Sulphur capture

The most described technique of this type is the addition of powdered limestone to combustion systems of the *fluidised bed* type. In these processes the fuel is burned in a bed made up of fine particles such as sand or ash, through which the combustion air is passed. This makes the bed appear like a boiling liquid – hence the name (Figure 71).

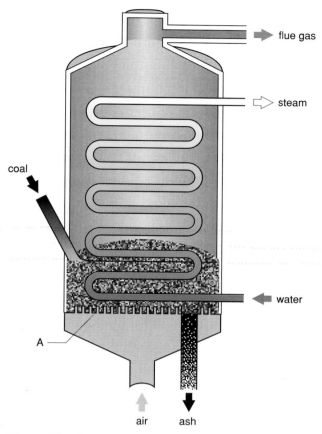

**Figure 71** *Representation of a fluidised bed combustion system. (A) distribution plate through which air is blown for fluidising.*

If powdered limestone is added to a fluidised bed, the limestone is converted to lime which then reacts with the sulphur dioxide:

$$CaCO_3 \rightarrow CaO + CO_2$$

$$CaO + SO_2 \rightarrow CaSO_3$$

$$2CaO + 2SO_2 + O_2 \rightarrow 2CaSO_4$$

This approach to sulphur capture has been described often, but has found relatively little use in the UK and so its scope for sulphur dioxide control is unclear. In particular, it is not known what effect the lime may have on the operation of the plant, what problems may be involved in the disposal of the ash and flue dust, and what sulphur control efficiency is available.

There is another option for sulphur dioxide capture that involves injecting limestone directly into the combustion zone of a conventional boiler. This approach was used in the USA in the 1960s, but with little success. European experience with lignite or brown coal has found much better removal, and this may be due to the somewhat lower temperatures at which such coal burns. This control option is a possible area for wider application in the future.

*Flue gas desulphurisation*

This general term applies to the processes that clean up the final boiler or furnace gases. Some of the processes that have been explored are dry, but most of those that have been developed commercially use an alkaline liquid or slurry to react with sulphur dioxide. For example, if we were to use sodium hydroxide:

$$2NaOH + SO_2 \rightarrow Na_2SO_3 + H_2O$$

We know that sulphur dioxide is an acidic gas which is present in flue gases at typically 0.1–0.2% by volume for average sulphur content fuels, but there is also another acidic gas – carbon dioxide. Although this is only weakly acidic, it will react with an alkali such as sodium hydroxide to produce sodium carbonate.

Scrubbing will be inefficient unless we continuously convert the sodium carbonate back to hydroxide by contact with lime.

$$Na_2CO_3 + Ca(OH)_2 \rightarrow CaCO_3 + 2NaOH$$

In addition, sodium sulphite is soluble in water and cannot be removed from the effluent. It is for these reasons that most of the commercial processes tend to use lime or limestone. While lime is more reactive than limestone and so allows smaller gas cleaning equipment to be used, it is also more expensive, so limestone tends to be favoured.

Very simply, these flue gas desulphurisation processes remove sulphur dioxide by converting it to calcium sulphite, some of which is further oxidised to calcium sulphate. This is difficult to separate from water and is usually disposed of as a sludge which has been described as having the consistency of toothpaste. British coal has a high chloride content and so some calcium chloride will be formed in the process. This is a soluble compound and will slowly leach out of the sludge with a resultant risk of water pollution if the sludge is disposed of to landfill. If the calcium sulphite is converted fully to calcium sulphate, or gypsum, this can be dewatered more easily and the gypsum may have a marketable use in plaster or plasterboard manufacture (Figure 72).

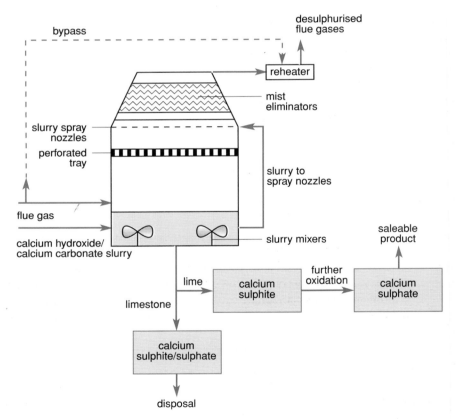

**Figure 72**  *Schematic representation of lime/limestone flue gas desulphurisation process.*

I should also mention two other approaches that have met commercial success. The Wellman–Lord process has been applied successfully in power stations and many industrial processes in several countries. It uses a sodium sulphite solution which is continuously regenerated according to the following chemical equation sequence:

$$Na_2SO_3 + H_2O + SO_2 \rightarrow 2NaHSO_3$$

$$\text{heat}$$
$$2NaHSO_3 \rightarrow Na_2SO_3 + H_2O + SO_2$$

The Wellman–Lord process is more expensive than the limestone process in terms of energy consumption. It is really a recovery system because the sulphur from the fuel is recovered as sulphur dioxide for use, converted to sulphuric acid or reacted with natural gas to produce sulphur. Obviously, the use of this method depends on a market for the recovered product, or on cheap and plentiful supplies of natural gas. One problem in the UK would be the high chloride content of coals, which would necessitate a pre-scrubber to remove the chlorides, and treatment of the liquid effluent so produced.

Absorption of sulphur dioxide in spray driers is the second approach deserving mention. For a long time, dry flue gas cleaning remained largely unpromising, and attention was focused on alternative scrubbing techniques using alkaline slurries or liquids, such as those described above.

In the dry scrubbing process a lime slurry reagent is prepared with an excess of undissolved solids of about 10%. The slurry is first dispersed as an abundant spray of fine droplets in the size range of 50–80 μm diameter. At typical flue gas temperatures of 160–190 °C, water evaporates rapidly from the droplets to precipitate out some of the dissolved lime. When the water content has been reduced to about one quarter of the original, the solids within each droplet begin to touch and hinder continued evaporation. Throughout this rapid drying process, the rate of $SO_2$ absorption depends critically on the changing geometry of the slurry droplets and the speed with which $SO_2$ diffuses through the different gas/liquid/solid constituents and their boundaries. With continued evaporation, pore spaces begin to open up between the minute grains of solid material so enabling gas to diffuse directly into the lime reagent and increase the rate of absorption.

The end product is a dry powder mixture of unreacted calcium hydroxide, together with calcium sulphite ($CaSO_3$), calcium sulphate ($CaSO_4$), and the dry products of combustion from the furnace (fly ash). For economy, a part of this material is returned to the slurry tank; the remainder is discarded.

In the arrangement shown in Figure 73, a rotary atomiser is mounted in the top of a large spray chamber. It has specially hardened wheel surfaces to resist abrasion by fly ash in the recirculated fraction of the regenerated slurry. In a representative installation, the flow rate of the slurry could be in the range of 20 to 40 tonnes per hour. This large throughput needs appropriate equipment to handle it, as shown by the scale of the atomiser in Figure 73. Part of the dry solids is recovered from the spray absorber module; the remaining gas-borne fraction is trapped in the dry collector, which can be either a bag filter or an electrostatic precipitator.

While there may be gaps in our understanding of the physics and chemistry of the process at a detailed and sophisticated level, it has been claimed to have substantial advantages over some competitive wet scrubbing systems. The process is essentially dry, simple to control and flexible in meeting the demand of varying furnace loads. Automatic control can be applied relatively easily in order to maintain, for example, sulphur dioxide removal efficiencies at better than 90% in a single unit. This performance can be upgraded if necessary, with a corresponding penalty of an increased consumption of the lime absorbent, leading to more waste for disposal.

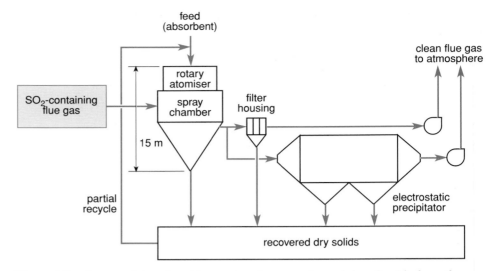

**Figure 73**  *A spray drier absorbing system for removing sulphur dioxide from the waste gases discharged from a furnace.*

The spray drying absorbing process is reliable and applicable to the control of other acidic gases. There are few moving parts and no significant corrosion problems requiring special materials of construction. With no direct wet and dry interface, troubles associated with wet scrubbing, such as flow-line blockage or scale deposition, are virtually absent. As the waste gases are not excessively cooled, plume rise suffers little, and the nuisance of wet acidic deposits is largely eliminated. The end-product is a dry powder that can be handled and disposed of relatively easily, without sludge handling equipment. Fly ash and metal contaminants are incorporated within a waste that may be disposed in landfill (more of this later).

*Technical aspects concerning raw materials for desulphurisation and disposal of products*

A large modern 2000 MW power station burns some 4.5–5 million tonnes of coal each year, and so you can imagine that the raw material and disposal quantities will be large. One estimate of the amounts of materials associated with a limestone/gypsum plant for a typical station (2000 MW) is summarised in Figure 74, while Table 25 compares the flows associated with two of the desulphurisation options.

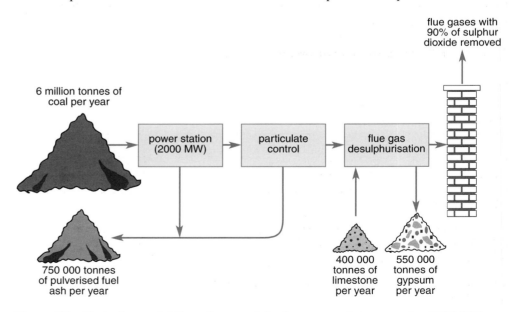

**Figure 74**  *Typical material flows for a coal-fired power station generating 2000 MW.*

**Table 25** *Principal annual imports and exports (tonnes) from flue gas desulphurisation at a 2000-MW power station*

| Process | Wellman–Lord | Limestone/gypsum |
|---|---|---|
| $SO_2$ removal efficiency | 90% | 90% |
| *Imports:* | | |
| limestone (solid) | 30 000 | 400 000 |
| lime (solid) | 3000 | 3000 |
| caustic soda (liquid) | 40 000 | |
| natural gas | $3 \times 10^7 \, m^3$ | |
| *Exports:* | | |
| sulphur (solid) | 75 000 | |
| or sulphuric acid (liquid) | 280 000 | |
| gypsum (solid) | | 560 000 |
| *By-products:* | | |
| calcium chloride (solid) | 25 000 | 25 000 |
| sodium sulphate (solid) | 30 000 | |
| *Waste water:* | | |
| treated | $2 \times 10^6$ | $2 \times 10^6$ |
| wastewater sludge | 15 000 | 40 000 |

76% **load factor**, coal 2% S, 0.4% Cl, no S retention in ash.

### SAQ 52

Write a balanced chemical equation for the limestone/gypsum desulphurisation reaction, and confirm by calculation the limestone requirements and gypsum production indicated in Figure 74 and Table 25.

Obviously, the supply of raw materials and the disposal of waste products must be in an environmentally acceptable manner, and marketable products can help achieve this. Unfortunately there are limited markets in the UK, as Table 26 for the 2000-MW power station example shows.

**Table 26** *FGD products as a proportion of existing UK markets*

| | |
|---|---|
| $H_2SO_4$ | 10–12% |
| Sulphur | 10–12% |
| Gypsum | 15–20% |

For sulphuric acid it would be difficult to put the equivalent of one power station's output into a single chemical works. A similar problem exists for gypsum, of which over 500 000 tonnes per year of marketable product could be produced from a 2000-MW station.

It is evident that solving one pollution problem may cause others, and the best practicable environmental option must be followed, although social, political and economic issues also play influential roles.

To remind you again of the options for dealing with $SO_2$, we have essentially to decide between:

- removing sulphur from the fuel;
- desulphurising combustion products;.

- using low sulphur fuels (e.g. natural gas);

- eliminating fossil fuels (e.g. go nuclear);

- dispersing combustion products from tall chimneys.

In addition, improving the user efficiency of electricity use reduces the demand and thereby reduces the primary fuel requirement.

By now, you may be aware that the UK plan for achieving these reductions involves fitting flue gas desulphurisation on power stations (8000 MW$_e$) to achieve one-third of the sulphur dioxide emissions required by the 1988 EC directive. The balance is to be achieved through measures such as construction of combined cycle gas turbines (see **combined heat and power** entry in set book), and the use of low sulphur-content fuels. These may be cheaper but have associated political and social implications beyond the scope of this course.

*Options for nitrogen oxides control*

Inexpensive combustion modifications can lower NO$_x$ emissions by up to 50% for new plant and 30–40% for existing plant, and the UK plan involves fitting low-NO$_x$ burners (e.g. Figure 50) to 12 large coal-fired power stations. Other countries plan to use selective catalytic reduction (SCR) or selective non-catalytic reduction (SNCR) to achieve greater reductions. The non-catalytic method is an application of a reaction such as:

$$4NO + 4NH_3 + O_2 = 4N_2 + 6H_2O$$

Ammonia (NH$_3$) is introduced into the furnace or flue at 800–1000 °C in the presence of oxygen which occurs as a result of the excess air supply for efficient combustion. The above reaction occurs and NO is reduced within 0.5 s, although poor mixing may impede efficient control of the pollutant. Use of a catalyst in the SCR option has been more successful. The chemical reaction is the same, but occurs more efficiently in the presence of a catalyst such as copper oxide (CuO) on titanium dioxide (TiO$_2$), the latter carrier being preferred to alternatives owing to its sulphur resistance. Problems with these options for control of NO include cost and the corrosion that may occur owing to reaction of excess ammonia with sulphur trioxide to produce ammonium hydrogen sulphate, which is acidic.

---

### SAQ 53

A packed bed absorption system for gas cleaning is to meet the following specification. Determine the flow rate of the sodium hydroxide solution to achieve this specification.

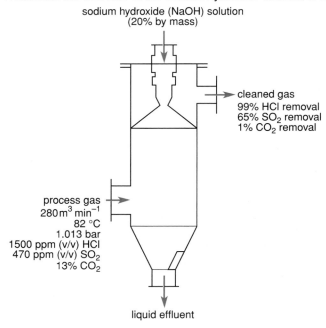

---

## 5.4   Dispersion from chimneys

The dispersion and behaviour of pollutants in the atmosphere is fundamental to the study of air pollution and its control. However, I have left the consideration of dispersion from chimneys until this late stage because it should be considered as a control option only after all others have been examined and applied.

### 5.4.1   Plume rise

The gases emitted from a chimney have a certain efflux velocity caused by a fan within the system, and may be buoyant if they are warmer than the surrounding air. Thus, in the absence of downwash and downdraught (see below), the gases rise above the physical height of the chimney owing to their momentum and buoyancy. The plume continues to rise by virtue of the density difference between the hot gases and the atmosphere, and the path of the plume bends over in the direction of the wind (Figure 75). The plume grows larger by turbulent diffusion, drawing air into it from its surroundings, and continues to rise until buoyancy effects are outweighed by the turbulence effects. The effective chimney height is the sum of the actual chimney height and the plume rise, and the benefit is that the chimney structure itself may be lower than would otherwise be required for effective dispersion.

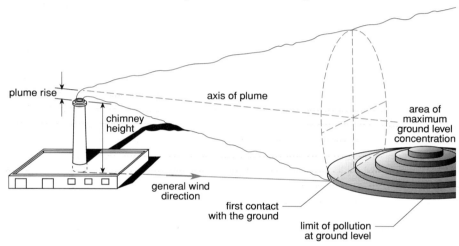

**Figure 75**   *Ideal plume behaviour showing plume rise.*

### 5.4.2   Lapse rate and plume behaviour

In the absence of local effects described next, the behaviour of a plume is influenced primarily by the stability of the atmosphere, and examples of this were given in Section 3.

### 5.4.3   Effects of buildings

The turbulence around buildings can have a major influence on the behaviour of a plume from a chimney. For most sharp-edged buildings the air flow separates immediately at the front edge of the building and the resulting region of disturbed flow surrounds the building up to twice its height and between five to ten times its height downwind (Figure 76).

A reverse flow zone is known as the cavity zone, in which a high level of turbulence exists. Beyond the cavity zone a strong mixing motion still exists, although the flow gradually reverts to the undisturbed flow pattern. Two aspects are significant in terms of the positive and negative pressure zones and eddies existing around buildings. First, there is the possibility that the release may re-enter the building, and second there is the impact on dispersion. Re-entry is clearly undesirable, and discharge above the cavity zone should avoid this problem. As the height of the eddy on the lee of the building extends to 1.3–2 times the building height, the chimney needs discharge at this height to avoid re-entry.

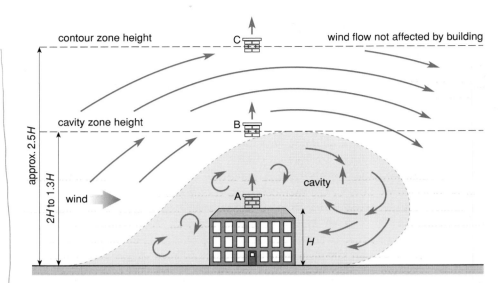

**Figure 76** *Building wake effects on plume behaviour. A chimney discharge at A may allow re-entry of emissions to the building. Discharge at B will avoid re-entry, but air pollution at ground level may result. Discharge at C avoids re-entry and gives maximal dispersion.* ↙ *thru dowdraught*

There is still the possibility that the plume may be drawn to ground level in the low pressure region by the effect known as *downdraught*. A general rule in use since 1932 suggests that a chimney should be 2.5 times the height of any building within a radius of twice the chimney height to be reasonably confident that downdraught will not occur. However, a chimney is a structure itself, and will therefore interfere with the wind flow. A low pressure region is formed immediately downwind, and this effect, known as *downwash*, may cause the plume to be drawn into this. Downwash effectively lowers the height of a chimney and so is to be avoided. Wind tunnel studies have shown that if the efflux velocity is 1.5 times the wind speed, downwash is minimised. The drag of the ground reduces the wind speed, and so the taller the chimney the greater the windspeed at its top. It would be too cumbersome to have a scale of efflux velocity with chimney height and according to location, so recommendations in project guidance notes and other guides suggest that chimneys and vents should be designed to have an efflux velocity not less than 15 m s$^{-1}$. Lower values are allowed in special circumstances such as for small boilers.

Another problem may occur when a wet gas cleaning system is in use. The liquid, typically water, may allow a thin film to form on the inside chimney surface. This film may be broken by a high gas velocity, and droplets are stripped off, carried in the gas stream and fall to the ground near to the chimney. If pollutants are dissolved in the liquid, a local nuisance is possible, and to avoid this, a lower velocity of 9 m s$^{-1}$ is recommended in such systems.

---

### SAQ 54

Distinguish between downwash and downdraught.

### SAQ 55

How may downwash be avoided?

---

## 5.5 Odours – how to approach solving a common yet difficult type of air pollution problem

Unpleasant odours, like excessive noise, are an increasing source of complaint about air quality. They are often particularly difficult to deal with, but in view of their frequency, we will deal with them as a special case. Some offensive odours (such as **hydrogen sulphide**) are due to toxic gases, but others, perhaps more offensive, may be non-toxic at the concentrations in which we encounter them. Odours from processes are often complex mixtures of many substances, each of which may be present at very low concentrations, but above the **odour threshold**. One common definition refers to odour thresholds as representing the lowest concentration at which the smell can be detected by 50% of the members of a testing panel. The sense of smell is remarkably sensitive, but is a subjective response for which there is no equivalent instrumental method of measurement; we cannot apply an 'A-weighting' as we do to represent human response to noise. For this reason, we use an odour panel to assess odour strengths. Certain chemical analysis techniques, such as gas chromatography and mass spectrometry, may help identify individual components in a process odour in order to assist in the choice of an abatement method involving chemical reaction, but the ultimate criterion is smell. It is important to remember the point made previously that since the time period over which we respond to a smell may be of the order of seconds, any representation of concentration over longer periods is inappropriate because peaks may be missed. Refer back to Figure 40 if you are not clear about this important point.

One way of assessing an odour emission is to collect a sample from a chimney or duct into a special container that will not adsorb components from the sample. The sample is then diluted with known amounts of air and the diluted mixture presented to panellists who judge whether they can detect the smell. The procedure is repeated until a dilution is reached at which half of the panel members detect no odour. This 'dilution to threshold' is used as a measure of odour strength, which is expressed in *odour units*, a dimensionless ratio. As an example, if the odour of 1 volume of carbon tetrachloride diluted with 10 000 volumes of uncontaminated air is not detected by half an odour panel, the strength of the odour is 10 000 odour units. So, the greater the number of dilutions with odour-free air necessary to bring an odorous emission to the threshold, the stronger the odour. The number of odour units, therefore, is analogous to pollutant concentration. Some typical odour strengths are shown in Table 27. Background odours in rural areas are typically 30 odour units in concentration.

**Table 27  *Typical odour strengths***

| Process | Odour strength (odour units) |
| --- | --- |
| Chicken farming (15 000 birds) | 600 |
| Fishmeal processing (white fish) | 150 000 |
| Potato crisps (1 000 000 t y$^{-1}$) | 275 000 |
| Animal waste rendering: | |
| ventilation | 6000 |
| process | 1 350 000 |

Dilution with air may offer a solution to an odour problem, but dispersion alone is not good practice for controlling air pollution as many odour thresholds are very low indeed (odour strengths very high).

What can we do about an odour problem? The sequence we will follow demonstrates a typical route towards solving many air pollution problems, and is represented in Figure 77.

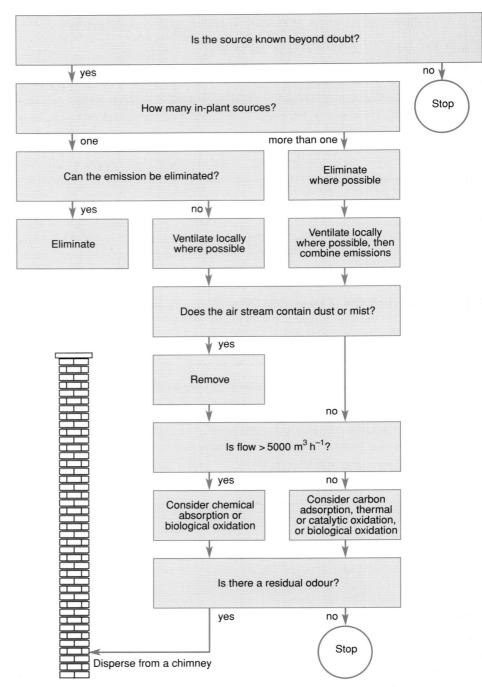

**Figure 77**   *Flow diagram for solving an air pollution problem.*

If there have been complaints about odours, the first thing is to analyse the complaints. Do they relate to wind directions as shown by a wind rose? Plotting a pollution rose should indicate the direction of the source, and may indicate that the suspected process is not in fact the cause of the problem.

When the source is identified, the most important step is to see if emissions can be prevented or eliminated at its origin. Potentially, this approach works towards a guarantee of limiting pollution from the process forever. However, some escape of air pollutants is likely to be unavoidable, and so the next step is to capture these emissions. Total enclosure or local ventilation of the process(es) can be designed to capture the emissions in the smallest volume of air. The more dilute the pollutant the more difficult its removal from an air stream. Then we have to consider the most appropriate removal method, bearing in mind the odour strength and the flow rate. For flows up to around 5000 $m^3$ $h^{-1}$ the cheapest option is often adsorption in carbon. As odours are often due to organic compounds, they can often be destroyed by burning, so incineration is usually effective. Unfortunately, it is also expensive owing to the fuel supply required, for the concentration of organics is rarely high enough to burn without auxiliary fuel. Temperatures over around 800 °C for a residence time of 1 second are typical requirements for good combustion of the odorous components (you should remember the essentials of good combustion from earlier in the course). The temperature may be lowered by about 200 °C by using a catalytic incinerator.

Other oxidation routes can employ biological or chemical oxidation. Chemical oxidation uses sodium hypochlorite or potassium permanganate in wet absorption systems of the type considered previously. As you may imagine, skilled attention is necessary for chemical methods.

Soil or peat beds offer a biological oxidation route. The microorganisms in soil can destroy odours, and soil beds have been used for odour control for several decades. Their main problem is the large area required (typically 1 m$^2$ can handle flows of only 10 m$^3$ h$^{-1}$). Fibrous peat beds are an alternative and are widely used throughout Europe. Their ease of operation and maintenance make them attractive for smaller organisations.

Only after considering all of these options and applying the most appropriate is dispersion from a chimney considered. It may offer the cheapest solution to the faint, residual odour remaining after treatment.

## SAQ 56

As a revision exercise, identify the appropriate units for expressing concentrations of the following air pollutants.

(a) Carbon monoxide.

(b) Stratospheric ozone.

(c) The odour from intensive chicken farming.

(d) Suspended particulate matter.

## 5.6 Some examples of best available technology

Some examples will now be given of the type of control considered best available technology (BAT) for selected processes at the time of writing. These examples are adapted from current guidance notes from HMIP.

### 5.6.1 Gas turbines

An industrial gas turbine engine is an internal combustion engine which produces power by the controlled burning of fuel. Fuel is fed to a compressed air supply in a combustion chamber and ignited. The heat produced causes the gas to expand rapidly, and further compressed air defines the flame and controls the temperature. The expanding gases drive a turbine which drives the air compressor, and the extra power drives a load such as an alternator. Most of the energy is removed from the gas flow by the turbine, but the gases are still sufficiently hot (typically 500 °C) to justify recovery of heat in a waste heat boiler which can generate steam to drive an additional turbine and alternator. The overall efficiency is therefore increased. (See **combined heat and power** in set book.) The use of gas or distillate fuel oils in combined-cycle gas turbine installations is much more energy efficient (over 50%) than conventional fossil-fuel-fired generation plant (about 35%), and this inherently reduces air pollution emissions.

## SAQ 57

Consider why fuels such as coal (and residual fuel oils) tend to be precluded from the direct firing to drive the turbine, and suggest a route for dealing with the problem.

With gas turbines, the main source of air pollution is the formation of oxides of nitrogen. It is not possible to prevent their formation, and therefore it is necessary to use BAT to minimise the emissions.

The least expensive system to install is water or steam injection, which reduces the temperature of the combustor by absorption of heat, and so reduces the formation of thermal oxides of nitrogen. You should recall the temperature dependence of the process generating this pollutant, as illustrated in Figure 3. A 50-MW$_{th}$ input installation typically requires about 3 t h$^{-1}$ of water to achieve 65% reduction in nitrogen oxides formation.

A potential option being developed for the future involves staged combustion by either burning fuel rich and then quenching with air (see Figure 50), or burning lean and injecting fuel at a second stage. Avoiding burning close to the stoichiometric ratio reduces oxides of nitrogen formation, but introduces technical problems of flame stability.

Selective catalytic reduction, as outlined previously, is a post-combustion technique which is expensive to install and to operate, but is the only option for dealing with oxides of nitrogen from fuel-bound nitrogen compounds.

### 5.6.2  Chemical waste incinerators

The gases released from a chemical waste incinerator include HCl, HF and SO$_2$. These gases differ in their physico-chemical properties, and so two stages of gas scrubbing are preferred. In the first stage, HCl and HF, together with metal vapours such as mercury, are washed out with water at low pH (0–3), while the second stage removes SO$_2$ with NaOH (pH 6–8). Spray towers, venturis and packed or plate towers are suitable for these wet absorption methods, which are the most expensive owing to the need for circulation and liquor treatment systems, as well as plume reheating to restore buoyancy. You will find a flow diagram of such a system in Unit 10.

Spray absorption techniques are also suitable for pollution control in these plant. In spray absorption, the absorbent is injected as a solution (such as NaOH) or a suspension (e.g. 'milk of lime' – a suspension of calcium hydroxide in water) into a spray drier where it reacts with the acidic gases and converts them to a dry particulate state by the processes described previously. The final, and cheapest, option is to use a dry method in which powdered lime is injected into the gas stream passing through a reaction tower. In both cases, particulate control techniques must follow the spray drier or reactor.

The residues from a wet scrubber are in the form of a slurry. The solids separated from this can normally be landfilled at a suitable licensed site, because heavy metals are usually as hydroxides or are retained in the liquid. The liquid wastes themselves may be minimised by using heat from the flue gases to evaporate water from the slurry. The resulting solid residue may be treated as that from a semi-dry scrubber. These and dry scrubbers produce residues from which the metals are leachable, and so are unsuitable for landfill.

Particulate matter may be controlled by electrostatic precipitators or fabric filters. In terms of removal efficiency, the preference is for fabric filters, which also allow further neutralisation reactions between the trapped solids and the gas stream. As *TCDD*s (see the set book and Unit 3, Section 9.1.3 if you cannot remember what these pollutants are) may also be associated with particulate matter, the better retention on fabric filters is a further advantage. The residues from the bag filter serving dry or semi-dry systems contain leachable heavy metals and so may not be landfilled.

---

### SAQ 58

Combustion of waste in a hazardous waste incinerator produces 280 cubic metres per minute of flue gas at 400 °C and 101.3 kPa, with hydrogen chloride and sulphur dioxide being present at 20 000 and 350 ppm (v/v) respectively. Process guidance notes indicate that the release limits expressed as half-hourly average values are 10 mg m$^{-3}$ for

HCl and 50 mg m$^{-3}$ for SO$_2$ at standard conditions of 273 K and 101.3kPa. It is proposed to achieve these limits by cleaning the flue gases with a spray drier using Ca(OH)$_2$ as the reactant. Assuming stoichiometric relationships between the reactants, determine the feed rate of absorbent required. You may need to refer back to Unit 3, Section 5 for help with this question.

### 5.6.3 Municipal waste incineration/sewage sludge incineration

Efficient combustion using the essentials of adequate reaction time, high temperature, turbulence and sufficient air ensures that most combustion generated pollutants are avoided, but TCDDs present more of a problem. There have been suggestions that although they are not stable at high temperatures, they have nevertheless been detected under such conditions, and can also be formed from basic building blocks in post-combustion regions (Figure 78).

The combustion gases are rapidly cooled to below 250 °C by a water spray, often followed by a caustic soda spray, to minimise the formation of TCDDs in cooling stages of the process. Priority is given to preventing TCDD formation, rather than their removal, which is difficult, although spray driers or activated carbon beds achieve some success.

Acid gases may be removed from the combustion gases by wet absorption, semi-dry or dry systems. In wet systems, the use of spray towers, venturi systems, packed towers or plate towers are the options. Semi-dry systems use spray driers fed with a lime slurry from which the water is evaporated by the heat of the exhaust gases. Dry systems involve the injection of lime powder into the exhaust gases in a tower, where most of the powder is entrained and subsequently removed in the downstream particulate control equipment. Costs decline in the sequence given, with wet systems being most expensive owing to circulation and treatment equipment for the liquor, and plume reheat equipment to avoid a visible plume through water vapour condensation.

Particulate matter is removed by wet or dry electrostatic precipitators or fabric filters. The last is most efficient and allows further neutralisation between the exhaust gas and trapped particulate matter. Fabric filters also prevent a notorious problem from incinerators, namely the passage of paper char through electrostatic precipitators. Despite a relatively large physical size, paper char behaves as a relatively small cross-sectional area in an electrostatic precipitator and may escape collection. Fabric filters avoid this problem.

### 5.6.4 Waste oil burners

Waste oils are defined (EC Directive 87/101) as 'any mineral-based lubricating or industrial oils which have become unfit for the use for which they were originally intended, and in particular used combustion engine oils and gear box oils, and also mineral lubricating oils from turbines and hydraulic oils.' If controlled in an acceptable manner, burning of waste oil may represent BPEO.

Typical requirements for waste oil burners include having plant that enables oil fuels to be burned efficiently. A fuel specification agreed between the operator and Inspectorate depends on the plant and arrestment equipment used at a site. Thus, fuel specification will be more exacting where minimal pollution abatement is offered. The abatement systems available for gaseous emissions include wet scrubbers, bag filters and electrostatic precipitators, and, as ever, the choice depends on the specific application and fuel quality. These systems should deal with the large number of metals and metalloids which may be found in waste oils and can be released in aerosol form during combustion.

Gaseous emissions may include acidic gases such as hydrogen chloride. Wet arrestment plant may be needed to comply with the emission limits set in the guidance note. Oxides of nitrogen are limited by design of the combustion system and by specifying low nitrogen oxide-forming burners.

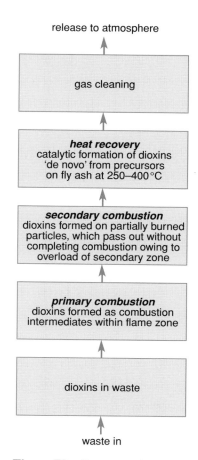

**Figure 78** *Routes to the formation of TCDDs or dioxins.*

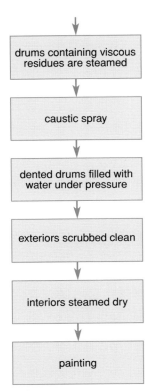

**Figure 79** *Typical sequence of operations in drum recovery by liquid cleaning.*

### 5.6.5  *Drum reclamation*

From the waste management units you will recall that drum reuse provides a good model for resource conservation. However, this activity is not without its environmental implications; indeed 'drum manufacturing and reconditioning' is a prescribed process under the provisions made in the Environmental Protection Act 1990. Here, we will consider only the reconditioning process.

Drum reconditioning involves two distinct phases – drum recovery and cleaning, followed by repainting. Drums may originate from a wide variety of sources and via a chain of handlers, and so may contain many different types of residue with a great potential for causing odour nuisance. The recovery and cleaning phase may be achieved by two routes – liquid cleaning or drum burning. This introduces some legal complications. Drum burning is controlled by HMIP; liquid cleaning techniques are subject to control under Part I of the Control of Pollution Act 1974; and the repainting or 'coating process' is subject to local authority control over air pollution. Here, however, we are concerned only with the processes rather than the detailed legal implications.

Drum recovery by liquid cleaning may follow a sequence similar to that in Figure 79. The first stage of cleaning can give rise to serious nuisance, although there is also a constant potential problem from drums awaiting treatment. Bearing in mind the potential costs of gas cleaning systems for odour abatement, one solution may be to avoid handling drums with serious odour nuisance potential; they may be better handled by drum burning. Drums containing residues with lower odour potential may be better treated by washing out water-miscible materials before steaming. Clearly, liquid wastes themselves have the potential for both odour and water pollution, and must be contained for appropriate treatment.

Drum burning is a more complicated process because it involves a furnace operation (Figure 80). Typically, drums have their lids removed by machine and are placed open end down on a conveyor belt passing through the furnace. The speed of the conveyor may be varied to ensure that the residence time in the furnace is sufficient to allow complete combustion of the residues. The furnace is typically heated by oil burners and an ***after-burner*** chamber is similarly heated. An after-burner is effectively a thermal incinerator incorporated into the furnace system, and its purpose is to ensure that combustible materials are completely burnt to ensure an emission free from visible smoke, which in no circumstances should exceed the equivalent of Ringelmann Shade 1 as described in BS 2742: 1969. You should recall this phraseology from Section 4.1.

After burning, drums may pass to an abrasive blasting chamber where they are subjected to both external and internal cleaning. Dust from the process is considerable and is subject to an emission limit for particulate concentration of 50 mg m$^{-3}$. A fabric filter will provide control to this standard and a low level discharge will minimise any impact on the local community should there be an abnormal release of particulate matter. The drums then pass to a repair section and are finally painted in a paint spray booth. This coating process is one of several for which guidance notes provide emission limits for several pollutants including volatile organic compounds, which must not exceed 50 mg m$^{-3}$ expressed as a 15-minute mean concentration in terms of total carbon. The expressed aim in the guidance note is for the reduction and eventual elimination of the use of volatile organic substances in surface coatings. Alternative approaches to achieve this may be:

(a)  water-based coatings containing a low organic solvent content (typically less than 10% by mass);

(b)  higher solids content coatings;

(c)  powder coatings;

(d)  organic solvent-free liquid coatings;

(e)  radiation-curing coatings (e.g. UV and electron beam curing).

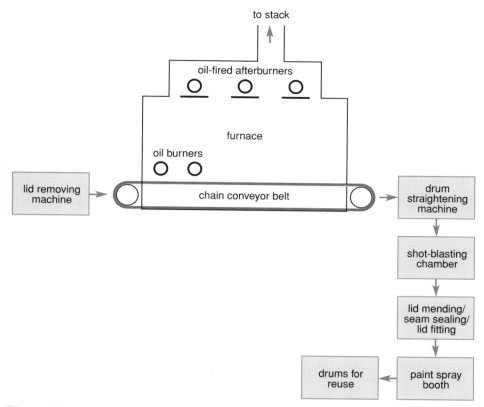

**Figure 80**   *Typical sequence of operations in drum reconditioning by drum burning.*

---

### SAQ 59

Some, but not all, of the potential releases of pollutants to atmosphere have been mentioned in the description of drum reclamation involving drum burning. Examine the description of the process again and consider from where releases may arise; mark these on a modified version of Figure 80. Also consider what air pollution control systems may be appropriate to deal with the unavoidable emissions.

---

## 5.6.6   Motor vehicle respraying

It is important to draw a distinction here between the spraying of motor vehicles during manufacture and the re-spraying of road vehicles. The scale of operation during manufacture is considerably greater; consequently, more demanding controls are required over the emissions. Thus, as we saw in the solution to SAQ 50(c), incineration is an option for the control of odours from manufacturing, but this is not appropriate for the scale of respraying activities. Nor are alternatives to organic solvent-based paints available at present.

Processes for the respraying of road vehicles are common and are prescribed for local authority control under the Environmental Protection (Prescribed Processes and Substances) Regulations 1991 (SI472: 1991) if more than a specified amount of organic solvents are likely to be used in any 12-month period. The paint spraying is typically carried out in a totally enclosed proprietary-type spray booth. Figure 81 illustrates such a booth, which is designed to meet emission concentrations set out in the guidance note for the process.

The main features of such a spray booth are that spraying is carried out in a totally enclosed area to minimise fugitive emissions, and the booth is maintained under negative pressure. The extracted air passes through filters and a water spray system before discharge from a stack. The stack must be 3 m above the roof ridge height of any building, within five times its uncorrected height, and never less than 8 m above ground level. Notice also that the paint curing or baking is carried out at a temperature

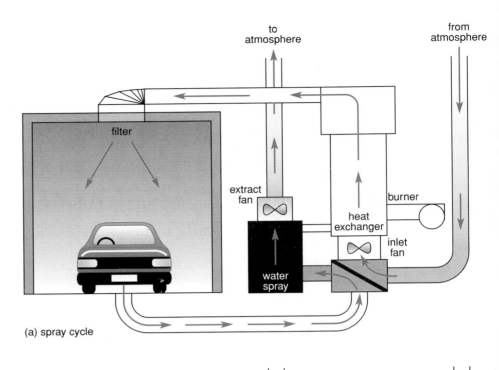

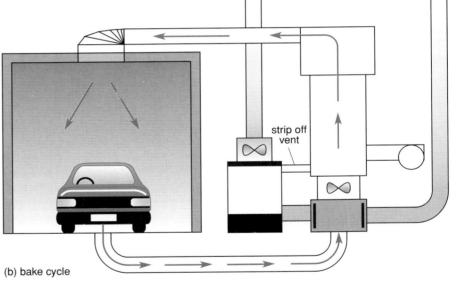

**Figure 81** *Representation of a typical paint spray booth for vehicle respraying. (a) During the spray cycle fresh air is drawn into the booth and the extract air passes through a water spray before discharge from a stack. (b) During the bake cycle the air is recirculated.*

of around 80 °C. Heat recovery is practised by recycling the bulk of the gas stream while the baking takes place. Although designed for economy of operation, this has a side benefit of reducing carbon dioxide emissions.

Paint mixing and equipment cleaning is usually carried out in a separate area which is provided with local extract ventilation. The discharge from this should not result in an offensive odour outside the process boundary.

### SAQ 60

Justify the height requirements for the flue serving a paint spray booth, and comment on the efflux velocity you would expect through the flue. Also comment on the suggestion made previously that the discharge from abrasive blast cleaning should be at low level to minimise impact on the community.

---

**SAQ 61**

Work through the scheme in Figure 77 and suggest how the requirement of no offensive odour at the process boundary may be met for the paint mixing area.

---

## 5.7 Summary

The design of ventilation systems is primarily concerned with the effective removal of offensive or hazardous components from a workplace or other indoor environment, but the potential impact on the external environment must not be ignored. Air quality requirements for the workplace are less demanding than for the external atmosphere, because people not at work include the old, the young and the sick, all of whom may be more susceptible to air pollutants than those at work. However, the first step in air pollution control is to study the process releasing pollutants. Can the releases be minimised or their nature changed to a less objectionable or less harmful form? We examined some options for minimising releases in Section 5.2.

If waste minimisation still allows releases to occur, the emissions collected by the ventilation system should so far as is practicable be treated to reduce the amount of undesirable component in the emission. In Section 5.3 we examined some of the technologies available for control. A variety of devices is available to treat waste gases to prevent discharge of potential pollutants, and only after these have been applied should the residual emission be discharged to atmosphere. This sequence has long been established in air pollution control law, and is clearly set out in the Environmental Protection Act 1990.

Upon release to the atmosphere, transport and dispersion mechanisms (introduced in Section 3) lead to a reduction in concentration of components in the plume. Ideally this occurs to such a degree that by the time the components reach ground level, their concentration is so low that there will be no adverse effect on a receptor, whether it be animal, plant or material. Dispersion is only appropriate for dealing with gaseous pollutants; particulate matter should be controlled by gas cleaning systems.

# 6  TRANSPORT AND AIR POLLUTION – AN OUTLINE

The classic air pollution episodes in the first half of this century were associated with emissions from stationary sources of air pollutants accumulating under stable atmospheric conditions, as we saw from Section 2. Nowadays we find the same weather conditions causing different problems, and the episode on 13 December 1991 provides ample evidence. (You should recall this episode of high nitrogen oxides pollution from Section 2 and TV 7.) In fact, the motor car and other forms of transport often get bad press coverage, as examples earlier in these units have shown. Most of this text has been concerned with stationary sources of air pollution, and to cover mobile sources in equal detail would expand it beyond reasonable limits. In this section, therefore, we will review only some of the issues relating to transport.

## 6.1  The role of traffic as a pollution source

If you refer back to Figure 5 you will be reminded of the major contribution that road transport makes to total emissions of air pollutants in the UK. If you combine this information with the trends in air pollutant emissions you calculated in SAQ 42, the significant role of transport to air pollution in the UK should be apparent to you. Contributions elsewhere may be more striking. In Melbourne, Victoria, for example, motor vehicles contribute 75% of the nitrogen oxides in the air.

Cars are the major source of nitrogen oxides emissions, and increasingly demanding emission limits in the UK came into force in 1992 as a result of EC directives. Some EC countries want more demanding standards, and plan measures such as reductions in car populations, encouragement to use smaller cars and developments in fuel efficiency. Such pressures make it likely that EC regulations will tighten continually, and similar controls will spread to eastern Europe, where low vehicle densities at present are likely to grow in the future. This raises the important point that nitrogen oxides and hydrocarbons (or VOCs) are precursors to secondary pollutants such as ozone, as we discussed in detail in Section 3.4.3. Transfrontier transport of the primary pollutants makes international agreements important.

Statistics suggest that the overall health and environmental impact of transport includes 100 000 annual deaths from accidents, a greater number of injuries, and an estimated 110 million people seriously affected by traffic noise above 65 dB (OECD, 1987). In the UK alone, estimates have been made that one-third of the population is at risk from traffic pollution, yet cars are predicted to increase in number from around 20 million in the early 1990s to 35 million in 2025.

## 6.2  Where does the pollution come from?

Burning fuel in an internal combustion engine produces three principal pollutants: carbon monoxide, nitrogen oxides and hydrocarbons, although the last is a generic term for many different compounds. Broadly, car exhaust gases include 1% by volume of hydrocarbons/carbon monoxide/nitrogen oxides, and 18% carbon dioxide.

Internal combustion engines run on a mixture of air and fuel. As with any combustion process, the air/fuel ratio is a most important variable in determining the amount of emissions and in developing technological solutions to reducing them.

Figure 82 shows the amount of carbon monoxide in the exhaust of a typical engine as a function of the air/fuel ratio. You will notice the similarity with the behaviour of a stationary furnace shown in Figure 51, in terms of the declining carbon monoxide concentration with increasing air supply. Typically, every kilogram of fuel requires 15 kg of air for a stoichiometric mixture, as you should recall from the Example in Section 1.1. This air/fuel ratio of around 15:1 is optimal for a conventional petrol

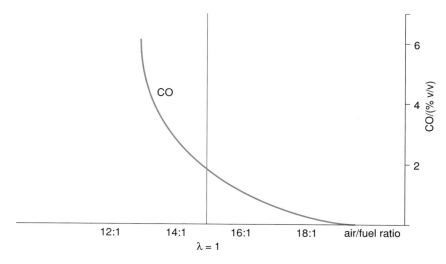

**Figure 82** *Carbon monoxide content of exhaust gases from a petrol-fuelled vehicle as a function of air/fuel ratio.*

engine, and is often expressed as $\lambda = 1$, with $\lambda$ (lambda) values above it being 'lean', while values below it are 'rich'.

We can draw similar curves for the other pollutants, and can combine them all on the same diagram to build up Figure 83 below. Carbon dioxide is an inevitable product of the combustion process, and can only be reduced by running fewer cars more economically in terms of fuel.

---

## SAQ 62

The magnitude of the units of pollutant concentrations need not be remembered, but study Figure 83 and rate the relative magnitude of emissions of the three pollutants.

---

## SAQ 63

Assuming an annual mileage of 10 000 miles, calculate the impact on the annual amount of carbon dioxide produced by the present and predicted vehicle population in the UK for 2025. Assume that current energy consumption is 35 miles to the gallon, but fuel efficiency is increased to 60 miles per gallon by 2025.

---

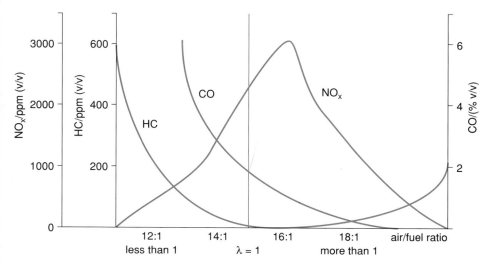

**Figure 83** *Gaseous pollutants in petrol-fuelled vehicle exhaust gases related to air/fuel ratio.*

The other pollutants may be controlled by various techniques. The first option is to adjust the air/fuel ratio to a region in which pollutant formation is minimised. Notice from Figure 83 that if we adjust the $\lambda$ value to more than 1, carbon monoxide and hydrocarbon concentrations in the exhaust gas initially decrease, but the hydrocarbon level then increases. Conversely, the nitrogen oxides increase and then decrease. So operating in a 'lean-burn' condition can reduce the emissions of two of the pollutants of concern. Unfortunately, hydrocarbon emissions increase, as we can see from Figure 84, which repeats Figure 83, but for convenience superimposes the lean-burn conditions.

As you may know from experience, it can be difficult to get a car to operate satisfactorily under lean-burn conditions – a cold engine misfiring is the result of not enough fuel vaporising in the cylinder and so behaving as a 'lean' mixture. You will also notice from Figure 84 that fuel efficiency increases as lean conditions are used, and this has been used as an argument in favour of this control option, since carbon dioxide emissions will also be reduced when fuel economy increases. However, the consensus has been that lean-burn conditions are unsuitable for meeting the increasingly demanding emission limits for the other pollutants, and especially the limits in the USA. To see why this is the case, we need to explore the other option for control – the catalytic converter.

Catalytic converters are similar to the catalysts used for catalytic incinerators described in Section 5.3.4, but of course are smaller. The modern catalyst is contained in a stainless steel box, similar in appearance to an exhaust silencer. A ceramic block within the box has a large surface area, such as is found in a honeycomb, with the result that the effective surface area has been equated to that of a football pitch. A coating of precious metal on this large surface area serves as the catalyst, which brings about the oxidation of hydrocarbons and carbon monoxide, while simultaneously promoting the reduction of nitrogen oxides. The simplest catalysts capable of being fitted to existing cars are uncontrolled and have no link to the air/fuel ratio. Consequently, they may remove only up to 50% of the pollutants ($CO/HC/NO_x$), since there is no engine management system to optimise engine efficiency. Three-way catalysts achieve cleanest exhaust emissions when they operate with an engine management system. A 'lambda probe' is located between the engine and catalyst and measures the oxygen in the exhaust gases. The air/fuel mixture may then be adjusted appropriately to ensure most efficient operation of the catalyst.

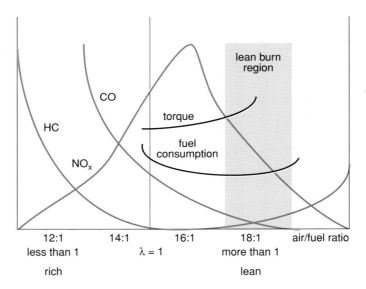

**Figure 84**  *Gaseous pollutants in petrol-fuelled vehicle exhaust gases related to air/ fuel ratio and lean-burn conditions.*

Catalysts are not necessarily the panacea that they may appear to be. Unfortunately, while three-way catalysts eliminate 90% of CO/HC/NO$_x$, it is reported that they make the engine 7% less efficient. Thus carbon dioxide emissions increase. Catalysts also need to reach a temperature of 300 °C in order for them to become active, and since many journeys are over short distances, the catalyst may not be performing optimally as it requires time to warm up. There is also the need to protect the catalyst from poisoning – the problem you should recall from catalytic incinerators. In the specific case of car catalysts, the main concern is to avoid use of leaded petrol, as the lead additives will poison the catalyst.

### SAQ 64

Analyse the outlines of lean-burn and three-way catalyst approaches to emission control, and determine why they are incompatible for meeting stringent vehicle emission limits.

## 6.3   Exhausts are not the only source of air pollutants from cars

The gradual introduction of catalytic converters will significantly reduce pollution from individual vehicle exhausts, although the overall effect on atmospheric pollution will be slow as the existing fleet will only slowly be replaced by vehicles with catalysts. In addition, exhaust pipes are not the sole source of concern. Look at Figure 85, which relates to contributions to hydrocarbon emissions in western Europe.

Car exhausts and solvent use may be the major sources of hydrocarbons (VOCs), but controls over the lesser sources are also being introduced. Pressures for these developments stem both from the involvement of VOCs in photochemical reactions, and from concerns over substances such as benzene, which is a genotoxic carcinogen. Proposed EC controls will require the fitting of carbon canisters to cars. Canisters contain activated carbon and trap pollutants by adsorption using the same principles that we met in Section 5.3.4. They are standard in Japan and USA, and two types of canister design are possible (Figure 86). 'Small' canisters have a nominal capacity of 1 litre and are effective at controlling the normal 'breathing' of the fuel system caused by the expansion of vapour through solar heating, or from residual engine heat immediately after the vehicle is parked. Petrol vapour is trapped and returned to the fuel system as it breathes in. Pollution is thereby reduced and energy saved. 'Large' canisters have a capacity of 4–5 litres and offer the additional advantage of controlling evaporative losses during refuelling the vehicle.

Hydrocarbon emissions also arise from the petrol storage and distribution system. 'Stage I' controls relate to the distribution chain from refinery to filling station, while 'Stage II' controls deal with the point of refuelling at the petrol pump and involve suction systems attached to fuel pump nozzles. At present, EC proposals only require small canisters, but Stage II controls have been used for several years in Sweden, Switzerland and parts of the USA. Debate on the merits of Stage II and large canisters for the control of refuelling emissions continues, with oil companies favouring the

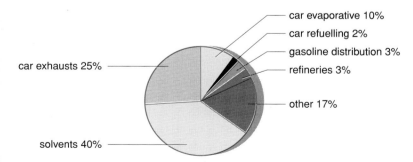

car evaporative 10%
car refuelling 2%
gasoline distribution 3%
refineries 3%
other 17%
car exhausts 25%
solvents 40%

**Figure 85**   *Contributions to hydrocarbon emissions in western Europe.*

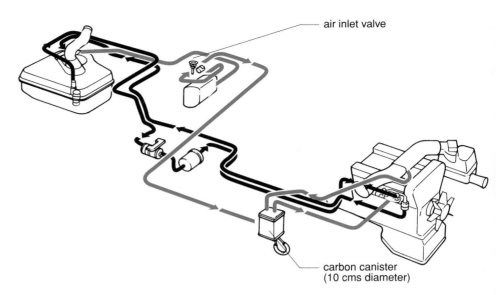

**Figure 86**  *Fuel and evaporative control systems. Additions for emission control over refuelling include: nozzle-actuated fuel tank vapour vent; enlarged carbon canister (20 cm diam.); purge control valve.*

large canister option, while car manufacturers prefer Stage II controls. The future requirements are uncertain, but it is noteworthy that large canisters as well as Stage II controls are being required in California to address the persistent problem of VOCs.

## 6.4   The diesel distinction

If we compare air pollutant emissions from diesel engines with those from equivalent petrol engines, we find that the former produce:

- fewer nitrogen oxides;

- considerably less carbon monoxide;

- fewer hydrocarbons;

- much greater particulate emissions.

While diesel emissions of $NO_x$ are less than from an uncontrolled petrol engine, they are greater than from a petrol vehicle with three-way catalyst. Hydrocarbons in the VOC context are less of a problem owing to the lower volatility of diesel fuel than petrol hydrocarbons, but are associated with carbonaceous particles formed by incomplete combustion. Exploring this point further, we need to note that a diesel engine operates by injecting fuel into a compressed air mass within the engine (hence the term 'compression ignition engine'). The diesel fuel must be broken into very fine droplets (atomised) which burn in the high temperature air (heated by compression). High temperatures and long combustion times will minimise the formation of particulate pollution in the exhaust, but high temperatures favour the formation of $NO_x$, as you will recall from Figure 3. Simultaneous control of both particulate and $NO_x$ formation is therefore thermodynamically and kinetically impossible. From the data in SAQ 42 it was apparent that 'smoke' pollution is increasing in urban areas, and this is attributed to diesel emissions of particulate matter. Excessive smoke from diesel engines can be caused by several factors, any of which result in incomplete combustion. A fault in the fuel management system, the ignition system, or excessive amounts of engine oil or transmission fluid leaking into the combustion chamber are possible causes. In general, smoke emissions indicate poor tuning or maintenance. Department of the Environment advice is for the public to report smoking diesel vehicles to the Department of Transport, but at present it is uncertain what action should be taken to deal with the problem.

## 6.5  *The magnitude of the emissions*

The magnitude of vehicle emissions of the various pollutants depends on the driving mode (Figure 87). For this reason, an instantaneous measurement of emissions is of relatively little use in an air pollution study, although a vehicle engineer may require such information.

For air pollution studies, aggregate pollution levels over driving cycles are most relevant. Typical cycles represent urban driving and high speed driving, and TV 7 shows a car undergoing an emission test on a chassis dynamometer. Differences between vehicles are significant, and the advent of catalyst and other engine modifications bring about changes over time. Emission factors are therefore continually in need of updating, and any figures quoted must be regarded as transient. As an illustration, however, Table 28 gives some examples of emission factors representing European averages.

*details not assessed*

**Table 28**  *Pollutant emission factors and energy consumption for representative vehicles*

| Transport mode | Fuel | Emission factors/(g km⁻¹) | | | | | | Energy consumption/ (MJ km⁻¹) |
| --- | --- | --- | --- | --- | --- | --- | --- | --- |
| | | $CO_2$ | $NO_x$ | VOC | CO | Particulates | $SO_2$ | |
| Light duty truck, <3.5 t: | petrol | | | | | | | |
| urban | | 590.7 | 4.5 | 7.0 | 70.0 | 0 | 0 | 10.7 |
| rural | | 265.0 | 7.5 | 5.5 | 55.0 | 0 | 0 | 4.8 |
| motorway | | 436 | 7.5 | 3.5 | 50.0 | 0 | 0 | 7.9 |
| Heavy duty truck, >16t: | diesel | | | | | | | |
| urban | | 1130.2 | 18.2 | 5.8 | 7.3 | 1.6 | 3.8 | 16.2 |
| rural | | 1158.1 | 24.1 | 3.0 | 3.7 | 1.6 | 3.9 | 16.6 |
| motorway | | 948.8 | 19.8 | 2.4 | 3.1 | 1.3 | 3.2 | 13.6 |

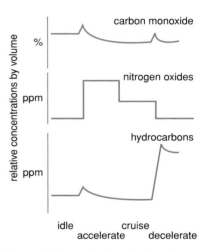

**Figure 87**  *Typical variations in emissions from petrol-fuelled vehicles related to driving mode.*

Emission factors are conventionally expressed in relation to distance travelled, but it is possible to relate the emissions to energy used. Taking $NO_x$ as an example, a petrol-engined truck in an urban area emits 4.5 g km⁻¹ and has an energy consumption of 10.7 MJ km⁻¹; hence the emission expressed as a function of energy use is:

$$4.5 \text{ g km}^{-1}/10.7 \text{ MJ km}^{-1} = 0.42 \text{ g MJ}^{-1}$$

Similarly, for the diesel vehicle, the $NO_x$ emission factor may be recalculated as:

$$18.2 \text{ g km}^{-1}/16.2 \text{ MJ km}^{-1} = 1.12 \text{ g MJ}^{-1}$$

This does not contradict the statement made previously that diesel vehicles emit lower $NO_x$ than equivalent petrol ones, because you should notice that our calculation here is comparing light-duty with heavy-duty vehicles. An advantage of expressing the emissions in relation to energy use is that we can now compare vehicle emissions with those from other energy sources. As an illustration, consider the emission factors for air pollutants from fossil-fuelled power stations in western Europe, as presented in Table 29.

**Table 29   *Emission factors per petajoule of electricity consumed for air pollutants emitted by fossil-fuelled power plant in western Europe***

| $CO_2/(kt\ PJ^{-1})$ | $CO/(t\ PJ^{-1})$ | $SO_2/(t\ PJ^{-1})$ | $NO_x/(t\ PJ^{-1})$ | $VOC/(t\ PJ^{-1})$ |
|---|---|---|---|---|
| 126.4 | 22 | 1514 | 375 | 8 |

PJ (petajoule) = $10^{15}$ J.

Let's return to our example of the diesel vehicle with the emission factor for $NO_x$ of 1.12 g $MJ^{-1}$. This equates to

$$1.12\ g\ MJ^{-1} \times 10^9\ MJ\ PJ^{-1} = 1.12 \times 10^9\ g\ PJ^{-1}$$
$$= 1.12 \times 10^3\ t\ PJ^{-1}$$

Notice how this compares with the emission factor from power plant. This illustrates why vehicle emissions contribute such a significant amount to air pollution in urban areas.

---

### SAQ 65

Follow a similar procedure to that in the example above to convert the emission factors in g $km^{-1}$ for all vehicle and driving modes to equivalent energy-based factors. When you have done this, compare the results with those for power plant.

---

## 6.6   Future perspectives

One policy dilemma was discussed in 1989 in a study carried out by the International Institute for Applied Systems Analysis, on future environments for Europe. The coming decades were expected to show a large increase in passenger and freight transport, particularly for cars, trucks and aircraft. By that time, supplies of clean oils may be relatively scarce, clean liquid fuels for transport may be prohibitively expensive, and choices will have to be made between environmental concerns and meeting the demands for transport. Even if abundant and relatively cheap liquid or gaseous fuels were to become available, the problems of $NO_x$ emissions as a by-product of high temperature combustion may not be solved. Hydrogen and methanol fuels may have attractions, but may also have as yet unknown environmental effects. Electric vehicles have many attractions, but the air pollution is transferred to the power station. The main disadvantage of electric vehicles is their range, but for deliveries in urban areas this is not unacceptable. In parts of the USA, a proportion of all new vehicle registrations must be electric powered.

Another view of the future was published by the Policy Studies Institute. Personal mobility was noted as one of the most keenly sought-after goals of most people, who want to travel to better jobs, to better shops, to places for leisure and so on. The motor car has brought about much of this mobility. Since the 1970s, total annual car mileage has more than doubled, growing at about three times the rate for coaches and buses, and twice the rate for heavy goods vehicles. Car ownership has also grown, but experience from overseas suggests that saturation is not yet near.

---

### SAQ 66

If projections of car population are valid, what will be the impact on emissions of controls such as catalytic converters?

---

# 7)   AS SAFE AS HOUSES?

*Modern societies are not simply urban societies; they are intra-mural societies.*

(Bull. NY Acad. Med., 1981, 57, 826–44)

It would be very remiss if in our consideration of air pollution we did not acknowledge the widely held view that no more than 10–30% of our activities take place outside buildings. In the case of home-based persons, only about 2.5 h may be spent out of doors each day, implying an occupancy factor of 0.9. The time spent at school, in the office or elsewhere under cover of buildings may lead to a similar occupancy factor, and so indoor air pollution deserves consideration.

Usually we would expect that the air quality in a building is closely related to that outside, for it is unusual to clean air before admitting it to a building. The rate of production or release of a pollutant, the rate of absorption or inactivation and the ventilation also play their parts in modifying indoor air quality.

Of course, similar relationships apply in the outside environment, but because the mixing volume is relatively so large, it is only the pollutants that we generate in large amounts that are of primary concern. Pollutants that are generated in small quantities do not reach high enough concentrations to be of concern to health. However, indoors, the relatively small volume makes even small releases of pollutants likely to produce concentrations of significance to health.

As few inhabited buildings are sealed from the outside air, ventilation will allow us to find inside all the pollutants found outside. In addition, however, there are many internally generated pollutants which are ultimately all the result of our own actions or choice. Some of these pollutants may come from building materials, and the concentrations of these tend to be constant over time, given that the ventilation is constant. Other pollutants come from our activities, and the concentrations of these vary with our actions.

## Exercise

Before continuing, make a list of sources of air pollutants in your own home.

My list includes hobbies and craft activities, which may introduce pollutants usually associated with the workplace into the home, and of course this is usually without the safety precautions that legislation may require at work. Non-flued cooking appliances and heaters will generate oxides of nitrogen and carbon monoxide, as well as increasing the water vapour content in the home. Smoking cigarettes is another major source of indoor air pollution, both to smokers and non-smokers through passive smoking. Other sources of pollution to which hypersensitivity of individuals has been reported include hair spray, plastic furniture and curtains, pesticides, foam rubber and its adhesives, refrigerants, aerosol propellants, creosote, ammonia, bleaches, mothballs, insulation materials, etc. I should also mention the problem of **radon**, a radioactive gas produced from building materials and the soil beneath our home. Whereas the other indoor air pollutants are mostly from human activities, radon arises naturally, and this makes its control rather more difficult, and beyond the scope of this course. At this point you should look back at the case study on indoor air pollution in China, as summarised in Section 5 of Unit 4.

You can see that there are many air pollutants in our homes, but because of space and time limits, I will only look at one in detail. You will remember that carbon monoxide is produced primarily from motor cars, and as we saw above, any pollutant outside will enter buildings. We have also got several sources of carbon monoxide indoors: can you think what they are?

I hope that you identified tobacco smoking, heating and cooking, although the last two don't apply if you only use electricity. You can also have carbon monoxide entering your home from an attached garage.

Carbon monoxide is a colourless, odourless gas produced as a product of incomplete combustion of carbon-containing fuels. Like lead, it is an example of a pollutant that affects us according to how much of the substance is in our body. Unlike sulphur dioxide, carbon monoxide is not irritating. It is also produced naturally in the body by the breakdown of haemoglobin; it is this substance that also binds and transports carbon monoxide in the body, as we saw in Units 2 and 3. You will remember that carbon monoxide can bind to haemoglobin about 240 times more readily than oxygen. The main result of this reversible combination is to decrease the capacity of blood to carry oxygen from the lungs to the body tissues. Essentially, the acute and chronic effects of carbon monoxide are due to 'hypoxia' or oxygen deficiency. As the central nervous system is particularly sensitive to oxygen shortage, carbon monoxide poisoning produces impairment of vigilance, alertness and the ability to carry out tasks involving precision. Fortunately, the formation of carboxyhaemoglobin is reversible, and so when we move away from exposure to high concentrations we are able to lower the level in our blood. However, some people are more susceptible to the effects than others. Thus people with diseases of the heart and lungs, the anaemic, elderly and pregnant women are among those who may be at special risk.

I have already mentioned that carbon monoxide acts by combining with haemoglobin, and the product formed is carboxyhaemoglobin. Most assessments of health risks relate to the carboxyhaemoglobin formed as a percentage of the maximum possible. There is general agreement that any individual should be protected from exposure to carbon monoxide that would result in carboxyhaemoglobin levels of 5% for any but transient periods, whereas especially susceptible people should not exceed 2.5%. It is relatively easy to measure carbon monoxide in the air, and many scientists have derived equations to relate the concentrations and time of exposure to carbon monoxide to the concentrations of carboxyhaemoglobin produced. Such applications are one form of air pollution model, and such models play a major role in air quality management nowadays. I have chosen one of the simpler equations to use as an introduction to the technique of modelling, but remember that there are others which may be more reliable for certain situations. We will use the equation to predict the effect of exposure to carbon monoxide on a person.

The equation we will use is:

$$[COHb]\,(\%) = K[CO]t$$

where [CO] is carbon monoxide concentration in ppm (v/v);

[COHb] is the percentage of carboxyhaemoglobin in blood;

$t$ is exposure time in minutes;

$K$ is a constant selected from Table 30.

**Table 30**   *Deriving the value for constant, K, in the carbon monoxide model*

|  | Individual at rest | Light activity | Light work | Heavy work |
|---|---|---|---|---|
| Alveolar ventilation rate (litres per minute) | 6 | 9.5 | 18 | 30 |
| Pulse rate | 70 | 80 | 110 | 135 |
| K | 0.0003 | 0.0005 | 0.0008 | 0.0011 |

As you will recall from earlier in this text, air quality varies continuously, and Figure 26 showed typical variations of carbon monoxide over a period of continuous measurement. Let us now look at a typical daily routine with representative carbon monoxide concentrations for various periods of the day (Table 31).

**Table 31**   *A daily diary of carbon monoxide concentrations*

| Time | Duration/h | Activity | Concentration | |
|---|---|---|---|---|
| | | | CO (ppm) | COHb (%) |
| 00.00–07.00 | 7.0 | sleep (bedroom) | 2.5 | 0.3 |
| 07.00–08.00 | 1.0 | eat (kitchen) | 12.0 | 0.4 |
| 08.00–08.15 | 0.25 | exercise dog | 15.0 | 0.2 |
| 08.15-08.30 | 0.25 | domestic | 5.0 | 0.04 |
| 08.30–09.00 | 0.5 | drive to work | 30.0 | 0.5 |
| 09.00–12.30 | 3.5 | office | 7.0 | 1.2 |
| 12.30–13.15 | 0.75 | walk in town | 12.0 | 0.4 |
| 13.15-17.00 | 3.75 | office | 7.0 | 1.3 |
| 17.00–17.30 | 0.5 | drive home | 35.0 | 0.5 |
| 17.30–18.00 | 0.5 | domestic | 5.0 | 0.1 |
| 18.00–19.00 | 1.0 | eat (kitchen) | 14.5 | 0.4 |
| 19.00–22.30 | 3.5 | domestic | 6.0 | 0.4 |
| 22.30–23.00 | 0.5 | exercise dog | 5.0 | 0.1 |
| 23.00–24.00 | 1.0 | sleep | 2.5 | 0.05 |

These illustrative concentrations of carbon monoxide show you how the levels to which we are exposed vary all the time, and I have calculated the carboxyhaemoglobin concentrations from the equation and using values of $K$ from Table 30. Check some of these calculations yourself before continuing.

The next thing we need to consider is what may be the effect on our health, and some signs and symptoms are set out in Table 32. Remember, however that we are all different, and some people may be more susceptible to the pollutant than others.

**Table 32**   *Health effects of carbon monoxide*

| [COHb] (%) | Signs and symptoms |
|---|---|
| 0–10 | No sign of symptoms. |
| 10–20 | Tightness across forehead, possible slight headache, dilation of cutaneous blood vessels. |
| 20–30 | Headache and throbbing of temples. |
| 30–40 | Severe headache, weakness, dizziness, dimness of vision, nausea, vomiting, collapse. |
| 40–50 | Same as above, greater risk of collapse, cerebral anaemia and increased pulse and respiration rates. |
| 50–60 | Cerebral anaemia, increased respiration and pulse rates, coma, intermittent convulsions. |
| 60–70 | Coma, intermittent convulsions, depressed heart action and respiration rate, possible death. |
| 70–80 | Weak pulse and slow respiration, leading to death within hours. |
| 80–90 | Death in less than one hour. |
| 90–100 | Death within a few minutes. |

In fact, while I have indicated no signs of effects below 10% carboxyhaemoglobin, controlled studies have found some less obvious effects, and some are mentioned in Table 33.

**Table 33** *Health effects of carbon monoxide at low exposure levels*

| [COHb] (%) | Reported effects |
|---|---|
| 2-3 | Impaired performance in time discrimination; shortened time to angina response in those with cardiovascular disease; decrease in exercise time in non-smokers. |
| 3-5 | Decrease in exercise time to exhaustion; longer reaction times. |
| 5-8 | Vigilance decrement; disturbance in certain perceptual and cognitive processes; decrease in maximal work time. |

You should now be able to predict any likely effects of exposure to carbon monoxide in our subject going through a normal daily routine. My interpretation is that with a maximal carboxyhaemoglobin concentration of 1.3%, there is unlikely to be much noticeable effect. Certainly we have not breached the 2.5% guideline.

### SAQ 67

Look at some measurements I made in another 'internal' environment, a multi-storey car park in a shopping precinct (Table 34). Try going through the above procedure to estimate any likely effects on people in that environment.

**Table 34** *Carbon monoxide levels in a car park during the day*

| | 09.00 to 10.00 | 10.00 to 11.00 | 11.00 to 12.00 | 12.00 to 13.00 | 13.00 to 14.00 | 14.00 to 15.00 | 15.00 to 16.00 | 16.00 to 17.00 | 17.00 to 18.00 |
|---|---|---|---|---|---|---|---|---|---|
| CO (ppm) | 10 | 100 | 220 | 300 | 270 | 200 | 200 | 300 | 500 |
| COHb (%) | | | | | | | | | |

There is little doubt that the carbon monoxide levels in the situation in SAQ 67 were very high, and you can see that the effect is to produce carboxyhaemoglobin levels of up to 24%. You won't be surprised to learn, therefore, that the reason why I was called in to make these investigations was because an older member of the car park staff had collapsed on several occasions. Being older, he was obviously a member of the section of the population more susceptible to the health effects of carbon monoxide. At this point I should admit that I have not given you a true representation of the carbon monoxide concentrations in the car park: the above table shows not the average values for each hourly period, but the *minimum* values!

I hope that you appreciate that this was a dramatic illustration of the acute effects of air pollution that may occur, but fortunately levels such as this are only likely where there is poor ventilation. In the open air it is unlikely that such high concentrations as those given in Table 34 would occur. Nevertheless, you can now see the potential significance of faulty combustion appliances in the home and the justification for improving combustion efficiency overall to avoid producing carbon monoxide.

# 8 CONCLUSION

The air is one of our most precious resources, vital both to sustain and to protect life on Earth, but its quality is under threat from many different forms of pollution. The evolution of legislation over the years has sought not so much to protect us, but more to protect the environment from harm caused by human activities. Although air quality has without doubt improved in many respects throughout this century, new problems have also emerged, among them being the concerns over global warming and changes in ozone concentrations.

Prevention is increasingly being recognised as the best solution for dealing with the newer problems as well as the traditional forms of air pollution such as smoke. Much air pollution is associated with combustion processes, and inefficient combustion leads to increased emissions of pollutants to atmosphere. Application of the prevention approach involves optimising combustion conditions.

Cleaning up waste gas streams from the unavoidable pollutants will always be necessary, however, and this usually involves add-on technology. Ultimately, some pollutants may be discharged to atmosphere and the natural dilution and dispersion processes serve to avoid risks to health or nuisance. In cleaning up waste gases and in dispersion, the close links between pollution of the air, land and water must always be borne in mind. Any abatement method must avoid conversion of one form of pollution into another: the guiding concept is to use the best practicable environmental option.

Information of air quality through more extensive monitoring programmes and networks provides information on the extent of pollution and the magnitude of releases from the variety of sources. TV 7 illustrated some of these aspects. It also showed some ways in which information is disseminated through the communication media to inform the public. This in turn increases public expectations and the pressure for further improvements. It also provides the public with the information to act towards minimising pollution – we all contribute towards pollution and so have a part to play in preventing further environmental harm.

## References

BOUTRON, C. F. *et al.* (1991) *Nature*, **353**, pp. 153–6.

MOLINA, M. F. AND ROWLAND, F. S. (1974) *Nature*, **249**, pp. 810–12.

OECD (1987) *Statistical Report on Road Accidents*, and *OECD Compendium of Environmental Data*, OECD Paris.

PORTEOUS, A. (1992) *Dictionary of Environmental Science and Technology*, John Wiley & Sons (T237 set book).

## Acknowledgements

Grateful acknowledgement is made to the following sources for permission to reproduce material in these units.

### Figures

*Cover illustration:* Based on an original by Ian Howatson, courtesy of Ian Howatson Illustration, Buckingham; *cover photograph:* The Environmental Picture Library/© Stan Gamester; *Figure 2: Report on the Current Work of the air Pollution and Pollution Abatement Divisions*, 16 December 1991, Warren Spring Laboratory; *Figure 19:* Lowry, S. 'Paris drivers urged to walk or stay home', *The Daily Telegraph*, 4 February 1989, © *The Telegraph*, London, 1989; 'Foggy days, everywhere but in London town', *The Times*, 7 February 1989, © Times Newspapers Ltd, 1989; *(map):* Reproduced with the permission of the Controller of Her Majesty's Stationery Office; *Figure 20(a):* Nuttall, N. (1991) 'London endures worst air pollution on record', *The Times*, 14 December 1991, © Times Newspapers Ltd, 1991; *Figure 20(b):* 'Weather log for Dec 1991, *Weather*, Vol 47, No 2, February 1992, Royal Meteorological Society; *Figure 21:* Ricketts, J.N. (1988) 'The use of satellite imagery to detect a cloud of noxious vapour', *Weather*, Vol 43, Royal Meteorological Society; *Figure 33:* From *BS 2742, Notes on the Use of the Ringelmann and Miniature Smoke Charts*, courtesy of the British Standards Institute; *Figure 44:* Warren Spring Laboratory (1990) *UK Smoke and Sulphur Dioxide Monitoring Networks*, April 1989-March 1990; *Figure 49:* Reprinted with permission from *Nature*, Vol 353, 12 September 1991. Copyright 1991 Macmillan Magazines Ltd; *Figures 54, 60, 61, 63:* Strauss, W. (1975) *Industrial Gas Cleaning*, Pergamon Press, © W Strauss; *Figures 57, 59, 67:* From *A User Guide to Dust and Fume Control*, The Institute of Chemical Engineers; *Figure 69 (right):* Buoniore, A.J. and Theodore, L. (1975) *Industrial Control Equipment for Gaseous Pollutants*, CRC Press Inc; *Figure 71:* From the *Fluidised Bed Combustion of Coal - NCB Report* (1980), British Coal; *Figure 77:* Valentin F.H. (1990) 'Making chemical process plants odour free', *Chemical Engineering*, January 1990, McGraw-Hill Inc.

### Table

*Table 17:* WHO (1987) Air Quality Guidelines for Europe, WHO Regional Publications European Series No 23, World Health Organization.

# ANSWERS TO SELF-ASSESSMENT QUESTIONS

## SAQ 1

Figure 3 shows that less NO is produced at lower flame temperatures. By modifying fuel burners to give lower flame temperatures it is possible to reduce nitrogen oxides emissions. We will see later (Section 5) how this may be done.

## SAQ 2

(a) The tables indicate that the pollutants from incomplete combustion will include smoke, sulphur dioxide, nitrogen oxides, carbon dioxide, non-methane hydrocarbons and carbon monoxide. The first three in this list are produced whether combustion is complete or incomplete, and so you may have listed only the last two pollutants. You should realise, however, that the others are also produced.

(b) The main pollutants will be non-methane hydrocarbons. Oxidants are also produced indirectly, as described in answer (c).

(c) Oxidants are produced from photochemical reactions, but nitrogen oxides are also implicated.

## SAQ 3

Your completed table should read as in Table 36. You will notice that the total number of excess deaths suggested by these data amounts to 1597, but when mortality over following weeks and the greater London area are considered, it is usually claimed that the smog caused over 4000 excess deaths.

**Table 36** *Mortality in the London fog of 1952 (central London)*

| Cause | Seasonal norm (deaths per week) | Deaths in week after fog | Excess deaths |
|---|---|---|---|
| Bronchitis | 75 | 704 | 629 |
| Other lung diseases | 98 | 366 | 268 |
| Coronary heart disease, myocardial degeneration | 206 | 525 | 319 |
| Other diseases | 508 | 889 | 381 |
| Total | 887 | 2484 | 1597 |

## SAQ 4

The major sources of the principal pollutants are as follows:

black smoke – 46% from road transport;

carbon dioxide – 34% from power generation;

carbon monoxide – 90% from road transport;

nitrogen oxides – 51% from road transport;

sulphur dioxide – 72% from electrical power generation;

volatile organic compounds -50% from processes and solvents.

On the basis of fuels, the principal sources are:

black smoke – 42% from diesel fuel use;

carbon dioxide – 40% from coal burning;

carbon monoxide – 87% from motor spirit use;

nitrogen oxides – coal and motor spirit make equal contributions of 29%;

sulphur dioxide – 75% from coal combustion;

volatile organic compounds – 62% from sources other than coal and petroleum.

## SAQ 5

(a) The emissions of lead in 1979 may be calculated from:

$$18.7 \times 10^6 \text{ tonnes} \times \frac{1\,l}{0.7\text{ kg}} \times 0.4 \text{ g } l^{-1} \times \frac{1\text{ kg}}{1000\text{ g}} \times \frac{70}{100}$$

= 7.5 thousand tonnes

Using the consumption rate of 23.9 million tonnes of fuel and 0.15 g $l^{-1}$, the 1989 emission is calculated as 3.6 thousand tonnes of lead. Thus, despite an increase in the fuel consumption, the gross emissions of lead to the atmosphere were almost halved as a result of the introduction of a more demanding fuel quality standard. In fact, UK government statistics estimate the lead emissions in 1989 as 2.6 thousand tonnes. This figure is lower than the one we have calculated here because we have not accounted for the increasing proportion of unleaded petrol being sold. Consequently, the reduction in lead emissions to atmosphere is even greater than our calculation suggests.

(b) If the total motor spirit consumption in 1991 was 24 million tonnes of which 9.85 million tonnes were unleaded, the amount of leaded fuel used was $14.15 \times 10^6$ tonnes. Assuming the lead content to be 0.15 g $l^{-1}$, calculation of the lead emission in a similar manner to that in (a) gives a total emission of $2.1 \times 10^3$ tonnes for 1991. I hope that you notice the continuing downward trend brought about by the changes occurring in fuel use.

## SAQ 6

The parcel of air cools according to the dry adiabatic lapse rate, and so becomes cooler than its surroundings. Consequently, there is a net downward force on the parcel.

## SAQ 7

The types of meteorological inversion mentioned in the text and from which you should have identified three are:

- radiation inversions – caused by surface cooling by radiation loss;
- advective inversions – caused by the horizontal movement of a warm air mass over a cool surface;
- frontal inversions – caused when warm air overrides cold air at a weather front;
- subsidence inversions – caused by an air mass dropping down at the centre of an anticyclone.

All inversions may lead to deterioration in air quality by trapping pollutants under the inversion layer or 'lid'.

## SAQ 8

The answer should include reference to the anticyclone causing a ground-based inversion and a subsidence inversion aloft. Both are clear from the environmental lapse rate shown. The inversions and the absence of wind allowed the unidentified chemical pollutant to build up to nuisance proportions in Nottinghamshire.

## SAQ 9

Your wind rose should look like this:

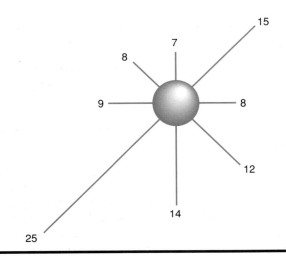

## SAQ 10

The pollution rose should look like the following diagram. This indicates that the highest pollution levels occur when the wind blows from the south-east, and so the source of pollution is likely to be in that direction from the monitoring station.

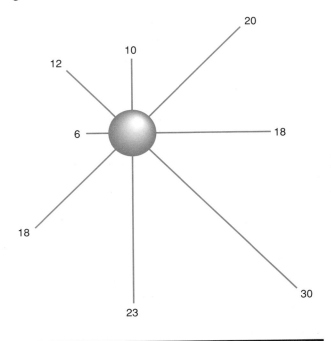

## SAQ 11

Ozone is produced by

$$O + O_2 + M \rightarrow O_3 + M$$

$$\Delta H = -100 \text{ kJ mol}^{-1}$$

and consumed by

$$O + O_3 \rightarrow 2O_2$$

$$\Delta H = -390 \text{ kJ mol}^{-1}$$

and

$$O_3 + E \rightarrow O_2 + O$$

I hope that you remember from Unit 3 that a negative heat of reaction indicates that energy is lost from the chemical system, i.e. the reactions are exothermic.

The heat lost by the reaction system is gained by the stratosphere, and this explains the temperature increase in that region, as was shown in Figure 23.

## SAQ 12

You should see from Figure 5 and recall from the answer to SAQ 4 that nitrogen oxides come primarily from road transport and power stations, and so minimising releases from these are important. Hydrocarbons (or volatile organic compounds) also come from motor vehicles in large proportion, but processes and solvent use are greater contributors. All these releases should be minimised, and Section 5 and TV 8 show some ways of doing this.

## SAQ 13

(a) To derive a formula for CFC-12 we first add 90 to 12 to give 102. This implies one carbon and hence the methane skeleton. No hydrogen and two fluorine atoms are indicated by the remaining two digits. This leaves two vacant bonds on the methane skeleton and these must be occupied by chlorine atoms. The formula of CFC-12 is therefore $CF_2Cl_2$, which is dichlorodifluoromethane.

(b) $CHClFCF_3$ has 2 carbon, 1 hydrogen and 4 fluorine atoms, which gives a number 214. Subtract 90 gives 124, and so this is CFC-124.

$CCl_2FCClF_2$ has 2 carbon, no hydrogen and 3 fluorine, which implies 203. Subtracting 90 gives 113 and so this compound is CFC-113.

## SAQ 14

The impact of carbon dioxide and the magnitude of its emissions, combined with the links with fossil fuel burning through direct emissions of $CO_2$ and precursor gases, suggests fuel burning as the dominant area for attention. CFCs are already being phased out owing to their effects on stratospheric ozone (Section 3.4.2) and so the fractional impact of energy use will grow. Energy consumption is therefore the area for great attention.

## SAQ 15

If it is impracticable to capture the $CO_2$ produced, one option is to produce less. We may do this by changing to fuels that contain less carbon, and hence which will produce less $CO_2$. We can go one step further and replace fossil fuels by renewable energy sources such as solar, tidal or wind power that produce no $CO_2$. Yet another option is to burn less fossil fuel. The last option implies improving the efficiency with which we use energy (see *energy efficiency* and *greenhouse effect* entries in the set book). Recycling is another important way of attacking global warming, because the amount of energy needed to make new products, such as aluminium cans, from raw materials is considerably greater than that needed for manufacture from recycled material.

## SAQ 16

Oxygen is present in waste gases from combustion plant as a result of the excess air supply required for combustion. Measuring the oxygen content can serve as a check on the performance of a combustion system.

## SAQ 17

From the entry in the set book, 'dark smoke' is defined in law as being as dark as or darker than Ringelmann Shade 2.

Black smoke is as dark as or darker than Ringelmann Shade 4.

In Section 4.1 it was quoted that guidance notes require that the emission from combustion processes should not exceed the equivalent of Ringelmann Shade 1.

## SAQ 18

The fuel consumption is known to be 0.024 tonne min$^{-1}$, which equates to 1.44 tonne h$^{-1}$. Hence the emissions over one hour of constant speed cruising are:

$NO_x$     1.44 t h$^{-1}$ × 59 kg t$^{-1}$ = 85 kg h$^{-1}$

CO     1.44 t h$^{-1}$ × 8 kg t$^{-1}$ = 11.5 kg h$^{-1}$

Hydrocarbons 1.44 t h$^{-1}$ × 2.7 kg t$^{-1}$ = 4 kg h$^{-1}$

$SO_2$     1.44 t h$^{-1}$ × ((21.9 × 3.8) − 2.1) kg t$^{-1}$
    = 117 kg h$^{-1}$

Notice from this calculation how considerable is the carbon dioxide emission compared with those of the other pollutants.

## SAQ 19

If the energy savings by efficiency improvements total 1070 GJ y$^{-1}$, the reductions in $NO_x$ emissions are given by:

$$44 \text{ g GJ}^{-1} \times 1070 \text{ GJ y}^{-1} = 47 \text{ kg y}^{-1}$$

## SAQ 20

The smoke stain method depends on the difference in the reflectance of light from clean filter paper and paper soiled by particulate matter. The calibration was originally based on coal smoke, which is very dark and has a high soiling power. However, nowadays airborne particles come from many sources, and coal smoke is no longer dominant, as you will see later. Consequently the smoke stain method may not give a representative result. In addition, light coloured particles, such as cement dust, have a lower soiling power. Clearly, the smoke stain is not directly related to the mass of particles.

## SAQ 21

The graph shows concentration as a function of time over which the averaging is done. As the averaging time decreases, higher concentrations result. From a graph such as this we could deduce the ratios between maximum concentrations for different averaging times, and if we know the concentration for one averaging time, we may then be able to predict the value for another. Similar techniques apply for means and minima over different averaging times.

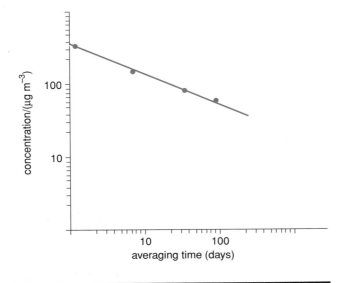

## SAQ 22

We have seen that air contains water and carbon dioxide, both of which absorb infra-red radiation (Section 3.1, Figure 7). The absorption regions of CO and $CO_2$ are reasonably well separated and there is no problem in separating them, but water can interfere. This problem is overcome by removing water by a freeze-drier or an absorbent in the sampling line to the instrument. Carbon monoxide is not soluble in water, so none is lost before measurement.

## SAQ 23

Both are equal to the median value.

## SAQ 24

(a)  The range is the difference between 44 and 5, i.e. 39.

(b)  In this set of data, $N$ is even, and the median value is the average of 24 and 25, i.e. 24.5.

(c)  As there are 40 data points, the first quartile value lies between the 10th and 11th value and is 14.5. Similarly, the third quartile value is 34.5.

(d)  As there are four data points in each decile, the seventh decile value occurs between the values 32 and 33, i.e. 32.5.

## SAQ 25

You should notice that the time-weighted average concentration decreases as the averaging time increases. This is to allow for the occurrence of short-term peak values and the effects of averaging times indicated in Figure 40. You may also have noticed that while the 8-h average matches the WHO long-term goal, the 1-h average has been lowered from 40 to 30 mg m$^{-3}$.

## SAQ 26

Consider the median of the daily values for the year, which you will remember is the same as the 50th percentile. A median smoke concentration of 22 µg m$^{-3}$ does not exceed the EC median limit value of 68 µg m$^{-3}$. There is no breach on this account.

As the median smoke value of 22 is less than 34, the median $SO_2$ concentration must not exceed 120. It is 45 µg m$^{-3}$, so there is no breach.

Now consider the winter median values of smoke (28 µg m$^{-3}$) and $SO_2$ (55 µg m$^{-3}$) which appear against the letters WMD. Again, neither is in breach of the corresponding EC *limit* values of 111 and 180 respectively.

Consider next the 98th percentile values of smoke (194 µg m$^{-3}$) and $SO_2$ (342 µg m$^{-3}$). Again the EC *limit* value of 213 for smoke has not been exceeded, but the limit of 250 for $SO_2$ has been breached at this site.

The arithmetic means (AM) of the daily mean values are 37 µg m$^{-3}$ for smoke and 63 µg m$^{-3}$ for $SO_2$. Both are greater than the corresponding guide values for the arithmetic mean. The sequence of daily values also exceeds the guide values set by the EEC directive in several respects. For example, the 90th percentile $SO_2$ concentration is 118 µg m$^{-3}$; so for almost 10% of the year, i.e. 36 days, the minimum $SO_2$ guide value of 100 is likely to be exceeded. Even the upper smoke guide value of 150 is exceeded for more than 18 days a year.

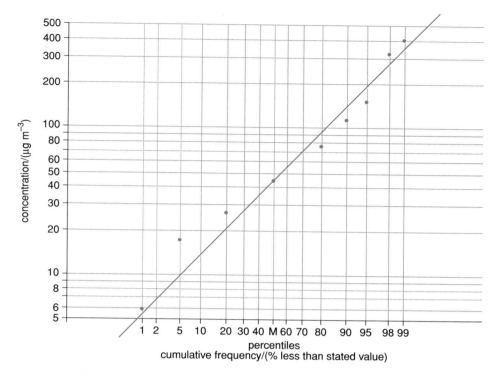

**Figure 88** *For SAQ 27.*

## SAQ 27

Your graph should look like Figure 88.

(a) Notice that the sulphur dioxide range is greater than that for smoke, and the peak 99th percentile for sulphur dioxide is 405 µg m$^{-3}$.

(b) From your graph you may deduce by interpolation that the 10% background level of sulphur dioxide is about 13 µg m$^{-3}$ compared with a corresponding smoke concentration of 10 µg m$^{-3}$ shown in Figure 45.

These observations indicate that the main differences are at high concentrations, which may cause acute harm to vegetation or human health. The differences are due to smoke being controlled by combustion efficiency modifications, while sulphur dioxide emissions are generally uncontrolled and depend on the type and amount of fuel burned.

## SAQ 28

You should note that the directive specifies two peak (98th percentile) values for $SO_2$ depending on the associated smoke level. In this case, with over 128 µg m$^{-3}$ smoke, the limit is 250 µg m$^{-3}$, which is under the line, and so the standard is breached.

## SAQ 29

The figures show that nitrogen dioxide levels of 300 ppb and above represent 'very poor' air quality. Such levels are characteristic of prolonged inversions.

## SAQ 30

The difference is in part due to the averaging time. The shorter the averaging time, the higher the value. However, there is also the fact that ozone has a significant effect on vegetation, and acute exposure may cause injury, as shown in Figure 47. The means for the two time periods are therefore relatively close.

## SAQ 31

An emission of smoke from a chimney is an offence unless statutory defences apply as set out in Section 5.1. In particular there is a defence that the smoke emission resulted from the unavoidable use of a fuel for which the furnace was not designed owing to suitable fuel not being available. The important factor is that the furnace was designed for coal, and so waste material is an 'unsuitable fuel'. It therefore is likely that an offence has been committed.

## SAQ 32

1.25 million Btu h$^{-1}$ = 1.25 × 10$^6$/3600

$$= 347 \text{ Btu s}^{-1}$$

$$= 347 \text{ Btu s}^{-1} × 1.055 \text{ kJ Btu}^{-1}$$

$$= 366 \text{ kW}$$

Similarly, 28 million Btu h$^{-1}$ = 7778 Btu s$^{-1}$

$$= 8.2 \text{ MW}$$

## SAQ 33

Coal, logs and oil are not authorised fuels, and may only be burned in an exempted fireplace in a smoke control area.

Gas is an authorised fuel and may be used in a smoke control area.

## SAQ 34

The rise in lead concentration between around 1750 to the beginning of this century is attributed to the Industrial Revolution. This is followed by a more rapid rise in pollution following the sharp increase in motor vehicle use. The decline in pollution since policy decisions began in the 1970s is clear.

## SAQ 35

If the amount of excess air is too low, complete combustion will not occur. This is because no burner or grate provides perfect mixing, and so the stoichiometric amount of air is likely to leave some fuel unburnt simply because molecules in the fuel fail to contact oxygen molecules. If the amount of excess air is too great, the excess has to be heated and carries this heat from the furnace or boiler. It therefore makes the plant less efficient. It is also possible for the surplus air to cool some of the furnace below the ignition temperature, and so allow unburnt or partial combustion products to be discharged to the atmosphere.

## SAQ 36

We can write an equation as:

$$C + O_2 + 3.76N_2 + \underset{\text{excess air}}{O_2} + 3.76N_2$$

$$= CO_2 + 3.76N_2 + \underset{\text{excess air}}{O_2} + 3.76N_2$$

from which

$$\% \; CO_2 = 1/9.52 = 10.5\%$$

## SAQ 37

You should remember from Unit 3 that burning carbon-containing fuels with insufficient air for complete combustion may produce carbon monoxide (CO). The amount produced tends to increase as the excess fuel diminishes, but as more air is added there comes a point when the CO itself burns readily, and so its concentration decreases. The minimum carbon monoxide remains in the flue gases beyond the stoichiometric point.

## SAQ 38

As $CO_2$ concentrations rise and then fall as the amount of air increases, certain $CO_2$ values correspond to either excess fuel or excess air (i.e. to the left or right of the stoichiometric point respectively). For coal and oil the excess fuel situation is indicated by smoke, but not so with gas, for which excess fuel may present a safety hazard.

## SAQ 39

Optimal efficiency of the boiler is a balance between incomplete combustion and heat loss by too much excess air. These conditions prevail with 100–300 ppm CO by volume.

## SAQ 40

If you recall the definitions of the mole, you will recall that 1 kilogram mole occupies 22.4 m$^3$ at NTP. To calculate the volume of the $CO_2$ produced in a year, divide the mass of $CO_2$ by the molecular mass of $CO_2$ (i.e. 44), and multiply the answer by 22.4 to give the volume in cubic metres at NTP.

## SAQ 41

Your answer should include cost savings in energy, in avoiding cleaning costs (in electronics), in avoiding pollution control plant and operating costs, as well as additional waste disposal costs for dealing with solid waste or liquid effluents from gas cleaning plant.

## SAQ 42

Your completed table should read as follows.

| Pollutant | Emission (thousand tonnes) | | Percentage of current UK emissions (%) | 1979–1989 10-y rise (%) |
| --- | --- | --- | --- | --- |
| | 1979 | 1989 | | |
| black smoke | 121 | 198 | 39 | 64 |
| sulphur dioxide | 55 | 60 | 2 | 9 |
| nitrogen oxides | 908 | 1298 | 48 | 43 |
| volatile organics | 490 | 762 | 37 | 56 |
| carbon monoxide | 3992 | 5751 | 88 | 44 |
| carbon dioxide | 21 000 | 29 000 | 19 | 38 |

Source: adapted from *Clean Air*, Vol. 21(2), p.55 (1991).

## SAQ 43

You should be aware of the fuller descriptions in the set book, but in summary:

- Grit is defined in BS 3405 as solid particles retained on a 200-mesh sieve, and therefore of size 76 μm and above.

- Dust is not defined in law, but is usually regarded as particulate matter between 1 and 75 μm.

- Fume is defined in the 1968 Clean Air Act as 'solid particulate matter smaller than dust'. It is therefore regarded as of size below 1 μm.

## SAQ 44

(a) From Table 21, you should notice that for mining and rock products, the usual technique for control of particulate matter is a wet deduster. Venturi systems are the wet system often used in this application, and give high efficiency control. Fabric filters are also used considerably for dealing with dry dusts, but when coating stone with tar to produce roadstone, any tarry matter would blind the fabric filter, so wet arresters are preferred for this application. Electrostatic precipitators would be too costly for such applications which do not produce heavy concentrations of dust.

(b) Wood-sanding operations generate fine dusts for which fabric filters are the preferred mode of gas cleaning. Cyclones are suitable for coarse wood dusts from activities such as sawing, but are less suitable for sander dust, which requires high-efficiency cyclones. Unfortunately, the high gas velocities in these can carry out fine wood dust, and so fabric filters are my preference. As sander dust is flammable, care must be taken to avoid the risk of fire or explosion in the gas cleaning plant.

(c) Grinding of metal can generate fine dust which is notorious for causing rust spotting on cars parked nearby. High efficiency control is therefore required, and as Table 21 indicates, the choice is usually between wet arresters or fabric filters. Of the wet gas cleaning options, the self-induced spray is common. As the burden generated is relatively light in concentration, small gas cleaning systems are commonly used.

(d) Galvanising of steel has often been associated with a local nuisance owing to the fine fume generated from the flux. As a fine particulate matter, the fume is ideally collected by a device such as a fabric filter, but unfortunately the hygroscopic nature of the fume may lead to blinding of the bags. The problem has often been a difficult one to solve, but some success has been achieved with knitted wire devices of the type shown in Figure 58. Irrigation of the mesh dissolves the ammonium chloride and prevents blockage.

(e) Pulverised coal burning generates high concentrations of dust of fine particle size. High-efficiency gas cleaning is therefore required, and while high-efficiency cyclones have been used, the preference is for electrostatic precipitators.

## SAQ 45

As in the example, the efficiency of collection

= (concentration removed/total concentration) × 100

In this case, the efficiency

= ((400 − 0.03)/400) × 100

= 99.99%

Notice that this example illustrates that while the efficiency has increased by only 0.01%, the emission has been reduced by about one-third of the previous value. Refer to the *electrostatic precipitator* entry in the set book to see a further illustration of this important point.

## SAQ 46

Many of these causes may be investigated by physical inspection of the plant, together with regular pressure and velocity tests. Isokinetic sampling may be needed to determine whether the plant is capable of the duty expected. Sampling before and after the gas cleaning plant would indicate the efficiency of collection offered, which could be matched against the specification. Equipment similar to that shown in Figure 35 is commonly used to check the performance of the plant, and Figure 37 illustrates typical sampling positions before and after the arrestment plant.

## SAQ 47

Fabric filters collect particulate matter by a combination of electrostatic, molecular and possibly capillary forces of attraction.

Dust removal is achieved at intervals by:

- mechanical shaking or displacing the filter bags;
- temporarily reversing the air flow; or
- using a high-pressure reverse jet of air.

## SAQ 48

A   It is an offence for the occupier of premises in a smoke control area to allow smoke emissions from a chimney unless (a) the emission is caused by the use of an authorised fuel or (b) the appliance discharging into the chimney is on a list of exempted fireplaces.

B   In venturi and certain tower scrubbers the particle collection efficiency is maximised if the upstream gas flow is saturated with water vapour before passing through the device.

C   The complete cleaning of fabric filters is neither necessary nor desirable since material retained within the filter reduces the pore size and increases the gas cleaning efficiency.

D   The purpose of the high voltage across the electrodes of an electrostatic precipitator is to maintain a space charge of electrons so that dust particles become negatively charged and are attracted to the positive electrode.

## SAQ 49

You will recall from Unit 3 that the air supply for efficient combustion must be controlled and depends upon the fuel supply. Ventilation air is perfectly satisfactory for providing the air for combustion, and organic compounds are indeed likely to be destroyed. Unfortunately, the amount of ventilation air may exceed the air requirements for efficient combustion in a boiler. Too much air will carry away heat from the furnace and reduce its efficiency, even to the extent of causing smoke pollution through inefficient combustion of the fuel. This may be a particular problem in the summer, when a boiler may be required to produce less heat, so burning less fuel and therefore needing less air.

## SAQ 50

(a) As shown in TV 8, vapour degreasing using trichloroethylene is conventionally controlled by a combination of condensing coils and lip extraction to a chimney for dispersion. Covers on the degreasing tanks help to contain the vapour, while a large freeboard (space above the liquid and below the top of the tank) also helps minimise release of vapour. Adsorption is an option for incorporation in the extraction system.

(b) Dry cleaning solvents in a retail premises can be recovered in carbon adsorption systems and the solvent recycled. Residual emissions are dispersed from a chimney.

(c) The large-scale operations of car body manufacture may generate considerable odour emissions, and justify the application of incineration systems since low residual concentrations may still cause an odour problem. Catalytic incineration is suitable provided that contamination of the catalyst is unlikely to shorten its life.

The long-term policy should be to deal with the problem at source by replacing solvent based paints with low solvent or aqueous based ones, and manufacturers are moving in this direction.

(d) Odours caused by hydrogen sulphide at an oil refinery will often be dealt with by combustion. Incineration is an option and may be achieved in an incinerator or at a flare, depending on the nature of the source. Notice that the hydrogen sulphide burns to produce sulphur dioxide, and so dispersion from well above ground is essential. Some waste gases in an oil refinery are controlled by absorption in solvents followed by recovery of the sulphur content.

## SAQ 51

(a) According to Figure 5, the power industry accounted for 72% $SO_2$ and 28% $NO_x$ in 1990.

(b) First we need to know how much fuel is burnt by the power station. It generates 2000 MW of electricity, which is 2000 MJ s$^{-1}$.

The fuel has a calorific value of 25 MJ kg$^{-1}$, so the amount required is

$$\frac{2000 \text{ MJ s}^{-1}}{25 \text{ MJ kg}^{-1}} = 80 \text{ kg s}^{-1}$$

However, the station is only 30% efficient, and so the actual fuel requirement is

80 kg s$^{-1}$ × 100/30 = 267 kg s$^{-1}$

The fuel has a specification sulphur content of 1.7%; therefore, the emission of sulphur is

267 kg s$^{-1}$ × 1.7% = 4.5 kg s$^{-1}$

But as the relative masses of sulphur and sulphur dioxide are 1:2, the emission of sulphur dioxide is 9 kg s$^{-1}$.

## SAQ 52

A balanced chemical equation to summarise the limestone gypsum process is:

$$2CaCO_3 + 2SO_2 + O_2 \rightarrow 2CaSO_4 + 2CO_2$$

From this equation, we can conclude that:

$2(40 + 12 + (3 \times 16))$ mass units of $CaCO_3$ react with $2(32 + (2 \times 16))$ mass units of $SO_2$ to produce $2(40 + 32 + (4 \times 16))$ mass units of $CaSO_4$.

That is, 200 mass units of $CaCO_3$ react with 128 mass units of $SO_2$ to produce 272 mass units of $CaSO_4$.

Figure 74 indicates that 6 million tonnes of coal are used each year, while Table 25 indicates that the coal contains 2% sulphur. Therefore, the sulphur released amounts to $2\% \times 6 \times 10^6$ tonnes. For simplicity we will ignore the sulphur retention in the ash, although you may have allowed for this in your calculation. The sulphur dioxide emission is twice the mass of sulphur released, and equates to

$$2 \times 2\% \times 6 \times 10^6 \text{ tonnes} = 240\,000 \text{ tonnes of } SO_2$$

From the stoichiometric proportions in the chemical equation, we can determine that:

240 000 tonnes of $SO_2$ react with $240\,000 \times 200/128$ = 375 000 tonnes of limestone

and produce

$240\,000 \times 272/128 = 510\,000$ tonnes of gypsum

Figure 74 indicates a slightly higher amount of limestone, and an excess over the stoichiometric amount would improve the removal of sulphur. Similarly, our calculated amount of gypsum is lower than in Figure 74, but in our calculation we have not accounted for the mass of water present in gypsum. We have confirmed to a first approximation, therefore, the quantities given in Figure 74.

## SAQ 53

We start with the balanced chemical equations for the reactions on which the gas cleaning depends. These equations are:

$$HCl + NaOH \rightarrow NaCl + H_2O$$

$$SO_2 + 2NaOH \rightarrow Na_2SO_3 + H_2O$$

$$CO_2 + NaOH \rightarrow NaHCO_3$$

Then we convert the gas flow to standard conditions of 0 °C and 1.013 bar.

280 m$^3$ min$^{-1}$ at 82 °C and 1.013 bar

$$= 280 \times \frac{273}{(273 + 82)}$$

$$= 215 \text{ m}^3 \text{ min}^{-1} \text{ at standard conditions}$$

Basic stoichiometric relationships and unit conversions introduced in Unit 3 allow us to write an expression for the total NaOH requirement to achieve the desired removal efficiencies.

NaOH required =

$$\left(\frac{215 \text{ m}^3 \text{ min}^{-1}}{22.4 \text{ m}^3 (\text{kg mol})^{-1}}\right)\left(\frac{1500 \text{ ppm HCl}}{10^6 \text{ ppm}} \times 99\% \times \frac{1 \text{ mol NaOH}}{1 \text{ mol HCl}}\right)$$

$$+ \left(\frac{470 \text{ ppm } SO_2}{10^6 \text{ppm}} \times 65\% \times \frac{2 \text{ mol NaOH}}{1 \text{ mol } SO_2}\right)$$

$$+ \left(\frac{13\% \ CO_2}{100\%} \times 1\% \times \frac{1 \text{ mol NaOH}}{1 \text{ mol } CO_2}\right)$$

$$= 9.6(0.0015 + 0.0006 + 0.0013) \text{ kg mol NaOH min}^{-1}$$

$$= 0.033 \text{ kg mol NaOH min}^{-1}$$

On a mass basis, this is equivalent to

$$0.033 \text{ kg mol NaOH min}^{-1} \times \frac{40 \text{ kg NaOH}}{1 \text{ kg mol NaOH}}$$

$$= 1.32 \text{ kg min}^{-1}$$

If for simplicity we assume that the specific gravity of the solution is 1, the flow rate of the solution containing 20% by mass of the sodium hydroxide becomes

$$1.32 \times \frac{100}{20} = 6.6 \text{ l min}^{-1}$$

## SAQ 54

Downdraught is the downward current of air to the lee of a building, a hill or of a chimney structure itself. An effect of downdraught is that it may cause downwash, which is when a plume rise is negative – i.e. the plume does not rise above the chimney but is drawn down below the chimney top.

## SAQ 55

Downwash may be avoided by the correct siting of a chimney out of the influence of downdraught effects, but this will not solve a problem of downwash due to the low pressure to the lee of the chimney itself. A high efflux velocity may assist in avoiding the problem for most common wind speeds.

## SAQ 56

(a) The preferred units for carbon monoxide are μg m$^{-3}$ or its derivatives, although the dimensionless ratio of ppm by volume (ppm v/v) is sometimes used.

(b) Stratospheric ozone concentrations are usually expressed in Dobson units.

(c) Odours are expressed in odour units based on the dilutions to the odour threshold.

(d) Concentrations of suspended particulate matter are usually described in units of μg m$^{-3}$.

## SAQ 57

The cheaper, less clean fuels such as coal are usually precluded from generating the hot gas to drive the turbine owing to the technical difficulties of removing particulate matter to minimise damage to the turbine. A recent development is the use of coal gas as a fuel. The coal is first gasified, sulphur compounds and other impurities are removed, and the cleaned gas is used to drive the turbine. (For some extra technical information, see the box below.)

---

*Technical note for SAQ 57*

This process of converting coal into gas (mainly carbon monoxide and hydrogen) which drives a gas turbine offers an efficiency of up to 46%, and can operate on a variety of coal types, including high sulphur fuels. The environmental impact is low owing to removal of 99% of the sulphur and up to 25% lower carbon dioxide emissions than conventional plant, as less coal is needed for a given power output. Cooling water requirements are also low and effluents are clean and can be eliminated. The process is to be used on a 250 MW$_e$ integrated gasification combined cycle power plant being built in the Netherlands.

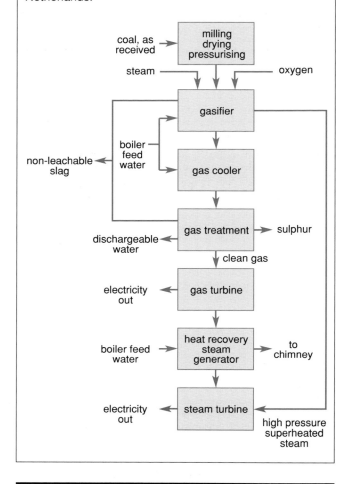

---

## SAQ 58

We first note that the incinerator flue gas flow rate is quoted at actual rather than standard conditions, and so we must convert to the same conditions to allow comparison. Using the principles covered in Unit 3, Section 5, we can determine that:

280 m$^3$ min$^{-1}$ at standard conditions becomes:

280 m$^3$ × 273/(273 + 400) = 114 m$^3$

Hence in 30 minutes the emission is 30 × 114 = 3420 m$^3$.

The emission of HCl in this volume is

3420 × 20 000/1 000 000 = 68.4 m$^3$

Likewise, the SO$_2$ emission is

3420 × 350/1 000 000 = 1.2 m$^3$

However, the permitted emission over this time period is given by:

for HCl, 3420 m$^3$ × 10 mg m$^{-3}$ = 34.2 g

and for SO$_2$, 3420 m$^3$ × 50 mg m$^{-3}$ = 171 g

We now need to determine the mass of pollutants emitted over this time period. This again draws on the principles learned in Unit 3.

68.4 m$^3$ of HCl converts to:

68.4 m$^3$ × (1 + 35.5) kg/22.4 m$^3$ = 111.5 kg

since one mole of gas (36.5 kg in the case of HCl) occupies 22.4 m$^3$ at standard conditions.

Likewise, 1.2 m$^3$ of SO$_2$ converts to

$$\frac{1.2 \text{ m}^3 \times (32 + (2 \times 16)) \text{ kg}}{22.4 \text{ m}^3} = 3.4 \text{ kg}$$

Hence, the minimum amount of HCl to be removed in the spray drier in order to meet the emission limit is

111.5 kg – 34.2 g = 111.47 kg

and for SO$_2$ we need to remove

3.4 kg – 171 g = 3.23 kg

We now need to consider the stoichiometry of the chemical equations. We write these as:

2HCl + Ca(OH)$_2$ → CaCl$_2$ + 2H$_2$O

2SO$_2$ + O$_2$ + 2Ca(OH)$_2$ → 2CaSO$_4$ + 2H$_2$O

From which we can determine that for complete reaction:

2 × 36.5 kg of HCl requires (40 + (2(16 + 1)) kg of Ca(OH)$_2$, which is 74 kg

and 128 kg of SO$_2$ requires 2(40 + (2(16 + 1)) kg of Ca(OH)$_2$, which is 148 kg.

Hence, over our 30-minute period,

111.47 kg of HCl requires 111.47 × 74/73 = 113 kg of Ca(OH)$_2$

and 3.23 kg of SO$_2$ requires 3.23 × 148/128 = 3.7 kg of Ca(OH)$_2$

giving a total amount of 113 + 3.7 = 117 kg of Ca(OH)$_2$ to the nearest kg.

Therefore, the feed rate of Ca(OH)$_2$ to the spray drier should be at least (117/30) = 3.9 kg per minute. In practice, a higher dose would be desirable to provide an excess of reactant which would ensure a high efficiency of conversion in a similar manner to the supply of excess air for combustion.

## SAQ 59

In addition to the emissions from the furnace and which are controlled by the afterburner, you may have noted the following sources of air pollution.

1   Fugitive emissions when the drums are opened.

2   Fugitive emissions from each end of the furnace when drums enter and leave. No mention was made of the openings at each end of the furnace, but clearly they must be open to allow drums to enter and leave. Local ventilation may help contain these emissions, which may then pass to the afterburner chamber.

3   The sand blasting chamber will generate considerable amounts of fine dust. These emissions will not be hot, moist or corrosive, so fabric filters offer good control.

4   The paint spray booth causes several potential problems. Paint is mixed with thinners, and these volatile organic compound emissions may be effectively controlled by carbon adsorption systems which offer the potential for solvent recovery. An alternative at the site in question may be to direct the ventilation air from the paint mixing area to the afterburner chamber. The same options may apply to the paint spray booth itself. Note the longer term aim of avoiding VOC emissions.

The potential releases to atmosphere are shown on the modified scheme in Figure 89.

## SAQ 60

You should recall that the discharge height for the flue serving a paint spray oven should be at least 8 m above ground level in order that dilution and dispersion may reduce any unavoidable odour to a concentration that will not cause nuisance. However, if the flue is attached or close to a building, there will be building wake and down-draught effects which reduce the effective plume height. In these circumstances, the flue should terminate at least 3 m above the ridge height.

As a typical paint spray booth incorporates wet gas cleaning, an efflux velocity no greater than 9 m s$^{-1}$ is preferred to avoid water droplets being carried out with the gas stream.

The discharge from abrasive cleaning is preferred at low level in order that any particulate matter is not dispersed over a wide area, but allowed to settle close to the source and within the process boundary.

## SAQ 61

If we work through the scheme in Figure 77 and apply it to the paint mixing area, we note first of all that the potential source is known, and that at present there is no alternative to a solvent-based paint; therefore the emission cannot be eliminated. Local ventilation is therefore appropriate, and in a paint mixing room we do not expect a high dust burden, nor do we expect a high ventilation rate. Consequently, the options for control suggested are carbon

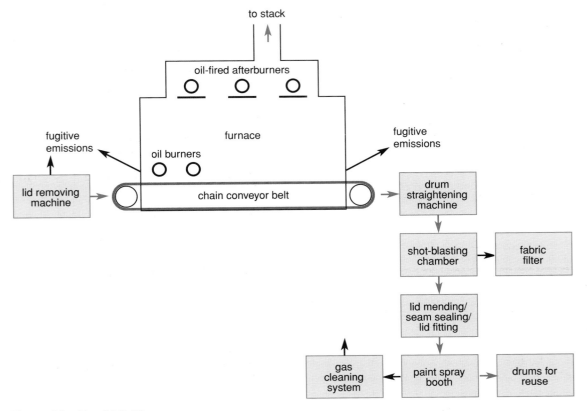

**Figure 89**  *For SAQ 59.*

adsorption, thermal or catalytic oxidation or biological oxidation. In practice, none of the oxidation options would normally be practicable through cost or space constraints, and so we are left with carbon adsorption. This would be the common means for controlling such a source, with the final discharge from a chimney to allow dilution.

## SAQ 62

You should notice that carbon monoxide is the greatest in concentration, followed by $NO_x$; hydrocarbons (HC) are last.

## SAQ 63

You should recall from the beginning of this section that the number of cars in the UK is predicted to increase from a current population of $20 \times 10^6$ to $35 \times 10^6$ by 2025.

In this example, the fuel consumption per vehicle is

$$\frac{10\,000 \text{ miles}}{35 \text{ miles gal}^{-1}} = 286 \text{ gallons}$$

so the total vehicle population consumes

$$286 \times 20 \times 10^6 \text{ gallons} = 5.7 \times 10^9 \text{ gallons}$$

In 2025, fuel efficiency is assumed to have increased to 60 miles gal$^{-1}$, but the number of vehicles has increased to 35 million. The fuel consumption will therefore be

$$\frac{10\,000 \text{ miles}}{60 \text{ miles gal}^{-1}} (35 \times 10^6) = 5.8 \times 10^9 \text{ gallons}$$

It is unnecessary for us to calculate the carbon dioxide emission, because on the fuel consumption rate alone we can predict that the increase in vehicle numbers will overwhelm the benefits of greater fuel economy, and carbon dioxide emissions will increase.

## SAQ 64

You will recall that pollutants such as carbon monoxide and hydrocarbons are produced as a result of incomplete oxidation, so their removal may be achieved by further oxidation. Conversely, nitrogen oxides are formed by the oxidation of nitrogen from the air, and removal of this pollutant may involve chemical reduction, or removal of the oxygen. In general, cars need 'three-way catalysts' to achieve present-day emission standards. Such catalysts balance the oxidation needs for the control of carbon monoxide and hydrocarbon against the oxygen released when nitrogen oxides are reduced. Only by controlling an engine to run exactly at stoichiometric conditions can both process occur simultaneously. In addition, the presence of excess oxygen, as will occur in lean burn conditions, makes $NO_x$ reduction impossible. Thus, lean burn conditions and three way catalysts are incompatible to meet stringent emission standards.

## SAQ 65

The recalculated emission factors on a PJ basis are presented in the revised version of Table 28 in Table 37 below.

**Table 37**   *Pollutant emission factors and energy consumption for representative vehicles*

| Transport mode | Fuel | Emission factors/(g km$^{-1}$) Emission factor/($10^3$ t PJ$^{-1}$) | | | | | | Energy consumption/ (MJ km$^{-1}$) |
|---|---|---|---|---|---|---|---|---|
| | | $CO_2$ | $NO_x$ | VOC | CO | Particulates | $SO_2$ | |
| *Light duty truck, <3.5 t:* | petrol | | | | | | | |
| urban | | 590.7 | 4.5 | 7.0 | 70.0 | 0 | 0 | 10.7 |
| | | **55.2** | **0.42** | **0.65** | **6.54** | | | |
| rural | | 265.0 | 7.5 | 5.5 | 55.0 | 0 | 0 | 4.8 |
| | | **55.2** | **1.56** | **1.15** | **11.45** | | | |
| motorway | | 436 | 7.5 | 3.5 | 50.0 | 0 | 0 | 7.9 |
| | | **55.2** | **0.95** | **0.44** | **6.33** | | | |
| *Heavy duty truck, >16 t:* | diesel | | | | | | | |
| urban | | 1130.2 | 18.2 | 5.8 | 7.3 | 1.6 | 3.8 | 16.2 |
| | | **69.77** | **1.12** | **0.36** | **0.45** | **0.1** | **0.23** | |
| rural | | 1158.1 | 24.1 | 3.0 | 3.7 | 1.6 | 3.9 | 16.6 |
| | | **69.77** | **1.45** | **0.18** | **0.22** | **0.1** | **0.23** | |
| motorway | | 948.8 | 19.8 | 2.4 | 3.1 | 1.3 | 3.2 | 13.6 |
| | | **69.77** | **1.46** | **0.18** | **0.28** | **0.1** | **0.24** | |

The data for power stations in Table 29 are repeated in Table 38. From this, we note that only the emission factors for carbon dioxide and sulphur dioxide are greater from power stations than the vehicles considered. This should place the role of mobile source emissions in perspective.

**Table 38** *Emission factors per petajoule of electricity consumed for air pollutants emitted by fossil-fuelled power plant in western Europe*

| $CO_2$/ (kt PJ$^{-1}$) | $CO$/ (t PJ$^{-1}$) | $SO_2$/ (t PJ$^{-1}$) | $NO_x$/ (t PJ$^{-1}$) | $VOC$/ (t PJ$^{-1}$) |
|---|---|---|---|---|
| 126.4 | 22 | 1514 | 375 | 8 |

## SAQ 66

Just as we saw for carbon dioxide emissions in the solution to SAQ 63, the predicted increase of 75% in traffic by 2025 may well outweigh the benefits of catalytic converters. You should recall the problems of converters needing to reach their optimal operating temperature, and the fact that the vehicle fleet will only slowly be replaced with vehicles with converters. In addition, there is the problem of carbon dioxide emissions, which is not addressed and is even aggravated by catalysts.

## SAQ 67

My predictions of carboxyhaemoglobin concentrations are as below. I hope that you noticed first of all that the concentrations peaked around lunchtime and late afternoon when traffic flow would be greatest.

|  | 09.00 to 10.00 | 10.00 to 11.00 | 11.00 to 12.00 | 12.00 to 13.00 | 13.00 to 14.00 | 14.00 to 15.00 | 15.00 to 16.00 | 16.00 to 17.00 | 17.00 to 18.00 |
|---|---|---|---|---|---|---|---|---|---|
| CO (ppm) | 10 | 100 | 220 | 300 | 270 | 200 | 200 | 300 | 500 |
| COHb (%) | 0.48 | 4.8 | 10.6 | 14.4 | 13.0 | 9.6 | 9.6 | 14.4 | 24 |

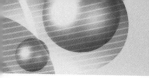

# Contents

KU-791-283

# WELCOME AND INTRODUCTION

Welcome to the Revision Guide for OCR A2 Chemistry.

We've tried to package the course in such a way as to help you more easily go into the examination room with added confidence for success.

You'll find details on:

- how OCR assess you through the examinations together with how examinations work
- there's all the content from the course presented in Specification order (with a handy list of Specification references for easy location)
- revision guidance.

*Sandra Clinton*

*Emma Poole*

2011

# A2 GCE SCHEME OF ASSESSMENT

The table below shows how the marks are allocated in the OCR A2 Chemistry course.

AS Unit F321 *Atoms, Bonds and Groups* counts 15%, Unit F322 *Chains, Energy and Resources* counts 25% and Unit F323 *Practical Skills in Chemistry 1* counts 10% of the Advanced GCE marks.

| Unit | Method of assessment | % of A2 |
|------|---------------------|---------|
| **A2 Unit F324:** *Rings, Polymers and Analysis* | 1 hour 15 minutes written paper Candidates answer all questions. 60 marks | 15% |
| **A2 Unit F325:** *Equilibria, Energetics and Elements* | 2 hour written paper Candidates answer all questions. 100 marks | 25% |
| **A2 Unit F326:** *Practical Skills In Chemistry 2* | Coursework Candidates complete three tasks set by the exam board and marked internally. 40 marks | 10% |

## Assessment objectives

Candidates are expected to demonstrate the following in the context of the chemical content of A2 Chemistry:

### Knowledge and understanding

- recognise, recall and show understanding of scientific knowledge;
- select, organise and communicate relevant information in a variety of forms.

### Application of knowledge and understanding

- analyse and evaluate scientific knowledge and processes;
- apply scientific knowledge and processes to unfamiliar situations including those related to issues;
- assess the validity, reliability and credibility of scientific information.

### How science works

- demonstrate and describe ethical, safe and skilful practical techniques and processes, selecting appropriate qualitative and quantitative methods;
- make, record and communicate reliable and valid observations and measurements with appropriate precision and accuracy;
- analyse, interpret, explain and evaluate the methodology, results and impact of their own and others' experimental and investigative activities in a variety of ways.

## Quality of written communication

It's all very well knowing lots of facts but you need to be able to communicate what you know and get your ideas across to the examiner. You might not think it but the examiner has your interests at the centre of their job – you need to give them the easiest route to maximizing your marks.

You should:

- ensure that text is legible and that spelling, punctuation, and grammar are accurate so that meaning is clear
- select and use a form and style of writing appropriate to purpose and to complex subject matter
- organise information clearly and coherently, using specialist vocabulary where appropriate

Quality of written communication is assessed across all externally assessed Units; if you write clear, well explained answers then you should obtain any marks assigned to it.

# HOW EXAMINATIONS WORK

Part of your course involves understanding/knowing *how science works*. Well, for maximum marks in your exam you need to know *how examinations work*. And in much the same way as science there are in-built rules that form the foundation of how examinations are constructed.

**Get and speak the *lingo*: know exam-speak, play the game**. Here are some popular terms which are often used in exam questions. Make sure you know what each of these terms means. For a term that requires a written answer it is most unlikely that one/two words will do!

- **Calculate**: means calculate and write down the numerical answer to the question. Remember to include your working and the units.
- **Define**: write down what a chemical/term means. Remember to include any conditions involved.
- **Describe**: write down using words and, where appropriate diagrams, all the key points. Think about the number of marks that are available when you write your answer.
- **Discuss**: write down details of the points in the given topic.
- **Explain**: write down a supporting argument using your chemical knowledge. Think about the number of marks that are available when you write your answer.
- **List**: write down a number of points. Think about the number of points required. Remember, incorrect answers will cost you marks.
- **Sketch**: when this term is used a simple freehand answer is acceptable. Remember to make sure that you include any important labels.
- **State**: write down the answer. Remember a short answer rather than a long explanation is required.
- **Suggest**: use your chemical knowledge to answer the question. This term is used when there is more than one possible answer or when the question involves an unfamiliar context.

# GETTING DOWN TO REVISION

OK, you're committed to preparing for your examination! How do *you* go about it? Remember, there are almost as many ways to revise as there are students revising. Underneath the methods of revising there are some common goals that the revising has to achieve.

**1 Boost your confidence**

Careful revision will enable you to perform at your best in your examinations. So give yourself the easiest route through the work. Organise the work into small, manageable chunks and set it out in a timetable. Then each time you finish a chunk you can say to yourself 'done it', and then move on to the next one. **And give yourself a reward too!** It's amazing how much of a lift it gives you by working in this way.

## 2 Be successful

To be successful in A2 level chemistry you must be able to:

- recall information
- apply your knowledge to new and unfamiliar situations
- carry out precise and accurate experimental work*
- interpret and analyse both your own experimental data and that of others*

*experience gained with practical work will help you with answering questions in the examination so don't set aside all this valuable knowledge and understanding

### How this revision guide can help

This book will provide you with the facts which you need to recall and some examination practice.

**Use it as a working book.** Start with the Contents list that shows you each of the topics covered. Print them and highlight the areas which you are already confident about. Then, in a different colour mark off the sections one at a time as your revision progresses. By doing this you will feel positive about what you have achieved rather than negative about what you still have to do.

For your revision programme you might like to use some or all of the following strategies:

- read through the topics one at a time and try the quick questions
- choose a topic and make your own condensed summary notes
- print or sketch and then colour important diagrams
- highlight key definitions or write them onto flash cards
- work through facts until you can recall them
- constantly test your recall by covering up sections and writing them from memory
- ask your friends and family to test your recall
- make posters for your bedroom walls
- use the 'objectives' as a self-test list
- carry out exam practice
- work carefully through the material on each page
- make 'to do' lists and tick them off.

Whatever strategies you use, measure your revision in terms of the progress you are making rather than the length of time you have spent working. You will feel much more positive if you are able to say specific things you have achieved at the end of a day's revision rather than thinking, 'I spent eight hours inside on a sunny day!'. Don't sit for extended periods of time. Plan your day so that you have regular breaks, fresh air, and things to look forward to.

**Watch out**: revision is an active occupation - just reading information is not enough! You will need to be active in your work for your revision to be successful.

**Improving your recall**: A good strategy for recalling information is to focus on a small number of facts for five minutes. Copy out the facts repeatedly in silence for five minutes then turn your piece of paper over and write them from memory. If you get any wrong then just write these out for five minutes. Finally test your recall of all the facts. Come back to the same facts later in the day and test yourself again. Then revisit them the next day and again later in the week. By carrying out this process they will become part of your long term memory – you will have learnt them!

**Past paper practice**: Once you have built up a solid factual knowledge base you need to test it by completing past paper practice. It might be a good idea to tackle several questions on the same topic from a number of papers rather than working through a whole paper at once. This will enable you to identify any weak areas so that you can work on them in more detail. Finally, remember to complete some mock exam papers under exam conditions.

## A final word (or two) for the examination room

Be prepared to answer questions on all the topics outlined in the Specification. Here are some obvious, and not so obvious thoughts:

- read through all the questions (*obvious*)
- identify which questions you can answer well (*obvious*)
  - start by answering these questions (*not so obvious*)
- once you have read a question carefully make sure you answer that question and NOT something you might think is the question (*not so obvious*)
- look at the number of marks that are available for each question and take this into account when you write your answer (*obvious and not so obvious*)
- answer space: the amount of space left for the answer will give you an indication of the length of answer the examiner expects (*obvious*)
  - short space = short answer (*obvious*)
  - longer space(1) = extended answer probably required; perhaps a sentence, or two; a calculation with working; a list containing a selection items (*obvious*)
  - longer space(2) = one word answer unlikely to be sufficient (*not so obvious*)
- answer all the questions, even if you have to guess at some (*obvious*)
- pace yourself and try to leave enough time to check your answers at the end (*obvious*)

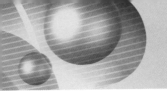

# 1.01 Naming organic compounds

## Some definitions

- **Displayed formula**: the relative positioning of atoms and the bonds between them.
- **Empirical formula**: the simplest whole number ratio of atoms of each element present in a compound.
- **Functional group**: the group of atoms responsible for the characteristic reactions of a compound. The functional group in a propan-2-ol molecule is the hydroxyl, OH group.
- **General formula**: the simplest algebraic formula of a member of a homologous series. The general formula for alkenes is $C_nH_{2n}$.
- **Homologous group**: a series of organic compounds having the same functional group but with each successive member differing by $CH_2$.
- **Molecular formula**: the actual number of atoms of each element in a molecule.
- **Skeletal formula**: The simplified organic formula, shown by removing hydrogen from alkyl chains, leaving just the carbon skeleton and associated functional groups.
- **Structural formula**: the minimal detail that shows the arrangement of the atoms in a molecule. The structural formula for propane is $CH_3CH_2CH_3$.

## Naming unbranched organic compounds

The names of unbranched organic compounds have three parts.
- The first part tells you the number of carbon atoms in the compound.

| number of carbon atoms | prefix (first part of name) |
|---|---|
| 1 | meth- |
| 2 | eth- |
| 3 | prop- |
| 4 | but- |
| 5 | pent- |
| 6 | hex- |

- The middle part tells you the bonding in the chain
  -an- means there are only single bonds
  -en- means there is a double bond in the carbon chain.

- The last part of the name tells you which functional groups are attached to the carbon chain.
  -ol means that a hydroxyl, –OH, group is attached to the carbon chain.
  -al means there is a carbonyl, >C=O, group at the end of the carbon chain.
  -oic acid means there is a carboxyl, COOH, group attached to the carbon chain.
  -one means there is a carbonyl, >C=O, group in the carbon chain but not at the end.
- We use a number to give the position of the functional group along the carbon chain. When numbers are needed we add hyphens between the parts of the names.

## Naming branched organic compounds

- To name an organic compound with a branched chain, first find the number of carbon atoms in the main (longest) chain.
- The branches that come off the main chain are called **side chains**.

| number of C atoms in side chain | side chain | name |
|---|---|---|
| 1 | $-CH_3$ | methyl |
| 2 | $-CH_2CH_3$ | ethyl |
| 3 | $-CH_2CH_2CH_3$ | propyl |
| 4 | $-CH_2CH_2CH_2CH_3$ | butyl |

- We use numbers to give the positions of the side chains.

### Questions

1 Look at the diagram below.

H—C—H with H—C—C—C—C chain, carbons bearing H atoms, and C double bonded to O with OH

a How many carbon atoms are in the main chain of this molecule?

b Circle the functional group in this compound.

c Name this compound.

# OCR

**Updated**

# Chemistry

## REVISION GUIDE

**Sandra Clinton**
**Emma Poole**

**A2**

# OXFORD
UNIVERSITY PRESS

Oxford University Press is a department of the University of Oxford. It furthers the University's objective of excellence in research, scholarship, and education by publishing worldwide in

Oxford New York Auckland Cape Town Dar es Salaam Hong Kong Karachi
Kuala Lumpur Madrid Melbourne Mexico City Nairobi
New Delhi Shanghai Taipei Toronto

With offices in
Argentina Austria Brazil Chile Czech Republic France Greece
Guatamala Hungary Italy Japan South Korea Poland Portugal Singapore
Switzerland Thailand Turkey Ukraine Vietnam

Oxford is a registered trade mark of Oxford University Press in the UK and in certain other countries

British Library Cataloguing in Publication Data
Data available

ISBN: 978-0-19913629-2

10 9 8 7 6 5 4 3 2 1

Printed by Bell and Bain Ltd., Glasgow

**Acknowledgements:**
Authors, editors, co-ordinators and contributors: Sandra Clinton, Emma Poole, Ruth Holmes.
Project managed by Elektra Media Ltd. Typeset by Wearset Ltd.

Paper used in the production of this book is a natural, recyclable product made from wood grown in sustainable forests. The manufacturing process conforms to the environmental regulations of the country of origin.

| class of compound | prefix | suffix | example name | displayed formula | functional group |
|---|---|---|---|---|---|
| alkane | | ane | propane | | |
| alkene | | ene | propene | | |
| halogenoalkane | halogeno | | 1-chloropropane | | |
| primary alcohol | | ol | propan-1-ol | | |
| secondary alcohol | | ol | propan-2-ol | | |
| tertiary alcohol | | ol | methylpropan-2-ol | | |
| nitrile | cyano | nitrile | propanenitrile | | |
| amine | amino | amine | propylamine | | |
| aldehydes | | al | propanal | | |
| ketones | | one | propanone | | |
| carboxylic acids | | oic acid | propanoic acid | | |
| acyl chloride | | oyl chloride | propanoyl chloride | | |
| amide | | amide | propanamide | | |
| ester | | oate | ethyl propanoate | | |
| acid anhydride | | anhydride | propanoic anhydride | | |
| arenes and aromatics | phenyl | benzene | phenylamine | | |
| | | | nitrobenzene | | |

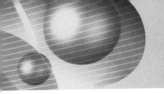 

## Arenes

Arene molecules contain at least one **benzene** ring. In the past arenes were called **aromatic compounds** because of their distinctive smells.

## Benzene

**Reminder**

Benzene must not be used in schools because it is highly toxic. Repeated contact with benzene can cause leukaemia.

- Benzene has the molecular formula $C_6H_6$.
- It is a planar molecule with six carbon atoms arranged in a hexagonal ring.
- The bond angle between the atoms is 120°.

Ideas about the structure of benzene have developed over time.

Kékule suggested that benzene molecules contained a ring of six carbon atoms with alternating single and double bonds.

The displayed formula of the Kékule structure of benzene.

The skeletal formula of the Kékule structure of benzene.

## The modern structure of benzene

All the carbon bonds are the same length.

| bond | bond length (nm) |
| --- | --- |
| mean C–C | 0.154 |
| mean C=C | 0.134 |
| C–C bonds in benzene | 0.140 |

- The carbon bonds in benzene are **intermediate** between single and double bonds.
- Benzene has six carbon atoms joined by single bonds with **delocalized** electrons above and below the plane.
- Each carbon atom contributes one electron to form a bond that is spread over all six carbon atoms.

- These electrons are delocalized.
- Benzene is a **planar** (flat) molecule, which allows the p orbitals to overlap, forming pi bonds.

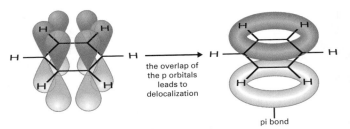

the overlap of the p orbitals leads to delocalization

pi bond

Benzene is often represented by its skeletal formula.

## Delocalization and stability

The delocalization of the electrons in pi bonds means that benzene is more stable than might be expected. Benzene does not readily undergo addition reactions, as this would require a lot of energy to break up the delocalized electron system.

Instead most of the reactions of benzene are substitution reactions. In these reactions a new group replaces a hydrogen atom and the delocalized electron system is maintained.

### The delocalization enthalpy of benzene

A cyclohexene molecule has one double bond. It reacts with hydrogen in a **hydrogenation** reaction to form cyclohexane.

cyclohexene + $H_2$ ⟶ cyclohexane

The enthalpy change for the hydrogenation of cyclohexene is $-120$ kJ mol$^{-1}$

If a benzene molecule contained alternating single and double bonds as shown by the Kékule structure it could be called cyclohexatriene.

cyclohexatriene + $3H_2$ ⟶ cyclohexane

We could predict that the enthalpy change for the hydrogenation of cyclohexatriene would be equal to three times the enthalpy change for the hydrogenation of cyclohexene, which would be $-360$ kJ mol$^{-1}$

The experimental value for the enthalpy change for the hydrogenation of benzene is $-208$ kJ mol$^{-1}$

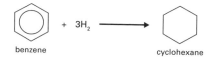

- Benzene does not contain three double bonds.
- Instead it has a delocalized electron system.
  - As a result benzene is more stable than might be expected.
- More energy is required to break the delocalized electron system than is required to break three double bonds
  - As a result the overall enthalpy change for the reaction is much lower than might be expected.

The difference between the predicted enthalpy of hydrogenation of cyclohexatriene and the enthalpy of hydrogenation of benzene is called the delocalization enthalpy and is equal to $-152$ kJ mol$^{-1}$

It is the amount of energy that must be supplied to break the delocalized electron system.

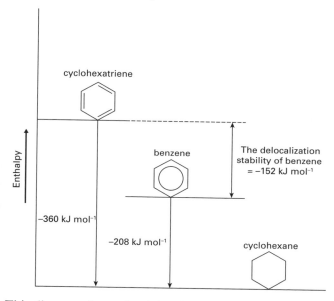

This diagram shows the delocalization enthalpy of benzene.

## Electrophilic substitution

Benzene mainly undergoes **electrophilic substitution** reactions with **electrophiles** such as $NO_2^+$, $Cl^+$, and $CH_3^+$.

- An electrophile is a species that can accept a lone pair of electrons.
- Benzene's delocalized electron system makes it very stable.
- By undergoing substitution reactions rather than addition reactions benzene retains the stability associated with a delocalized system.

Electrophilic substitution reactions take place in two steps.

**Step 1** An electrophile, $E^+$, is added to the benzene ring.

**Step 2** A hydrogen ion is eliminated.

- In step 1 a dative covalent bond is formed between a carbon atom in the benzene molecule and the electrophile.
- Note that the curly arrow represents the movement of a pair of electrons.

- The hexagon diagram represents a benzene molecule, $C_6H_6$.
- This produces an unstable intermediate which has a positive charge.
- In step 2 the bond between the carbon atom in the benzene ring and the hydrogen atom is broken. A hydrogen ion is released and the pair of electrons is used to restore the delocalized electron system.

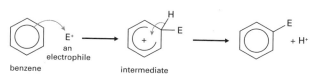

## The nitration of benzene

**Nitrobenzene** is made by the nitration of benzene. During nitration a nitro group, $NO_2$, is substituted onto the benzene molecule. The overall equation for the reaction is:

$$C_6H_6 + NO_2^+ \rightarrow C_6H_5NO_2 + H^+$$

- $NO_2^+$ is called a **nitronium** ion. It is an electrophile, which is generated by using a nitrating mixture.
- A nitrating mixture consists of a mixture of concentrated sulfuric acid and concentrated nitric acid.
- Sulfuric acid is a stronger acid than nitric acid, so sulfuric acid will protonate the nitric acid:

$$H_2SO_4 + HNO_3 \rightarrow HSO_4^- + H_2NO_3^+$$

- The protonated nitric acid, $H_2NO_3^+$ then decomposes to form a nitronium ion, $NO_2^+$:

$$H_2NO_3^+ + H_2SO_4 \rightarrow NO_2^+ + H_3O^+ + HSO_4^-$$

- The nitronium ion electrophile then reacts with benzene.
- The reaction is carried out at about 50 °C. If higher temperatures are used further nitration may occur.

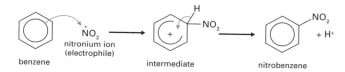

- Finally, the catalyst, sulfuric acid, is regenerated:

$$H^+ + HSO_4^- \rightarrow H_2SO_4$$

- Overall a nitro group is added to the benzene molecule and hydrogen is lost.

Nitration is an important step in the synthesis of many useful new substances.

## Questions

1 Name these compounds

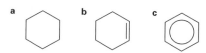

2 Why haven't you done any practical work using benzene?

3 Why does benzene typically undergo substitution reactions rather than addition reactions?

### The halogenation of benzene

Alkenes that contain C=C double bonds react readily with bromine. In fact, bromine water is used to test for the presence of C=C bonds in alkenes. The bromine adds across the double bond of the alkene molecule.

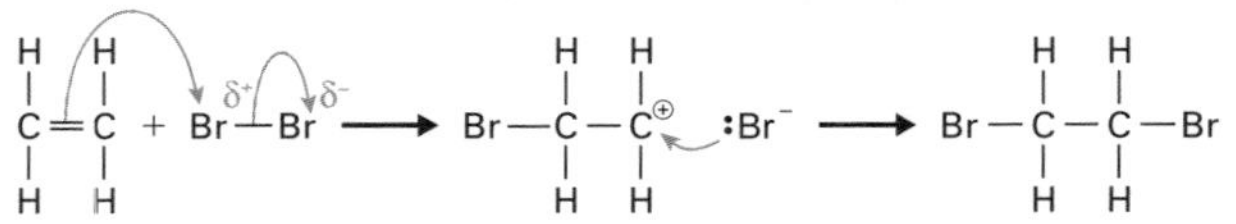

The pi electron pair in the alkene molecule attacks the slightly positively charged bromine in the bromine molecule. The double bond in the alkene is broken and a new bond is formed between the alkene and bromine.

However, benzene does not react with bromine unless a catalyst known as a halogen carrier is present. This is due to the delocalized pi electron system in benzene molecules. This lowers the pi electron density and prevents the benzene molecule from being able to polarize the bromine molecule sufficiently to be able to break the Br-Br bond. This means that no reaction takes place without a catalyst.

Benzene does react with halogens in the presence of a halogen carrier.

- In bromination reactions $AlBr_3$ or $FeBr_3$ can be used as a halogen carriers.
- In chlorination reactions $AlCl_3$ or $FeCl_3$ can be used as a halogen carrier.
- Iron can be used as a halogen carrier in bromination or chlorination reactions. The iron reacts with bromine to form $FeBr_3$ and with chlorine to form $FeCl_3$.

### The bromination of benzene

In the bromination of benzene the halogen carrier $AlBr_3$ is used to produce the bromonium ion, $Br^+$, which is an electrophile.

$$AlBr_3 + Br_2 \rightarrow AlBr_4^- + Br^+$$

The bromonium electrophile now reacts with benzene in an electrophilic substitution reaction.

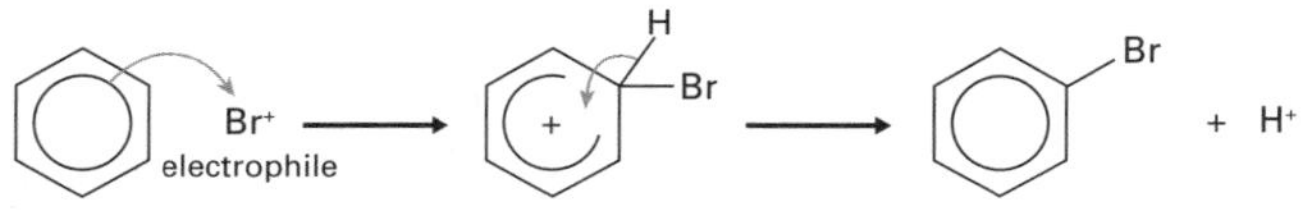

benzene      intermediate      bromobenzene

The reaction produces $H^+$ which reacts with the $AlBr_4^-$ to regenerate the $AlBr_3$ catalyst.

$$H^+ + AlBr_4^- \rightarrow AlBr_3 + HBr$$

## Phenol

Phenols are compounds that have a hydroxyl group, OH, attached directly to the benzene ring.

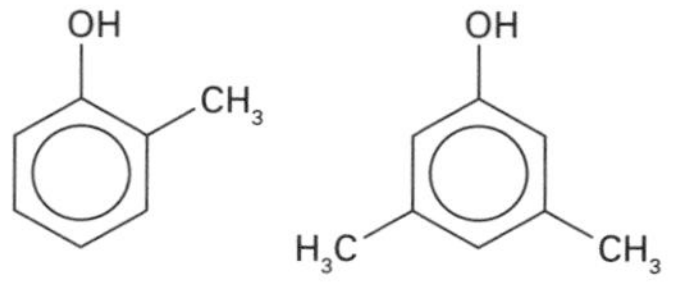

phenols

The simplest phenol, benzenol, is always known as phenol.

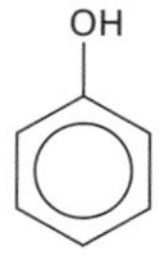

'phenol'

Phenol dissolves in water to form a very weak acid.

$$C_6H_5OH(l) + H_2O(l) \rightleftharpoons C_6H_5O^-(aq) + H_3O^+(aq)$$

## Reaction of phenol with sodium hydroxide

Phenol reacts with sodium hydroxide to form a solution of sodium phenoxide.

$$C_6H_5OH(l) + NaOH(aq) \rightleftharpoons C_6H_5O^-Na^+(aq) + H_2O(l)$$

| phenol | sodium hydroxide | | sodium phenoxide | water |

This is a neutralization reaction.

## Reaction of phenol with reactive metals

Phenol reacts with sodium to form a salt called sodium phenoxide and hydrogen.

$$2C_6H_5OH(l) + 2Na(s) \rightarrow 2C_6H_5O^-Na^+(aq) + H_2(g)$$

| phenol | sodium | | sodium | hydrogen |

As hydrogen gas is produced in the reaction, effervescence is observed.

## Reaction of phenol with bromine

For benzene to react with halogens a catalyst called a halogen carrier must be present. However, no catalyst is required for the bromination of phenol. The reaction takes place readily at room temperature. If bromine water is reacted with phenol a precipitate of 2,4,6-tribromophenol is produced and the bromine water is decolorized.

$$C_6H_5OH(l) + 3Br_2(aq) \rightarrow C_6H_2Br_3OH(s) + 3HBr(aq)$$

| phenol | bromine water | 2,4,6-trinitrophenol | |

Phenol reacts more readily with bromine than benzene does because the lone pair of electrons found in the p-orbital of the oxygen interacts with the delocalized pi electrons of the benzene ring. This increases the electron density to the extent that the pi electrons are now able to polarize the bromine molecule and produce an electrophile that is then able to carry out an electrophilic substitution reaction with the benzene ring.

## Uses of phenol

Phenol is an important chemical feedstock and is used make a wide range of new chemicals including:

* plastics such as melamine
* antiseptics such as 'TCP'
* disinfectants such as 'Dettol'
* resins for making paints

# Questions

1 Why will benzene only react with a halogen if a halogen carrier is present?

2 Give the equation for the reaction between phenol and water.

3 Explain why phenol reacts more readily with bromine than benzene does.

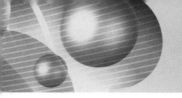

# 1.04  Aldehydes and ketones

## Aldehydes

Aldehydes and ketones both contain a **carbonyl**, >C=O, group.

Aldehydes have the general formula

$$R - \overset{\displaystyle O}{\underset{\displaystyle H}{C}}$$

Examples include

$$H - \overset{H}{\underset{H}{C}} - \overset{O}{C} \overset{}{\underset{H}{}}$$
ethanal

$$H - \overset{H}{\underset{H}{C}} - \overset{H}{\underset{H}{C}} - \overset{O}{C} \overset{}{\underset{H}{}}$$
propanal

## Ketones

Ketones have the general formula

$$\overset{R_1}{\underset{R_2}{C}} = O$$

Examples include

$$H - \overset{H}{\underset{H}{C}} - \overset{O}{\overset{\|}{C}} - \overset{H}{\underset{H}{C}} - H$$
propanone

$$H - \overset{H}{\underset{H}{C}} - \overset{H}{\underset{H}{C}} - \overset{O}{\overset{\|}{C}} - \overset{H}{\underset{H}{C}} - H$$
butanone

Ketones that have five or more carbon atoms have isomers with the carbonyl group on different carbon atoms, so numbers are used to indicate the position of the carbonyl group.

### Worked example

*Look at the displayed and skeletal formula for the compound, **A**, below.*

compound **A**

1 *Identify the functional group present in this compound.*
2 *Name the class of compound that **A** belongs to.*
3 *Name compound **A**.*

1 A contains the carbonyl, >C=O, functional group.
2 A is a ketone
3 hexan-3-one

## Oxidation and reduction

**Oxidation** can be described as:
- loss of electrons
- gain of oxygen atoms
- loss of hydrogen atoms

**Reduction** can be described as:
- gain of electrons
- loss of oxygen atoms
- gain of hydrogen atoms

Aldehydes are made by the oxidation of primary alcohols while ketones are made by the oxidation of secondary alcohols. Aldehydes are readily oxidized, while ketones cannot readily be oxidized.

primary alcohol $\xrightarrow{\text{oxidation}}$ $\xleftarrow{\text{reduction}}$ aldehyde $\xrightarrow{\text{oxidation}}$ $\xleftarrow{\text{reduction}}$ carboxylic acid

secondary alcohol $\xrightarrow{\text{oxidation}}$ $\xleftarrow{\text{reduction}}$ ketone

## Distinguishing between aldehydes and ketones

Aldehydes are readily oxidized by oxidizing agents such as **acidified potassium dichromate(VI)**, $K_2Cr_2O_7$, to carboxylic acids.

For example propanal is oxidized to propanoic acid:
$$CH_3CH_2CHO + [O] \rightarrow CH_3CH_2COOH$$
Notice how the symbol [O] is used to represent the oxidizing agent.

During the reaction the dichromate(VI) ions are reduced to chromium(III) ions, so there is a colour change from orange to green.

By contrast, ketones are not readily oxidized.

These observations can be used to distinguish between aldehydes and ketones.

### Tollens' reagent

**Tollens' reagent** contains ammoniacal silver nitrate, $AgNO_3$. When Tollens' reagent is added to an aldehyde and then gently warmed in a water bath at around 60 °C the aldehyde is oxidized to a carboxylic acid, while the silver ions, $Ag^+$, are reduced to silver atoms, Ag, which form a layer called a silver mirror:
$$Ag^+(aq) + e^- \rightarrow Ag(s)$$
If a ketone is warmed with Tollens' reagent there is no reaction and so no colour change.

## Reduction of aldehydes

Aldehydes can be reduced to primary alcohols by a reducing agent such as sodium tetrahydridoborate(III), $NaBH_4$, also known as sodium borohydride.

The reducing agent is added and then heated under reflux. Water or ethanol can be used as solvents.

$NaBH_4$ reduces the carbonyl, C=O, bond but it does not reduce C=C bonds. It produces hydride, $H^-$, ions.

The general equation for this reaction is:
$$RCHO + 2[H] \rightarrow RCH_2OH$$
Notice how the symbol [H] is used to represent the reducing agent.

## Reduction of ketones

Ketones can also be reduced by reducing agents such as sodium tetrahydridoborate(III). Ketones are reduced to secondary alcohols.

The general equation for this reaction is:

$$R_1COR_2 + 2[H] \rightarrow R_1CH(OH)R_2$$

### Example

The ketone propanone can be reduced to the secondary alcohol propan-2-ol:

$$CH_3COCH_3 + 2[H] \rightarrow CH_3CH(OH)CH_3$$

## The carbonyl group

Aldehydes and ketones both contain the carbonyl group.

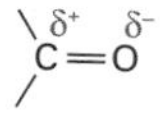

This group is polar and undergoes nucleophilic addition reactions.

### Nucleophilic addition reactions

The mechanism for the reduction of aldehydes is shown below.

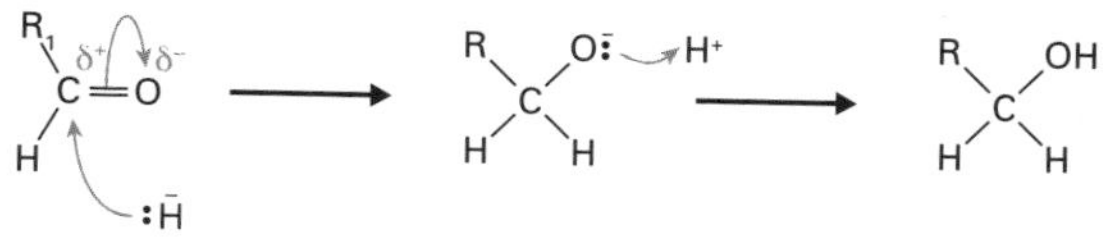

The mechanism for the reduction of ketones is shown below.

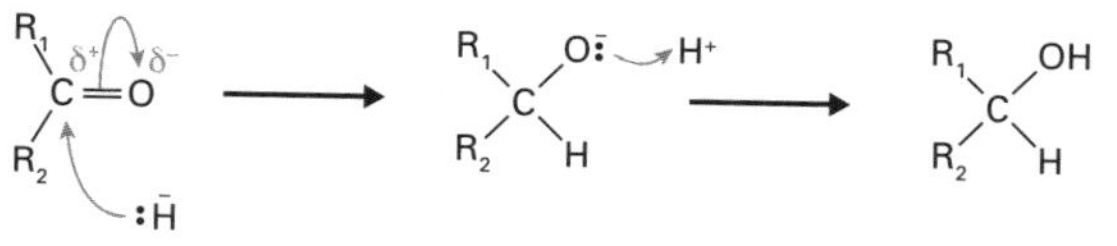

Notice how

- the relevant dipoles and lone pairs of electrons are included
- curly arrows are used to show the movement of pairs of electrons

## 2,4-dinitrophenylhydrazine

2,4-dinitrophenylhydrazine or 2,4-DNP is used to test for the presence of a carbonyl group. Aldehydes and ketones both react with 2,4-DNP.

Brady's reagent is a solution of 2,4-DNP in methanol and sulfuric acid. When Brady's reagent is added to an organic compound that contains a carbonyl group an orange or yellow precipitate is formed.

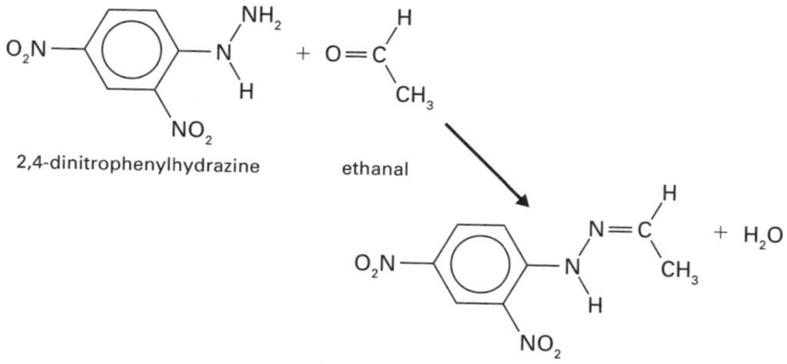

2,4-dinitrophenylhydrazine          ethanal

the 2,4-dinitrophenylhydrazine derivative of ethanal

The melting point of the precipitate formed in this reaction can be used to identify the aldehyde or ketone present.

- The precipitate formed is impure so first it must be purified by recrystallization.
- Then the melting point of the precipitate is determined.
- This melting point is compared with the melting points of other 2,4-DNP derivatives to positively identify the aldehyde or ketone.

---

### Questions

1  Describe how you could use Tollens' reagent to distinguish between an aldehyde and a ketone.
2  Name the carboxylic acid formed when ethanal is oxidized.
3  Give the equation for the reduction of butanal.

---

# 1.05 Carboxylic acids

## The carboxyl group

Carboxylic acids contain the carboxyl group, –COOH.

$$R-C\underset{OH}{\overset{O}{<}}$$

The **carboxyl** group contains both the hydroxyl group, –OH, and the carbonyl group, >C=O.

The presence of both groups modifies the properties of each so that carboxylic acids have their own set of chemical properties.

$$\overset{\delta^+}{\underset{/}{\setminus}}C=\overset{\delta^-}{O} \qquad -\overset{\delta^+}{C}-\overset{\delta^-}{O}H$$

Both the hydroxyl group and the carbonyl group are polar. This means that the carboxyl group is even more polar than either a carbonyl or an alcohol.

$$-\overset{\delta^+}{C}\underset{\delta^-\ \ \delta^+}{\overset{O\ \ \delta^-}{<}}$$

## The water solubility of carboxylic acids

Carboxylic acids with short carbon chains are very soluble in water. Carboxylic acids contain C=O and O–H bonds. These bonds are very polar. Hydrogen bonds form between the carboxylic acid molecules and water molecules.

Figure showing hydrogen bonding between a carboxylic acid molecule and water molecules, labelled "hydrogen bond".

As the carbon chain length increases, carboxylic acids become less soluble as the non-polar carbon chain does not interact with water molecules.

## Naming carboxylic acids

Unbranched **carboxylic acids** are named according to the number of carbon atoms they have.

**Example**

Structural formulae of propanoic acid.

This is propanoic acid.

If the carboxylic acid has a branched chain we use numbers to indicate the position of the side chains. We number the carbon atoms starting from the carbon atom in the carboxyl group.

Structural formulae of 2-methylbutanoic acid.

This is 2-methylbutanoic acid.

## Making carboxylic acids

Carboxylic acids are made by the oxidation of primary alcohols or aldehydes.

Propan-1-ol is oxidized by acidified potassium dichromate(VI) to propanal:

$$CH_3CH_2CH_2OH + [O] \rightarrow CH_3CH_2CHO + H_2O$$

If the oxidizing agent is in excess, the propanal is further oxidized to propanoic acid:

$$CH_3CH_2CHO + [O] \rightarrow CH_3CH_2COOH$$

## Acidic reactions of carboxylic acids

Carboxylic acids are weak acids. They partially dissociate in water.

**Example**

Ethanoic acid is a weak acid:

$$CH_3COOH \rightleftharpoons CH_3COO^- + H^+$$

Notice that the symbol $\rightleftharpoons$ is used to show that the reaction does not go to completion. In fact, the position of equilibrium lies well to the left.

Carboxylic acids react with carbonates to form a salt, water, and carbon dioxide. This reaction can be used to test for the presence of the carboxyl group.

**Example**

Ethanoic acid + sodium carbonate → sodium ethanoate + water and carbon dioxide:

$$2CH_3COOH + Na_2CO_3 \rightarrow 2CH_3COONa + H_2O + CO_2$$

This is a neutralization reaction.

Fizzing is seen as the sodium carbonate is added to the carboxylic acid.

Carboxylic acids react with reactive metals such as sodium to form a salt and hydrogen. Fizzing is seen as the hydrogen gas is made. This is a redox reaction.

**Example**

ethanoic acid + sodium → sodium ethanoate + hydrogen

$$CH_3COOH + Na \rightarrow CH_3COO^-Na^+ + \tfrac{1}{2}H_2$$

Carboxylic acids react with aqueous bases such as sodium hydroxide solution to form a salt and water.

**Example**

ethanoic acid + sodium hydroxide → sodium ethanoate + water

$$CH_3COOH + NaOH \rightarrow CH_3COO^-Na^+ + H_2O$$

This is a neutralization reaction.

### Carboxylate ions

Carboxylic acids react to form **carboxylate ions**.

**Example**

Ethanoic acid reacts with an alkali to form an ethanoate ion.

Reaction scheme showing ethanoic acid + OH⁻ → ethanoate ion + H₂O.

The lone pair of electrons on the oxygen atom and the pi electrons in the C=O bond form a **delocalized system**. This means the negative charge on the oxygen is delocalized and each carbon–oxygen bond is the same length and strength. This stabilizes the carboxylate ion and explains why carboxylic acids are acidic while alcohols, which cannot form delocalized structures, are neutral.

## Esters

Esters contain the group –COOR.

### Naming esters

The names of esters are based on the carboxylic acid they are made from and the alkyl group of the alcohol that has replaced the acid proton.

### Example

The first part of the name is the alkyl group that has replaced the acid proton; in this case it is methyl.

The second part of the name comes from the carboxylic acid that has been used to make the ester; in this case ethanoic acid.

So this is methyl ethanoate.

### Worked example

*Name the ester made from propanoic acid and methanol.*

Methyl propanoate

### Making esters

Esters are made by **esterification** reactions in which carboxylic acids, $R_1COOH$, react with alcohols, $R_2OH$, in the presence of a concentrated sulfuric acid or hydrochloric acid catalyst.

$$R_1COOH + R_2OH \xrightleftharpoons{H^+} R_1COOR_2 + H_2O$$

Note that this reaction is reversible.

In the reaction, a molecule of water is made for each molecule of ester.

these atoms form
the water molecule

### The hydrolysis of esters

The esterification reaction is reversible, and the backwards reaction is called **hydrolysis**.

• Hydrolysis is the breaking down of a compound using water.

$$\text{carboxylic acid} + \text{alcohol} \xrightleftharpoons[\text{hydrolysis}]{\text{esterification}} \text{ester} + \text{water}$$

The reaction can be carried out in a solution of a dilute acid or of a dilute alkali.

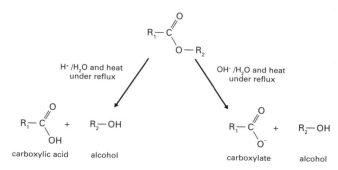

Hydrolysis using an alkali is the preferred method because the reaction happens more quickly. In this method, as the carboxylic acid is made it reacts with the alkali to form the salt of the carboxylic acid.

### Useful esters

**Esters** are found in nature as oils and fats.

They are very useful compounds which have pleasant, fruity smells and are often used as synthetic food flavourings. It is often cheaper to produce these flavourings than to extract natural flavourings. However, some people can tell the difference between the synthetic and the natural versions.

Esters are also used as solvents in perfumes and also as plasticizers (chemicals that are added to plastics to make them softer and more flexible).

---

## Questions

1 Name the functional group present in carboxylic acids.
2 Why are esters added to plastics?
3 Name the ester made from ethanoic acid and methanol.

---

# 1.06 Esters

## Biodiesel

**Biodiesel** is a fuel increasingly used in diesel engines that is not made from crude oil. As well as being a good fuel, biodiesel has good lubricating properties so it helps to reduce engine damage.

Biodiesel is a mixture of the methyl esters of long-chain carboxylic acids. It is usually made from vegetable oils. Rape methyl ester (RME) is made by reacting rape seed oil with methanol. This renewable fuel is almost identical to the non-renewable diesel made from crude oil.

## Acid anhydrides

**Acid anhydrides** contain the functional group –COOCO

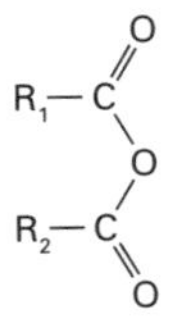

Acid anhydrides are fairly reactive organic compounds and are useful in organic synthesis.

### Naming acid anhydrides

The names of acid anhydrides are based on the names of the carboxylic acids they are derived from.

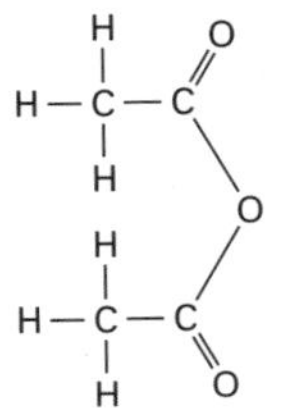

ethanoic anhydride 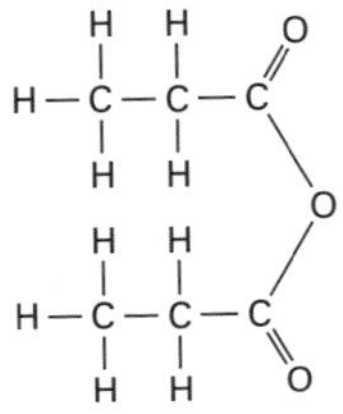        propanoic anhydride

## Reactions of acid anhydrides

Acid anhydrides react with alcohols to produce an ester and a carboxylic acid.

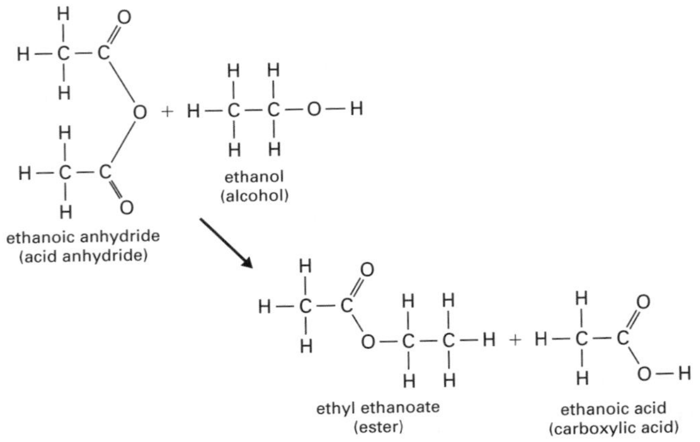

ethanoic anhydride
(acid anhydride)

ethanol
(alcohol)

ethyl ethanoate
(ester)

ethanoic acid
(carboxylic acid)

## Triglycerides

**Triglycerides** are found in vegetable oils and animal fats. They are the triesters of
- long-chain carboxylic acids (fatty acids)
- propane-1,2,3-triol (glycerol)

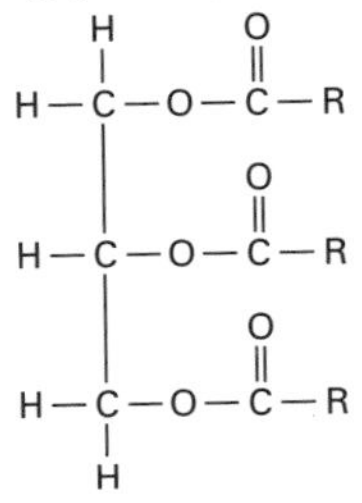

a triglyceride

Each glycerol molecule is joined to three long carbon chain carboxylic acids. The carboxylic acids joined to the glycerol can be the same or different.

A shorthand formula can be used to describe the structure of fatty acids.
- The first number shows the number of carbon atoms in the fatty acids.
- The second number shows the number of double bonds
- Finally the position of any double bonds is given in brackets.

**Example**

octadecanoic acid, 18,0

This shows that this fatty acid contains 18 carbon atoms and no double bonds (it is saturated).

octadec-9-enoic acid, 18,1 (9)

This shows that this fatty acid contains 18 carbon atoms and one double bond, between carbon 9 and carbon 10.

octadec-9,12-enoic acid, 18,2 (9,12)

This shows that this fatty acid contains 18 carbon atoms and two double bonds, the first between carbon 9 and carbon 10 and the second between carbon 12 and carbon 13.

Fatty acids are long-carbon-chain carboxylic acids. The carbon chains they contain can be saturated or unsaturated. In vegetable oils the carbon chains are normally unsaturated (contain C=C double bonds), while in animal fats the chains are normally saturated (do not contain C=C double bonds). *Cis-trans* isomerism can occur in unsaturated fats.

*Cis-trans* isomerism is a special type of *E/Z* isomerism. *E/Z* isomerism occurs because there is restricted rotation about C=C double bonds. In *cis-trans* isomerism both of the carbon atoms involved in the C=C double bond are attached to the same group or atom.

In the *trans* isomer the same groups are placed diagonally across the double bond, while in the *cis* form the same groups are either both on top of or both below the double C=C bond.

The *cis* form    The *trans* form

The C=C double bonds in naturally occurring vegetable oils are normally in the *cis* form. This means the molecules are bent and the fatty acid molecules cannot pack closely together. They have melting points below room temperature and so are liquids at room temperature.

In the *trans* form the molecules are more linear and the fatty acid molecules pack closer together. They have higher melting points and may be solid at room temperature.

## Making margarine

Many vegetable oils contain many double C=C bonds and are known as **polyunsaturated fats**. However for many uses, such as spreading a fat on bread or making cakes and pastries, a fat that is solid at room temperature is desirable. Vegetable oils can be made into margarine by adding hydrogen across some of the double C=C bonds in a process known as **hydrogenation**. A nickel catalyst is used. As hydrogen is added to the unsaturated vegetable oil the oil's melting point increases so that it becomes solid at room temperature. In addition the remaining C=C double bonds can be changed from the *cis* form to the *trans* form. There are concerns that the *trans* forms of unsaturated fats are linked to an increase in the levels of harmful cholesterol in the blood and that this in turn may lead to a greater risk of coronary heart disease and stroke.

## Questions

1 Name these compounds:

2 Name the two organic products made when ethanoic anhydride is reacted with ethanol.

# 1.07  Isomers

## Structural isomers

**Structural isomers** have the same number of each type of atom (same molecular formula) but a different structural arrangement.

### Worked example

Three carbonyl compounds have the same molecular formula, $C_4H_8O$. Name and give the displayed formula of these three compounds.

The compounds contain a >C=O group.

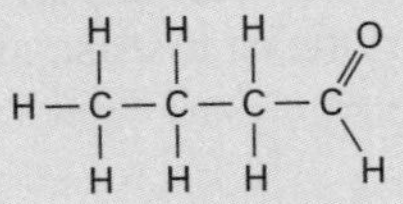

butanal

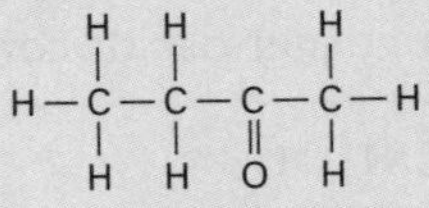

butanone

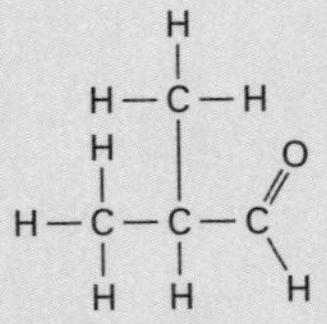

methyl propanal

In some structural isomers the carbon chains are arranged in different ways. For example, methylpropane and butane are isomers.

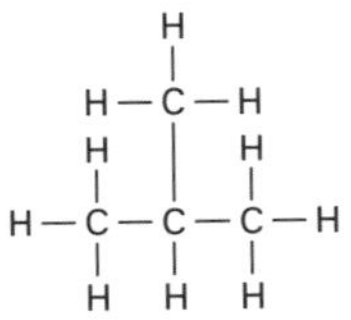

methylpropane

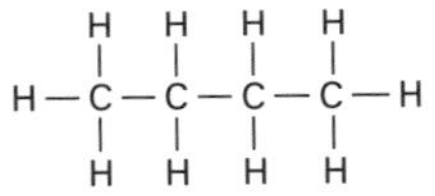

butane

In other structural isomers the same functional group is positioned at different places along the carbon chain. Butan-1-ol and butan-2-ol are examples.

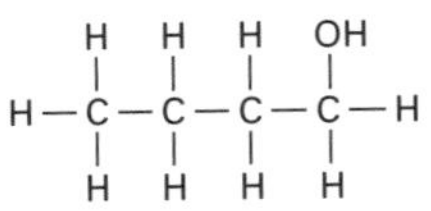

butan-1-ol

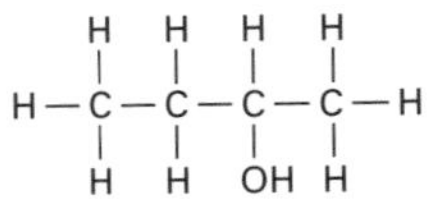

butan-2-ol

## Stereoisomers

**Stereoisomers** have the same molecular formula and the same structural formula but the atoms have a different arrangement in space. Stereoisomers include:

* **Cis-trans** or *E/Z* isomers (these have a C–C bond)
* **Optical isomers** (these have an **asymmetric** carbon atom)

### Cis-trans or E/Z isomers

* Although there is normally free rotation about a C–C bond there is restricted rotation about a C=C bond. ℝ As a result it is possible for alkene molecules to exist as stereoisomers.

For stereoisomers (*E/Z* isomers) to exist a molecule must have:

* a C=C bond
* two different groups attached to the carbon atoms involved in the double bond

### Example

But-2-ene has two stereoisomers.

The *E* isomer is

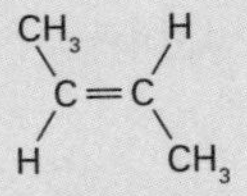

*E* comes from the German word *entgegen*. It means opposite.

The *Z* isomer is

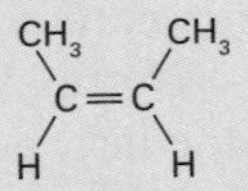

*Z* comes from the German word *zusammen*. It means together.

Notice that but-1-ene does not exist as stereoisomers.

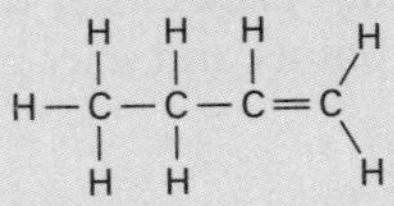

This is because one of the carbon atoms involved in the double bond is attached to two identical groups (two hydrogen atoms).

## Optical isomers

**Optical isomers** are another type of stereoisomers. Optical isomers are **non-superimposable** mirror images of each other. Optical isomers do not have to contain C=C bonds. They occur when a molecule contains a carbon atom which is attached to four different groups. This carbon atom is called an asymmetric carbon and it is a chiral centre.

### Example

This is the displayed formula of 2-iodobutane

* asymmetric carbon – a carbon atom attached to four different groups.

2-Iodobutane has two optical isomers. Notice how they are non-superimposable mirror images of each other.

### Distinguishing between optical isomers of a compound

Although they are chemically identical we can tell optical isomers apart by their optical activity. One optical isomer will rotate the plane of plane-polarized light clockwise while the other optical isomer will rotate the plane anticlockwise.

A mixture of optical isomers that contains equal amounts of each isomer will not show optical activity as the rotating effect of one optical isomer is cancelled out by the other optical isomer.

### Synthetic and natural organic molecules

Chemicals produced in the laboratory, such as synthetic amino acids, are not optically active because equal amounts of each optical isomer are produced.

However, if the same amino acid is produced by a living organism it will be optically active because only one optical isomer will be produced. This has important consequences in the manufacture of drugs. If a drug containing a chiral centre is produced in the laboratory it is likely that both optical isomers will be produced. Although one of these optical isomers may be very beneficial the other may be harmful. This was the case with the drug thalidomide. Introduced in the late 1950s one optical isomer relieved the symptoms of morning sickness. Unfortunately the other optical isomer caused serious birth defects. Although thalidomide is still used to treat leprosy, it is never given to pregnant women.

Pharmaceutical companies are now more aware of the importance of producing drugs that contain single optical isomers.

This can increase the cost of making drugs if both optical isomers are produced and the optical isomers then need to be separated.

However, it does reduce the chance of side-effects from the drug if the unwanted optical isomer is removed, and the pharmaceutical activity (effectiveness) of the drug will increase if only the desired optical isomer is present.

Modern synthesis of pharmaceuticals that contain only single optical isomers can be carried out by

* using enzymes or bacteria
* using chemical chiral synthesis or chiral catalysts
* using molecules that have a chiral centre and exist as a single optical isomer such as natural α-amino acids and sugars as starting materials. These molecules can be used to produce pharmaceuticals which also contain a single optical isomer.

### Questions

1 Does pent-1-ene have two stereoisomers? Explain your answer.

2 What is the difference between the E and the Z forms of but-2-ene?

3 Will a compound that has optical isomers always be optically active? Explain your answer.

# 1.08 Amines

## Naming amines

**Amines** are fishy-smelling compounds which contain nitrogen atoms and are derived from ammonia, $NH_3$. Amines are classified as primary, secondary, or tertiary depending on the number of hydrogen atoms in the ammonia that have been replaced by organic groups.

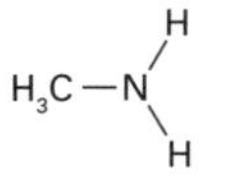

methylamine

1 hydrogen is replaced so this is a primary amine

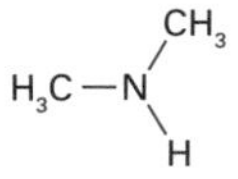

N-methylmethanamine

2 hydrogens are replaced so this is a secondary amine

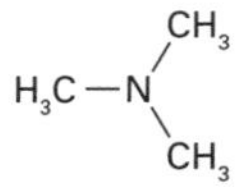

N,N-dimethylmethanamine

3 hydrogens are replaced so this is a tertiary amine

**Aromatic amines** contain a benzene ring.

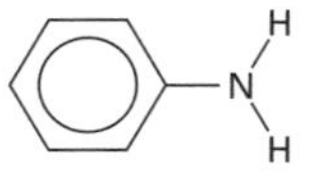

phenylamine

The primary amine propanamine exists as two isomers.

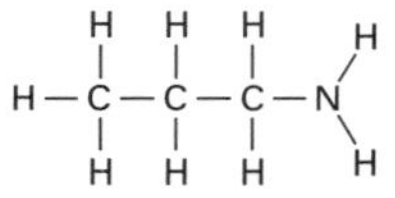

propylamine

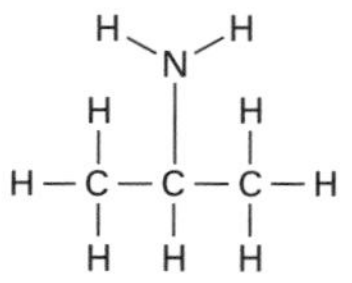

propan-2-amine

## The basic properties of amines

- Ammonia, primary amines, and primary aromatic amines are **Brønsted–Lowry bases** because they can accept protons.
- The nitrogen atom in an ammonia molecule has a lone pair of electrons that can accept a hydrogen ion (or proton) to form an ammonium ion.

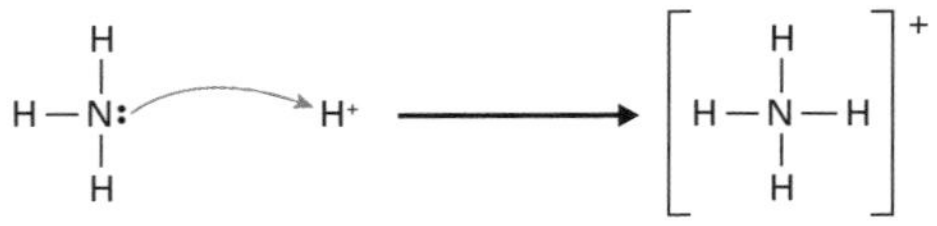

- When ammonia dissolves in water it reacts with the water molecules:
$$NH_3(aq) + H_2O(l) \rightleftharpoons NH_4^+(aq) + OH^-(aq)$$
- The solution formed is alkaline because hydroxide, $OH^-$, ions are formed. However, the reaction does not go to completion, so ammonia is only a weak base.
- Primary amines also dissolve in water and form alkaline solutions.
- Primary amines are stronger bases than ammonia.
$$CH_3NH_2(aq) + H_2O(l) \rightleftharpoons CH_3\overset{+}{N}H_3(aq) + OH^-(aq)$$
- **Primary aromatic amines** such as phenylamine are weaker bases than ammonia.

## Nucleophilic properties of amines

Ammonia and amines also act as **nucleophiles**. They have a lone pairs of electrons which can be donated to form a dative covalent bond.

Halogenoalkanes react with an excess of ammonia to form primary amines. Ethanol is used as a solvent.

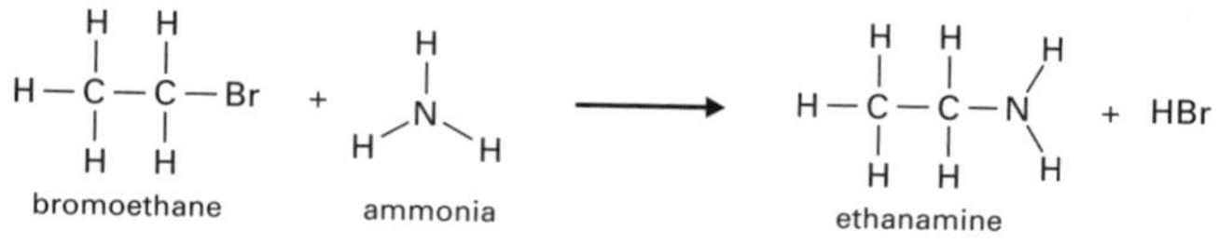

bromoethane        ammonia                        ethanamine

- The reactivity of the halogenoalkane depends on the strength of the carbon–halogen bond.
- This means that fluoroalkanes are least reactive and iodoalkanes are most reactive.

However, if ammonia is not in excess the primary amine produced will react with another halogenoalkane molecule and further substitution can take place.

### Making aromatic amines

Aromatic amines such as phenylamine can be made by the reduction of nitroarenes such as nitrobenzene using tin and concentrated hydrochloric acid.

## Dye stuffs

So-called azo dyes can be made by nitrating benzene to produce nitrobenzene.

- First the nitrobenzene is reduced to **phenylamine**, $C_6H_5NH_2$, an aromatic amine.

$$C_6H_5NO_2 + 6[H] \longrightarrow C_6H_5NH_2 + 2H_2O$$
nitrobenzene                                phenylamine

- Then the aromatic amine is converted to a **diazonium salt**. Sodium nitrate(III) and hydrochloric acid are used to produce nitrous acid, $HNO_2$:

$$NaNO_2 + HCl \rightarrow HNO_2 + NaCl$$

- The reaction must be cooled in an ice bath so that it is kept below 10 °C. This stops the diazonium salt decomposing.

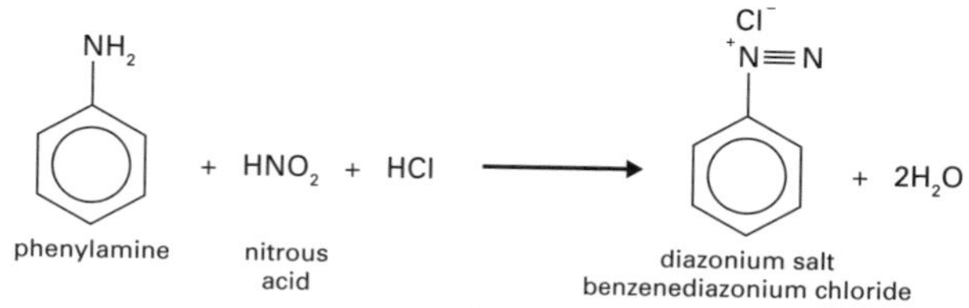

phenylamine    nitrous            diazonium salt
               acid               benzenediazonium chloride

- Finally the diazonium salt is reacted with another suitable aromatic compound to form an **azo dye**.

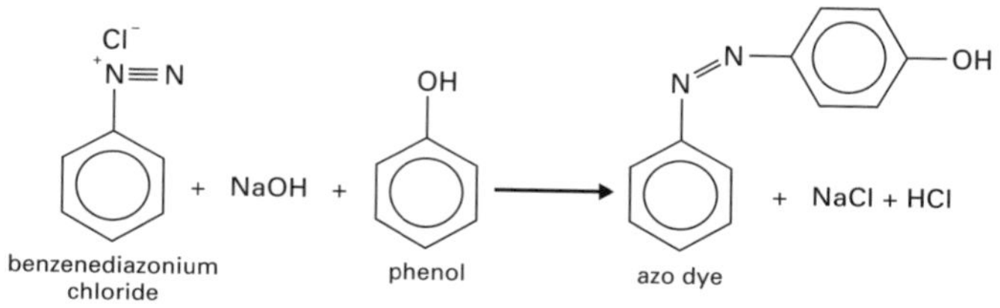

benzenediazonium          phenol        azo dye
chloride

- This is a coupling reaction. Again the reaction must be cooled to stop the diazonium salt from decomposing.

Azo dyes are useful dyes that can be used to colour synthetic or natural fibres. Different coloured dyes are formed by coupling the diazonium salt with different aromatic compounds.

---

## Questions

1 Why do amines act as bases?
2 Why do amines react as nucleophiles?

---

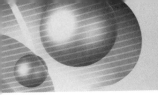

# 1.09 Amino acids and polymers

## Amino acids

- **Amino acids** have an amino, $-NH_2$, group and a carboxyl, $-COOH$, group.
- The amino group is basic and the carboxyl group is acidic so amino acids are amphoteric – they react with both acids and bases.
- There are about twenty naturally occurring amino acids.

- Different amino acids have different R groups.
- α-Amino acids have an –R group bonded to a carbon atom that directly carries the amino and carboxyl groups.
- α-Amino acids join together to form proteins.

The general formula for an α-amino acid is $RCH(NH_2)COOH$.

## Zwitterions

- Amino acids can exist as **zwitterions** in which both the functional groups are charged.

- The **isoelectric point** is the pH at which both the amino group and the carboxyl group are most likely to be charged.
  - As a result the amino acid will be electrically neutral overall.
- Different α-amino acids have different R groups and this means that they have different isoelectric points.

- At lower pH values the amino group is more likely to be protonated.
- At higher pH values the carboxyl group is more likely to have lost its proton.
- The existence of zwitterions means that amino acids are readily soluble in water (which is a polar solvent).
- The existence of zwitterions means that amino acids have quite high melting points and are solid at room temperature.

## Proteins and polypeptides

Amino acids can join together to form **polypeptides** or **proteins**.

- Proteins are made up of more than about twenty different amino acids.
- Most common proteins contain more than a hundred amino acid units.
- Polypeptides are made up of less than about twenty amino acid units.

## Making proteins

- Proteins are made by a **condensation polymerization** reaction.
- In these reactions, bonds form between the monomers, in this case amino acids, so that they join together to form a larger molecule.
- Another small molecule, in this case water, $H_2O$, is also made. As each amino acid is added one water molecule is also formed.
- Proteins are examples of natural polymers.

## The peptide link

Amino acids contain the amine group, $-NH_2$, and the carboxyl group, $-COOH$.

The amine group of one amino acid reacts with the carboxyl group of the next amino acid to form a dipeptide. A water molecule is lost and a **peptide link**, $-CONH-$, is formed.

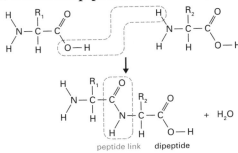

- Note the R groups may be the same or they may be different.
- In proteins the bonds named peptide bonds are really amide groups. So proteins and polypeptides are actually polyamides.
- The dipeptide produced in this reaction has an amino group at one end and a carboxyl group at the other end so the dipeptide can react with more amino acids.

Proteins have complicated structures. The primary structure of a protein is the order of the amino acids which make up the proteins.

The polypeptide chain is folded in various ways to form the 3D structure of the functional protein. This structure is held in place largely by hydrogen bonds.

At high temperatures or in acidic or alkaline conditions the hydrogen bonds can be broken. This disrupts the structure of the protein and it becomes denatured.

24

# Hydrolysis of the peptide link

- Proteins are made by the condensation polymerization of amino acids.
- Proteins can be broken down into amino acids by **hydrolysis**. Hydrolysis is the reverse of the condensation polymerization of amino acids.
- First the protein is reacted with 6 mol dm$^{-3}$ hydrochloric acid for 24 hours.
- Then the reaction mixture is neutralized.

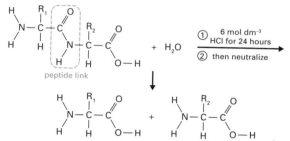

# Addition polymers

- Addition polymers are made when many unsaturated molecules join together.
- In **addition polymerization** the only product formed is the polymer.
- In condensation polymerization a small molecule such as water or hydrogen chloride is made at the same time as the polymer is made.

# Making addition polymers

- The monomer ethene is used to produce the polymer poly(ethene) or polythene.
- The names of polymers can be written either with or without the brackets.
- Here three ethene molecules join together to form a section of poly(ethene).

ethene molecules join together to form        poly(ethene)

- Notice that the monomers are unsaturated but the polymer is saturated.
- In a similar way phenylethene molecules can join together to form poly(phenylethene).

phenylethene molecules join together to form        poly(phenylethene)

- Phenylethene used to be called styrene, so its polymer was called polystyrene.

# The repeat unit

Because polymers can be made from enormous numbers of monomers we use the idea of a **repeat unit** to represent the structure of a polymer.

## *The repeat unit from the polymer*

To work out the repeat unit of a polymer, for example propene

- Redraw it so that the carbon–carbon double bond is horizontal and the bond angles are changed to 90°.
- Replace the carbon–carbon double bond with a single bond and draw a line (representing a **trailing bond**) to the left and the right of the carbon atoms that had been involved in the double bond.
- Note that the brackets are not essential, but if brackets are used the trailing bonds must extend through the brackets.

The use of the repeat unit makes it much easier to write equations for the formation of addition polymers. Here is the equation for the formation of poly(chloroethene) from its monomer chloroethene:

chloroethene        poly(chloroethene)

Chloroethene used to be called vinyl chloride so its polymer was poly(vinyl chloride) or PVC.

## *The monomer from the repeat unit*

To work out the monomer from the repeat unit of polytetrafluoroethene or PTFE

- Identify the carbon atoms which have trailing bonds.
- Remove the trailing bonds and add a double bond between these two carbon atoms.
- Finally change the bond angle from 90° to 120°.

---

## Questions

1 Identify the two functional groups found in all amino acids.

2 What are the conditions required for the hydrolysis of proteins?

3 Name the polymer formed from the addition polymerization of chloroethene.

# 1.10  Condensation polymers

## Natural and synthetic condensation polymers

In **condensation polymerization** reactions monomers join together.

- Each monomer has at least two functional groups and every time a link is made to extend the polymer a small molecule, such as water, is lost.
- Natural condensation polymers include proteins and silk.
- Synthetic condensation polymers include nylon and Kevlar.

Polyester and polyamide fibres are used to make clothes.

## Dicarboxylic acids and diols

**Dicarboxylic** acids contain two carboxyl, –COOH, groups. Ethanedioic acid is an example.

- Note that even the carbon atoms involved in the carboxyl group are included in the name.
- The suffix dioic acid is used to indicate that there are two carboxyl groups.

**Diols** contain two hydroxyl, OH, groups.

- The carbon atoms bonded to the hydroxyl functional groups are included in the name.
- The positions of both the hydroxyl groups are also given in the name.

Propane-1,3-diol is an example.

## Making polyesters

Esters can be made by reacting alcohols with carboxylic acids.

$$R_1-\overset{\overset{O}{\|}}{C}-OH \;+\; HO-R_2 \;\longrightarrow\; R_1-\overset{\overset{O}{\|}}{C}-O-R_2 \;+\; H_2O$$

- **Polyesters** can be made by reacting dicarboxylic acids with diols.
- When a dicarboxylic acid reacts with a diol an ester and water are made.

$$\underset{\text{dicarboxylic acid}}{HO-\overset{O}{\overset{\|}{C}}-R_1-\overset{O}{\overset{\|}{C}}-OH} \;+\; \underset{\text{diol}}{HO-R_2-OH} \;\longrightarrow\; \underset{\text{ester}}{\overset{O}{\overset{\|}{C}}-R_1-\overset{O}{\overset{\|}{C}}-O+R_2-OH} \;+\; \underset{\text{water}}{H_2O}$$

*ester link*

- Notice how one end of the ester still has a carboxyl group while the other end still has a hydroxyl group.
  - ⊛ As a result the ester can react with more molecules to form a long polyester molecule.

## Terylene

**Terylene** is made from the dicarboxylic acid benzene-1,4-dicarboxylic acid and the diol ethane-1,2-diol.

$$n \underset{\text{benzene-1,4-dicarboxylic acid}}{\overset{O}{\overset{\|}{C}}\cdots\overset{O}{\overset{\|}{C}}} \;+\; n \underset{\text{ethane-1,2-diol}}{HO-\overset{H}{\underset{H}{C}}-\overset{H}{\underset{H}{C}}-OH}$$

$$\underset{\text{repeat unit of Terylene}}{\left(\!\!-\overset{O}{\overset{\|}{C}}\cdots\overset{O}{\overset{\|}{C}}-O-\overset{H}{\underset{H}{C}}-\overset{H}{\underset{H}{C}}-O-\!\!\right)}$$

Benzene-1,4 dicarboxylic acid used to be called terephthalic acid while ethane-1,2-diol used to be called ethylene glycol.

- The polymer is called polyethylene terephthalate or PET.
- It is used to make plastic drinks bottles.
- It can also be drawn into fibres which are known as Terylene which is used in fabrics that are used to make clothes.
- The inclusion of Terylene makes the fabric less likely to crease and more likely to last longer.

## The repeat unit of a polyester

$$\left(\!\!-\overset{O}{\overset{\|}{C}}-\underset{\text{acid}}{\text{from carboxylic}}-\overset{O}{\overset{\|}{C}}-O-\underset{\text{diol}}{\text{from}}-O-\!\!\right)$$

- The trailing bonds go from the carbon atom of the C=O group of the carboxylic acid on one side and from the oxygen atom of the diol group on the other side.
- If brackets are used the trailing bonds should extend through the brackets.

## Diamines

**Diamines** have two amine, –NH₂, groups.
Propane-1,3 diamine is an example.

$$\overset{H}{\underset{H}{N}}-\overset{H}{\underset{H}{C}}-\overset{H}{\underset{H}{C}}-\overset{H}{\underset{H}{C}}-\overset{H}{\underset{H}{N}}$$

- Note that the position of both functional groups is given.
- The suffix diamine is used to indicate that there are two amine groups.

## Proteins

- Amino acids can join together to form proteins.
- Amino acids have at least two different functional groups. One is an amine, $-NH_2$, and the other is a carboxyl, $-COOH$, group.
- Amino acids can be described as being difunctional compounds.

## Making synthetic polyamides

- An amide link is made between a molecule which has a carboxyl group and another molecule which has an amine group.

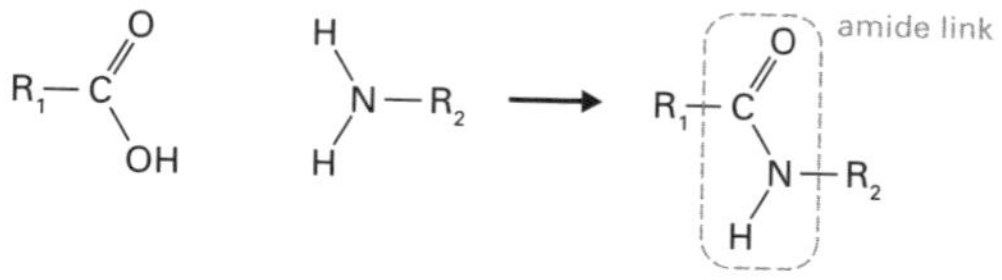

- Polyamides are made by reacting dicarboxylic acids with diamines.

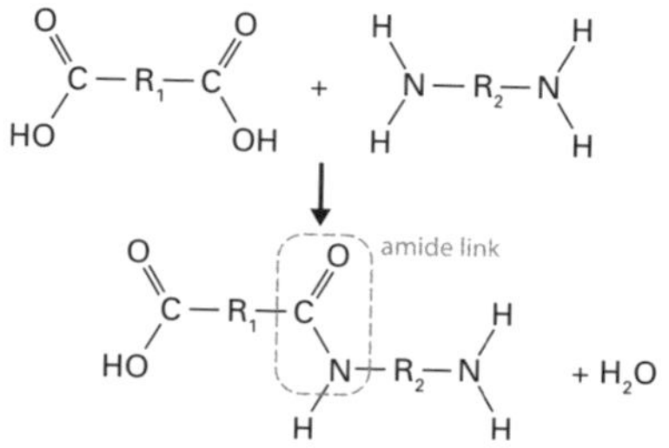

- As these molecules have a functional group at each end of the molecule they can form very long polymer chains.

## The repeat unit of a polyamide

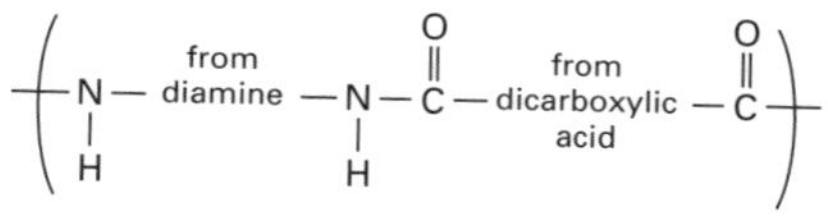

- The trailing bonds go from the nitrogen atom of the amine on one side and from the carbon atom of the C=O group of the carboxylic acid on the other side.
- If brackets are used the trailing bonds should extend through the brackets.

## Nylon

- **Nylon** 6,6 is a synthetic **polyamide** used to make ropes and clothes.
- It is made from the diamine 1,6-diaminohexane and hexane-1,6-dicarboxylic acid.
- The first part of "6,6" in the name comes from the number of carbon atoms in the diamine and the second comes from the number of carbon atoms in the dicarboxylic acid.

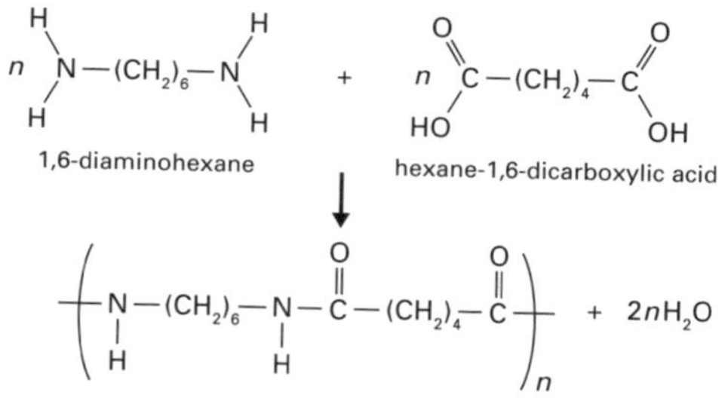

nylon 6,6

## Kevlar

**Kevlar** is another useful synthetic polyamide.

- It is used to make bullet-proof vests.
- It is light, very strong, and has a high melting point.
- It is made by a condensation polymerization between benzene-1,4-diamine and benzene-1,4-dicarboxylic acid.

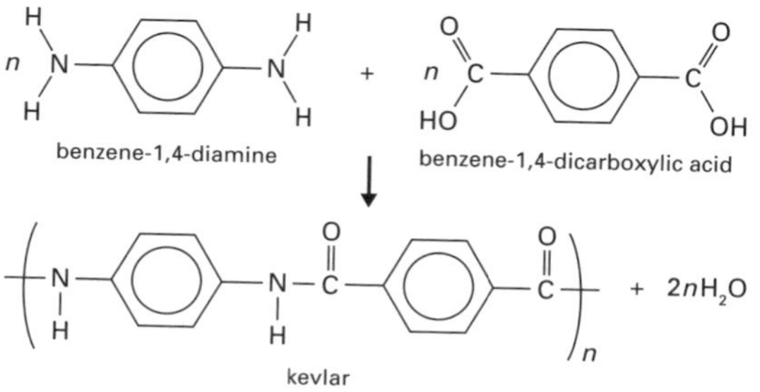

kevlar

## Biodegradable and non-biodegradable plastics

- **Biodegradable** materials can be broken down by micro-organisms.
- Polyalkenes such as poly(ethene) and poly(propene) are made by addition polymerization. Addition polymers are saturated. This makes them chemically inert.
  As a result these plastics are **non-biodegradable**.
- Polyesters and polyamides are biodegradable and can be hydrolysed by acids or alkalis.
  As a result it is much easier to dispose of these plastics.

Poly(lactic acid) is a condensation polymer made from the hydroxycarboxylic acid 2-hydroxypropanoic acid (lactic acid) which is made from corn starch.

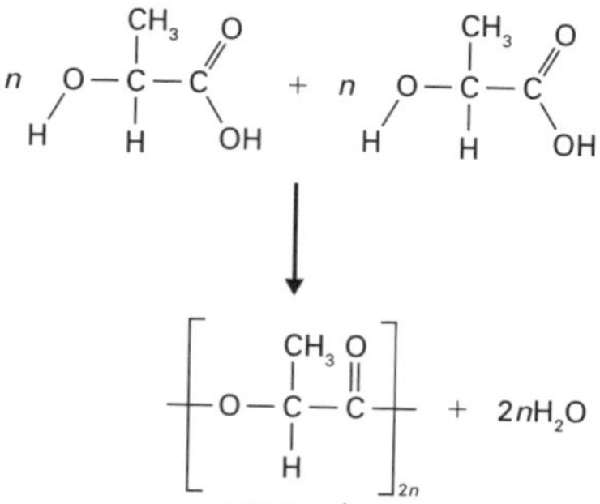

repeat unit

Poly(lactic acid) is used to make waste sacks and disposable eating utensils. Chemists have developed polymers such as poly(lactic acid) which degrade naturally in the environment because this reduces the amount of waste in landfill sites.

## Hydrolysis of polyesters

Polyesters can be hydrolysed by hot aqueous acids or alkalis. Each of the ester linkages in the polyester is hydrolysed.

- Hydrolysis by hot aqueous hydrochloric acid produces the monomers used to make the polyester.
- Hydrolysis by hot aqueous sodium hydroxide produces the sodium salt of the dicarboxylic acid and the diol.

the repeat unit of Terylene

acid hydrolysis
e.g. HCl(aq)

alkaline hydrolysis
e.g. NaOH(aq)

benzene-1,4-dicarboxylic acid

the sodium salt of
benzene-1,4-dicarboxylic acid

+

+

ethane-1,2-diol

ethane-1,2-diol

## Hydrolysis of polyamides

Polyamides can also be hydrolysed by hot aqueous acids or alkalis. The amide linkages in the polyamide are hydrolysed.

- Hydrolysis by hot aqueous hydrochloric acid produces the ammonium salt of the diamine and the dicarboxylic acid.
- Hydrolysis by hot aqueous sodium hydroxide produces the diamine and the sodium salt of the dicarboxylic acid.

repeat unit of nylon 6,6

acid hydrolysis
e.g. HCl (aq)

alkaline hydrolysis
e.g. NaOH (aq)

ammonium salt
of the diamine

diamine

+

+

dicarboxylic acid

sodium salt of
dicarboxylic acid

# Photodegradable polymers

Photodegradable polymers break down when exposed to sunlight. Condensation polymers, which contain C=O bonds, absorb ultraviolet radiation. Photodegradable polymers are designed so that when this happens the polymer chains are broken. These chains are then decomposed further by bacteria to form carbon dioxide and water.

| Questions |
| --- |
| 1 Name the type of compound that can be reacted with a dicarboxylic acid to form a polyester. <br> 2 Name a synthetic polyamide used to make ropes and clothes. <br> 3 Name a natural polyamide made from amino acids. |

# 1.11 Synthetic routes

## Synthesis

Chemists are interested in making new chemicals from existing ones. In your examination you may be asked to suggest a way to synthesize a new compound.

This will involve you showing a good understanding of the chemistry of the range of organic compounds covered in the AS course and A2 course is. So it is important to revise these sections very thoroughly.

If a reaction from the AS course is used in a question then details of the reagents and the conditions used will be included. Some questions could introduce chemicals that are not mentioned in the specification to see how you can apply your knowledge in new situations. In such questions information about reagents and conditions will be supplied in the question.

There are often several ways to produce a certain chemical so chemists choose routes which

- don't involve too many steps, as the more steps there are the lower the yield of the desired product is likely to be
- keep costs down by not using expensive starting materials or expensive techniques
- are less likely to result in competing reactions that will decrease the yield of the desired product.

**Safety** also needs to be considered. Think about the specific hazards of the chemicals involved, for example they may be volatile, flammable, toxic by inhalation, or corrosive.

Then think about steps that could sensibly be used to reduce these hazards, for example

- You could heat a volatile flammable liquid under reflux using an electrical heater.
- You could wear gloves when using a corrosive chemical.
- You could use a fume cupboard when using a chemical that should not be breathed in.
- It will be assumed that a lab coat and goggles will be worn.

### Worked example 1

*Consider the series of reaction below.*

$$H-\underset{\underset{H}{|}}{\overset{\overset{H}{|}}{C}}-\underset{\underset{H}{|}}{\overset{\overset{H}{|}}{C}}-\underset{\underset{H}{|}}{\overset{\overset{H}{|}}{C}}-Br \xrightarrow{step\ 1} H-\underset{\underset{H}{|}}{\overset{\overset{H}{|}}{C}}-\underset{\underset{H}{|}}{\overset{\overset{H}{|}}{C}}-\underset{\underset{H}{|}}{\overset{\overset{H}{|}}{C}}-OH \xrightarrow{step\ 2} H-\underset{\underset{H}{|}}{\overset{\overset{H}{|}}{C}}-\underset{\underset{H}{|}}{\overset{\overset{H}{|}}{C}}-C\underset{H}{\overset{O}{\nwarrow}}$$

1-bromompropane    compound **Y**    propanal

*1 Name compound **Y**.*

*2 Give the reagents and conditions required for step 2.*

*3 Identify the functional group present in:*

  *a compound Y*

  *b propanal.*

1 **Y** is propan-1-ol

2 Step 2 acidified potassium dichromate(VI) and distil off the product

3 **a** Hydroxyl

  **b** Carbonyl.

### Worked example 2

*Consider the following reaction series.*

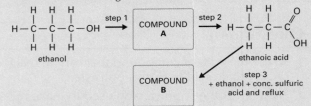

*1 Name compounds **A** and **B**.*

*2 Name the type of reaction occurring in*

  *a step 1*

  *b step 3*

*3 Give the reagents and conditions required for step 2 and describe what you would see.*

1 Compound **A** is ethanal and compound **B** is ethyl ethanoate.

2 **a** Step 1 is oxidation.

  **b** Step 3 is esterification.

3 Warm with acidified potassium dichromate(VI) solution. There would be a colour change of orange to green.

## Identifying functional groups

Chemical tests can be used to identify a range of **functional groups**.

### Identifying alkenes

- Aqueous bromine can be used to test for the presence of **alkenes**.
- If an alkene is present the aqueous bromine is decolorized (brown to colourless) because of an addition reaction between the alkene and the bromine.
- **Alkanes** are saturated so there is no change when alkanes are mixed with aqueous bromine.
- Benzene also does not react because the high stability of the delocalized electron system means it is resistant to addition reactions.

## Identifying aldehydes and ketones

**Aldehydes** and **ketones** both contain a carbonyl, >CO, group. Aldehydes can be oxidized to carboxylic acids while ketones are not easily oxidized. This can be used to distinguish between these two groups.

### Tollens' reagent

- Tollens' reagent is a solution of silver nitrate in aqueous ammonia. Tollens' reagent contains silver, $Ag^+$, ions.
- Aldehydes reduce these silver ions to silver atoms:

$$Ag^+(aq) + e^- \rightarrow Ag(s)$$

- A silver mirror is produced inside the test tube.
- There is no change for ketones.

### Acidified potassium dichromate(VI)

- Acidified potassium dichromate(VI) can also be used to distinguish between aldehydes and ketones. Aldehydes reduce the orange $Cr_2O_7^{2-}$ ions to green $Cr^{3+}$ ions.
- There is no change for ketones.

## Identifying carboxylic acids

**Carboxylic acids** are weak organic acids that contain the carboxyl group, –COOH.

- Carboxylic acids have a pH of around 3 which means that they turn universal indicator orange/red.
- Carboxylic acids react with carbonates to form a salt, water, and carbon dioxide. For example ethanoic acid reacts with calcium carbonate:

$$2CH_3COOH(aq) + CaCO_3(s) \rightarrow (CH_3COO)_2Ca(aq) + CO_2(g) + H_2O(l)$$

- To confirm that the gas produced is carbon dioxide it can be bubbled through limewater. If the gas is carbon dioxide it will turn the limewater cloudy.

## Identifying alcohols

**Alcohols** contain the hydroxyl, –OH, group. These compounds can be classified as being primary, secondary, or tertiary alcohols.

- First the alcohol is heated with acidified potassium dichromate(VI).
- Tertiary alcohols are not easily oxidized so when they are heated with acidified potassium dichromate(VI) there is no change.
- Primary and secondary alcohols are both oxidized so when they are heated with acidified potassium dichromate(VI) the orange $Cr_2O_7^{2-}$ ions are reduced to green $Cr^{3+}$ ions.
- Primary alcohols are oxidized to aldehydes, while secondary alcohols are oxidized to ketones. Tollens' reagent or acidified potassium dichromate(VI) can be used to distinguish between these two types of compound.

## Questions

1 Suggest a safety precaution that could be used when using concentrated sulfuric acid.

2 How could a tertiary alcohol be distinguished from a primary or secondary alcohol?

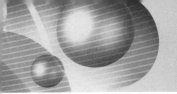

# 1.12 Mass spectrometry and chromatography

## Mass spectrometry

**Mass spectrometry** can be used to identify organic compounds. When an organic compound is placed in a mass spectrometer it is bombarded by high-energy electrons and different electrons are knocked out of the organic molecule. This is called ionization.

- When a sample is bombarded with electrons it forms a cation with an unpaired electron, $M^{+\bullet}$. This species is a radical.
- The peak on the mass spectrum with the highest mass/charge ratio is called the molecular ion peak or M.
- The highest peak is called the base peak.
- The more stable the cation (positive ion) the higher its peak will be.
- The molecular ion may also fragment, to produce ions with lower mass/charge ratios.

$$M^{+\bullet} \longrightarrow X^+ \ + \ Y^{\bullet}$$

this fragment is shown in the mass spectrum    this fragment has no charge so it is not shown in the mass spectrum

When organic molecules pass through a mass spectrometer they fragment (break up).

By studying the position of the peaks caused by fragmentation chemists can suggest the identity of the ions responsible. This allows chemists to build up an idea of the structure of the organic compound being investigated.

| mass/charge ratio | ion responsible for the peak |
|---|---|
| 15 | $CH_3^+$ |
| 29 | $C_2H_5^+$ |
| 43 | $C_3H_7^+$ |
| 17 | $OH^+$ |

### Worked example

The mass spectrum of an alcohol shows peaks at

- 15 m/z
- 17 m/z
- 29 m/z
- 31 m/z
- 46 m/z

a) What is the $M_r$ of the compound?

b) Suggest the identity of the ions responsible for each of the peaks observed.

c) Suggest the name of this compound.

### Answer

a) The peak with the highest mass/charge ratio has a value of 46 m/z, so the $M_r$ of the compound is 46.

b) 15 m/z = $CH_3^+$
   17 m/z = $OH^+$
   29 m/z = $C_2H_5^+$
   31 m/z = $CH_2OH^+$
   46 m/z = $C_2H_5OH^+$

c) Ethanol

Even if two compounds have the same $M_r$ and the same atoms, if they have different structures they will fragment in different ways.

## Chromatography

**Chromatography** is an analytical technique used to separate components in a mixture.

In gas chromatography:

- The stationary phase is a liquid or solid on a solid support.
- The mobile phase is a gas.

In thin-layer chromatography:

- The stationary phase is a solid.
- The mobile phase is a liquid.

If the stationary phase is solid the components in the mixture are separated by adsorption – how strongly each of the components interacts with the surface of the stationary phase.

If the stationary phase is liquid the components in the mixture are separated by the relative solubility of each of the components in the mobile phase.

### $R_f$ values

$R_f$ values are used to compare the distance that a component moves compared with the distance that the solvent front moves.

$$R_f = \frac{\text{distance moved by component}}{\text{distance moved by solvent front}}$$

### Example

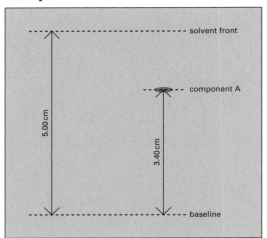

Component A has moved 3.40 cm from the baseline while the solvent front has moved 5.00 cm.

This means that component A has an $R_f$ value of
3.40/5.00 = 0.68.

Provided the same solvent and the same conditions are
used, component A will always give an $R_f$ value of 0.68.

## Gas chromatography

**Gas chromatography** (GC) is used to separate mixtures
of volatile liquids. In GC, the components move through
the apparatus at different speeds. The retention time
is the time it takes for a component to pass through
the apparatus from the inlet to the detector. In gas
chromatography each component produces a separate
peak. Once separated the components in the mixture can
be identified. Gas chromatography is so accurate that
the area under the peaks indicates the relative amount of
each component in a sample. It is used to measure the
level of alcohol in blood or urine samples in court cases.
However, it has some limitations:

- Similar compounds often have similar retention times.
- New compounds will have no reference times for
  comparison.

## Combining techniques

Mass spectrometry can be combined with
chromatography in a technique known as GC-MS to
provide a powerful analytic tool.

Gas chromatography can be used to separate the
components of the mixture, then mass spectrometry can
be used to positively identify each of the components
either by analysing the mass spectra produced or by
comparing the mass spectra with a spectral database.
GC-MS can be used

- in forensic science to identify drugs
- in environmental analysis to monitor water quality
- in airport security to detect explosives
- by space probes to analyse materials on other planets

## Questions

1 In mass spectrometry what is the name given
to the peak which has the highest mass/charge
ratio?

2 What are the limitations with gas
chromatography?

3 Suggest how GC-MS could be used as part of
airport security.

# 1.13 Spectroscopy

## Infrared spectroscopy

- **Infrared** (IR) spectroscopy is usually used to identify the functional groups in organic compounds.
- Different bonds absorb infrared radiation with slightly different wavenumbers.
- By examining the wavenumbers of the radiation that have been absorbed by a compound we can work out which bonds must be present.

### Reminder

Information about the wavenumber of radiation which a particular bond absorbs will be provided in an exam question.

- Transmittance–wavenumber graphs are used to show the wavenumber of the radiation that has been absorbed.
- Concentrate on the strong peaks where transmission falls below 70%.
- Note that O–H and N–H bonds produce very broad peaks due to hydrogen bonding.
- The section between 400 $cm^{-1}$ and 1500 $cm^{-1}$ is known as the **fingerprint region**.
- The fingerprint region is unique for every compound.
  - As a result, if the fingerprint region of an unknown sample is found to be identical to the fingerprint of a known compound the unknown sample can be identified.

## Nuclear magnetic resonance spectroscopy

**Nuclear magnetic resonance** (NMR) spectroscopy is a powerful technique which gives information about the position of $^1H$ or $^{13}C$ atoms in a molecule.

NMR spectroscopy is the same technology that is used in magnetic resonance imaging (MRI).

MRI scans are a non-invasive method of diagnosing medical conditions in patients. These scans allow medical staff to build up an image of what is happening inside a patient's body but without the possible complications associated with operating on a patient. The technique is very useful but due to the strong magnetic fields used is unsuitable for patients with heart pacemakers.

### The chemical shift

- If atoms have an odd mass number such as $^1H$ or $^{13}C$ then their nuclei will have spin. This spin can be detected using radio frequencies.
- Depending on the molecular environment around the $^1H$ or $^{13}C$, their precise resonance frequency will vary slightly.
- This slight variation can be used to give information about the structure of a compound.
- To allow chemists to compare the spectra produced on different machines, a reference compound is added to the sample.
- The differences between the resonance frequencies of the $^1H$ or $^{13}C$ atoms in the sample and in the reference are measured. These are known as the shifts.

The **chemical shift**, $\delta$, is given by

$$\delta = \frac{\text{shift (hertz)}}{\text{spectrometer frequency (MHz)}}$$

Note that the chemical shift is measured in parts per million (ppm)

### The reference standard

Tetramethylsilane, TMS, is used as the reference standard for NMR.

TMS is chosen because

$$CH_3-Si\underset{\underset{CH_3}{|}}{\overset{\overset{CH_3}{|}}{|}}CH_3$$

- It is fairly cheap.
- It does not react with the sample being analysed.
- All the carbon atoms are equivalent so it only produces one strong peak, which is usually upfield from the peaks produced by the other $^1H$ or $^{13}C$ nuclei.

### Spectra

The carbon-13 NMR spectrum of ethanol gives two peaks because ethanol contains carbon atoms in two different environments. These are labelled 1 and 2.

In carbon-13 NMR spectra the size of the chemical shift reveals information about the type of carbon environment. In the exam remember to refer to the data sheet which is provided.

In the carbon-13 NMR spectra of ethanol we would expect to see one peak at $\delta = 50$–70 ppm for C–O and another peak at $\delta = 5$–55 ppm for C–C.

### $^{13}C$ NMR chemical shifts relative to TMS

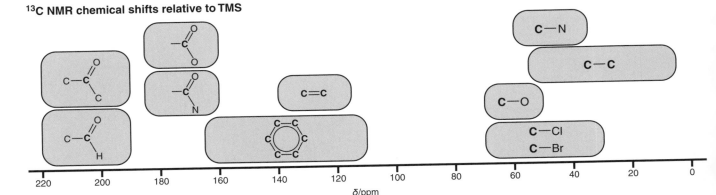

Chemical shifts are typical values and can vary slightly depending on the solvent, concentration, and substituents.

## ¹H NMR chemical shifts relative to TMS

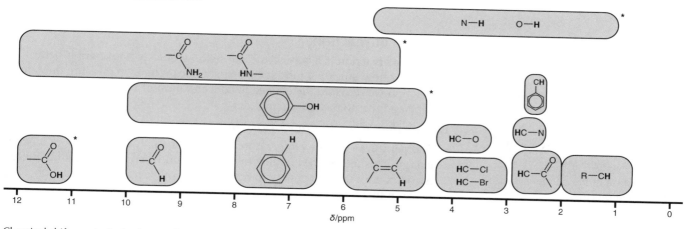

Chemical shifts are typical values and can vary slightly depending on the solvent, concentration, and substituents.
*OH and NH chemical shifts are very variable (sometimes outside these limits) and are often broad. Signals are not usually seen as split peaks.

Proton NMR gives more information about the compound being analysed.

The proton NMR spectrum of ethanol gives three peaks because ethanol contains hydrogen atoms in three different environments. These are labelled a, b, and c. The relative areas of these peaks reveal the proportions of the hydrogen atoms in these different environments. In the proton NMR spectra of ethanol we would expect the three peaks to be in the ratio 1:2:3 because this is the ratio of $H_a:H_b:H_c$

In proton NMR spectra the size of the chemical shift reveals information about the type of hydrogen environment. Remember to refer to the data sheet which is provided in the exam.

### Choosing a solvent

- Care must be taken when choosing a solvent for ¹H NMR as many solvents that contain protons will produce peaks in the spectrum.
- Tetrachloromethane, $CCl_4$, is often used.

### Deuterated solvents

The sample is normally dissolved in a solvent before NMR analysis is carried out. Deuterium, D, is an isotope of hydrogen that contains two nucleons: one proton and one neutron. This means that deuterium does not produce a signal in NMR spectra. $CDCl_3$ is a deuterated solvent and samples are often dissolved in $CDCl_3$.

It can be difficult to identify OH and NH protons in NMR spectra because these protons produce broad signals that can occur over a wide range of different chemical shifts. Deuterium oxide, $D_2O$, is used to filter out these peaks.

- First the NMR spectrum is run normally.
- Then a small amount of $D_2O$ is added and mixed with the sample. The $D_2O$ exchanges deuterium ions (which do not produce a signal) with the hydrogen in the OH or NH group and the NMR spectrum is run again.
- The two spectra are compared and any peaks caused by NH or OH will appear in the first spectra but will have disappeared from the second spectra. This allows these peaks to be identified.

### Spin–spin splitting patterns

The hydrogen atoms on one carbon atom affect the hydrogen atoms on the next (the adjacent) carbon atom. So in our ethanol molecule the hydrogen atoms labelled $H_c$ influence the hydrogen atoms labelled $H_b$. This happens throughout the molecule and is called **spin–spin coupling**. It leads to peak splitting. This can be seen using high-resolution NMR

- The $n + 1$ rule is used to deduce the spin coupling pattern, where $n$ is the number of hydrogen atoms on an adjacent carbon atom.
- Each of the peaks in the high-resolution NMR spectrum of ethanol will be affected differently.
  - $H_a$ is not attached to a carbon atom so this peak does not undergo spin–spin coupling and remains a single peak.
  - The $H_b$ atoms are attached to a carbon atom that is adjacent to a carbon atom which is bonded to three hydrogen atoms. This peak is split into $(3 + 1) = 4$ peaks. This is called a quartet.
  - The $H_c$ atoms are attached to a carbon atom that is adjacent to a carbon atom which is bonded to two hydrogen atoms. This peak is split into $(2 + 1) = 3$ peaks. This is called a triplet.
- Note: a single hydrogen atom bonded to an adjacent carbon atom would split a peak into a doublet.

## Combining techniques

Chemists often combine evidence from nuclear magnetic resonance, infrared spectroscopy and mass spectroscopy to deduce the structure of organic compounds.

### Questions

1  The diagram shows a molecule of propane.

$$
\begin{array}{c}
\phantom{H-}\overset{\displaystyle H}{\underset{\displaystyle H}{|}}\ \overset{\displaystyle H}{\underset{\displaystyle H}{|}}\ \overset{\displaystyle H}{\underset{\displaystyle H}{|}} \\
H-C-C-C-H
\end{array}
$$

Suggest what the ¹³C NMR spectrum of propane would look like.

2  Why is TMS used as the reference standard for NMR?

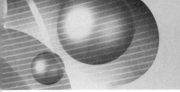

# 2.01 Kinetics 1

## Key terms

**Rate of reaction:** change in concentration of a species over time, units mol dm$^{-3}$ s$^{-1}$

**Reaction order:** power to which the concentration of a species is raised in the rate equation

**Rate constant:** the constant $k$ in the rate equation

**Half time:** time taken for the concentration of a species to fall by half

**Rate determining step:** the slowest step in a reaction

## Questions

1 The rate equation for a reaction is

Rate = $k[A]^2[B]^2$

What is the overall order of reaction?

2 The rate equation for a reaction is

Rate = $k[A][B]$

What are the units of the rate constant $k$?

3 A reaction is first order with respect to A and zero order with respect to B. What is the rate equation for this reaction?

## The rate of reaction

The rate of reaction is a way of measuring how quickly a reactant is being used up or how quickly a product is being made. When we measure the rate of reaction we measure the change in concentration of a species over a period of time and the units used are mol dm$^{-3}$ s$^{-1}$

### Factors that affect the rate of reaction

- **Temperature** – As the temperature increases the particles gain more kinetic energy. This means they collide more often and when they do collide more particles have enough energy to react (activation energy) so the rate of reaction increases.
- **Catalysts** – A catalyst increases the rate of reaction by offering an alternative reaction pathway with a lower activation energy. This means that more particles have energy equal to, or greater than, the activation energy, so more of the collisions are successful and the rate of reaction increases.
- **Concentration** – As the concentration of solutions of reactants increases the particles become closer together. This means that the particles collide more often so the rate of reaction increases.
- **Pressure** – As the pressure of gaseous reactants increases the particles are closer together. This means that the particles collide more often so the rate of reaction increases.
- **Surface area** – Increasing the surface area of a solid reactant increases the rate of reaction. As the surface area increases the collision frequency increases so the rate of reaction goes up.

## The rate equation

The **rate equation** is written in the form:

$$\text{rate} = k[A]^m[B]^n$$

- Notice the square brackets which indicate that we are measuring concentrations in units of mol dm$^{-3}$.
- [A] is the concentration of species A.
- [B] is the concentration of species B.
- $k$ is the rate constant, which can have different units
- $m$ is the order of reaction with respect to A.
- $n$ is the order of reaction with respect to B.

The rate equation cannot be worked out by looking at the stoichiometric equation. In fact, there may be species that appear on the stoichiometric equation that do not appear in the rate equation and there may be species, such as a catalyst, that appear in the rate equation but do not appear in the stoichiometric equation. The rate equation can only be determined by experimental methods.

### The overall order of reaction

The overall order of the reaction is the sum of the orders of reaction with respect to the individual species. In this example:

$$\text{rate} = k[A]^2[B]$$

The reaction is second order with respect to A and first order with respect to B. The overall order of reaction is given by 2+1, so the overall order of this reaction is 3.

## Orders of reaction

### Zero order

If the order of reaction with respect to a species is zero then changing the concentration of that species has no effect on the rate of reaction. The species is not involved in the **rate determining step**.

ZERO ORDER

rate of reaction (mol dm$^{-3}$ s$^{-1}$)

concentration (mol dm$^{-3}$)

If a reaction is second order with respect to A and zero order with respect to B, the rate equation is:

$$\text{rate} = k[A]^2[B]^0$$

Since anything to the power of zero is equal to 1 this equation simplifies to:

$$\text{rate} = k[A]^2$$

### First order

If a reaction is first order with respect to a species then the concentration of that species has a direct effect on the rate of reaction. If the concentration of the species is doubled the rate of reaction will also be doubled. If the concentration of the species is tripled then the rate of reaction is also tripled. Note that the line has a positive gradient and that it goes through the origin.

If a reaction is first order with respect to A and first order with respect to B the rate equation is:

$$\text{rate} = k[A]^1[B]^1$$

Since anything to the power of 1 remains unchanged this is simplified to:

$$\text{rate} = k[A][B]$$

### Second order

If a reaction is found to be second order with respect to a species then the concentration of that species also has a direct effect on the rate of reaction. If the concentration of the species is doubled the rate of reaction increases four times ($2^2 = 4$).

If the concentration of the species is tripled the rate of reaction increases nine times ($3^2 = 9$).

Note that the line curves upwards and that it goes through the origin.

If a reaction is second order with respect to A the rate equation is:

$$\text{rate} = k[A]^2$$

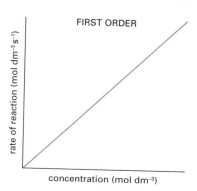

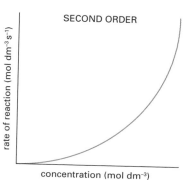

## Finding the order of reaction

The order of reaction for a species can be worked out using **the initial rates method**.

In this method the experiment is carried out several times using different concentrations of the reactants and any other species that might affect the rate of reaction, such as a catalyst.

The concentrations of all species except one are kept constant and the initial rate of reaction is measured with different values of the concentration of that one species.

Any changes in the initial rate of reaction must have been caused by the change in the concentration of that particular species. This information can be used to calculate the order of reaction with respect to that species.

The experiment is then repeated, with the concentration of the next species to be investigated being changed.

### Calculating $k$

The value of $k$, the rate constant, can be determined by substitution of data into a rate equation.

For the worked example below, using the first line of data from the table:

$k$ = rate / $[CH_3COCH_3][H^+]$
= 1 / (0.5)(0.5) = 4 $dm^3$ $mol^{-1}$ $s^{-1}$

## Worked example

*Iodine reacts with propanone in the presence of an acid catalyst. From the data in the table work out the order of the reaction with respect to propanone, iodine, and hydrogen ions. Write the rate equation for the reaction.*

$$CH_3COCH_3 + I_2 \xrightarrow{H^+} CH_3COCH_2I + HI$$

| concentration of $CH_3COCH_3$ (mol dm$^{-3}$) | concentration of $I_2$ (mol dm$^{-3}$) | concentration of $H^+$ (mol dm$^{-3}$) | initial rate of reaction (mol dm$^{-3}$ s$^{-1}$) |
|---|---|---|---|
| 0.5 | 0.5 | 0.5 | 1 |
| 0.5 | 1.0 | 0.5 | 1 |
| 1.0 | 0.5 | 0.5 | 2 |
| 0.5 | 0.5 | 1.0 | 2 |

**Answer**

The reaction is first order with respect to $CH_3COCH_3$

The reaction is zero order with respect to $I_2$

The reaction is first order with respect to $H^+$

So the rate equation is

Rate = $k[CH_3COCH_3][H^+]$

## The rate constant and temperature

- An increase in temperature increases the rate of reaction.
- The rate equation is:

$$\text{rate} = k[A]^m[B]^n$$

Changing the temperature does not affect the concentrations of A or B. Therefore the rate constant $k$ must increase as the temperature increases. This is true for exothermic and for endothermic reactions.

 As a result it is very important that if we are investigating the effect of changing the concentration of A or B on the rate of reaction that we keep the temperature constant.

- A large value of $k$ means a fast rate of reaction.
- A small value of $k$ means a slow rate of reaction.
- A catalyst provides an alternative reaction pathway with a lower activation energy so it increases the value of the rate constant, $k$.

## Finding the order of reaction

The order of reaction for a species can also be worked out using the graphical method.

In this method the experiment is carried out once and the concentration of the reactant is measured at different times. These results are used to draw a concentration–time graph.

Tangents are drawn and the gradient of these tangents gives the rate of reaction.

The gradient at the initial concentration of 1.0 mol dm$^{-3}$ is given by 0.22 mol dm$^{-3}$/5 s = 0.044 mol dm$^{-3}$ s$^{-1}$

The gradient is then worked out at another point in the graph, normally at half the initial concentration.

The gradient at half the initial concentration (0.5 mol dm$^{-3}$) is given by 0.20 mol dm$^{-3}$/9.5 s = 0.021 mol dm$^{-3}$ s$^{-1}$

The second rate of reaction is approximately half of the value of the initial rate of reaction.

As the rate of reaction has halved as the concentration has halved, the reaction is first order.

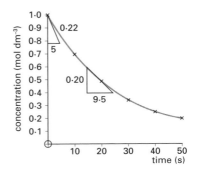

## Using half-lives

The half-life of a reaction is the time it takes for the concentration of a reactant to halve.

The half-life of a reaction can be determined from a concentration–time graph.

### First order reactions

First order reactions have a constant half-life.

It takes 20 seconds for the concentration to halve from 0.8 mol dm$^{-3}$ to 0.4 mol dm$^{-3}$.

It takes a further 20 seconds for the concentration to halve from 0.4 mol dm$^{-3}$ to 0.2 mol dm$^{-3}$.

As the half-life remains constant this means that this is a first order reaction.

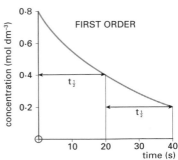

### Zero order reactions

By contrast this is the concentration–time graph for a zero order reaction The gradient of the line is constant. This means that the rate of reaction is constant. It shows that the amount of the reactant has no effect on the rate of reaction.

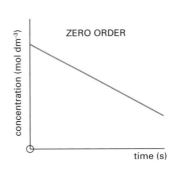

### Second order reactions

For a second order reaction the half-life increases as the concentration decreases.

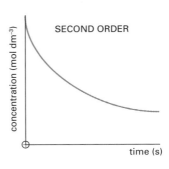

# Rate equations and mechanisms

Although some reactions involve just one step many reactions involve a number of steps that happen in order. The slowest step in the reaction is called the **rate determining step** (or rate limiting step). This step has the highest activation energy.

Chemists are very interested in the mechanisms of a reaction. If they know which bonds are being broken and which bonds are being made and the order in which this is happening it helps them to understand how the new compound is made and helps them to design useful new compounds.

The rate equation gives us information about the mechanisms because it tells us the species that are involved in the rate determining step.

The order of reaction with respect to a species tells us the number of molecules of that species in the rate determining step.

For example if the rate equation for a reaction is:

$$\text{rate} = k[A]^2[B]$$

It tells us the reaction is second order with respect to A and first order with respect to B.

This means that the rate determining step involves two molecules of A and one molecule of B or something that is made from two molecules of A and one molecule of B.

## Worked example 1

In a reaction A reacts with B in the presence of a catalyst, C, to produce G.

$$A + B \xrightarrow{\text{catalyst, C}} G$$

*Two possible mechanisms are proposed for the reaction*

Mechanism 1   **Step 1**   $A + C \xrightarrow{\text{slow}} D$

**Step 2**   $D \xrightarrow{\text{fast}} E + C$

**Step 3**   $E + B \xrightarrow{\text{fast}} G$

Mechanism 2   **Step 1**   $A + B + C \xrightarrow{\text{slow}} G$

*The rate equation is found to be:* rate = $k[A][C]$

*Which, if either, of these mechanisms is consistent with the rate equation?*

In mechanism 1 the rate determining step involves reactant A and the catalyst C. As these both appear in the rate equation, mechanism 1 is consistent with the rate equation.

However, in mechanism 2 the rate determining step involves both the reactants A and B plus the catalyst C. As B does not appear in the rate determining step this mechanism is not consistent with the rate equation.

## Worked example 2

*In a reaction P reacts with Q to produce Z.*

$$P + Q \rightarrow Z$$

*The rate equation for this reaction is:* rate = $k[P]^2[Q]$

*Write an equation for the slow step and the fast step of this reaction.*

The rate equation shows that 2 moles of P react with 1 mole of Q in the slow step. We cannot know the structure of the product so it is written simply as $P_2Q$.

$$\text{slow step} \quad 2P + Q \rightarrow P_2Q$$

$P_2Q$ is clearly not a product of the reaction; it is an intermediate which breaks down in the fast step. Since Z is not formed in the slow step it must be formed in the fast step. As only 1 mole of P is given in the overall equation, 1 mole of P must be formed in the fast step:

$$\text{fast step} \quad P_2Q \rightarrow P + Z$$

## Worked example 3

*The reaction of propanone with iodine in the presence of an acid catalyst is shown to be first order with respect to $CH_3COCH_3$, zero order with respect to $I_2$ and first order with respect to $H^+$. Using the overall equation below write an equation for the fast step and for the slow step in the reaction.*

*Overall equation:* $CH_3COCH_3 + I_2 \rightarrow CH_3COCH_2I + HI$

In the slow step 1 mole of $CH_3COCH_3$ reacts with 1 mole of $H^+$. A molecular formula is used for the product of the slow step as its structure cannot be determined from the information given.

$$\text{slow step} \quad CH_3COCH_3 + H^+ \rightarrow C_3H_7O^+$$

In the fast step the $C_3H_7O^+$ intermediate breaks up, giving the products from the overall equation and releasing an $H^+$ (this is a catalyst and is therefore regenerated in the reaction).

$$\text{fast step} \quad C_3H_7O^+ + I_2 \rightarrow CH_2COCH_2I + HI + H^+$$

## Methods of measuring the rate of a reaction

Methods of following the rate of reaction include:

- titration
- colorimetry
- collecting the volume of a gas produced

## Questions

1  What is the half-life of a reaction?

2  How can a concentration–time graph be used to prove that a reaction is first order?

3  What does a high value for the rate constant $k$ indicate?

4  In a reaction A reacts with B and C forming Z. The overall equation for the reaction is $A + B + C \rightarrow Z$. The rate equation is rate = $k[A]^2[B]$. Write equations for the slow step and the fast step of this reaction.

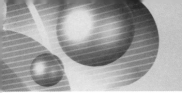

# 2.03 Equilibria 1

## Le Chatelier's Principle

Many chemical reactions are reversible. When a reversible reaction reaches a dynamic equilibrium the rate of the forward reaction is equal to the rate of the backward reaction. If the temperature is changed the position of equilibrium moves. We can apply Le Chatelier's Principle to work out how the position of equilibrium will change. If the temperature is increased the equilibrium moves in the endothermic direction. In a reaction which is exothermic in the forward direction, increasing the temperature moves the equilibrium towards the endothermic side and reduces the yield of the product made.

### Le Chatelier's Principle

Le Chatelier's Principle states that if a small change is applied to a system in dynamic equilibrium, the position of the equilibrium moves in such a way as to minimize the effect of the change

### Worked example

*Explain the term 'dynamic equilibrium'.*

In a dynamic equilibrium the rate of the forward reaction is equal to the rate of the backward reaction so that there is no change in the concentrations of the products and reactants.

## Concentration

Concentration is equal to the number of moles of a substance in 1 dm³ of a solution. It is measured in units of mol dm⁻³

[A] means the concentration of substance A in units of mol dm⁻³. Notice how square brackets are used.

### Worked example

*At equilibrium a mixture was found to contain 0.001 moles of A and 0.02 moles of B. The total volume was 2.0 dm³. What are the concentrations of A and B?*

Concentration of A = $\dfrac{0.001 \text{ moles}}{2 \text{ dm}^3}$ = 0.0005 mol dm⁻³

Concentration of B = $\dfrac{0.02 \text{ moles}}{2 \text{ dm}^3}$ = 0.01 mol dm⁻³

### Worked example

*The following system is at equilibrium.*

$X + Y \rightleftharpoons Z$

*At equilibrium there was found to be 0.04 moles of X, 0.02 moles of Y, and 0.005 moles of Z. The total volume is 500 cm³. What are the concentrations of X, Y, and Z?*

500 cm³ is equal to 0.5 dm³.

Concentration of X = $\dfrac{0.04 \text{ moles}}{0.5 \text{ dm}^3}$ = 0.08 mol dm⁻³

Concentration of Y = $\dfrac{0.02 \text{ moles}}{0.5 \text{ dm}^3}$ = 0.04 mol dm⁻³

Concentration of Z = $\dfrac{0.005 \text{ moles}}{0.5 \text{ dm}^3}$ = 0.01 mol dm⁻³

## The equilibrium constant

- The equilibrium constant, $K_c$, has a fixed value for any particular equilibrium reaction at a given temperature.
- It is a measure of how far a reaction has proceeded but gives no information about the rate of the reaction.
- A high value of $K_c$ indicates that the equilibrium favours the products.
- A low value of $K_c$ indicates that the equilibrium favours the reactants.

### Finding the equilibrium constant

The equilibrium constant is written in terms of the equilibrium concentrations. For the reaction:

$$aA + bB \rightleftharpoons cC + dD$$

$$K_c = \frac{[C]^c \, [D]^d}{[A]^a \, [B]^b}$$

- All the concentration must be equilibrium concentrations.
- If the system has yet to reach equilibrium this equation will not apply. The system will continue to react until equilibrium is established.
- The equilibrium concentration of each term is raised to the power of the number used in the balanced equation.
- The equilibrium concentrations of the products are written on the top of the fraction.
- The equilibrium concentrations of the reactants are written on the bottom of the fraction.
- $K_c$ is a concentration term, so it can only be applied to gases and solutions.

## Worked example

*Write the $K_c$ expression for this reaction.*

$N_2(g) + 3H_2(g) \rightleftharpoons 2NH_3(g)$

$$K_c = \frac{[NH_3]^2}{[N_2][H_2]^3}$$

The products are written on the top of the fraction.

The reactants are written on the bottom of the fraction.

The equilibrium concentration of ammonia is raised to the power of 2.

The equilibrium concentration of hydrogen is raised to the power of 3.

## Homogeneous equilibria

In homogeneous equilibria all the species are in the same phase. For example they are

- all gases
- all solutions

### Working out the units of $K_c$

$H_2(g) + Cl_2(g) \rightleftharpoons 2HCl(g)$

$$K_c = \frac{[HCl]^2}{[H_2][Cl_2]}$$

$$= \frac{(\cancel{mol\ dm^{-3}})\ (\cancel{mol\ dm^{-3}})}{(\cancel{mol\ dm^{-3}})\ (\cancel{mol\ dm^{-3}})}$$

For this equation the units cancel so there are no units for $K_c$, and this is written as 'no units'. However, this is not always the case and the units must be worked out each time.

## Worked example

*Dinitrogen tetroxide, $N_2O_4(g)$, decomposes to form nitrogen dioxide, $NO_2(g)$.*

$N_2O_4(g) \rightleftharpoons 2NO_2(g)$

*Give the expression for $K_c$ for this reaction. Include the units.*

$$K_c = \frac{[NO_2]^2}{[N_2O_4]}$$

$$= \frac{(\cancel{mol\ dm^{-3}}) \times (mol\ dm^{-3})}{(\cancel{mol\ dm^{-3}})}$$

$$= mol\ dm^{-3}$$

## Factors that affect the value of $K_c$

A catalyst will not affect the position of equilibrium so it will not affect the value of $K_c$. It will simply mean that we reach the position of equilibrium more quickly.

For solutions, if the concentration of one of the substances is changed then the system will no longer be in equilibrium so it will adjust until it re-establishes equilibrium. At that point the value of $K_c$ will not have changed.

For gases, if the pressure is changed and the number of molecules on each side of the balanced equation is not the same then the system will no longer be in equilibrium.

It will adjust until it re-establishes equilibrium, at which point the value of $K_c$ will not have changed.

However **temperature** will affect the position of equilibrium. If the reaction is exothermic in the forward direction increasing the temperature will move the position of equilibrium in the endothermic direction:

- reducing the amount of products
- increasing the amount of reactants

$$K_c = \frac{[products] \leftarrow \boxed{less}}{[reactants] \leftarrow \boxed{more}}$$

Increasing the temperature of an exothermic reaction will decrease the value of $K_c$.

Increasing the temperature of an endothermic reaction will increase the value of $K_c$.

## Worked example

*Sulfur dioxide reacts with oxygen to form sulfur trioxide. The reaction is reversible.*

$2SO_2(g) + O_2(g) \rightleftharpoons 2SO_3(g)$

*Give the expression for $K_c$ for this reaction. Include the units.*

$$K_c = \frac{[SO_3]^2}{[SO_2]^2[O_2]}$$

$$units = \frac{(\cancel{mol\ dm^{-3}}) \times (\cancel{mol\ dm^{-3}})}{(\cancel{mol\ dm^{-3}}) \times (\cancel{mol\ dm^{-3}}) \times (mol\ dm^{-3})}$$

$$= \frac{1}{mol\ dm^{-3}}$$

$$= dm^3\ mol^{-1}$$

## Worked example

*The manufacture of ammonia is based on this equilibrium.*

$N_2(g) + 3H_2(g) \rightleftharpoons 2NH_3(g)$

*What is the effect of adding a catalyst on:*

**a** *the rate at which equilibrium is attained*

**b** *the position of equilibrium*

**c** *the value of $K_c$?*

**a** The rate is faster so it takes less time to reach equilibrium.

**b** There is no change to the position of equilibrium.

**c** There is no change in the value of $K_c$.

## Questions

1 How is concentration calculated?

2 Which factor or factors will affect the value of $K_c$ for a given reaction?

3 Write the equilibrium expression for the reaction:

$2A + 3B \rightleftharpoons 2C$

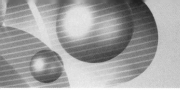

# 2.04 Equilibria 2

## The equilibrium constant, $K_c$

$K_c$ values can be calculated readily from the concentrations of each of the reactants and products at equilibrium. Work through all of the following examples to make sure you are confident about doing this..

## Calculating the value of $K_c$

### When we know the number of moles at equilibrium

**Step 1**  Write the expression for $K_c$.

**Step 2**  Work out the concentrations (this is given by the number of moles divided by the volume).

**Step 3**  Substitute in the values.

**Step 4**  Calculate the answer. Remember to include the units.

---

**Worked example**

*Find the value of $K_c$ for this equilibrium:*

*$A + 2B \rightleftharpoons 2C$*

*The equilibrium mixture contained 0.3 moles of A, 0.4 moles of B, and 6.0 moles of C. The total volume was 2.0 dm³.*

$$K_c = \frac{[C]^2}{[A][B]^2}$$

Concentration of A $= \dfrac{0.3 \text{ mol}}{2.0 \text{ dm}^3} = 0.15 \text{ mol dm}^{-3}$

Concentration of B $= \dfrac{0.4 \text{ mol}}{2.0 \text{ dm}^3} = 0.20 \text{ mol dm}^{-3}$

Concentration of C $= \dfrac{6.0 \text{ mol}}{2.0 \text{ dm}^3} = 3.0 \text{ mol dm}^{-3}$

$$K_c = \frac{3.0 \text{ mol dm}^{-3} \times 3.0 \text{ mol dm}^{-3}}{0.15 \text{ mol dm}^{-3} \times 0.20 \text{ mol dm}^{-3} \times 0.20 \text{ mol dm}^{-3}}$$

$$K_c = 1500 \text{ dm}^3 \text{ mol}^{-1}$$

---

**Worked example**

*Find the value of $K_c$ for this equilibrium:*

*$A + 2B \rightleftharpoons C + D$*

*The equilibrium mixture contained 0.4 moles of A, 0.3 moles of B, 0.10 moles of C, and 0.10 moles of D. The total volume was 2.5 dm³.*

$$K_c = \frac{[C][D]}{[A][B]^2}$$

Concentration of A $= \dfrac{0.4 \text{ mol}}{2.5 \text{ dm}^3} = 0.16 \text{ mol dm}^{-3}$

Concentration of B $= \dfrac{0.3 \text{ mol}}{2.5 \text{ dm}^3} = 0.12 \text{ mol dm}^{-3}$

Concentration of C and D $= \dfrac{0.1 \text{ mol}}{2.5 \text{ dm}^3} = 0.04 \text{ mol dm}^{-3}$

$$K_c = \frac{(0.04 \text{ mol dm}^{-3}) \times (0.04 \text{ mol dm}^{-3})}{(0.16 \text{ mol dm}^{-3}) \times (0.12 \text{ mol dm}^{-3}) \times (0.12 \text{ mol dm}^{-3})}$$

$$K_c = \frac{0.0016}{0.002304} = 0.694 \text{ dm}^3 \text{ mol}^{-1}$$

---

### When we only know the number of moles at the start of the experiment

**Step 1**  Write the expression for $K_c$.

**Step 2**  State the number of moles of each reactant and product at the start.

**Step 3**  Calculate the number of moles of each reactant and product present at equilibrium.

**Step 4**  Work out the concentrations (number of moles divided by the volume).

**Step 5**  Substitute in the values.

**Step 6**  Calculate the answer. Remember to include the units.

---

**Worked example**

*Find the value of $K_c$ for this equilibrium:*

*$A + B \rightleftharpoons C$*

*In an experiment 0.5 moles of A and 0.3 moles of B were mixed in a 5 dm³ container. At equilibrium there was found to be 0.3 moles of A.*

$$A + B \rightleftharpoons C$$

$$K_c = \frac{[C]}{[A][B]}$$

| number of moles | | | |
|---|---|---|---|
| | **A** | **B** | **C** |
| at start | 0·5 | 0·3 | 0·0 |
| at equilibrium | 0·3 | | |

In the reaction, A : B : C is 1 : 1 : 1.

The number of moles of A that have reacted is 0.2, which means that 0.2 moles of B will also have reacted leaving

0.1 moles of B at equilibrium.

0.2 moles of C will have been made so there is 0.2 moles of C present at equilibrium.

$$A + B \rightleftharpoons C$$

$$K_c = \frac{[C]}{[A]\,[B]}$$

|  | A | B | C |
|---|---|---|---|
| at equilibrium | 0·3 mol | 0·1 mol | 0·2 mol |

Concentration of A = $\dfrac{0·3\ \text{mol}}{5\ \text{dm}^3}$ = 0·06 mol dm$^{-3}$

Concentration of B = $\dfrac{0·1\ \text{mol}}{5\ \text{dm}^3}$ = 0·02 mol dm$^{-3}$

Concentration of C = $\dfrac{0·2\ \text{mol}}{5\ \text{dm}^3}$ = 0·04 mol dm$^{-3}$

$$K_c = \frac{[C]}{[A]\,[B]}$$

$$K_c = \frac{0·04\ \text{mol dm}^{-3}}{0·06\ \text{mol dm}^{-3} \times 0·02\ \text{mol dm}^{-3}}$$

$$= 33\ \text{dm}^3\ \text{mol}^{-1}$$

## Finding equilibrium amounts from $K_c$ values

For the reaction A $\rightleftharpoons$ B  $K_c$ = 5.0

If 10 moles of A were allowed to reach equilibrium how many moles of B would be present in the equilibrium mixture?

At equilibrium there are $x$ moles of B. So we can work out the number of moles of the other substances in terms of $x$.

| number of moles | | |
|---|---|---|
|  | A | B |
| at start | 10 | 0 |
| at equilibrium | 10 − x | x |

We can find the equilibrium concentrations by dividing the number of moles by the volume, but as we do not know the volume we will call it $V$.

Concentration of A = $\dfrac{10 - x}{V}$

Concentration of B = $\dfrac{x}{V}$

$$K_c = \frac{[B]}{[A]} = 5·0$$

$$5·0 = \frac{\left(\dfrac{x}{V}\right)}{\left(\dfrac{10 - x}{V}\right)}$$

$$50 - 5x = x$$

$$50 = 6x$$

$$x = 8·3$$

So there are 8.3 moles of B in the equilibrium mixture.

## Worked example

*Calculate the value of $K_c$ for the reaction from the data given:*

$$A \rightleftharpoons B + C$$

*0.08 moles of A was placed into a 2.0 dm$^3$ vessel and heated. At equilibrium 75% of the A had dissociated.*

If 75% of the A that was originally present has dissociated it leaves 25% or 0.02 moles of A. We can now work out the equilibrium amounts of the other species.

$$A \rightleftharpoons B + C$$

$$K_c = \frac{[B]\,[C]}{[A]}$$

| number of moles | | | |
|---|---|---|---|
|  | A | B | C |
| at start | 0·08 | 0 | 0 |
| at equilibrium | 0·02 | 0·06 | 0·06 |

down by 0·06              B and C will be
                          up by 0·06 moles

Concentration of A = $\dfrac{0·02\ \text{mol}}{2\ \text{dm}^3}$ = 0·01 mol dm$^{-3}$

B = $\dfrac{0·06\ \text{mol}}{2\ \text{dm}^3}$ = 0·03 mol dm$^{-3}$

C = $\dfrac{0·06\ \text{mol}}{2\ \text{dm}^3}$ = 0·03 mol dm$^{-3}$

$$K_c = \frac{(0·03\ \text{mol dm}^{-3}) \times (0·03\ \text{mol dm}^{-3})}{(0·01\ \text{mol dm}^{-3})}$$

$$K_c = \frac{0·0009\ \text{mol dm}^{-3}}{0·01}$$

$$K_c = 0·09\ \text{mol dm}^{-3}$$

## Questions

1  In the reaction:

   A + 2B $\rightleftharpoons$ C

   the equilibrium mixture contained 0.03 moles of A, 0.2 moles of B, and 0.04 moles of C. The total volume was 0.5 dm$^3$

   a  Write the expression for $K_c$ including units.

   b  Find the concentration of A, B, and C at equilibrium

   c  Calculate the value of $K_c$.

2  For the equilibrium X + 2Y $\rightleftharpoons$ Z

   0.5 moles of X and 0.8 moles of Y were reacted together. At equilibrium there was found to be 0.3 moles of X. Calculate the number of moles of Y and Z present at equilibrium.

3  For the equilibrium A + 2B $\rightleftharpoons$ 2C

   0.02 moles of A and 0.10 moles of B were reacted together. At equilibrium 50% of A had reacted.

   Calculate the number of moles of A, B, and C present at equilibrium.

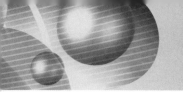

# 2.05 Acids and bases 1

## Ionic equations

Acids are $H^+$ donors. Work through the equations below. Note that in the ionic equations only those ions that have undergone a chemical change are shown. The spectator ions are not included.

Metal and acid:

$$Mg(s) + 2HCl(aq) \rightarrow MgCl_2(aq) + H_2(g)$$
$$Mg(s) + 2H^+(aq) \rightarrow Mg^{2+}(aq) + H_2(g)$$

Carbonate and acid:

$$CaCO_3(s) + 2HCl(aq) \rightarrow CaCl_2(aq) + H_2O(l) + CO_2(g)$$
$$CaCO_3(s) + 2H^+(aq) \rightarrow Ca^{2+}(aq) + H_2O(l) + CO_2(g)$$

Base and acid:

$$MgO(s) + H_2SO_4(aq) \rightarrow MgSO_4(aq) + H_2O(l)$$
$$MgO(s) + 2H^+(aq) \rightarrow Mg^{2+}(aq) + H_2O(l)$$

Alkali and acid:

$$NaOH(aq) + HCl(aq) \rightarrow NaCl(aq) + H_2O(l)$$
$$OH^-(aq) + H^+(aq) \rightarrow H_2O(l)$$

## Brønsted–Lowry acids and bases

- An acid is a proton ($H^+$) donor.
- A base is a proton acceptor.
- The species formed when an acid loses an $H^+$ ion is the acid's **conjugate base**.
- The species formed when a base gains an $H^+$ is the base's **conjugate acid**.

In the equilibrium:

$$HCl + H_2O \rightleftharpoons H_3O^+ + Cl^-$$

- $Cl^-$ is the conjugate base of HCl.
- $H_3O^+$ is the conjugate acid of $H_2O$.
- The pair is linked by the gain or loss of a $H^+$ ion.

$$HCl + H_2O \rightleftharpoons H_3O^+ + Cl^-$$
$$\text{acid 1 base 2 \quad base 1 \quad acid 2}$$

## Definition and determination of pH

**pH** is equal to –log base 10 of the concentration of hydrogen ions.

$$pH = -\log_{10}[H^+]$$

> **Reminder**
>
> Make sure you press the log key not the ln key on your calculator.

Strong acids like hydrochloric acid, HCl, are completely ionized in water.

$$HCl \rightarrow H^+ + Cl^-$$

So we can use the concentration of the acid to calculate the concentration of the $H^+$ ions and then use this to find the pH.

> **Worked example**
>
> *Find the pH of a 0.2 mol dm$^{-3}$ solution of HCl.*
>
> HCl is a strong acid so it is completely ionized in water.

> $$HCl \rightarrow H^+ + Cl^-$$
> $$0.2 \qquad 0.2$$
> $$pH = -\log_{10}[H^+]$$
> $$pH = -\log_{10}0.2$$
> $$pH = 0.70$$

> **Worked example**
>
> *Find the pH of a 0.5 mol dm$^{-3}$ solution of HNO$_3$.*
>
> HNO$_3$ is a strong acid so it is completely ionized in water.
>
> $$HNO_3 \rightarrow H^+ + NO_3^-$$
> $$0.5 \qquad 0.5$$
> $$pH = -\log_{10}[H^+]$$
> $$pH = -\log_{10}0.5$$
> $$pH = 0.30$$

## Finding the pH

We can rearrange the equation to find the concentration of $H^+$ ions if we know the pH.

$$[H^+] = 10^{-pH}$$

> **Reminder**
>
> To get $10^x$ using a calculator, press the inverse or shift key and then the log key.

> **Worked example**
>
> *A strong acid has a pH of 1. What is the value of [H$^+$]?*
>
> $$[H^+] = 10^{-pH}$$
> $$[H^+] = 10^{-1}$$
> $$[H^+] = 0.1 \text{ mol dm}^{-3}$$

## The ionic product of water

Water will naturally partially ionize.

$$H_2O \rightleftharpoons H^+ + OH^-$$

The equilibrium expression for this reaction is

$$K_c = \frac{[H^+][OH^-]}{[H_2O]}$$

As the concentration of water is very large we can consider it to be constant and the expression simplifies to:

$$K_w = [H^+][OH^-]$$
$$\text{where } K_w = K_c \times [H_2O]$$

- $K_w$ is called the **ionic product of water**.
- At 298 K or 25 °C it has a value of $1 \times 10^{-14}$ mol$^2$ dm$^{-6}$.
- The value of $K_w$ changes with temperature.

### Neutral solutions

In neutral solutions the concentration of $H^+$ ions is equal to the concentration of $OH^-$ ions

$[H^+] = [OH^-]$

$[H^+]^2 = 1 \times 10^{-14} \text{ mol}^2 \text{ dm}^{-6}$

$[H^+] = 1 \times 10^{-7} \text{ mol dm}^{-3}$

$pH = -\log_{10}[H^+]$

$pH = -\log_{10}(1 \times 10^{-7})$

$pH = 7$

So neutral solutions have a pH of 7 at 25 °C.

### Finding the pH of strong bases

We can use the ionic product of water to find the pH of solutions of strong bases such as sodium hydroxide and potassium hydroxide.

#### Worked example

*Find the pH of 0.2 mol dm$^{-3}$ sodium hydroxide solution. Sodium hydroxide is a strong alkali so it is fully ionized in water.*

$NaOH \rightarrow Na^+ + OH^-$

0.2

$K_w = [H^+][OH^-]$

$1 \times 10^{-14} \text{ mol}^2 \text{ dm}^{-6} = [H^+] \times 0.2 \text{ mol dm}^{-3}$

$[H^+] = \dfrac{1 \times 10^{-14} \text{ mol}^2 \text{ dm}^{-6}}{0{\cdot}2 \text{ mol dm}^{-3}}$

$[H^+] = 5 \times 10^{-14} \text{ mol dm}^{-3}$

$pH = -\log_{10}[H^+]$

$pH = -\log_{10}(5 \times 10^{-14})$

$pH = 13.3$

#### Reminder

A high value for $[H^+]$ means a low value for pH.

A low value for $[H^+]$ means a high value for pH.

## $K_a$ for weak acids

Organic acids such as methanoic acid, ethanoic acid, and propanoic acid are all weak acids (see section on carboxylic acids).

- Weak acids have a pH of around 3.
- Weak acids are only partially ionized in water.
- A weak acid can be represented by HA.

$$HA \rightleftharpoons H^+ + A^-$$

- As a result we cannot work out $[H^+]$ directly from the concentration of the weak acid, as we could with strong acids.

- Instead we use the **acid dissociation constant, $K_a$**

$$K_a = \frac{[H^+][A^-]}{[HA]}$$

- Note that the expression does not include water, $H_2O$.
- $K_a$ shows us the extent to which the acid has dissociated.

When using this expression we assume that:

- $[HA]$ = the initial concentration of the weak acid (even though some of the acid will actually have dissociated).
- $[A^-] = [H^+]$ (even though some of the $H^+$ ions will actually have come from the ionization of water)

As a result the expression for $K_a$ simplifies to:

$$K_a = \frac{[H^+]^2}{[HA]} \quad \text{or} \quad [H^+]^2 = K_a \times [HA]$$

- This allows us to find the value of $[H^+]$ and from this we can calculate the pH of the solution.

#### Worked example

*Calculate the pH of a 0.2 mol dm$^{-3}$ solution of a weak acid, given that K$_a$ = 1.7 × 10$^{-5}$ mol dm$^{-3}$.*

$$K_a = \frac{[H^+][A^-]}{[HA]}$$

$$K_a = \frac{[H^+]^2}{[HA]}$$

$[H^+]^2 = K_a \times [HA]$

$[H^+]^2 = 1.7 \times 10^{-5} \text{ mol dm}^{-3} \times 0.2 \text{ mol dm}^{-3}$

$[H^+]^2 = 3.4 \times 10^{-6} \text{ mol}^2 \text{ dm}^{-6}$

$[H^+] = 1.84 \times 10^{-3} \text{ mol dm}^{-3}$

$pH = -\log_{10}[H^+]$

$pH = -\log_{10}(1.84 \times 10^{-3})$

$pH = 2.73$

## p$K_a$

$pK_a = -\log_{10}K_a$

$K_a = 10^{-pK_a}$

- A high value for $K_a$ means a low value for $pK_a$.
- A low value for $K_a$ means a high value for $pK_a$.

## Weak bases

Ammonium hydroxide, $NH_4OH$, is a weak base. It is only partially ionized in water.

$NH_4OH \rightleftharpoons NH_4^+ + OH^-$

---

## Questions

1 Give the definition for pH.
2 What is the pH of the following solutions:
  a 0.1 mol dm$^{-3}$ of HCl
  b 0.5 mol dm$^{-3}$ of $HNO_3$
  c 0.6 mol dm$^{-3}$ of HCl
3 Name three weak acids.
4 Write an ionic equation for the reaction of calcium oxide with sulfuric acid.

# 2.06 Acids and bases 2

## Titrations

In titrations:
- A known volume of an acid is placed in a flask.
- An **indicator** is added.
- An alkali (a soluble base) is added from a burette.
- The indicator is used to show the endpoint. This is when exactly the right amount of alkali has been added so that neither the acid nor the base is in excess.
  - As a result the volume of alkali that had to be added can then be accurately measured.

Titrations can also be carried out by placing the alkali in the flask and adding the acid from the burette.

## Titration curves

**Titration curves** can be used to show how the pH changes as alkali is added to an acid. The shape of the curves depends on whether the acid and alkali used are weak or strong.

### Strong acid and strong base

- A strong acid will have a pH of around 1 and a strong base will have a pH of around 13.
  - As a result the graph starts at 1 and ends at 13.
- The graph is vertical between pH 3 and pH 11
- The equivalence point (when neither acid nor alkali is present in excess) is at pH 7, which is the middle of the vertical part of the graph.

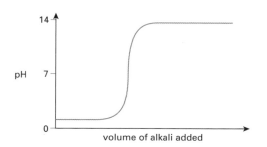

### Weak acid and strong base

- A weak acid will have a pH of around 3 and a strong base will have a pH of around 13.
  - As a result the graph starts at 3 and ends at 13.
- The graph is vertical between pH 5 and pH 11
- The equivalence point (when neither acid nor alkali is present in excess) is at pH 9.

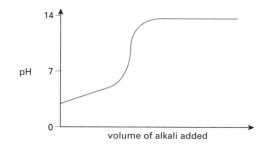

### Strong acid and weak base

- A strong acid will have a pH of around 1 and a weak base will have a pH of around 11.
  - As a result the graph starts at 1 and ends at 11.
- The graph is vertical between pH 3 and pH 9
- The equivalence point (when neither acid nor alkali is present in excess) is at pH 5.

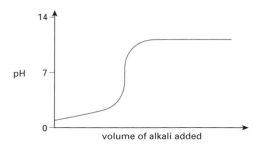

### Weak acid and weak base

- A weak acid will have a pH of around 3 and a weak base will have a pH of around 11.
  - As a result the graph starts at 3 and ends at 11.

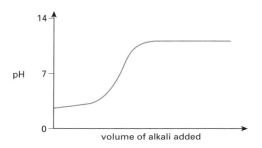

- Unfortunately there is no vertical section for this titration curve, so this method is not suitable for weak acids and weak bases.

Note that titration curves can also be drawn for titrations where acids are added to bases.

## Indicators

You will not be expected to recall how indicators work but you should be able to work through the outline below applying your knowledge of acid dissociation and Le Chatelier's Principle.

Indicators are weak acids. When they are placed in water they partially dissociate forming an $H^+$ ion and an anion.
- The undissociated indicator is one colour and the anion is a different colour.
- When the indicator is placed in acid the equilibrium shifts to the left-hand side and the colour of the undissociated indicator is seen.
- When the indicator is placed in alkali the equilibrium shifts to the right-hand side and the colour of the anion is seen.
- At the endpoint of the titration the concentrations of the undissociated and dissociated species are equal.
- As a result a mixture of the two colours is seen.

The pH range over which an indicator changes colour can be determined.

In order to be suitable for use in a titration the indicator must change colour during the vertical portion of the titration curve.

- Methyl orange changes colour in the pH range 3.1–4.4.
- Phenolphthalein changes colour in the pH range 8.3–10.0.

Either indicator is suitable for a strong acid/strong base titration. Methyl orange is not suitable for a weak acid/strong base titration as it changes colour outside the vertical portion.

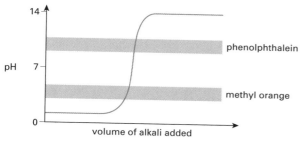

Strong acid and strong base

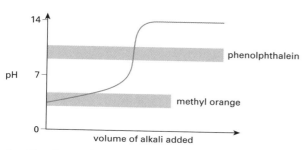

Weak acid and strong base

You are not required to remember the pH ranges for the indicators but you should be able to choose suitable indicators from a list. Have a look at the list below and make sure you can select a suitable indicator for each of the titration curves shown on page 48.

| indicator | pH range |
|---|---|
| methyl orange | 3.1–4.4 |
| bromothymol blue | 6.0–7.6 |
| phenolphthalein | 8.3–10.0 |
| bromophenol blue | 3.0–4.6 |
| cresol red | 7.2–8.8 |

## Buffer solutions

A **buffer solution** minimizes a change in pH when small amounts of acid or base are added to it.

Buffers are made of an acid–base conjugate pair.

An **acidic buffer** is made by dissolving the salt of a weak acid in the acid itself, for example sodium ethanoate in ethanoic acid.

This gives the weak acid $CH_3COOH$ and its conjugate base $CH_3COO^-$.

Acidic buffers have a pH of less than 7. They work best when the concentration of the acid and the conjugate base are similar, for example $[CH_3COOH] = [CH_3COO^-]$

### How do acidic buffers work?

As discussed above, an acidic buffer can be made by dissolving sodium ethanoate in ethanoic acid.

When the salt of the weak acid sodium ethanoate is dissolved in the weak acid it is fully ionized.

$$CH_3COONa \rightarrow CH_3COO^- + Na^+$$

This means there is a large reservoir of $CH_3COO^-$ ions. Because ethanoic acid is a weak acid it is only partially ionized.

In addition, the high concentration of ethanoate ions from the dissolved salt shifts the equilibrium so very little ethanoic acid will dissociate:

$$CH_3COOH \rightleftharpoons CH_3COO^- + H^+$$

This means there is a large reservoir of $CH_3COOH$ molecules.

- $[CH_3COO^-]$ is given by the concentration of the salt of the weak acid.
- $[CH_3COOH]$ is given by the initial concentration of the weak acid.

Buffer solutions minimize changes to pH when small amounts of acid are added because the $H^+$ ions react with ethanoate ions, $CH_3COO^-$, to form ethanoic acid molecules:

$$H^+ + CH_3COO^- \rightleftharpoons CH_3COOH$$

Buffer solutions minimize changes to pH when small amounts of base are added because the $OH^-$ ions react with ethanoic acid molecules, $CH_3COOH$ to form ethanoate ions and water molecules, thus shifting the equilibrium:

$$CH_3COOH + OH^- \rightleftharpoons CH_3COO^- + H_2O$$

## Questions

1 Suggest the name of an indicator that would be suitable for a titration between a strong acid and a weak base.

2 What is a buffer solution?

3 Suggest how you could make an acidic buffer solution.

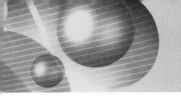

# 2.07 Acids and bases 3

## Important relationships

**pH**

$pH = -\log[H^+]$

$[H^+] = 10^{-pH}$

**Buffer equation**

$K_a = \dfrac{[H^+][A^-]}{[HA]}$

[HA] = concentration of weak acid

[A⁻] = concentration of salt

## Calculating the pH of an acidic buffer solution

We can work out the concentration of the hydrogen ions and use this to work out the pH of an acidic buffer solution.

- [HA] is the concentration of weak acid. We assume that it is the same as the initial concentration of the acid.
- [A⁻] is the concentration of conjugate base. We assume that it is the same as the concentration of the salt.

$K_a = \dfrac{[H^+][A^-]}{[HA]}$

$[H^+] = \dfrac{K_a \times [HA]}{[A^-]}$

$pH = -\log_{10}[H^+]$

### Worked example

*Calculate the pH of a buffer made by mixing 0.30 moles of a weak acid, HA, with 0.2 moles of its salt, NaA in 2.0 dm³ of solution.*

$K_a = 4.0 \times 10^{-6} \text{ mol dm}^{-3}$

The salt is fully ionized $NaA \rightarrow Na^+ + A^-$

The weak acid is partially ionized $HA \rightleftharpoons H^+ + A^-$

$$K_a = \dfrac{[H^+][A^-]}{[HA]}$$

$$\text{Concentration of } A^- = \dfrac{0.20 \text{ mol}}{2.0 \text{ dm}^3} = 0.1 \text{ mol dm}^{-3}$$

$$\text{Concentration of } HA = \dfrac{0.30 \text{ mol}}{2.0 \text{ dm}^3} = 0.15 \text{ mol dm}^{-3}$$

$$4 \times 10^{-6} \text{ mol dm}^{-3} = \dfrac{[H^+] \times 0.1 \text{ mol dm}^{-3}}{0.15 \text{ mol dm}^{-3}}$$

$$[H^+] = \dfrac{4 \times 10^{-6} \text{ mol dm}^{-3} \times 0.15}{0.1} = 6 \times 10^{-6} \text{ mol dm}^{-3}$$

$$pH = -\log_{10}[H^+] = 5.2$$

## Calculating the concentrations of solutions used to prepare a buffer solution

Calculate the concentration of sodium ethanoate needed to prepare a buffer solution of pH 4.2 if 1 dm³ of the sodium ethanoate is added to 1 dm³ of 0.010 mol dm⁻³ ethanoic acid. Give your answer to 2 signficant figures. $pK_a$ for ethanoic acid is 4.75.

**Step 1** Write down the buffer equation and rearrange it so that it is expressed in terms of [A⁻]:

$K_a = \dfrac{[H^+][A^-]}{[HA]}$

$[A^-] = \dfrac{K_a \times [HA]}{[H^+]}$

**Step 2** Convert all the data into the form needed for substitution into the buffer equation:

$K_a = 10^{-4.75} = 1.78 \times 10^{-5}$

$[H^+] = 10^{-4.2} = 6.31 \times 10^{-5}$

**Step 3** Calculate the concentration of the acid in the buffer mixture.

Since equal volumes of both ethanoic acid and sodium ethanoate are mixed to make the buffer solution, the concentration of the ethanoic acid in the buffer mixture is half of that in the original solution:

$[HA] = \dfrac{0.01}{2} = 0.005$

**Step 4** Substitute all the data into the rearranged buffer equation:

$$[A^-] = \frac{K_a \times [HA]}{[H^+]}$$

$$[A^-] = \frac{(1.78 \times 10^{-5}) \times (0.005)}{6.31 \times 10^{-5}}$$

$$[A^-] = 1.41 \times 10^{-3}$$

$[A^-]$ in original solution = $2.8 \times 10^{-3}$ mol dm$^{-3}$

Always remember to add units to your final answer and express it to the correct number of significant figures.

## Buffers in your blood

Human blood contains a number of different buffer mixtures in order to minimize pH changes. When carbon dioxide dissolves in water it forms carbonic acid, $H_2CO_3$:

$$CO_2(g) + H_2O(l) \rightleftharpoons H_2CO_3(aq)$$

Carbonic acid is a weak acid so dissociates in solution releasing $H^+$ ions:

$$H_2CO_3(aq) \rightleftharpoons H^+(aq) + HCO_3^-(aq)$$

The resulting $HCO_3^-$ ions dissolve in blood plasma.

### Worked example

*Blood contains a buffer mixture of carbonic acid and the hydrogencarbonate ion. Calculate the ratio of the concentration of hydrogencarbonate to carbonic acid needed for healthy blood with a pH of 7.4.*

*The $K_a$ for carbonic acid is $4.45 \times 10^{-7}$.*

**Step 1** Write out the $K_a$ expression for carbonic acid:

$$H_2CO_3(aq) \rightleftharpoons H^+(aq) + HCO_3^-(aq)$$

**Step 2** Write out the buffer equation and rearrange so it is expressed in terms of the ratio of $[HCO_3^-]$ to $[H_2CO_3]$:

$$K_a = \frac{[H^+][A^-]}{[HA]}$$

$$\frac{[HCO_3^-]}{[H_2CO_3]} = \frac{K_a}{[H^+]}$$

**Step 3** Convert the data into the correct format to use in the equation:

pH = 7.4

$[H^+] = 10^{-7.4} = 3.98 \times 10^{-8}$

**Step 4** Substitute the data into the equation:

$$\frac{[HCO_3^-]}{[H_2CO_3]} = \frac{(4.45 \times 10^{-7})}{(3.98 \times 10^{-8})} = 11.2$$

**Step 5** Express answer as a ratio:

$[HCO_3^-]:[H_2CO_3] = 11.2:1$

## Questions

1 Calculate the pH of a buffer solution made by mixing 1 dm$^3$ of propanoic acid of concentration 0.05 mol dm$^{-3}$ with 1 dm$^3$ of sodium propanoate of concentration 0.06 mol dm$^{-3}$. The p$K_a$ for propanoic acid is 4.87.

2 Calculate the ratio of butanoate to butanoic acid in a buffer solution of pH 3.45. The $K_a$ for butanoic acid is $1.51 \times 10^{-5}$.

3 Calculate the concentration of ethanoic acid used to prepare a buffer mixture of pH 4.20 when 500 cm$^3$ of ethanoic acid is mixed with 500 cm$^3$ of sodium ethanoate solution of concentration 0.01 mol dm$^{-3}$.

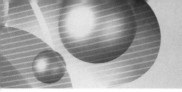

# 2.08 Enthalpy changes

## Standard enthalpy change of neutralization

The energy change that accompanies the neutralization of an aqueous acid by an aqueous base to form 1 mole of $H_2O(l)$, under standard conditions.

## Enthalpy change of neutralization

The neutralization of an aqueous acid by an aqueous base is an exothermic process in which water is formed:

$$H^+(aq) + OH^-(aq) \rightarrow H_2O(l)$$

The **standard enthalpy change of neutralization** is defined as the energy change that accompanies the neutralization of an aqueous acid by an aqueous base to form 1 mole of $H_2O(l)$, under standard conditions.

The standard enthalpy change of neutralization is the same for all strong acids as they fully dissociate in water. For weak acids, the value is less exothermic and is variable as some energy is required for the dissociation process.

Adding known quantities of acid and alkali together and measuring the maximum temperature rise can be used to measure the energy released in this process.

You should remember from AS how to calculate the enthalpy change of reaction from temperature measurements.

### Calculating the heat change of a reaction

The heat change for a reaction ($q$, measured in joules) is given by the equation:

$$q = mc\Delta T$$

where $m$ = mass of the solution (g), $c$ = specific heat capacity of the solution ($J\ g^{-1}\ K^{-1}$) and $\Delta T$ is the temperature change (final temperature – initial temperature) (K).

Since enthalpy of neutralization is measured in $kJ\ mol^{-1}$ of acid, the heat change needs to be divided by the number of moles of acid taking part in the reaction and then divided by 1000 to convert into kJ.

Remember to give your final value a negative sign as the enthalpy of neutralization is always exothermic.

## Worked example

*25.0 cm³ of sodium hydroxide solution was placed in a polystyrene beaker and the temperature of the solution recorded. 1.0 mol dm⁻³ hydrochloric acid was added, 5.0 cm³ at a time; the temperature was recorded after each addition. The temperature values were plotted against the volume of acid added obtaining the graph opposite.*

**a** *Use the graph to determine the volume of acid required to neutralize the sodium hydroxide solution.*
**b** *Calculate the concentration of the sodium hydroxide solution.*
**c** *From the graph, determine the temperature change for the neutralization reaction.*
**d** *Using your answers to parts b and c calculate the enthalpy of neutralization per mole of hydrochloric acid. Assume the specific heat capacity of the solution c = 4.2 J g⁻¹ K⁻¹.*

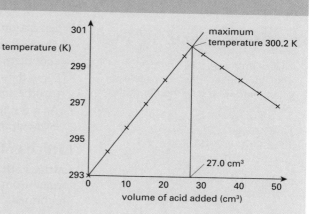

**a** The endpoint of the titration is shown by the maximum temperature on the graph. The volume at the endpoint is read from the graph by noting the volume where the lines cross. Draw a line on the graph to show how you have used it to obtain your answer.

Volume of acid needed = 27.0 cm³

**b** Number of moles of HCl used = $c \times V$ = 1.0 × (27.0/1000) = 0.027
Mole ratio      HCl:NaOH      1:1
Number of moles of NaOH used = 0.027
Concentration of NaOH = $n/V$ = 0.027/25.0 = 0.001 08 mol dm⁻³

**c** Temperature change  = maximum temperature – initial temperature
                = 300.2 – 293 = 7.2 K

**d** Be careful to calculate the correct mass value; remember it is the mass of the solution. In this case you must add together the initial amount of sodium hydroxide solution and the amount of hydrochloric acid at the neutralization point.
$q = mc\Delta T$ = (25.0 + 27.0) × 4.2 × 7.2 = 1572.48 J

**e** Enthalpy of neutralization is the enthalpy change per mole of acid. Make sure you use the number of moles of hydrochloric acid at the neutralization point.
$\Delta H$ = –1572.48/0.027 = –58 240 J mol⁻¹
    = –58.2 kJ mol⁻¹

## Questions

**1** Write out the definition for enthalpy of neutralization five times, then check you can remember it.

**2** 75 cm³ of sodium hydroxide solution was placed in an insulated beaker. 75 cm³ of 0.67 mol dm⁻³ hydrochloric acid was used to exactly neutralize the sodium hydroxide solution. The temperature rise during the neutralization was 4.5 °C. Calculate the enthalpy of neutralization per mole of hydrochloric acid.

# 2.09 Enthalpy change of solution

When an ionic solid dissolves in water two processes take place.

- The ions in the crystal lattice are separated from each other (an endothermic process).
- Then the separate ions form interactions with the water molecules (exothermic processes).
- As a result, the enthalpy change for dissolving, which is the difference between these two values, may be exothermic or endothermic.

## Lattice enthalpy, $\Delta H_L$

**Lattice enthalpy** is the enthalpy change when one mole of an ionic solid is formed from its gaseous ions; this process is always **exothermic** as ionic bonds are formed.

Lattice enthalpies

| compound | $\Delta H_L^{\ominus}$ (kJ mol$^{-1}$) | compound | $\Delta H_L^{\ominus}$ (kJ mol$^{-1}$) |
|---|---|---|---|
| NaF | −918 | MgCl$_2$ | −2493 |
| NaCl | −780 | MgO | −3889 |
| NaBr | −742 | | |

Lattice enthalpy is influenced by the distance between the ions and the charges on the ions.

- The larger the distance between the oppositely charged ions in a crystal lattice the weaker the force of attraction between them.
  - As a result the lattice enthalpy of NaCl is less exothermic than that of NaF.
- The greater the charge on the ions in a crystal lattice the greater the force of attraction between them.
  - As a result the lattice enthalpy of MgO is much more exothermic than that of MgCl$_2$.

## Enthalpy change of hydration, $\Delta H_{hyd}^{\ominus}$

Enthalpy of hydration is the enthalpy change when one mole of separated gaseous ions is dissolved fully in water to form one mole of aqueous ions. The formation of interactions between the ions and water molecules releases energy so this process is exothermic.

## Enthalpy change of solution, $\Delta H_{soln}^{\ominus}$

Enthalpy of solution is the enthalpy change when one mole of an ionic substance is dissolved in water so that the ions are totally separated and do not interact with each other. The enthalpy of solution is dependent on both lattice dissociation enthalpy and enthalpies of hydration so may be either endothermic or exothermic.

## Calculating enthalpy change of solution

When an ionic solid dissolves in water:

- the ionic bonds in the crystal lattice are broken (minus lattice enthalpy)
- the separated gaseous ions become surrounded by water molecules (hydration enthalpies)

## Worked example

Calculate the enthalpy change of solution of KCl using the given data

$\Delta H_L^\ominus$ KCl = -701 kJ mol$^{-1}$          $\Delta H_{hyd}^\ominus$ K$^+$ = -322 kJ mol$^{-1}$

$\Delta H_{hyd}^\ominus$ Cl$^-$ = -364 kJ mol$^{-1}$

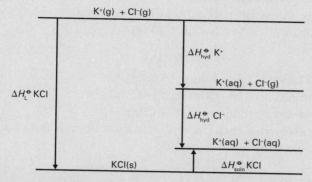

$\Delta H_{soln}^\ominus$ KCl = $-\Delta H_L^\ominus$ KCl + $\Delta H_{hyd}^\ominus$ K$^+$ + $\Delta H_{hyd}^\ominus$ Cl$^-$

$\Delta H_{soln}^\ominus$ KCl = +701 + (-322) + (-364) = +15 kJ mol$^{-1}$

Note that this value is endothermic so the solution becomes colder as the potassium chloride dissolves.

## Questions

1 a Use the data in the table to calculate the enthalpy change of solution of ammonium chloride

| quantity | value (kJ mol$^{-1}$) |
|---|---|
| $\Delta H_L^\ominus$ NH$_4$Cl | -640 |
| $\Delta H_{hyd}^\ominus$ NH$_4^+$ | -301 |
| $\Delta H_{hyd}^\ominus$ Cl$^-$ | -364 |

b Would ammonium chloride be suitable for use in an instant cold pack? Explain your answer

2 Explain the difference in the following lattice enthalpies:

| compound | value (kJ mol$^{-1}$) |
|---|---|
| MgCl$_2$ | -2493 |
| CaCl$_2$ | -2237 |
| SrCl$_2$ | -2112 |

## Cold packs

Solids with endothermic enthalpies of solution are used to make instant cold packs.

## The dissolving process

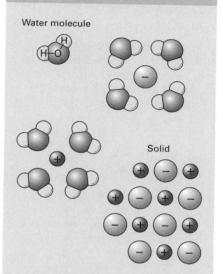

Water molecule

Solid

*Dissolving needs two processes: the break-up of the crystal lattice followed by the hydration of the ions.*

## Enthalpy change of solution, $\Delta H_{soln}^\ominus$

The enthalpy change when one mole of an ionic substance is dissolved in a volume of water large enough to ensure that the ions are separated and do not interact with each other.

For example

KCl(s) + aq → K$^+$(aq) + Cl$^-$(aq)

$\Delta H_{soln}^\ominus$ = +17.2 kJ mol$^{-1}$

# 2.10 Born–Haber cycles

## Ionization energies

First ionization energy, $\Delta H_{i1}^{\ominus}$: the enthalpy change when one mole of electrons is removed from one mole of gaseous atoms forming one mole of gaseous 1+ ions.
e.g. $Na(g) \rightarrow Na^+(g) + e^-$

Second ionization energy, $\Delta H_{i2}^{\ominus}$: the enthalpy change when one mole of electrons is removed from one mole of gaseous 1+ ions forming one mole of gaseous 2+ ions.
e.g. $Mg^+(g) \rightarrow Mg^{2+}(g) + e^-$

## Electron affinity

First electron affinity, $\Delta H_{ea1}^{\ominus}$: the enthalpy change when one mole of electrons is gained by one mole of gaseous atoms to form one mole of gaseous 1– ions.
e.g. $Cl(g) + e^- \rightarrow Cl^-(g)$

Second electron affinity, $\Delta H_{ea2}^{\ominus}$: the enthalpy change when one mole of electrons is gained by one mole of gaseous 1– ions forming one mole of gaseous 2– ions.
e.g. $O^-(g) + e^- \rightarrow O^{2-}(g)$

## Enthalpy of atomization, $\Delta H_{at}^{\ominus}$

The enthalpy change when one mole of gaseous atoms is formed from an element or compound.
e.g. $\frac{1}{2}Cl_2(g) \rightarrow Cl(g)$

$\Delta H_{at}^{\ominus} = + 122 \text{ kJ mol}^{-1}$

Note that this value is half that of the bond dissociation enthalpy of chlorine.

A **Born–Haber cycle** is an enthalpy level diagram that enables you to calculate the enthalpy changes involved in the formation of **ionic compounds**. It is essential that you can recall definitions for and use the following enthalpy changes (examples are given for sodium, chlorine, and sodium chloride):
* Enthalpy of formation    $Na(s) + \frac{1}{2}Cl_2(g) \rightarrow NaCl(s)$
* Lattice enthalpy    $Na^+(g) + Cl^-(g)$
                            $\downarrow$
                     $NaCl(s)$
* Ionization energy    $Na(g) \rightarrow Na^+(g) + e^-$
* Electron affinity    $Cl(g) + e^- \rightarrow Cl^-(g)$
* Enthalpy of atomization   $\frac{1}{2}Cl_2(g) \rightarrow Cl(g)$

You must be able to use these definitions to draw Born–Haber cycles and then use the cycle to calculate lattice enthalpies.

### Born and Haber

Born–Haber cycles are named after Max Born and Fritz Haber who published their ideas in 1919. Born started his working life in Germany but settled in Britain and shared the Nobel Prize in Physics in 1954 for research into quantum mechanics. Haber won the Nobel Prize in Chemistry in 1918 for developing the Haber Process.

## Constructing a Born–Haber cycle for sodium chloride

Born–Haber cycles are always drawn with the enthalpy changes in the same order. Remember that endothermic processes are shown with upwards pointing arrows and exothermic processes are shown with downwards pointing arrows. Cycles can be drawn roughly to scale with the length of each arrow proportional to the enthalpy change but you will not be examined on this.

Work through the enthalpy cycle below making sure you understand each label, and then practise writing it from memory.

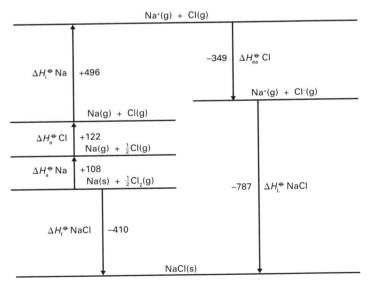

Try covering up one of the values on the cycle then work it out from the rest of the data. Remember to subtract the data if you are moving against the arrow head.

For example: To calculate $\Delta H_L^{\ominus}$ NaCl

$$\Delta H_L^{\ominus} \text{ NaCl} = -(-349) - 496 - 122 - 108 + (-410) = -787 \text{ kJ mol}^{-1}$$

# The Born–Haber cycle for calcium chloride

The table below contains the data needed to construct the Born–Haber cycle for calcium chloride, $CaCl_2$. Since this contains $Ca^{2+}$ ions both the first and second Ionization energies of calcium need to be used.

| | standard enthalpy change | value (kJ mol$^{-1}$) |
|---|---|---|
| $\Delta H_f^\ominus$ | Enthalpy of formation of calcium chloride | −795 |
| $\Delta H_{at}^\ominus$ | Enthalpy of atomization of calcium | 193 |
| $\Delta H_{at}^\ominus$ | Enthalapy of atomization of chlorine | 122 |
| $\Delta H_{ie1}^\ominus$ | First ionization energy of calcium | 590 |
| $\Delta H_{ie2}^\ominus$ | Second ionization energy of calcium | 1150 |
| $\Delta H_{ea}^\ominus$ | First electron affinity of chlorine | −349 |

Note that the bond dissociation enthalpy of chlorine has been given – this will form two moles of gaseous chlorine atoms so is the same as doubling the enthalpy of atomization.

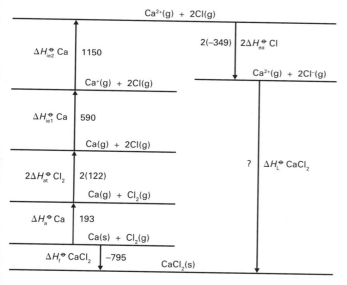

$$\Delta H_L^\ominus\ CaCl_2(s) = -2(-349) - 1150 - 590 - 244 - 193 - 795$$
$$= -2274\ kJ\ mo^{l-1}$$

This value is highly exothermic so $CaCl_2$ is stable. The lattice enthalpy for CaCl is −719 kJ mol$^{-1}$ so is less stable.

## Questions

1 a Draw a Born–Haber cycle and use it to calculate the lattice dissociation enthalpy of MgCl.

| enthalpy change | value (kJ mol$^{-1}$) | enthalpy change | value (kJ mol$^{-1}$) |
|---|---|---|---|
| $\Delta H_f^\ominus$ MgCl | −94 | $\Delta H_{at}^\ominus$ Mg | +148 |
| $\Delta H_{at}^\ominus$ Cl | +122 | $\Delta H_{ie1}^\ominus$ Mg | +738 |
| $\Delta H_{ea}^\ominus$ Cl | −349 | $\Delta H_{ie2}^\ominus$ Mg | +1451 |

b The lattice enthalpy of $MgCl_2$ is −2524 kJ mol$^{-1}$. Explain why $MgCl_2$ is formed in preference to MgCl.

2 Use the data given to construct a Born–Haber cycle for sodium oxide, then use your cycle to calculate the second electron affinity of oxygen.

| enthalpy change | value (kJ mol$^{-1}$) | enthalpy change | value (kJ mol$^{-1}$) |
|---|---|---|---|
| $\Delta H_f^\ominus$ Na$_2$O | −416 | $\Delta H_{at}^\ominus$ Na | +109 |
| $\Delta H_{at}^\ominus$ O | +248 | $\Delta H_{ie1}^\ominus$ Na | +495 |
| $\Delta H_{ea1}^\ominus$ O | −142 | $\Delta H_L^\ominus$ Na$_2$O | −1917 |

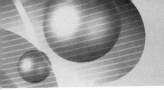
Entropy is a measure of the disorder in a system. An organized room has low **entropy** while a typical teenager's bedroom has high entropy! At absolute zero the entropy of a pure substance is zero.

## Entropy

### Entropy diagram for heating water

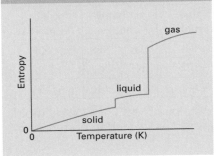

When a substance changes state there is a change in entropy:

* Solids have a regular arrangement of particles.
* The particles in a solid are close to each other.
  * As a result solids have low entropies because they are very ordered.
* Liquids have a greater entropy than solids because the particles are disordered – there are many ways they can be arranged.
* Gases have a high entropy because they are highly disordered – the particles can be arranged in a large number of ways.

Examine the diagram showing the entropy changes on heating water. Note the increases in entropy when the state changes. This increase is much larger when the water boils as all the hydrogen bonds between the water particles are broken.

## Entropy changes

There will be an overall increase in entropy in a reaction if:

* there are more particles of products than reactants and they are in the same state
* the reactants are solids or liquids and the products include a gas

There is an increase in entropy when the following reactions take place. Work through each one applying the rules above:

$$CaCO_3(s) \rightarrow CaO(s) + CO_2(g)$$
$$KHCO_3(s) + HCl(aq) \rightarrow KCl(aq) + H_2O(l) + CO_2(g)$$
$$C_3H_8(g) + 5O_2(g) \rightarrow 3CO_2(g) + 4H_2O(g)$$

When substances are dissolved in water there is an increase in entropy because the separated ions or molecules in solution have a high degree of disorder.
$$CuSO_4(s) + aq \rightarrow Cu^{2+}(aq) + SO_4^{2-}(aq)$$
The standard entropy change for a reaction is readily calculated from absolute entropy values using the relationship $\Delta S^{\ominus} = \Sigma S^{\ominus}$ **(products)** $- \Sigma S^{\ominus}$ **(reactants)**

### Entropy data for water

| Substance | Standard entropy, $S$ (J K⁻¹ mol⁻¹) |
|---|---|
| $H_2O(s)$ | 62.1 |
| $H_2O(l)$ | 69.9 |
| $H_2O(g)$ | 188.7 |

### Worked example

Calculate the entropy change for the combustion of ethane $C_2H_6(g)$:

$$C_2H_6(g) + 3\tfrac{1}{2}O_2(g) \rightarrow 2CO_2(g) + 3H_2O(g)$$

| substance | $C_2H_6(g)$ | $O_2(g)$ | $CO_2(g)$ | $H_2O(g)$ |
|---|---|---|---|---|
| entropy, $S^{\ominus}$ (J K⁻¹ mol⁻¹) | 229.5 | 204.8 | 213.6 | 188.7 |

$\Delta S = \Sigma S^{\ominus}$ (products) $- \Sigma S^{\ominus}$ (reactants)

$\Sigma S^{\ominus}$ (products) $= (2 \times 213.6) + (3 \times 188.7) = 993.3$ J K⁻¹ mol⁻¹

$\Sigma S^{\ominus}$ (reactants) $= (229.5) + (3.5 \times 204.8) = 946.3$ J K⁻¹ mol⁻¹

$\Delta S^{\ominus} = 993.3 - 946.3 = +47$ J K⁻¹ mol⁻¹

Notice that this is a positive entropy change, which would be expected as the number of molecules has increased.

## Feasibility, enthalpy, and entropy

Spontaneous changes are those that happen in only one direction and cannot be reversed without an input of energy:

* Rusting and the reactions of acids with alkalis are spontaneous chemical reactions.

- The dissolving of sugar is a spontaneous process.
- An understanding of enthalpy changes alone is not enough to predict if a process will be spontaneous. We must also consider the entropy changes that occur.

For a reaction to occur both the entropy and enthalpy changes must be favourable.

Consider the combustion of ethane under standard conditions:

- The entropy change is positive.
- The enthalpy change is negative.
- Ⓡ As a result the reaction is feasible.

Note that the combustion of ethane is feasible but not spontaneous as it has a high activation energy. Ethane will not burn in air until a source of ignition is provided.

## Free energy and feasibility

The table below can be used to predict if a reaction is feasible under standard conditions. We often carry reactions out at other temperatures and can determine if a reaction will be feasible by using the idea of **free energy change**.

### Feasibility

| $\Delta H$ | $\Delta S$ | |
|---|---|---|
| | negative | positive |
| negative | feasible if $\Delta H < T\Delta S$ | always feasible |
| positive | never feasible | feasible if $\Delta H < T\Delta S$ |

Free energy change:

- is given the symbol $\Delta G$
- is also called Gibbs energy (after the scientist Willard Gibbs)
- is measured in kJ mol$^{-1}$
- is calculated by $\Delta G = \Delta H - T\Delta S$

A reaction is feasible when $\Delta G \leq 0$

---

### Entropy units

Entropy and entropy change are measured in J K$^{-1}$ mol$^{-1}$. Take care using the data as enthalpy and enthalpy changes are measured in kJ mol$^{-1}$.

### Worked example

Nitrogen gas can react with oxygen gas to form a mixture of oxides. The temperature at which this reaction will occur is very high. What is the minimum temperature at which nitrogen gas will react spontaneously with oxygen gas?

$\Delta H^{\ominus} = +180$ kJ mol$^{-1}$

$\Delta S^{\ominus} = +25$ J K$^{-1}$ mol$^{-1}$

For the reaction to be spontaneous $\Delta G^{\ominus} \leq 0$

Calculate the minimum temperature based on $\Delta G^{\ominus} = 0$

$0 = 180 - T(25/1000)$

$180 = 0.025T$

$T = 180/0.025 = 7200$ K

The minimum temperature at which this reaction will occur is 7200 K

---

### Worked example

Will the thermal dissociation of NH$_4$Cl proceed spontaneously at 245 K?

$NH_4Cl(s) \rightarrow NH_3(g) + HCl(g)$    $\Delta H^{\ominus} = +176$ kJmol$^{-1}$    $\Delta S^{\ominus} = +284$ J K$^{-1}$ mol$^{-1}$

$\Delta G^{\ominus} = \Delta H^{\ominus} - T\Delta S^{\ominus}$

$\Delta G^{\ominus} = 176 - (245 \times 284/1000) = +106$ kJmol$^{-1}$

$\Delta G^{\ominus}$ is positive so the reaction will not occur spontaneously

Note that $\Delta S^{\ominus}$ is in J K$^{-1}$ mol$^{-1}$ so is converted to kJ mol$^{-1}$

---

## Questions

1 Sketch a labelled diagram showing the entropy changes as solid chlorine is heated until it fully vaporizes.

2 Explain why the reaction of sodium hydrogencarbonate with nitric acid occurs at room temperature even though the reaction is endothermic.

3 Calculate the minimum temperature at which calcium carbonate will decompose to form calcium oxide and carbon dioxide.

$\Delta H^{\ominus} = +178$ kJ mol$^{-1}$        $\Delta S^{\ominus} = +165$ J K$^{-1}$ mol$^{-1}$

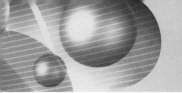

# 2.12 Redox reactions

Redox reactions involve both the loss of electrons (oxidation) and the gain of electrons (reduction). These processes always occur at the same time.

## Oxidation states

**Oxidation states** are used to find out the number of electrons that must be gained to make a neutral atom. For example, the oxidation state of magnesium in $Mg^{2+}$ is +2 because two electrons would need to be gained in order to make a neutral atom:

$$Mg^{2+} + 2e^- \rightarrow Mg$$

The oxidation state of chlorine in $Cl^-$ is –1 because one electron would need to be lost to make a neutral atom:

$$Cl^- \rightarrow Cl + e^-$$

The oxidation state of an element is 0.

It is important that you can apply the oxidation number rules. Work through the table below and make sure you can remember each one then work through the examples below to determine the oxidation states of various elements.

### OIL RIG

**O**xidation **i**s the **l**oss of electrons

Oxidation is shown by an increase in oxidation number

**R**eduction **i**s the **g**ain of electrons

Reduction is shown by a decrease in oxidation number

| Element | Oxidation state in compounds and ions | Exceptions |
|---------|:---:|---|
| H | +1 | Metal hydrides: oxidation state is –1, e.g. NaH |
| Li, Na, K | +1 | |
| Mg, Ca, Ba | +2 | |
| Al | +3 | |
| F | –1 | |
| Cl | –1 | Oxidation state varies when combined with F or O |
| O | –2 | Oxidation state is not –2 when combined with F. Oxidation state is –1 in peroxides e.g. $H_2O_2$ |

### Oxidizing and reducing agents

**Oxidizing agents** are species that undergo reduction.

**Reducing agents** are species that undergo oxidation.

**Step 1** Write down the formula.

**Step 2** Using the table write the known oxidation states above the symbol for each element.

**Step 3** Using the known oxidation states work out the total oxidation state.

**Step 4** Subtract the total oxidation states from zero for compounds or from the charge if the problem is about a polyatomic ion.

| Worked example 1 | |
|---|---|
| What is the oxidation state of aluminium in $Al_2O_3$? | |
| Step 1 | $Al_2O_3$ |
| Step 2 | $Al_2\overset{-2}{O_3}$ |
| Step 3 | $\underset{-6}{Al_2\overset{-2}{O_3}}$ |
| Step 4 | Total oxidation state of Al = 0 – (–6) = +6. Oxidation state of each Al = +6/2 = +3 |

| Worked example 2 | |
|---|---|
| What is the oxidation state of manganese in $MnO_4^-$ ? | |
| Step 1 | $MnO_4^-$ |
| Step 2 | $Mn\overset{-2}{O_4}^-$ |
| Step 3 | $\underset{-8}{Mn\overset{-2}{O_4}^-}$ |
| Step 4 | Total oxidation state of Mn = –1–(–8) = +7 |

## Half-equations

Half-equations show the loss or gain of electrons by one substance. For example, this is the full equation for the reaction between calcium and chlorine. Note that it can be split into two half-equations:

$$Ca(s) + Cl_2(g) \rightarrow CaCl_2(s)$$

The oxidation half-equation is: $Ca \rightarrow Ca^{2+} + 2e^-$

The reduction half-equation is: $Cl_2 + 2e^- \rightarrow 2Cl^-$

## Combining half-equations

Half-equations are straightforward to combine as long as you remember that the electrons on the left hand side and the right hand side of the equation must cancel out.

### Worked example 1

Complete the following half-equation: $Br_2 \rightarrow Br^-$
**Step 1** Write out the two species $\qquad$ $Br_2 \rightarrow Br^-$
**Step 2** Balance the atoms $\qquad$ $Br_2 \rightarrow 2Br^-$
**Step 3** Add enough electrons to make the total charges the same on each side
$Br_2 + \mathbf{2e^-} \rightarrow 2Br^-$

### Worked example 2

Complete the following half-equation: $Cr_2O_7^{2-} \rightarrow Cr^{3+}$
Half-equations involving d block elements may involve hydrogen ions. These are needed when the d block element is combined with oxygen in a polyatomic ion.
**Step 1** Write out the two species $\qquad$ $Cr_2O_7^{2-} \rightarrow Cr^{3+}$
**Step 2** Add enough water molecules to the right hand side to balance the oxygen atoms $\qquad$ $Cr_2O_7^{2-} \rightarrow Cr^{3+} + \mathbf{7H_2O}$
**Step 3** Add enough $H^+$ ions to the left hand side to account for the hydrogen atoms on the right $\qquad$ $Cr_2O_7^{2-} + \mathbf{14H^+} \rightarrow Cr^{3+} + 7H_2O$
**Step 4** Balance all the atoms in the equation $\quad$ $Cr_2O_7^{2-} + 14H^+ \rightarrow 2Cr^{3+} + 7H_2O$
**Step 5** Add enough electrons to make the total charges on each side the same
$Cr_2O_7^{2-} + 14H^+ + \mathbf{6e^-} \rightarrow 2Cr^{3+} + 7H_2O$

### Worked example 4

Half-equations can be constructed by using oxidation numbers to balance the equation.
Write a balanced half-equation for the reduction of acidified $MnO_4^-$ to $Mn^{2+}$.
**Step 1** Write out the two species: $MnO_4^- \rightarrow Mn^{2+}$
**Step 2** Add enough water molecules to the right-hand side to balance the oxygen atoms: $\qquad$ $MnO_4^- \rightarrow Mn^{2+} + \mathbf{4H_2O}$
**Step 3** Add enough $H^+$ ions to the left-hand side to account for the hydrogen atoms on the right: $\qquad$ $MnO_4^- + \mathbf{8H^+} \rightarrow Mn^{2+} + 4H_2O$
**Step 4** Determine the oxidation number of the manganese in both ions. Write the oxidation state above the formula:

$$\overset{+7}{Mn}O_4^- + 8H^+ \rightarrow \overset{+2}{Mn}^{2+} + 4H_2O$$

**Step 5** Use the change in oxidation number to determine the number of electrons being transferred. Add electrons to the relevant side of the equation: $\qquad$ $MnO_4^- + 8H^+ + \mathbf{5e^-} \rightarrow Mn^{2+} + 4H_2O$

An overall equation for a redox reaction can also be balanced using oxidation numbers. Work through the example below.
Write a balanced equation for the reaction of iron(II) ions with acidified manganate(VII) ions forming iron(III) ions and manganese(II) ions.
**Step 1** Write out the information given: $\quad$ $MnO_4^- + Fe^{2+} \rightarrow Mn^{2+} + Fe^{3+}$
**Step 2** Add enough water molecules to the right-hand side to balance the oxygen atoms: $\qquad$ $MnO_4^- + Fe^{2+} \rightarrow Mn^{2+} + Fe^{3+} + \mathbf{4H_2O}$
**Step 3** Add enough H+ ions to the left-hand side to account for the hydrogen atoms on the right: $\qquad$ $MnO_4^- + Fe^{2+} + \mathbf{8H^+} \rightarrow Mn^{2+} + Fe^{3+} + 4H_2O$
**Step 4** Determine the change in oxidation state for both ions. Write the oxidation states above the formula:

$$\overset{+7}{Mn}O_4^- + \overset{+2}{Fe}^{2+} + \mathbf{8H^+} \xrightarrow[\text{down by 5}]{\text{up by 1}} \overset{+2}{Mn}^{2+} + \overset{+3}{Fe}^{3+} + 4H_2O$$

**Step 5** Use the change in oxidation number to determine the number of electrons being transferred. Balance the equation so the increase in oxidation number is equal to the decrease in oxidation number:
$MnO_4^- + \mathbf{5}Fe^{2+} + 8H^+ \rightarrow Mn^{2+} + \mathbf{5}Fe^{3+} + 4H_2O$

### Worked example 3

Combine these two half-equations:

$Cr_2O_7^{2-} + 14H^+ + 6e^- \rightarrow 2Cr^{3+} + 7H_2O$

$Fe^{2+} \rightarrow Fe^{3+} + e^-$

In order to combine these equations the electrons must balance. So 6 moles of $Fe^{2+}$ are needed in order to reduce 1 mole of $Cr_2O_7^{2-}$:

$\mathbf{6}Fe^{2+} \rightarrow \mathbf{6}Fe^{3+} + \mathbf{6}e^-$

Overall:

$Cr_2O_7^{2-} + 14H^+ + 6Fe^{2+} \rightarrow 2Cr^{3+} + 7H_2O + 6Fe^{3+}$

---

## Questions

1 Work out the oxidation states of the element in bold in the following:
 a $\mathbf{Mn}O_4^-$
 b $\mathbf{Fe}^{2+}$
 c $\mathbf{Cl}O_3^-$
 d $\mathbf{N}H_4^+$
2 Balance the following half-equations:
 a $Cu^{2+} \rightarrow Cu^+$
 b $MnO_4^- \rightarrow Mn^{2+}$
 c $O^{2-} \rightarrow O_2$
3 Combine the pairs of half-equations below:
 a $Mg \rightarrow Mg^{2+} + 2e^-$
 $\quad Br_2 + 2e^- \rightarrow 2Br^-$
 b $Zn \rightarrow Zn^{2+} + 2e^-$
 $\quad Cr_2O_7^{2-} + 14H^+ + 6e^- \rightarrow 2Cr^{3+} + 7H_2O$

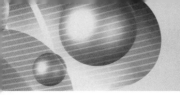

## Standard hydrogen electrode

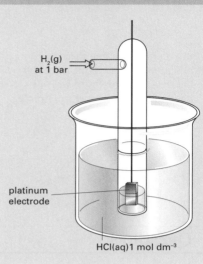

platinum
electrode

HCl(aq)1 mol dm⁻³

## Standard electrode potential

The standard electrode potential, $E^{\ominus}$, is the electromotive force of an electrochemical cell measured relative to the hydrogen half-cell under standard conditions, i.e.:

- a temperature of 298 K (25 °C)

- a pressure of 100 kPa (100,000 Pa)

- solutions of ions at a concentration of 1.00 mol dm⁻³

The hydrogen half-cell is assigned an $E^{\ominus} = 0\,V$
( $2H^+(aq) + 2e^- \rightleftharpoons H_2(g)$ )

When a strip of magnesium is placed into a solution of copper(II) sulfate, a redox reaction occurs:

$$Mg(s) + Cu^{2+}(aq) \rightarrow Mg^{2+}(aq) + Cu(s)$$

The magnesium is oxidized: $\qquad Mg(s) \rightarrow Mg^{2+}(aq) + 2e^-$

The copper(II) ions are reduced $\qquad Cu^{2+}(aq) + 2e^- \rightarrow Cu(s)$

- The sulfate ions are spectator ions and do not take part in the reaction.
  - As a result they are not included in the equations for the redox reaction.

If instead you were to put copper metal into a solution of magnesium(II) sulfate, no reaction would occur. An understanding of electrochemical cells enables you to predict whether a reaction will occur or not.

## Half-cells

The standard electrode potential, $E^{\ominus}$, for a redox reaction tells us whether a substance is readily oxidized or reduced.

To determine the $E^{\ominus}$ value a **half-cell** is made and connected to the standard hydrogen half-cell.

This hydrogen half-cell is assigned an $E^{\ominus}$ value of 0.00 V so every other half-cell is measured relative to hydrogen.

The diagram shows how the $E^{\ominus}$ value for a copper half-cell could be determined.

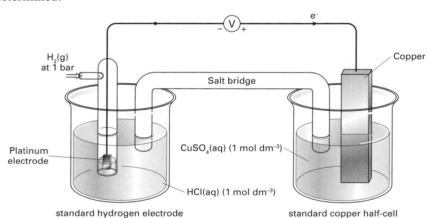

standard hydrogen electrode          standard copper half-cell

The $E^{\ominus}$ value for the copper half-cell is +0.34 V. The positive sign shows that the potential on the copper electrode is more positive than that on the standard hydrogen electrode. The electrons flow from the hydrogen half-cell to the copper half-cell.

Note that the equations representing half-cells are always written as **reduction reactions** with the use of an equilibrium arrow.

## Electrochemical cells

An **electrochemical cell** can be constructed for any pair of half-cells.

The diagram shows the electrochemical cell obtained when the magnesium and copper half-cells are connected together.

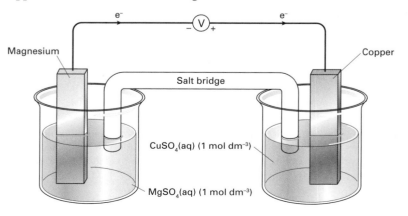

When this cell is connected up:

- the concentration of magnesium ions increases
- solid copper is deposited on the copper electrode
- a reading of +2.71 V is obtained

This tells us that

- In the magnesium half-cell oxidation occurs so the equilibrium
  $Mg^{2+}(aq) + 2e^- \rightleftharpoons Mg(s)$ lies to the left hand side.
- The $E^{\ominus}$ value for the magnesium half-cell is –2.37 V.
- In the copper half-cell reduction occurs so the equilibrium
  $Cu^{2+}(aq) + 2e^- \rightleftharpoons Cu(s)$ lies to the right hand side.
- The $E^{\ominus}$ value for the magnesium half-cell is +0.34 V
- Electrons flow from the magnesium half-cell to the copper half-cell.

In the next section you will revise how to calculate and interpret the voltmeter reading.

## Ions of the same element

An electrochemical cell can be used to look at the reaction of an ion to form another ion of the same element in a different oxidation state. The cell uses a platinum electrode to conduct electricity.

The diagram below shows the electrochemical cell made from the two half-equations:  $Fe^{3+}(aq) + e^- \rightleftharpoons Fe^{2+}(aq)$
$Mg^{2+}(aq) + 2e^- \rightleftharpoons Mg(s)$

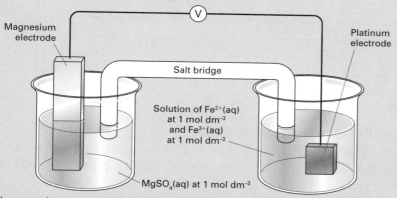

When you have worked through the next page, come back to this diagram and work out the direction of movement of the electrons. Calculate the reading on the voltmeter.

## Cell for a non-metal

The electrochemical cell for a non-metal uses the same electrode as for a hydrogen half-cell. Note that the gas is passed into the cell at a pressure of 1 bar. The diagram shows the electrochemical cell made from the two half-cells:

$$Zn^{2+}(aq) + 2e^- \rightleftharpoons Zn(s)$$
$$Cl_2(g) + 2e^- \rightleftharpoons 2Cl^-(aq)$$

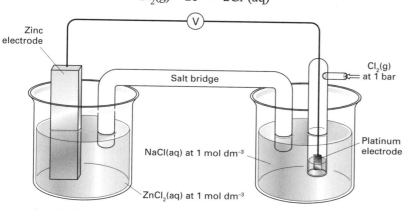

Take another look at this diagram after you have worked through the next page and work out the direction of movement of the electrons. Calculate the reading on the voltmeter.

### Salt bridge

The salt bridge in a simple cell is a piece of filter paper that has been soaked in saturated potassium chloride or potassium nitrate solution. The role of the salt bridge is to balance the charges of the electrochemical cell. Positive ions move into the half-cell in which reduction occurs and negative ions move into the half-cell in which oxidation occurs.

## Questions

1 Draw a labelled diagram to show how the standard electrode potential of the zinc half-cell could be determined
($Zn^{2+}(aq) + 2e^- \rightleftharpoons Zn(s)$)

2 Draw a labelled diagram showing the electrochemical cell obtained when the zinc and copper half-cells are connected.

3 Draw a labelled diagram showing the electrochemical cell made from the two half-cells:
$Mg^{2+}(aq) + 2e^- \rightleftharpoons Mg(s)$
$F_2(g) + 2e^- \rightleftharpoons 2F^-(aq)$

# 2.14 The electrochemical series

**Standard electrode potentials**, which are measured by connecting a half-cell to a standard hydrogen electrode, can be used to calculate the e.m.f. of a cell and to predict the direction of simple redox reactions.

## The electrochemical series

| electrode reaction | E (V) |
|---|---|
| $Li^+(aq) + e^- \rightleftharpoons Li(s)$ | −3.03 |
| $K^+(aq) + e^- \rightleftharpoons K(s)$ | −2.92 |
| $Na^+(aq) + e^- \rightleftharpoons Na(s)$ | −2.71 |
| $Mg^{2+}(aq) + 2e^- \rightleftharpoons Mg(s)$ | −2.37 |
| $Zn^{2+}(aq) + 2e^- \rightleftharpoons Zn(s)$ | −0.76 |
| $Fe^{2+}(aq) + 2e^- \rightleftharpoons Fe(s)$ | −0.44 |
| $Pb^{2+}(aq) + 2e^- \rightleftharpoons Pb(s)$ | −0.13 |
| $2H^+(aq) + 2e^- \rightleftharpoons H_2(g)$ | 0.00 |
| $Cu^{2+}(aq) + e^- \rightleftharpoons Cu^+(aq)$ | +0.15 |
| $Cu^{2+}(aq) + 2e^- \rightleftharpoons Cu(s)$ | +0.34 |
| $Cu^+(aq) + e^- \rightleftharpoons Cu(s)$ | +0.52 |
| $I_2(aq) + 2e^- \rightleftharpoons 2I^-(aq)$ | +0.54 |
| $Fe^{3+}(aq) + e^- \rightleftharpoons Fe^{2+}(aq)$ | +0.77 |
| $Br_2(aq) + 2e^- \rightleftharpoons 2Br^-(aq)$ | +1.09 |
| $Cr_2O_7^{2-}(aq) + 14H^+(aq) + 6e^- \rightleftharpoons 2Cr^{3+}(aq) + 7H_2O(l)$ | +1.33 |
| $Cl_2(aq) + 2e^- \rightleftharpoons 2Cl^-(aq)$ | +1.36 |
| $MnO_4^-(aq) + 8H^+(aq) + 5e^- \rightleftharpoons Mn^{2+}(aq) + 4H_2O(l)$ | +1.51 |
| $F_2(g) + 2e^- \rightleftharpoons 2F^-(aq)$ | +2.87 |

## Using the electrochemical series

The list of standard electrode potentials in order is called the electrochemical series. This is written in order of increasingly negative potential or increasingly positive potential.

Examine the electrochemical series on this page carefully. You need to be able to

- combine half-equations to write overall equations
- identify oxidizing agents and reducing agents for pairs of equations

Consider the half-equation and $E^\ominus$ value for chlorine/chloride

- The $E^\ominus$ value is positive.
- This means that the equilibrium lies a long way to the right hand side.
  - As a result chlorine is readily reduced to chloride ions.
- Consider the half-equation and $E^\ominus$ value for zinc ions/zinc.
- The $E^\ominus$ value is negative.
- This means that the equilibrium lies a long way to the left hand side.
  - As a result zinc is readily oxidized to zinc ions.

If we want to combine these two half-equations then we must reverse the half-equation for the zinc system before we add the equations together:

Reduction half-equation $Cl_2(aq) + 2e^- \rightarrow 2Cl^-(aq)$

Oxidation half-equation $Zn(s) \rightarrow Zn^{2+}(aq) + 2e^-$

Overall equation $\qquad Cl_2(aq) + Zn(s) \rightarrow Zn^{2+}(aq) + 2Cl^-(aq)$

If the number of electrons provided by the oxidation is not equal to the number needed for the reduction then the equations must be balanced carefully so that the number of electrons cancels on either side.

# Calculating cell e.m.f.

The e.m.f. of a cell is calculated simply from standard electrode potential values. You will see this calculated in many different ways in different books. If this method is very different from the method you have learnt, then refer to the method you have been taught!

**Example**

*Write an overall equation and calculate the cell e.m.f. for the cell formed by combining the $Mg^{2+}/Mg$ and $Cu^{2+}/Cu$ half-cells.*

**Step 1** Write out half-equations and $E^{\ominus}$ values from the list:
$$Mg^{2+} + 2e^{-} \rightleftharpoons Mg \qquad\qquad E^{\ominus} = -2.37 \text{ V}$$
$$Cu^{2+} + 2e^{-} \rightleftharpoons Cu \qquad\qquad E^{\ominus} = +0.34 \text{ V}$$

**Step 2** Reverse the half-equation for the cell with the most negative $E^{\ominus}$ value: This is the cell in which oxidation will occur.
$$Mg \rightleftharpoons Mg^{2+} + 2e^{-}$$

**Step 3** Combine the two half-equations. Check that the electrons balance:
$$Mg + Cu^{2+} \rightarrow Mg^{2+} + Cu$$

**Step 4** Use the equation
$$E^{\ominus}_{cell} = E^{\ominus}_{reduction} - E^{\ominus}_{oxidation}$$
$$= +0.34 - (-2.37) = +2.71 \text{ V}$$

# Feasibility of reactions

Electrochemical cells with large and positive e.m.f. values are **feasible**. However, the reaction may not occur **spontaneously** as the activation energy may be too high or the concentrations of the solutions may be so low that that the reaction takes place at a very slow rate.

# Predicting whether a reaction will occur

The possibility of a reaction taking place can be predicted from the electrochemical series.

**Example**

*Use $E^{\ominus}$ values to explain why chlorine gas will oxidize bromide ions but chlorine gas will not oxidize fluoride ions.*

The $E^{\ominus}$ value for the $Cl_2/Cl^-$ system has a more positive value than that for the $Br_2/Br^-$ ion so chlorine is more readily reduced than bromine. Therefore chlorine will oxidize bromide ions forming chloride ions and bromine.

The $E^{\ominus}$ value for the $Cl_2/Cl^-$ system has a more negative value than that for the $F_2/F^-$ system so fluorine is more readily reduced than chlorine. Therefore chlorine is unable to oxidize fluoride ions.

## Cell e.m.f.

The e.m.f. can be determined from a cell diagram and the relevant standard electrode potential data. Use the electrode potential data to determine what has been oxidized and what has been reduced.

$$E^{\ominus}_{cell} = E^{\ominus}_{reduction} - E^{\ominus}_{oxidation}$$

## Questions

1  For each of the pairs of substances below, state which one is the more powerful reducing agent.

   **a**  Li or Zn

   **b**  $F^-$ or $Br^-$

2  Calculate the cell e.m.f. for the electrochemical cell formed from combining the $Fe^{2+}/Fe$ and $Mg^{2+}/Mg$ half-cells. Is the reaction feasible?

3  Use $E^{\ominus}$ values to explain whether the following reactions will take place.

   **a**  zinc with magnesium ions

   **b**  bromine with iodide ions

   **c**  $MnO_4^-(aq)$ with $Zn(s)$

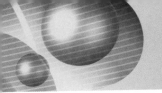

# 2.15 Commercial cells and fuel cell vehicles

**Fuel cell**

Fuel cells use the energy from the reaction of a fuel with oxygen to create a voltage.

## Modern storage cells

**Electrochemical cells** are a convenient source of energy. A battery is made from two or more cells connected in series.

There are three main types of commercial electrochemical cell:

- primary cells – these are not rechargeable and are thrown away when run down
- secondary cells – these can be recharged after they run down
- fuel cells – these produce electricity from gaseous or liquid fuels

Each electrochemical cell contains two **electrodes** and an **electrolyte** that acts as a salt bridge.

You are expected to be able to apply the principles of electrode potentials to modern **storage cells.** These are the secondary cells that are used in mp3 players, laptops and mobile telephones. You do not need to recall the details of any specific storage cells.

### Worked example

*The nickel–cadmium cell is the most common rechargeable cell in everyday use. The electrodes in the cell are made from cadmium and nickel hydroxide. The electrolyte in the cells is aqueous potassium hydroxide.*

*Use the standard electrode potentials given to write an equation for the process that takes place during the discharge of the cell.*

$$Cd(OH)_2 + 2e^- \rightleftharpoons Cd + 2OH^- \qquad E^\ominus = -0.80 \text{ V}$$

$$NiO(OH) + H_2O + e^- \rightleftharpoons Ni(OH)_2 + OH^- \qquad E^\ominus = +0.45 \text{ V}$$

**Step 1** Reverse the half-equation with the most negative $E^\ominus$ value:

$$Cd + 2OH^- \rightleftharpoons Cd(OH)_2 + 2e^-$$

**Step 2** Balance the electrons by multiplying the NiO(OH) half-equation by 2:

$$2NiO(OH) + 2H_2O + 2e^- \rightleftharpoons (OH)_2 + 2OH^-$$

**Step 3** Add together the two half-equations:

$$Cd + 2OH^- + 2NiO(OH) + 2H_2O \rightarrow 2Ni(OH)_2 + 2OH^- + Cd(OH)_2$$

**Step 4** Cancel out any species that appear on both sides of the equation:

$$Cd + 2NiO(OH) + 2H_2O \rightarrow 2Ni(OH)_2 + Cd(OH)_2$$

*Calculate the standard cell potential of this cell.*

Use the equation:

$$E^\ominus{}_{cell} = E^\ominus{}_{reduction} - E^\ominus{}_{oxidation}$$

$$E^\ominus{}_{cell} = +0.45 - (-0.80) = +1.25 \text{ V}$$

*Write an equation for the reaction that takes place in this cell under charge.*

Under charge electrons are put into the cell from a charger. This causes the cell reaction under discharge to be reversed.

$$2Ni(OH)_2 + Cd(OH)_2 \rightarrow Cd + 2NiO(OH) + 2H_2O$$

**Emissions from fuel cells**

Note that pure hydrogen emits only water as a by-product. Hydrogen-rich fuels produce only small amounts of air pollutants and $CO_2$.

## Fuel cells

**Fuel cells** convert the chemical energy in a fuel such as hydrogen or methanol directly into electrical energy. The fuel undergoes an oxidation reaction with oxygen from the air using electrochemical reactions in the fuel cell.

The hydrogen–oxygen fuel cell contains two flat electrodes, each coated with a thin layer of platinum catalyst. A proton exchange membrane is placed between the two electrodes allowing the movement of hydrogen ions. Hydrogen gas flows to one electrode and air to the other. Water vapour, the waste product, is pushed out by the stream of air.

The relevant electrode potentials are:

$2H^+ + 2e^- \rightleftharpoons H_2$ $\qquad E^{\ominus} = 0.00$ V

$2H^+ + \frac{1}{2}O_2 + 2e^- \rightleftharpoons H_2O$ $\qquad E^{\ominus} = 1.23$ V

Since the $H^+/H_2$ reaction has the more negative electrode potential, this half-equation is reversed, giving

$H_2 \rightleftharpoons 2H^+ + 2e^-$

The overall cell reaction is therefore:

$$\frac{1}{2}O_2 + H_2 \rightarrow H_2O$$

Note that the $H^+$ ions cancel out as they appear on both sides of the equation.

## Fuel cell vehicles

Scientists in the car industry are developing **fuel cell vehicles** (FCVs), which are fuelled by either:

- hydrogen gas, or
- hydrogen-rich fuels such as methanol, natural gas or petrol which are converted into hydrogen gas by a 'reformer' in the car

Fuel cell vehicles could present us with an alternative to the direct use of finite oil-based fuels in cars. There are limitations to their use as shown in the table below.

### Storage of hydrogen in fuel cells

The hydrogen for use in the fuel cell has to be stored in the FCV. This may be:

- as a liquid under pressure
- by adsorption onto the surface of a solid material
- by absorption within a solid material

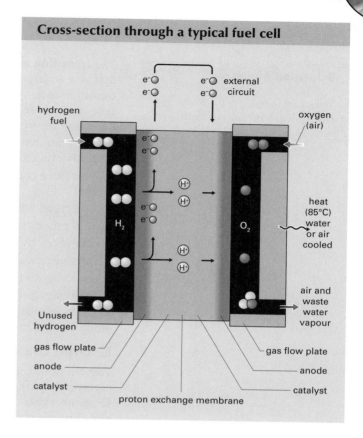

**Cross-section through a typical fuel cell**

## Advantages and disadvantages of fuel cell vehicles

| benefits | limitations |
|---|---|
| • FCVs are much more efficient than petrol- or diesel-powered vehicles.<br>• The only waste product is water.<br>• Energy is produced without fossil fuels.<br>• Pure hydrogen emits only water as a waste product.<br>• Hydrogen-rich fuels produce only small amounts of air pollutants. | • Hydrogen is highly flammable, so storing and transporting it has safety implications.<br>• Adsorbers and absorbers have limited life cycles.<br>• Hydrogen fuel cells have a limited lifetime and high production costs.<br>• Toxic chemicals are used in the production of the hydrogen cell. |

### A hydrogen economy?

There is a political and social desire to move to a hydrogen economy but there are many obstacles to be overcome. The main issues are:

- public and political acceptance of hydrogen as a fuel
- the safety risks and costs associated with the handling and maintenance of hydrogen systems
- the energy needed to manufacture the hydrogen in the first place

## Questions

1 It is thought by many people that fuel cell vehicles are the solution to our transport problems. State three benefits and three limitations of their use.

2 Write out equations for the reactions that occur at each electrode in a fuel cell.

3 State three methods of storing the hydrogen in a fuel cell.

# 2.16 The transition metals

**Transition metals**

Transition metals are elements that can form at least one stable ion with an incomplete d sub-level.

The **transition metals** are in the d block of the periodic table. It is important that you understand the distinction between a **d block element** and a transition metal. Transition metals are elements with an incomplete d sub-level that can form at least one stable ion with an incomplete d sub-level. Using this definition the first row transition elements are titanium to copper.

* Scandium has an incomplete d sub-level but forms $Sc^{3+}$ ions which have no d sub-level electrons.
* Zinc has a complete d sub-level and forms $Zn^{2+}$ ions with a complete d sub-level.
* As a result neither scandium nor zinc is a transition element.

Typical properties of the transition elements include:
* catalytic activity
* variable oxidation states
* the ability to form complexes
* the ability to form coloured ions

The transition metals are also stronger, more dense, and less reactive than group 1 and 2 metals.

## Electron configurations

The electron configurations of the transition metals are often written using an argon core, [Ar]. This represents the electron configuration $1s^2\ 2s^2\ 2p^6\ 3s^2\ 3p^6$. Remember that the 4s shell is filled before the 3d shell and note that copper and chromium are exceptions.

| element | symbol | electron configuration |
|---|---|---|
| titanium | Ti | [Ar] $3d^2\ 4s^2$ |
| vanadium | V | [Ar] $3d^3\ 4s^2$ |
| chromium | Cr | [Ar] $3d^5\ 4s^1$ |
| manganese | Mn | [Ar] $3d^5\ 4s^2$ |
| iron | Fe | [Ar] $3d^6\ 4s^2$ |
| cobalt | Co | [Ar] $3d^7\ 4s^2$ |
| nickel | Ni | [Ar] $3d^8\ 4s^2$ |
| copper | Cu | [Ar] $3d^{10}\ 4s^1$ |

### *Chromium and copper*

In chromium the electron configuration is [Ar] $3d^5\ 4s^1$ rather than [Ar] $3d^4\ 4s^2$. One of the 4s electrons is promoted to the 3d sub-level as this half-fills both the 4s and 3d sub-levels.

In copper the electron configuration is [Ar] $3d^{10}\ 4s^1$ rather than [Ar] $3d^9\ 4s^2$. One of the 4s electrons is promoted to the 3d sub-level. Again the 4s sub-level is half-filled.

## Formation of ions

When the transition metals in period 4 form ions, they lose electrons from their 4s sub-level first then from their 3d sub-level. Work through the electron configurations below for some transition metal ions and make sure you can write them.

| ion | electron configuration |
|---|---|
| $Ti^{2+}$ | [Ar] $3d^2$ |
| $Cu^+$ | [Ar] $3d^{10}$ |
| $Fe^{3+}$ | [Ar] $3d^5$ |
| $Mn^{2+}$ | [Ar] $3d^5$ |

The ions of transition metals usually have a colour and often exist as **complexes**.

## Variable oxidation states

The transition metals have variable oxidation states. This is possible because the d and s sub-levels are at similar energy levels. The table below shows the possible oxidation states of each element. The most important ones are shown in bold. Note that the maximum possible oxidation states increase to manganese then decrease again.

| Ti | V | Cr | Mn | Fe | Co | Ni | Cu |
|---|---|---|---|---|---|---|---|
| | | | + 7 | | | | |
| | | **+ 6** | + 6 | + 6 | | | |
| | **+ 5** | | | | | | |
| **+ 4** | **+ 4** | | | | | | |
| **+ 3** | + 3 | **+ 3** | + 3 | **+ 3** | **+ 3** | + 3 | |
| + 2 | + 2 | + 2 | **+ 2** | **+ 2** | **+ 2** | + 2 | **+ 2** |
| | | | | | | | + 1 |

### Uses of transition elements

Transition metals and their compounds are often used as catalysts. For example, vanadium(V) oxide is used in the contact process for manufacturing sulfuric acid.

Iron is used in the Haber process to manufacture ammonia.

## The transition metals titanium to copper

| 47·9 | 50·9 | 52·0 | 54·9 | 55·8 | 58·9 | 58·7 | 63·5 |
|---|---|---|---|---|---|---|---|
| Ti | V | Cr | Mn | Fe | Co | Ni | Cu |
| Titanium | Vanadium | Chromium | Manganese | Iron | Cobalt | Nickel | Copper |
| 22 | 23 | 24 | 25 | 26 | 27 | 28 | 29 |

## Questions

1 Write electron configurations for the following atoms and ions:

  a Cr

  b Ni

  c $Cu^{2+}$

  d $Ni^{2+}$

  e $V^{3+}$

2 Write out the common properties of the transition metals four times then check that you can recall them.

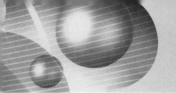

### Complex ion

A central metal ion bonded to one or more ligands by dative covalent bonds.

### Ligand

A molecule or ion that can donate a pair of electrons to a transition metal ion.

A **complex** is a central metal ion surrounded by **ligands**. The ligand donates a pair of electrons to the central metal ion forming a **dative covalent bond**. Transition metals form complexes with water in aqueous solution and with other ligands such as chloride ions, ammonia and cyanide ions. The next page explains complex ions and their shapes in more detail.

### Formation of coloured ions

The transition metals all form complex ions with water, where the central transition metal ion is surrounded by six water molecules. These are called hexaaqua complexes. Different transition metals form different coloured complexes. Make sure you can remember the colours given below.

| complex ion | colour |
| --- | --- |
| $[Fe(H_2O)_6]^{2+}(aq)$ | pale green |
| $[Fe(H_2O)_6]^{3+}(aq)$ | orange |
| $[Cu(H_2O)_6]^{2+}(aq)$ | blue |
| $[Co(H_2O)_6]^{2+}(aq)$ | pink |

If the water ligand is replaced by another ligand then the colour of the complex may change. You will read more about this on the ligand substitution page.

### Precipitation reactions of metal ions with hydroxide ions

When an alkali such as sodium hydroxide is added to an aqueous complex, hydroxide ions remove hydrogen ions from the water ligands, leaving a complex with no overall charge. These complexes are insoluble in water and so form a precipitate.

$$[Cu(H_2O)_6]^{2+}(aq) + 2OH^-(aq) \rightarrow [Cu(H_2O)_4(OH)_2](s) + 2H_2O(l)$$
blue solution          blue precipitate

It is acceptable to write these equations in a simplified form with the water ligands omitted. These are called ionic equations.

$$Cu^{2+}(aq) + 2OH^-(aq) \rightarrow Cu(OH)_2(s)$$

You must be able to write equations for precipitate formation and state the colours of the aqueous solutions and the precipitates formed from them.

| precipitate | colour of precipitate | equation |
| --- | --- | --- |
| $Cu(OH)_2(s)$ | blue | $Cu^{2+}(aq) + 2OH^-(aq) \rightarrow Cu(OH)_2(s)$ |
| $Co(OH)_2(s)$ | blue, turns pink on standing | $Co^{2+}(aq) + 2OH^-(aq) \rightarrow Co(OH)_2(s)$ |
| $Fe(OH)_2(s)$ | green, turns orange-brown on standing | $Fe^{2+}(aq) + 2OH^-(aq) \rightarrow Fe(OH)_2(s)$ |
| $Fe(OH)_3(s)$ | orange-brown | $Fe^{3+}(aq) + 3OH^-(aq) \rightarrow Fe(OH)_3(s)$ |

# Variable oxidation state

Transition metals have variable oxidation states. Remember that the d and s sub-levels are at similar energy levels so electrons can readily be removed from both sub-levels.

Consider the transition metal iron. The electron configuration of iron is $[Ar] 3d^6 4s^2$.

When iron is oxidized to $Fe^{2+}$ the two 4s electrons are removed:

$$Fe \rightarrow Fe^{2+} + 2e^-$$
$$[Ar] 3d^6 4s^2 \quad [Ar] 3d^6$$

When iron is oxidized to $Fe^{3+}$ the two 4s electrons and one of the d electrons are removed:

$$Fe \rightarrow Fe^{3+} + 2e^-$$
$$[Ar] 3d^6 4s^2 \quad [Ar] 3d^5$$

$Fe^{3+}$ is more stable than $Fe^{2+}$ as the 3d shell in $Fe^{3+}$ has one electron in each orbital. In $Fe^{2+}$ one of the orbitals contains paired electrons; these will repel each other.

Manganese has two stable oxidation states: $MnO_4^-(aq)$ contains manganese in a +7 oxidation state; $Mn^{2+}(aq)$ contains manganese in a +2 oxidation state. You should be able to construct and balance the half-equation linking these two species:

$$MnO_4^-(aq) + 8H^+(aq) + 5e^- \rightarrow Mn^{2+}(aq) + 4H_2O(l)$$

# Catalysis

A **catalyst** is a substance that increases the rate of a chemical reaction by providing an alternative reaction route with a lower activation energy. Transition metals and their compounds can act as catalysts.

You do not need to learn about how catalysts work in detail. You should work through the following examples and make sure you can understand each process.

## The Haber process

The Haber process is used to manufacture ammonia which is essential for making fertilizers. The ammonia is manufactured from nitrogen and hydrogen in the presence of an iron catalyst.

- The overall equation is $N_2(g) + 3H_2(g) \rightleftharpoons 2NH_3(g)$
- The iron is a heterogeneous catalyst: it acts as a surface on which the reaction take place.

## The contact process

The contact process is used to manufacture sulfuric acid. Vanadium(V) oxide is used as a heterogeneous catalyst in the second stage of the manufacturing process.

---

## Heterogeneous and homogeneous

Heterogeneous catalysts exist in a different physical state to the reactants in the reaction. Reactions occur at the surface of the catalyst in regions called active sites.

- *Reactants are* **adsorbed** *to the active site.*
- *The reaction takes place.*
- *Products are* **desorbed** *from the active site.*

Homogeneous catalysts are in the same physical state as the reactions. Their catalytic action involves variable oxidation states.

---

## Questions

1 Write out the table showing the colours of the ions five times until you can write the formulae and colours of the ions from memory.

2 Write out an ionic equation for the reaction of iron(II) chloride solution with sodium hydroxide solution.

3 Explain why iron(III) ions are more stable than iron(II) ions.

# 2.18 Complex ions and their shapes

A complex is a central metal ion surrounded by ligands. The ligand donates a pair of electrons to the central metal ion. You must know the formulae of common ligands and the structures of the complex ions that they form.

## Ligands

Ligands can be negative ions or uncharged molecules that have one or more lone pairs of electrons to donate.

Examples of ligands include:
- halide ions such as chloride ions, $Cl^-$
- cyanide ions, $CN^-$
- hydroxide ions, $OH^-$
- ammonia, $NH_3$
- water, $H_2O$

### Unidentate ligands

A **unidentate** ligand has one pair of electrons that it can donate.
- common unidentate ligands include: $Cl^-$, $CN^-$, $NH_3$, $H_2O$
- the donation of the pair of electrons to the complex ion is shown as an arrow pointing from the ligand to the metal ion.
- in the diamminesilver(I) complex ion each ammonia molecule donates a lone pair of electrons to the silver ion. This ion is commonly known as Tollens' reagent and is used to test for aldehydes.

### Bidentate ligands

A **bidentate** ligand has two pairs of electrons that it can donate.
- 1,2-diaminoethane is a bidentate ligand as each nitrogen atom has a lone pair of electrons.
- Each molecule can form two dative covalent bonds with the central metal ion.
- The abbreviation en may be used to show 1,2-diaminoethane in diagrams of complexes.

Another example of a bidentate ligand is the ethanedioate ion, $C_2O_4^{2-}$.

### Multidentate ligands

**Multidentate** ligands are able to donate more than two pairs of electrons.

The ligand $EDTA^{4-}$, shown on the left, can donate six pairs of electrons to the central metal ion. It has two lone pairs on nitrogen atoms, and four on oxygen atoms in the carboxylate groups.

Haemoglobin, found in red blood cells, is a protein that binds to oxygen allowing blood to carry it round the body. Each haemoglobin molecule is made from four smaller sub-units, each of which contains a haem group. This is a complex involving an iron(II) ion and a multidentate ligand that forms four co-ordinate bonds with a central metal ion.

## Ligands and dative covalent bonds

A ligand is an ion or molecule that can donate a pair of electrons to a central metal ion, forming a covalent bond.

A dative covalent bond is a covalent bond in which one atom donates both electrons.

## Octahedral complexes

Complexes that contain six dative bonds have an **octahedral** shape. They have a co-ordination number of 6 (this is the number of pairs of electrons donated to the central metal ion). Examples of octahedral complexes include $[Cu(H_2O)_6]^{2+}$, $[V(H_2O)_6]^{3+}$ and $[Cu(NH_3)_4(H_2O)_2]^{2+}$.

## Tetrahedral complexes

Complexes containing chloride or cyanide ions have only four dative bonds since the chloride and cyanide ligands are large. They have a tetrahedral shape and a co-ordination number of 4. Examples of tetrahedral complexes include $[CuCl_4]^{2-}$ and $[FeCl_4]^{2-}$.

## Square planar complexes

Some complexes with four ligands are square planar instead of tetrahedral. The tetracyanonickelate(II) ion. $[Ni(CN)_4]^{2-}$ is square planar.

# Cis-platin

The complex diamminedichloroplatinum(II), $[PtCl_2(NH_3)_2]$, is square planar and exists as *cis* and *trans* stereoisomers.

- The *cis* isomer has two ammine ligands next to each other.
- The *trans* isomer has two ammine ligands on opposite sides.

The *cis* isomer is commonly called cis-platin and is used as an anticancer drug.

- It is used to treat cancer of the ovaries, testes, bladder, stomach, and lungs.
- The side effects of cis-platin include nausea, vomiting, allergic reactions, hearing loss, and kidney problems.
- It is not entirely clear how the drug works but it is thought to be converted in cells into a reactive ion that binds to DNA and stops cancer cells dividing.

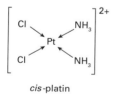

*cis*-platin          *trans*-platin

## Naming complexes

Work through the rules below making sure you can see how the following complex ions are named.

hexaaquacopper(II)   $[Cu(H_2O)_6]^{2+}$

tetraachlorocobaltate(II)   $[CoCl_4]^{2-}$

diamminesilver(I)   $[Ag(NH_3)_2]^+$

tetraamminediaquacopper(II) $[Cu(H_2O)_2(NH_3)_4]^{2+}$

| ligand | name in complex |
|--------|-----------------|
| water | aqua |
| ammonia | ammine |
| chloride | chloro |
| hydroxide | hydroxo |
| cyanide | cyano |

| metal | name in anionic complexes |
|-------|---------------------------|
| chromium | chromate |
| cobalt | cobaltate |
| copper | cuprate |
| iron | ferrate |
| silver | argentate |

A roman numeral in brackets shows the oxidation state of the metal.

Anionic complexes have a name ending in –ate, cationic complexes end with the normal name of the metal.

---

# Questions

1  State the co-ordination number and oxidation states of the central metal ion in:

   a  $[Cu(H_2O)_2(NH_3)_4]^{2+}$

   b  $[FeCl_4]^{2-}$

2  Name and predict the shapes of each of the complexes in question 1.

# 2.19 Isomerism in complex ions

Some transition metal complexes exist as **stereoisomers**. These are compounds with the same structural formula but with different arrangements of the atoms in space.

*Cis-trans* isomerism and optical isomerism are both examples of stereoisomerism.

> ### Stereoisomers
>
> Compounds with the same structural formula but with different arrangements of the atoms in space.

## *Cis-trans* isomerism

*Cis-trans* isomerism is a special kind of $E/Z$ isomerism. In transition metal complexes the *cis* isomer is the one with identical groups on the same side of the structure; the *trans* isomer is the one with identical groups on different sides of the structure.

> ### *Cis-trans* isomerism
>
> *Trans* isomers have identical atoms or groups of atoms opposite each other.
>
> *Cis* isomers have identical atoms or groups of atoms on the same side as each other.

Common examples of *cis-trans* isomerism in complex ions include *cis*-platin and the isomers of $[NiCl_2(NH_3)_2]$ and of $[CoCl_2(NH_3)_4]^+$.

Practise drawing these isomers:

*trans*-$[NiCl_2(NH_3)_2]$        *cis*-$[NiCl_2(NH_3)_2]$

*trans*-$[CoCl_2(NH_3)_4]^+$        *cis*-$[CoCl_2(NH_3)_4]^+$

# Optical isomerism

**Optical isomerism** occurs when a stereoisomer has non-superimposable mirror image forms. Octahedral complexes containing bidentate ligands often show this form of isomerism. Drawing these isomers is hard and will need careful practice. The diagram shows the two optical isomers of $[Ni(NH_2CH_2CH_2NH_2)_3]^{2+}$. Cover up the right hand diagram and practise drawing it yourself.

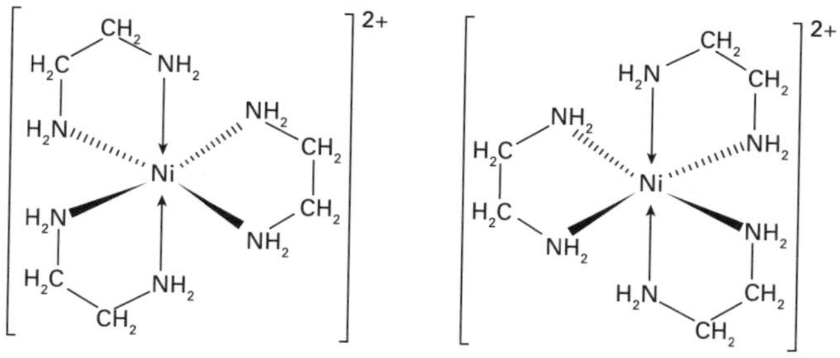

**Optical isomerism**

Optical isomers are stereoisomers that are non-superimposable mirror images of each other.

# Questions

1 Using the isomers of $[Pt(NH_3)_2Cl_2]$ explain what is meant by the term *cis-trans* isomerism.

2 Draw the optical isomers of $[Co(NH_2CH_2CH_2NH_2)_2Cl_2]^+$.

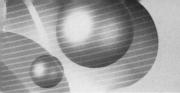

# 2.20 Ligand substitution

## Important colours

| complex ion | colour |
|---|---|
| $[Cu(H_2O)_6]^{2+}(aq)$ | blue |
| $[Cu(NH_3)_4(H_2O)_2]^{2+}(aq)$ | deep blue |
| $[CuCl_4]^{2-}(aq)$ | yellow |
| $[Co(H_2O)_6]^{2+}(aq)$ | pink |
| $[CoCl_4]^{2-}(aq)$ | blue |

A **ligand substitution** reaction takes place when one ligand in a complex ion is exchanged for another. You need to be able to write equations, draw the complex ions formed and state the colour changes for all of the ligand substitution reactions given on this spread.

Water and ammonia are both neutral unidentate ligands. Ammonia molecules are able to replace water molecules in ligand substitution reactions. As water and ammonia have a similar size, the co-ordination number remains 6 and the complexes are octahedral in shape. With excess ammonia four of the aqua ligands are replaced.

$$[Cu(H_2O)_6]^{2+}(aq) + 4NH_3(aq) \rightarrow [Cu(NH_3)_4(H_2O)_2]^{2+}(aq) + 4H_2O(l)$$
$$\text{blue} \qquad\qquad\qquad\qquad\qquad \text{deep blue}$$

It is also possible for chloride ions to substitute for water ligands. These reactions involve a change in co-ordination number from 6 to 4 and a change in shape from octahedral to tetrahedral, as well as a change in colour.

From hexaaquacopper(II) the complex formed is tetrachlorocuprate(II) which is yellow. Note that the reaction forms an equilibrium mixture so the colour is often observed as green.

$$[Cu(H_2O)_6]^{2+}(aq) + 4Cl^-(aq) \rightleftharpoons [CuCl_4]^{2-}(aq) + 6H_2O(l)$$
$$\text{blue} \qquad\qquad\qquad\qquad \text{yellow}$$

The ligand substitution reaction for hexaaquacobalt with chloride ions is used as the test for water due to the distinct colour change from pink to blue.

$$[Co(H_2O)_6]^{2+}(aq) + 4Cl^-(aq) \rightleftharpoons [CoCl_4]^{2-}(aq) + 6H_2O(l)$$
$$\text{pink} \qquad\qquad\qquad\qquad \text{blue}$$

## Iron and haemoglobin

The haemoglobin in blood uses ligand substitution reactions for the transport of oxygen.

- Haemoglobin has a central iron(II) ion surrounded by a quadridentate ligand called haem.
- Haem has 4 nitrogen atoms with lone pairs that form dative covalent bonds with the central iron(II) ion.
- Of the remaining two bonding sites one is occupied by globin.
- The remaining site is occupied by water, which can be replaced by $O_2$ which can then break away when needed.

If the carbon monoxide ligand attaches to the bonding site instead of water it forms a very stable complex and the carbon monoxide cannot break away again.

# Stability constants

We can write an equilibrium constant for ligand substitution reactions of aqueous transition metal ions. This is called a stability constant, $K_{stab}$. For example:

$$[Cu(H_2O)_6]^{2+}(aq) + 4Cl^-(aq) \rightleftharpoons [CuCl_4]^{2-}(aq) + 6H_2O(l)$$

$$K_{stab} = \frac{[[CuCl_4]^{2-}(aq)]}{[[Cu(H_2O)_6]^{2+}(aq)]\,[Cl^-(aq)]^4}$$

Note that the water released in the reaction is not written in the $K_{stab}$ expression as the whole reaction is carried out in aqueous solution.

The value of $K_{stab}$ tells you about the stability of the complex ion formed:

- Very stable complexes have high $K_{stab}$ values.
- The equation above has a $K_{stab}$ value of $4.17 \times 10^5$ dm$^{12}$ mol$^{-4}$.
- The units for $K_{stab}$ are calculated in the same way as units for $K_c$ values.

---

### Worked example

*The stability constants for the hexaammine complexes of cobalt(II) and cobalt(III) ions are given below. Write the $K_{stab}$ expression for the hexaammine complex of cobalt(II) and use the data to explain which complex is more stable.*

$[Co(NH_3)_6]^{2+}(aq)$          $K_{stab} = 7.7 \times 10^4$ mol$^{-6}$ dm$^{18}$

$[Co(NH_3)_6]^{3+}(aq)$          $K_{stab} = 4.5 \times 10^{33}$ mol$^{-6}$ dm$^{18}$

$[Co(H_2O)_6]^{2+}(aq) + 6NH_3(aq) \rightleftharpoons [Co(NH_3)_6]^{2+}(aq) + 6H_2O(l)$

$$K_{stab} = \frac{[[Co(NH_3)_6]^{2+}(aq)]}{[[Co(H_2O)_6]^{2+}(aq)]\,[NH_3(aq)]^6}$$

The stability constant for $[Co(NH_3)_6]^{3+}(aq)$ is significantly larger than for $[Co(NH_3)_6]^{2+}(aq)$ so the cobalt (III) complex is more stable.

---

### Stability constant $K_{stab}$

The stability constant $K_{stab}$ for a complex ion is the equilibrium constant for the equilibrium existing between an aqueous transition metal and the complex ion it forms when it has undergone ligand substitution.

---

## Questions

1 State the colour changes that occur when a small amount of aqueous ammonia is added to hexaaquacopper(II)(aq).

2 Explain why a green solution is often observed when concentrated hydrochloric acid is added to hexaaquacopper(II)(aq).

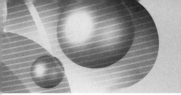

# 2.21    Redox titrations

## Mole relationships

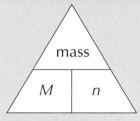

$M$ = molar mass

$n$ = number of moles

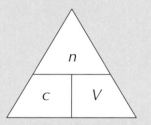

$c$ = concentration in mol dm⁻³

$V$ = volume in dm³

$n$ = number of moles

## Which acid?

Sulfuric acid is suitable for both dichromate(VI) and manganate(VII) titrations. However, hydrochloric acid is only suitable for dichromate(VI) titrations. This is because of the strength of manganate(VII) ions as an oxidizing agent. It is able to oxidize chloride ions to chlorine.

You have already learnt about acid–base titrations. **Redox titrations** are carried out using the same equipment and are similar in principle to acid–base titrations but rely on redox reactions. The most common oxidizing agents used in redox titrations are the manganate(VII) ion and the dichromate(VI) ion. The reducing agent thiosulfate, $S_2O_3^{2-}$, can also be used.

## Manganate(VII) in titrations

Acidified aqueous potassium manganate(VII), $KMnO_4$, can act as an oxidizing agent in redox titrations. Make sure you can write and balance the half-equation for the reduction of the manganate(VII) to the manganese(II) ion:

$$MnO_4^-(aq) + 8H^+(aq) + 5e^- \rightarrow Mn^{2+}(aq) + 4H_2O(l)$$

The hydrogen ions are supplied by dilute sulfuric acid. The most common use of manganate(VII) in redox titrations is to find the concentration of aqueous iron(II) ions. The iron(II) ions are oxidized to iron(III).

$$Fe^{2+}(aq) \rightarrow Fe^{3+}(aq) + e^-$$

When the two half-equations are combined the overall equation is:

$$MnO_4^-(aq) + 8H^+(aq) + 5Fe^{2+}(aq) \rightarrow Mn^{2+}(aq) + 4H_2O(l) + 5Fe^{3+}(aq)$$

When these titrations are carried out:

- Aqueous iron(II) ions are placed in the conical flask.
- Dilute sulfuric acid is added.
- Aqueous potassium manganate(VII) is added from a burette to the flask.
- The manganate(VII) loses its colour as it enters the iron(II) solution.
- The endpoint is when a permanent pale pink tinge caused by excess manganate(VII) is first seen.

### Worked example

*Calculate the concentration of a solution of potassium manganate(VII) if 20.0 cm³ of a solution of 0.10 mol dm⁻³ iron(II) sulfate reacts exactly with 23.4 cm³ of potassium manganate(VII).*

No of moles of iron(II) sulfate = $0.1 \times (20.0/1000) = 2 \times 10^{-3}$

No of moles of potassium manganate = $2 \times 10^{-3} \div 5 = 4 \times 10^{-4}$

Concentration of potassium manganate = $4 \times 10^{-4} \div (23.4/1000) = 0.017$ mol dm⁻³

## Dichromate(VI) in titrations

Acidified aqueous potassium dichromate(VI), $K_2Cr_2O_7$, can also be used as an oxidizing agent in redox titrations. The titration is carried out in the same way as with aqueous potassium manganate(VII).

The relevant half-equations and overall equations are:

$$Cr_2O_7^{2-}(aq) + 14H^+(aq) + 6e^- \rightarrow 2Cr^{3+}(aq) + 7H_2O(l)$$
$$Fe^{2+}(aq) \rightarrow Fe^{3+}(aq) + e^-$$
$$Cr_2O_7^{2-}(aq) + 14H^+(aq) + 6Fe^{2+}(aq) \rightarrow 2Cr^{3+}(aq) + 7H_2O(l) + 6Fe^{3+}(aq)$$

As with potassium managate(VII) this reaction is self-indicating but the colour change may be difficult to see so an indicator may be added.

## Thiosulfate in titrations

If a reducing agent is needed for a redox titration then the thiosulfate ion, $S_2O_3^{2-}$, is used. On oxidation of the thiosulfate ion the tetrathionate ion, $S_4O_6^{2-}$, is formed: $2S_2O_3^{2-}(aq) \rightarrow S_4O_6^{2-}(aq) + 2e^-$

Thiosulfate is frequently used to find the concentration of aqueous iodine, which is reduced to iodide ions: $I_2(aq) + 2e^- \rightarrow 2I^-(aq)$

Overall: $2S_2O_3^{2-}(aq) + I_2(aq) \rightarrow S_4O_6^{2-}(aq) + 2I^-(aq)$

Starch suspension is used as an indicator near the endpoint. It forms a deep purple colour with iodine; the endpoint is when this colour first disappears.

## Worked example

### Calculating the amount of copper in brass

Iodine thiosulfate titrations can be used for determining quantities of copper, as the copper(II) ion reacts with iodide ions to form iodine which can be titrated:

$$2Cu^{2+}(aq) + 4I^-(aq) \rightarrow 2CuI(s) + I_2(aq)$$

*A 0.50 g piece of brass is dissolved in nitric acid forming a mixture of zinc(II) nitrate and copper(II) nitrate. An excess of potassium iodide solution is added to the resulting mixture forming copper(I) iodide and iodine.*

$$2Cu^{2+}(aq) + 4I^-(aq) \rightarrow 2CuI(s) + I_2(aq)$$

*The iodine formed reacts with 22.40 cm³ of 0.200 mol dm⁻³ sodium thiosulfate solution.*

$$2S_2O_3^{2-}(aq) + I_2(aq) \rightarrow S_4O_6^{2-}(aq) + 2I^-(aq)$$

*Calculate the percentage of copper in the brass. Give your answer to 3 significant figures.*

**Step 1** Calculate the number of moles of sodium thiosulfate used in the titration. (For all unstructured calculations, always start by converting the data into moles.)

$n = (22.40/1000) \times 0.200 = 0.004\ 48$

**Step 2** Calculate the number of moles of $I_2$ the sodium thiosulfate reacted with in the titration.

mole ratio is $2S_2O_3^{2-}(aq) : 1\ I_2(aq)$

$n = 0.004\ 48/2 = 0.002\ 24$

**Step 3** The iodine that took part in the titration was formed in the first reaction so this value can be used to calculate the number of moles of $Cu^{2+}(aq)$:

mole ratio is $1\ I_2(aq)$ released : $2Cu^{2+}(aq)$ reacted

$n = 0.002\ 24 \times 2 = 0.004\ 48$

**Step 4** Calculate the mass of copper in 0.004 48 moles and then determine the percentage:

mass of copper = $0.004\ 48 \times 63.5 = 0.28$ g

percentage of copper in brass = $0.28/0.50 \times 100 = 56.9\%$

Note that the answer is expressed to 3 significant figures as required by the question.

## Colours of important ions

| ion | colour in aqueous solution |
|---|---|
| $MnO_4^-(aq)$ | purple |
| $Mn^{2+}(aq)$ | very pale pink |
| $Cr_2O_7^{2-}(aq)$ | orange |
| $Cr^{3+}$ | green |

## Questions

1 Calculate the concentration in mol dm⁻³ of a solution of potassium dichromate(VI) if 26.4 cm³ of 0.05 mol dm⁻³ iron(II) sulfate reacts exactly with 25.0 cm³ of the potassium dichromate(VI).

2 What volume of 0.1 mol dm⁻³ sulfuric acid would be needed to provide enough H⁺ ions for the reaction of 52.4 cm³ of 0.2 mol dm⁻³ potassium manganate(VII) with iron(II) ions?

3 Write out the half-equations for the following reactions:

  **a** manganate(VII) as an oxidizing agent

  **b** dichromate(VI) as an oxidizing agent

  **c** thiosulfate as a reducing agent

# Periodic table

## The Periodic Table of the Elements

**Key**

relative atomic mass
**atomic symbol**
name
atomic (proton) number

| 1.0 |
|---|
| **H** |
| hydrogen |
| 1 |

| Group 1 | Group 2 | 3 | 4 | 5 | 6 | 7 | Group 0 |
|---|---|---|---|---|---|---|---|
| | | | | | | | 4.0 **He** helium 2 |
| 6.9 **Li** lithium 3 | 9.0 **Be** beryllium 4 | 10.8 **B** boron 5 | 12.0 **C** carbon 6 | 14.0 **N** nitrogen 7 | 16.0 **O** oxygen 8 | 19.0 **F** fluorine 9 | 20.2 **Ne** neon 10 |
| 23.0 **Na** sodium 11 | 24.3 **Mg** magnesium 12 | 27.0 **Al** aluminium 13 | 28.1 **Si** silicon 14 | 31.0 **P** phosphorus 15 | 32.1 **S** sulfur 16 | 35.5 **Cl** chlorine 17 | 39.9 **Ar** argon 18 |

| 39.1 **K** potassium 19 | 40.1 **Ca** calcium 20 | 45.0 **Sc** scandium 21 | 47.9 **Ti** titanium 22 | 50.9 **V** vanadium 23 | 52.0 **Cr** chromium 24 | 54.9 **Mn** manganese 25 | 55.8 **Fe** iron 26 | 58.9 **Co** cobalt 27 | 58.7 **Ni** nickel 28 | 63.5 **Cu** copper 29 | 65.4 **Zn** zinc 30 | 69.7 **Ga** gallium 31 | 72.6 **Ge** germanium 32 | 74.9 **As** arsenic 33 | 79.0 **Se** selenium 34 | 79.9 **Br** bromine 35 | 83.8 **Kr** krypton 36 |
|---|---|---|---|---|---|---|---|---|---|---|---|---|---|---|---|---|---|
| 85.5 **Rb** rubidium 37 | 87.6 **Sr** strontium 38 | 88.9 **Y** yttrium 39 | 91.2 **Zr** zirconium 40 | 92.9 **Nb** niobium 41 | 95.9 **Mo** molybdenum 42 | [98] **Tc** technetium 43 | 101.1 **Ru** ruthenium 44 | 102.9 **Rh** rhodium 45 | 106.4 **Pd** palladium 46 | 107.9 **Ag** silver 47 | 112.4 **Cd** cadmium 48 | 114.8 **In** indium 49 | 118.7 **Sn** tin 50 | 121.8 **Sb** antimony 51 | 127.6 **Te** tellurium 52 | 126.9 **I** iodine 53 | 131.3 **Xe** xenon 54 |
| 132.9 **Cs** caesium 55 | 137.3 **Ba** barium 56 | 138.9 **La\*** lanthanum 57 | 178.5 **Hf** hafnium 72 | 180.9 **Ta** tantalum 73 | 183.9 **W** tungsten 74 | 186.2 **Re** rhenium 75 | 190.2 **Os** osmium 76 | 192.2 **Ir** iridium 77 | 195.1 **Pt** platinum 78 | 197.0 **Au** gold 79 | 200.6 **Hg** mercury 80 | 204.4 **Tl** thallium 81 | 207.2 **Pb** lead 82 | 209.0 **Bi** bismuth 83 | [209] **Po** polonium 84 | [210] **At** astatine 85 | [222] **Rn** radon 86 |
| [223] **Fr** francium 87 | [226] **Ra** radium 88 | [227] **Ac\*** actinium 89 | [261] **Rf** rutherfordium 104 | [262] **Db** dubnium 105 | [266] **Sg** seaborgium 106 | [264] **Bh** bohrium 107 | [277] **Hs** hassium 108 | [268] **Mt** meitnerium 109 | [271] **Ds** darmstadtium 110 | [272] **Rg** roentgenium 111 | | | | | | | |

Elements with atomic numbers 112–116 have been reported but not fully authenticated

| 140.1 **Ce** cerium 58 | 140.9 **Pr** praseodymium 59 | 144.2 **Nd** neodymium 60 | 144.9 **Pm** promethium 61 | 150.4 **Sm** samarium 62 | 152.0 **Eu** europium 63 | 157.2 **Gd** gadolinium 64 | 158.9 **Tb** terbium 65 | 162.5 **Dy** dysprosium 66 | 164.9 **Ho** holmium 67 | 167.3 **Er** erbium 68 | 168.9 **Tm** thulium 69 | 173.0 **Yb** ytterbium 70 | 175.0 **Lu** lutetium 71 |
|---|---|---|---|---|---|---|---|---|---|---|---|---|---|
| 232.0 **Th** thorium 90 | [231] **Pa** protactinium 91 | 238.1 **U** uranium 92 | [237] **Np** neptunium 93 | [242] **Pu** plutonium 94 | [243] **Am** americium 95 | [247] **Cm** curium 96 | [245] **Bk** berkelium 97 | [251] **Cf** californium 98 | [254] **Es** einsteinium 99 | [253] **Fm** fermium 100 | [256] **Md** mendelevium 101 | [254] **No** nobelium 102 | [257] **Lr** lawrencium 103 |

# Index

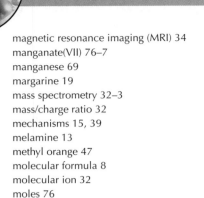